Convergence Strategies for Green Computing and Sustainable Development

Vishal Jain
Sharda University, India

Murali Raman
Asia Pacific University of Technology, Malaysia

Akshat Agrawal
Amity University, Guragon, India

Meenu Hans
K.R. Mangalam University, India

Swati Gupta
Center of Excellence, K.R. Mangalam University, India

A volume in the Advances in Environmental
Engineering and Green Technologies (AEEGT)
Book Series

Published in the United States of America by
IGI Global
Engineering Science Reference (an imprint of IGI Global)
701 E. Chocolate Avenue
Hershey PA, USA 17033
Tel: 717-533-8845
Fax: 717-533-8661
E-mail: cust@igi-global.com
Web site: http://www.igi-global.com

Library of Congress Cataloging-in-Publication Data

Names: Jain, Vishal, 1983- editor. | Raman, Murali, 1971- editor. |
  Agrawal, Akshat, 1986- editor. | Hans, Meenu, 1984- editor. | Gupta,
  Swati, 1987- editor.
Title: Convergence strategies for green computing and sustainable
  development / edited by Vishal Jain, Murali Raman, Akshat Agrawal, Meenu
  Hans, Swati Gupta.
Description: Hershey, PA : Engineering Science Reference, [2024] | Includes
  bibliographical references and index. | Summary: "The book highlights
  how the IoT can effectively contribute to pollution reduction using
  energy-efficient sensors. These sensors are crucial in measuring various
  components and monitoring trends in the current era. Additionally, AI
  techniques enable the computational analysis to envision systems that
  promote positive energy. On the other hand, cloud computing
  revolutionizes business models by providing flexibility, cost savings,
  enhanced security, efficiency, and unlimited storage while optimizing
  energy consumption and reducing carbon footprints"-- Provided by
  publisher.
Identifiers: LCCN 2023029595 (print) | LCCN 2023029596 (ebook) | ISBN
  9798369303382 (hardcover) | ISBN 9798369303399 (paperback) | ISBN
  9798369303405 (ebook)
Subjects: LCSH: Cloud computing. | Green technology. | Sustainable
  development.
Classification: LCC QA76.585 .C68 2024 (print) | LCC QA76.585 (ebook) |
  DDC 004.67/82--dc23/eng/20230927
LC record available at https://lccn.loc.gov/2023029595
LC ebook record available at https://lccn.loc.gov/2023029596

This book is published in the IGI Global book series Advances in Environmental Engineering and Green Technologies (AEEGT) (ISSN: 2326-9162; eISSN: 2326-9170)

British Cataloguing in Publication Data
A Cataloguing in Publication record for this book is available from the British Library.

For electronic access to this publication, please contact: eresources@igi-global.com.

Advances in Environmental Engineering and Green Technologies (AEEGT) Book Series

Sang-Bing Tsai
Zhongshan Institute, University of Electronic Science and Technology of China, China & Wuyi University, China
Ming-Lang Tseng
Lunghwa University of Science and Technology, Taiwan
Yuchi Wang
University of Electronic Science and Technology of China
Zhongshan Institute, China

ISSN:2326-9162
EISSN:2326-9170

MISSION

Growing awareness and an increased focus on environmental issues such as climate change, energy use, and loss of non-renewable resources have brought about a greater need for research that provides potential solutions to these problems. Research in environmental science and engineering continues to play a vital role in uncovering new opportunities for a "green" future.

The **Advances in Environmental Engineering and Green Technologies (AEEGT)** book series is a mouthpiece for research in all aspects of environmental science, earth science, and green initiatives. This series supports the ongoing research in this field through publishing books that discuss topics within environmental engineering or that deal with the interdisciplinary field of green technologies.

COVERAGE

- Pollution Management
- Waste Management
- Cleantech
- Air Quality
- Renewable Energy
- Green Technology
- Green Transportation
- Policies Involving Green Technologies and Environmental Engineering
- Sustainable Communities
- Alternative Power Sources

IGI Global is currently accepting manuscripts for publication within this series. To submit a proposal for a volume in this series, please contact our Acquisition Editors at Acquisitions@igi-global.com or visit: http://www.igi-global.com/publish/.

Titles in this Series

For a list of additional titles in this series, please visit: http://www.igi-global.com/book-series/advances-environmental-engineering-green-technologies/73679

Optimization Techniques for Hybrid Power Systems Renewable Energy, Electric Vehicles, and Smart Grid
Sunanda Hazra (Budge Budge Institute of Technology) Sneha Sultana (Dr. B. C. Roy Engineering College, Durgapur, India) and Provas Kumar Roy (Department of Electrical Engineering, Kalyani Government Engineering College, Kalyani, West Bengal, India)
Engineering Science Reference • copyright 2024 • 330pp • H/C (ISBN: 9798369304921) • US $300.00 (our price)

Agriculture and Aquaculture Applications of Biosensors and Bioelectronics
Alex Khang (Global Research Institute of Technology and Engineering, USA)
Engineering Science Reference • copyright 2024 • 576pp • H/C (ISBN: 9798369320693) • US $265.00 (our price)

Innovations in Engineering and Food Science
Shilpa Mehta (Auckland University of Technology, New Zealand) Fakhar Islam (NUR International University, Pakistan) and Ali Imran (Government College University, Pakistan)
Engineering Science Reference • copyright 2024 • 424pp • H/C (ISBN: 9798369308196) • US $265.00 (our price)

Modeling and Monitoring Extreme Hydrometeorological Events
Carmen Maftei (Transilvania University of Brasov, Romania) Radu Muntean (Transilvania University of Braşov, Romania) and Ashok Vaseashta (International Clean Water Institute, USA)
Engineering Science Reference • copyright 2024 • 338pp • H/C (ISBN: 9781668487716) • US $250.00 (our price)

Novel AI Applications for Advancing Earth Sciences
Sudesh Yadav (Department of Higher Education, Government PG College, Ateli, India) Satya Prakash Yadav (GL Bajaj Institute of Technology and Management, India) Pethuru Raj (Edge AI Division, Reliance Jio Platforms Ltd., Bangalore, India) Prabhakar Tiwari (Madan Mohan Malaviya University of Technology, India) and Victor Hugo C. de Albuquerque (Department of Teleinformatics Engineering (DETI), Federal University of Ceará, Brazil)
Engineering Science Reference • copyright 2024 • 405pp • H/C (ISBN: 9798369318508) • US $265.00 (our price)

Exploring Ethical Dimensions of Environmental Sustainability and Use of AI
Hemachandran Kannan (Woxsen University, India) Raul Villamarin Rodriguez (Woxsen University, India) Zita Zoltay Paprika (Corvinus University of Budapest, Hungary) and Abejide Ade-Ibijola (University of Johannesburg, South Africa)
Engineering Science Reference • copyright 2024 • 426pp • H/C (ISBN: 9798369308929) • US $265.00 (our price)

701 East Chocolate Avenue, Hershey, PA 17033, USA
Tel: 717-533-8845 x100 • Fax: 717-533-8661
E-Mail: cust@igi-global.com • www.igi-global.com

Table of Contents

A. Kistan, Department of Chemistry, Panimalar Engineering College, Chennai, India
R Puviarasi, Department of Electronics and Communication Engineering, Saveetha School of Engineering, Saveetha Institute of Medical and Technical Sciences (SIMATS), Thandalam, India
S. Gokul, YSR Technical Education, India

Detailed Table of Contents

Chapter 1
    Juhi Singh, Manipal University Jaipur, India
    Aarti Chugh, SGT University, India
    Arun Kumar Singh, Amity University, Gurgaon, India

Sustainable development objectives face substantial potential problems because of the fast development and use of artificial intelligence technology in a variety of fields. The purpose of this essay is to examine the difficulties and creative solutions related to sustainability in the era of AI. The chapter's first section examines how AI systems affect the environment, concentrating on their carbon footprint and energy use. AI applications spread are critical to address the rising energy needs of AI infrastructure and algorithms, as well as the environmental effects of producing and discarding AI hardware. The impact of many strategies, including eco-friendly data centers, energy-efficient algorithms, and sustainable design principles, on the environment is evaluated. The societal effects of AI on sustainability are examined in the second section. The chapter explores these concerns and offers creative solutions that use AI to deal with societal problems, such developing fair and open algorithms, assuring ethical AI application, and encouraging human-AI cooperation.

Chapter 2
    Sanusi Mohammed Sadiq, Federal University, Dutse, Nigeria
    Invinder Paul Singh, Swami Keshwanand Rajasthan Agricultural University, India
    Muhammad Makarfi Ahmad, Bayero University, Kano, Nigeria
    Ummulqulthum Ndatsu Usman, University of St. Andrews, UK

The sustainable development goals were underlined as needing significant societal changes, which were made even more urgent by the pandemic's advent. The future civilization should strive for sustainable growth, a strategy in which technology is a key component. Society 5.0 is a relatively new idea that serves as a framework for social development and has the potential to have a significant impact on societies at all aspects, including sustainability and quality of life. It seeks to maximize the capacity of the relationship between individuals and technology in the advocacy of the enhancement of everyone's quality of life through an incredibly smart society. Through the analysis of scientifically published works and the data from organizations and governments working on such schemes, it is possible to say that Industry 5.0 is far more than a pattern, and Society 5.0 would consequently open previously unimaginable prospects for the development of a highly smart globalized world.

    Jyoti Verma, Chitkara Business School, Chitkara University, India
    Yashna Sharma, Chitkara Business School, Chitkara University, India

Green technology is a game-changing strategy to solve urgent environmental issues while fostering economic and social well-being. This chapter dives into the vital role green technology plays in addressing the pressing need for sustainability at the national and international levels. The chapter emphasizes how many top businesses support ecological solutions, and how countries are increasingly seeing sustainability as a top concern. Additionally, it emphasizes how green technologies have a beneficial impact on a variety of industries and how they have the potential to lead global sustainability activities. The study showed the positive impact of green technologies in different fields. It will focus on applications, and success stories while emphasizing the beneficial effects of green technology across various industries. This chapter opens the path for a greater comprehension of sustainable technologies' crucial role in building a more sustainable future by focusing on their fundamental necessity.

    Arti Saxena, Manav Rachna International Institute of Reseacrh and Studies, India
    Kapil Gupta, Manav Rachna International Institute of Research and Studies, India
    Sasmita Pala, Manav Rachna International Institute of Reseacrh and Studies, India

This chapter outlines the journey that intertwines solar energy and artificial intelligence (AI), focusing on optimizing solar energy generation within India's dynamic landscape. Solar energy is abundant— its variability demands creative solutions to turn unpredictability into efficiency. In this context, as technology advances, AI emerges as a valuable tool capable of understanding complex weather patterns, forecasting energy generation, and dynamically adjusting solar panel setups. This study navigates the synergy between AI and solar energy in India. Each section sheds light on different aspects of AI's transformative potential, detailing methods, applications, and concrete results. As the chapter unravels the intricate connection between these two domains, it not only uncovers a more intelligent approach to energy generation, but also catches a glimpse of a future where renewable resources thrive in harmony with technological innovation.

    R. Pitchai, Department of Computer Science and Engineering, B.V. Raju Institute of
      Technology, Narsapur, India
    Suresh Tiwari, Department of Mechanical Engineering, Jharkhand University of Technology,
      Ranchi, India
    C. Viji, Department of Computer Science and Engineering, Alliance College of Engineering
      and Design, Alliance University, Bangalore, India
    A. Kistan, Department of Chemistry, Panimalar Engineering College, Chennai, India
    R Puviarasi, Department of Electronics and Communication Engineering, Saveetha School
      of Engineering, Saveetha Institute of Medical and Technical Sciences (SIMATS),

Thandalam, India
S. Gokul, YSR Technical Education, India

This chapter explores the complex issue of sustainable computing, focusing on its environmental implications. It outlines the principles of green computing, the carbon footprint associated with technology, and the role of data centers in minimizing it. The chapter also highlights the importance of energy efficiency in computing, highlighting the growing energy consumption in IT and outlines strategies for achieving it. It also discusses the role of emerging technologies like renewable energy, IoT, smart grids, quantum computing, and sustainable algorithms in promoting sustainability. The chapter also highlights the role of software solutions in sustainable computing, including green software development practices, virtualization, cloud computing, and power management software. The chapter discusses the practical application of sustainable computing in organizations, highlighting challenges, ethical considerations, and a roadmap for the future of sustainable computing, enriched with case studies.

Chapter 6

Green Computing: Building an Environmentally Sustainable Future Using Cloud and IoT With 6G111
Mala Shharma, Institute of Technology and Science, Ghaziabad, India

Green computing refers to strategies and procedures for creating, utilizing, and disposing of computer resources in an environmentally responsible manner while preserving overall computing performance. This entails using less hazardous materials, getting the most usage possible out of a product while using the least amount of energy possible, as well as making old items and garbage more reusable, recyclable, and biodegradable. Many businesses are making efforts to lessen the negative effects of their activities on the environment.

Chapter 7

Piyal Roy, Brainware University, India
Shivnath Ghosh, Brainware University, India
Amitava Podder, Brainware University, India
Subrata Paul, Brainware University, India

The concept of smart cities, powered by internet of things (IoT) technologies, has gained attraction in recent years as a means to address urban challenges and create sustainable urban environments. However, with the growing concern about environmental issues, there is a need to explore how IoT can be leveraged to make smart cities more eco-friendly and sustainable. This book chapter proposes to delve into the topic of green IoT for eco-friendly and sustainable smart cities by examining the role of IoT in enabling sustainable practices in various aspects of urban life, including energy management, waste management, transportation, and urban planning. The chapter will also highlight the challenges and opportunities of using IoT for sustainable smart cities and discuss potential solutions and best practices for building green IoT systems in urban environments.

Chapter 8

Yogita Yashveer Raghav, Dronacharya College of Engineering, Gurugram, India
Pallavi Pandey, K.R. Mangalam University, India

Individuals worldwide are increasingly embracing new technology, dedicating more time to portable devices, and contributing to high energy consumption and carbon emissions in the IT industry. Green cloud computing aims to optimize energy efficiency, promote renewable energy sources, and implement eco-friendly practices in cloud computing infrastructure. By prioritizing energy conservation and sustainable production, it plays a vital role in mitigating environmental challenges. This chapter analyzes factors impacting energy consumption in cloud computing, emphasizing power efficiency and energy-efficient mechanisms in data centers. It also highlights the role of cloud users in achieving sustainable cloud computing and emphasizes the importance of energy-performance. Authors have proposed steps to reduce carbon emissions in data centers and conserve power at home. Adopting green cloud computing practices contributes to protecting the environment and advancing sustainable development goals through advanced technologies.

This chapter explores the integration of applied artificial intelligence (AI), machine learning (ML), and edge computing in cloud environments, with a focus on leveraging these technologies for sustainable development. The first part of the thesis investigates the enhancement of cloud computing through the application of AI and ML techniques. The second part delves into the emerging paradigm of Edge AI in cloud computing, which examines the integration of AI and ML capabilities at the network edge to enable real-time analysis and decision-making. The thesis highlights the importance of sustainable development in cloud computing, emphasizing the need for energy-efficient and environmentally conscious solutions. Through comprehensive experimentation and analysis, this research contributes valuable insights into the development of sustainable cloud architectures and strategies. The findings provide a roadmap for organizations and researchers to leverage the synergistic potential of AI, ML, and edge computing, driving advancements in cloud technology for sustainable development.

Load balancing plays a vital role in the effective management of resources within cloud computing environments. As the use of cloud technologies continues to expand rapidly, it becomes increasingly important to ensure efficient allocation of resources and address performance issues. The utilization of load balancing techniques becomes crucial in the distribution of workloads across multiple servers, thereby optimizing resource usage and enhancing system performance. Swarm intelligence-based load balancing presents a promising approach to achieving sustainable resource allocation in cloud environments. By leveraging self-organization and decentralized decision-making principles, swarm intelligence algorithms can optimize resource utilization, minimize energy consumption, and improve overall system performance. This chapter offers a comprehensive overview of this topic, emphasizing the potential advantages, challenges, and future directions associated with load balancing using swarm intelligence within the context of sustainable development in cloud environments.

Chapter 11
 Kiritkumar Patel, Ganpat University, India
 Ajaykumar Patel, Ganpat University, India
 Bhavesh Patel, Ganpat University, India

Cloud computing refers to a network of computing resources (servers, networks, applications, hardware, and software) interconnected globally. A good usage technique for resource utilization is load balancing. The practice of reassigning the total load to the individual nodes in a particular network is known as task distribution in the cloud. Since there is now no specific research carried out to perform comparative analytics in terms of different parameters of scheduling of task-based algorithms, it is crucial to develop a consistent comparison mechanism among them. FCFS, SJF, OLB, and GPA are the scheduling algorithms that are explored. Distribution of tasks is the main concern of crucial elements that boosts performance and optimizes resource usage. This study surveys the various scheduling methods employed by cloud service providers. There are so many scheduling approaches available to optimize performance and minimize execution time. It also discusses the security challenges in the cloud according to infrastructure and services.

Chapter 12
 Anuj Kumar Gupta, CGC College of Engineering, India

In the adoption of cloud computing technology, the data security of customer data is prime research these days. The user gets access of the cloud resources that are hosted over the internet that can be hijacked by the attacker. In one example, the access of the virtual machine (VM) as a dedicated resource is given to the end user by the CSP; and when the end user is accessing these resources through an internet-connected PC, there is a possibility of security violation by the attacker, who can take full control of the data. Most of the intrusion detection and prevention system implemented over the cloud infrastructures is rule-based and therefore are only capable to detect the known threats. This research work addressed the security problem by a) selection of optimal data security algorithm, and b) data fragmentation and distribution of data blocks over the multiple cloud nodes that make it difficult to guess about the actual data and its location.

Chapter 13
 Varuna Kumara, Department of Electronics and Communication Engineering, Moodlakatte
 Institute of Technology, Kundapura, India
 Durgesh M Sharma, Shri Ramdeobaba College of Engineering and Management, Nagpur,
 India
 J. Samson Isaac, Department of Biomedical Engineering, Karunya Institute of Technology
 and Sciences, Coimbatore, India
 S. Saravanan, Department of Electrical and Electronics Engineering, B.V. Raju Institute of
 Technology, Narsapur, India
 D. Suganthi, Department of Computer Science, Saveetha College of Liberal Arts and

Sciences, SIMATS, Thandalam, India
Sampath Boopathi, Mechanical Engineering, Muthayammal Engineering College,
Namakkal, India

The book explores the use of artificial intelligence (AI) in power monitoring systems for SMEs to enhance energy efficiency, reduce operational costs, and ensure sustainability. It discusses current energy challenges faced by SMEs, emphasizes real-time monitoring, and highlights the benefits of AI integration. The chapter details the components of an AI-integrated power monitoring system, including data acquisition, analysis, and control strategies. It examines AI techniques like machine learning, deep learning, and predictive analytics for identifying energy usage patterns. The chapter also discusses successful cases of SMEs using AI-based systems, highlighting their optimization of energy consumption and reduced costs.

Chapter 14

R. Jeya, Department of Computing Technologies, School of Computing, SRM Institute of
Science and Technology, Kattankulathur, India
G. R. Venkatakrishnan, Department of Electrical and Electronics Engineering, Sri
Sivasubramaniya Nadar College of Engineering, Kalavakkam, India
R. Rengaraj, Department of Electrical and Electronics Engineering, Sri Sivasubramaniya
Nadar College of Engineering, Kalavakkam, India
M. Rajalakshmi, Department of Computing Technologies, School of Computing, SRM
Institute of Science and Technology, Kattankulathur, India
K. Pradeep Mohan Kumar, Department of Computing Technologies, School of Computing,
SRM Institute of Science and Technolog, Kattankulathur, India
Sampath Boopathi, Mechanical Engineering, Muthayammal Engineering College,
Namakkal, India

This chapter explores the integration of AI techniques in water resource management for soil-based and soilless irrigation systems in agriculture. It emphasizes the importance of AI in optimizing water use and data-driven decision-making. AI-powered techniques like machine learning and predictive analytics enable precise water optimization. Soilless systems like hydroponics, aquaponics, and aeroponics also contribute to water efficiency. AI is crucial in weather forecasting, climate adaptation, crop water estimation, and water use optimization in water-stressed environments. The chapter discusses successful AI implementations, cost-benefit analysis, ethical, social, environmental considerations, equity, access, and sustainability. Future prospects, advancements, and challenges in AI techniques for water management are explored, emphasizing the need for AI adoption in water-efficient farming practices.

Chapter 15

Manish Kumar Singh, School of Electronics Engineering (SENSE), VIT-AP University, India
Anamika Lata, School of Electronics Engineering (SENSE), VIT-AP University, India

This chapter explores the integration of AI and ML techniques in the design and manufacturing of green and flexible electronics. It emphasizes the significance of these technologies for sustainable development and discusses the challenges and opportunities they present. The chapter provides an overview of AI and ML algorithms applicable to the field, including materials selection, intelligent manufacturing, energy efficiency prediction, and design optimization. Case studies highlight successful applications of AI and ML in green and flexible electronics. Overall, this chapter demonstrates how AI and ML contribute to the sustainability, efficiency, and performance of electronic devices, including AI-assisted materials selection, intelligent manufacturing processes, predictive modeling for energy efficiency, and optimization of flexible electronic designs using machine learning. It demonstrates the effectiveness of AI and ML in achieving sustainable development in the field of green and flexible electronics.

Preface

As the editors of *Convergence Strategies for Green Computing and Sustainable Development*, we are delighted to present this comprehensive reference book that explores the convergence of emerging technologies to foster sustainable development. In an era defined by the rapid evolution of the Internet of Things (IoT), Artificial Intelligence (AI), Fog computing, and cloud computing, the need for innovative strategies to address environmental concerns has never been more critical.

The relentless pursuit of progress has brought about unprecedented challenges, affecting societies, the environment, and natural resources. However, this book sheds light on the transformative potential of technology to mitigate these challenges. From energy-efficient sensors in IoT that combat pollution to the computational analysis capabilities of AI driving positive energy systems, and the revolutionary impact of cloud computing on business models, the path to a sustainable future is paved with technological innovation.

The primary objective of this edited book is to provide a convergence strategy that holistically understands, transforms, and develops technological systems for emerging technologies in society. To achieve this, we have adhered to certain guiding principles in the preparation of this reference book:

1. **Accuracy and Rigorous Editing:** The information presented in this book is accurate and up-to-date, undergoing rigorous editing to ensure precision and reliability.
2. **Clarity and Conciseness:** Clear and concise language has been employed to facilitate easy comprehension for readers from diverse backgrounds.
3. **Well-Organized Content:** The content is well-organized to enable readers to swiftly locate the information they seek, featuring chapter summaries, tables of contents, and indexes.
4. **Practical Insight and Real-World Examples:** Practical advice and real-world examples are integrated to assist readers in applying the information to their own work or projects.
5. **Well-Designed Visuals:** Complex concepts are elucidated through well-designed visuals, enhancing reader understanding.

The target audience for this book includes Master's students, research scholars, faculty members, working professionals seeking knowledge, and industry experts exploring new trends. The carefully curated topics span various domains, reflecting the dynamic landscape of green computing and sustainable development.

Covered Topics

1. Sustainable Cloud Computing:
   - Introduction of Sustainable Emerging Technologies
   - Introduction of Sustainable Cloud Computing and IoT
   - Impacts of digital transformation on the Environment and Sustainability
   - Environmental sustainability and digital challenges
   - Security, privacy, and effectiveness of sustainable Cloud Computing technique for Big Data analysis and IoT
   - A Taxonomy and future directions for sustainable cloud computing
2. Artificial Intelligence and Machine Learning for Sustainable Development:
   - Introduction and Challenges in Green Artificial Intelligence and ML
   - Role of AI and ML in Achieving the Sustainable Development Goals
   - Sustainable AI- Environmental Implications, Challenges, and Opportunities
   - Efficient, Sustainable, and Equitable Technology for Smart Cities and Futures
   - Artificial Intelligence for Sustainability in Energy Industry
   - Application of Artificial Intelligence in efficient energy generation and Storage
   - AI and 5G Convergence for Energy-Efficiency Perspective
3. Sustainable Wireless Systems and Networks:
   - Green and sustainable communication techniques for Energy-Efficient Wireless networks and systems
   - Sustainable Approaches for Optimizing Performance of Wireless Networks
   - Sustainable Approaches for WSN Security I
   - Sustainability of 5G Networks
   - Energy and Battery Management
4. Green IoT and Edge-AI as Crucial Technological Facilitators for a Sustainable Digital Transition:
   - Energy-Efficient Communication Protocols, Interoperability
   - Green-Internet of Things for Smart Ecosphere
   - Green IoT for Eco-Friendly and Sustainable Smart Cities
   - Advancements and Sustainability with Environment Using Green IoT
   - Internet of Things (IoT) for Sustainable Ecosystem Expansion
   - Smart data acquisition systems for handling energy generation schemes

The chapters delve into diverse domains, each contributing a unique perspective to the overarching theme of fostering green computing for sustainable development. In the section on "Sustainable Cloud Computing," readers will embark on a journey through the foundations of emerging technologies, the integration of IoT with sustainable cloud computing, and the profound impacts of digital transformation on environmental sustainability. Moving to "Artificial Intelligence and Machine Learning for Sustainable Development," the chapters dissect the challenges and opportunities presented by green AI and ML, exploring their role in achieving sustainable development goals and their application in diverse industries, from smart cities to energy generation and storage. The section on "Sustainable Wireless Systems and Networks" intricately examines communication techniques, optimization strategies, and security measures in energy-efficient wireless networks, addressing the sustainability of 5G networks and effective energy management. Finally, the chapters on "Green IoT and Edge-AI" illuminate energy-efficient communication protocols, interoperability, and the pivotal role of IoT in fostering eco-friendly smart cities. Each chapter provides practical insights, real-world examples, and a forward-looking perspective, making this book an indispensable resource for those navigating the dynamic landscape of green computing and sustainable development.

Chapter 1: In this foundational chapter, the focus is on examining the intricate relationship between sustainable development objectives and the rapid evolution of artificial intelligence (AI) technology. The exploration begins with an in-depth analysis of how AI systems impact the environment, particularly in terms of carbon footprint and energy use. Various strategies, such as eco-friendly data centers, energy-efficient algorithms, and sustainable design principles, are evaluated for their environmental implications. The second section shifts the focus to societal effects, exploring the role of AI in addressing societal challenges through the development of fair and open algorithms, ethical AI applications, and fostering human-AI cooperation. This chapter serves as a critical introduction to the complexities and creative solutions associated with sustainability in the AI era.

Chapter 2: Against the backdrop of the Sustainable Development Goals and the transformative effects of the pandemic, this chapter navigates the concept of Society 5.0 as a key framework for social development. Delving into the idea that technology plays a pivotal role in sustainable growth, the chapter explores the potential of Society 5.0 to impact various aspects of society, including sustainability and quality of life. Drawing on scientific publications and data from governmental and organizational initiatives, the chapter argues that Society 5.0 goes beyond being a mere trend, offering unprecedented prospects for a highly smart globalized world. This chapter provides readers with a forward-looking perspective on the intersection of societal development, technology, and sustainability.

Chapter 3: Green technology emerges as a game-changing strategy in this chapter, addressing urgent environmental concerns while promoting economic and social well-being. The exploration centers on the pivotal role of green technology at both national and international levels, emphasizing its endorsement by leading businesses and its increasing recognition as a top global priority. The chapter examines the positive impact of green technologies across various industries, presenting specific applications and success stories. By focusing on the fundamental necessity of sustainable technologies, this chapter contributes to a greater understanding of their crucial role in building a more sustainable future.

Chapter 4: The synergy between solar energy and artificial intelligence takes center stage in this chapter, specifically focusing on optimizing solar energy generation within India's dynamic landscape. Acknowledging the abundance of solar energy but recognizing its variability, the chapter explores how AI serves as a valuable tool for understanding complex weather patterns, forecasting energy generation, and dynamically adjusting solar panel setups. With sections dedicated to various aspects of AI's transformative potential, this chapter not only sheds light on a more intelligent approach to energy generation but also envisions a future where renewable resources thrive in harmony with technological innovation.

Chapter 5: Tackling the complex issue of sustainable computing, this chapter delves into its environmental implications and outlines the principles of green computing. From the carbon footprint associated with technology to the role of data centers in minimizing environmental impact, the chapter emphasizes the importance of energy efficiency in computing. The exploration extends to emerging technologies such as renewable energy, IoT, smart grids, quantum computing, and sustainable algorithms, presenting a comprehensive overview of strategies for promoting sustainability. Practical applications in organizations, ethical considerations, and a roadmap for the future enrich this chapter, making it a valuable guide for navigating the landscape of sustainable computing.

Chapter 6: This chapter provides a concise overview of green computing strategies, emphasizing the responsible creation, utilization, and disposal of computer resources. It underscores the importance of using less hazardous materials, maximizing product usage while minimizing energy consumption, and making items more reusable, recyclable, and biodegradable. The chapter highlights ongoing efforts by businesses to mitigate the negative environmental impact of their activities, aligning with the overarching theme of green computing for sustainability.

Chapter 7: Focusing on the concept of smart cities powered by IoT technologies, this chapter explores the role of IoT in making smart cities more eco-friendly and sustainable. It delves into various aspects of urban life, including energy management, waste management, transportation, and urban planning. By proposing to unravel the topic of "Green IoT for Eco-Friendly and Sustainable Smart Cities," the chapter aims to provide insights into the challenges and opportunities associated with leveraging IoT for sustainable urban development, offering potential solutions and best practices.

Chapter 8: This chapter zooms in on the imperative of green cloud computing, emphasizing its role in optimizing energy efficiency, promoting renewable energy sources, and implementing eco-friendly practices in cloud computing infrastructure. It analyzes factors impacting energy consumption, highlights power efficiency and energy-efficient mechanisms in data centers, and underscores the role of cloud users in achieving sustainable cloud computing. By proposing steps to reduce carbon emissions in data centers and conserve power, the chapter advocates for the adoption of green cloud computing practices to advance environmental protection and sustainable development goals.

Chapter 9: Exploring the integration of Applied Artificial Intelligence (AI), Machine Learning (ML), and Edge Computing in cloud environments, this chapter underscores the importance of sustainable development in cloud computing. It investigates the enhancement of cloud computing through AI and ML techniques and delves into the emerging paradigm of Edge AI in cloud computing. The research contributes valuable insights into the development of sustainable cloud architectures and strategies, providing a roadmap for organizations and researchers to leverage the synergistic potential of AI, ML, and Edge Computing for sustainable development.

Chapter 10: Load balancing emerges as a vital aspect of effective resource management within cloud computing environments, and this chapter emphasizes its role in addressing performance issues and optimizing resource usage. By introducing swarm intelligence-based load balancing, the chapter explores how self-organization and decentralized decision-making principles can enhance resource utilization, minimize energy consumption, and improve overall system performance. Offering a comprehensive overview, the chapter highlights the potential advantages, challenges, and future directions associated with load balancing using swarm intelligence within the context of sustainable development in cloud environments.

Chapter 11: Focused on task distribution in the cloud, this chapter surveys various scheduling methods employed by cloud service providers to optimize performance and minimize execution time. Exploring scheduling algorithms such as FCFS, SJF, OLB, and GPA, the chapter delves into the crucial elements that boost performance and optimize resource usage. The study addresses the need for a consistent comparison mechanism among these scheduling methods, emphasizing their impact on performance and efficiency while discussing security challenges in the cloud infrastructure and services.

Chapter 12: This chapter addresses the prime research concern of data security in cloud computing, particularly the security of customer data. Acknowledging the potential security violations in cloud infrastructures, the chapter proposes optimal data security algorithms and data fragmentation techniques to make it challenging for attackers to gain control of data. By highlighting the limitations of rule-based intrusion detection and prevention systems, the research contributes to the understanding of enhanced security measures, emphasizing the importance of data security in the adoption of cloud computing technology.

Chapter 13: Exploring the use of Artificial Intelligence (AI) in power monitoring systems for Small and Medium-sized Enterprises (SMEs), this chapter focuses on enhancing energy efficiency, reducing operational costs, and ensuring sustainability. The chapter details the components of an AI-integrated power monitoring system, including data acquisition, analysis, and control strategies. It examines AI techniques like machine learning, deep learning, and predictive analytics for identifying energy usage patterns, showcasing successful cases of SMEs using AI-based systems to optimize energy consumption and reduce costs.

Chapter 14: This chapter explores the integration of AI techniques in water resource management for both soil-based and soilless irrigation systems in agriculture. Emphasizing the importance of AI in optimizing water use and data-driven decision-making, the chapter discusses AI-powered techniques like machine learning and predictive analytics. It explores soilless systems like hydroponics, aquaponics, and aeroponics, contributing to water efficiency. The chapter discusses successful AI implementations, cost-benefit analysis, ethical considerations, and future prospects, highlighting the need for AI adoption in water-efficient farming practices.

Chapter 15: The final chapter delves into the integration of AI and ML techniques in the design and manufacturing of green and flexible electronics. It underscores the significance of these technologies for sustainable development and discusses the challenges and opportunities they present. The chapter provides an overview of AI and ML algorithms applicable to the field, including materials selection, intelligent manufacturing, energy efficiency prediction, and design optimization. Case studies highlight successful applications of AI and ML in green and flexible electronics, demonstrating their effectiveness in achieving sustainability in electronic device manufacturing.

We trust that this book will serve as a valuable resource for readers seeking in-depth knowledge and practical insights into the convergence of green computing and sustainable development. The collective expertise of our esteemed contributors is woven into the fabric of each chapter, offering a rich tapestry of ideas and strategies to shape a more sustainable future.

Editors,

Vishal Jain
Sharda University, India

Murali Raman
Asia Pacific University, Malaysia

Akshat Agrawal
Amity University, India

Meenu Hans
K. R. Mangalam University, India

Swati Gupta
K. R. Mangalam University, India

Chapter 1
Sustainability in the Age of AI:
Exploring Challenges and Innovative Solutions

Juhi Singh
Manipal University Jaipur, India

Aarti Chugh
SGT University, India

Arun Kumar Singh
Amity University, Gurgaon, India

ABSTRACT

Sustainable development objectives face substantial potential problems because of the fast development and use of artificial intelligence technology in a variety of fields. The purpose of this essay is to examine the difficulties and creative solutions related to sustainability in the era of AI. The chapter's first section examines how AI systems affect the environment, concentrating on their carbon footprint and energy use. AI applications spread are critical to address the rising energy needs of AI infrastructure and algorithms, as well as the environmental effects of producing and discarding AI hardware. The impact of many strategies, including eco-friendly data centers, energy-efficient algorithms, and sustainable design principles, on the environment is evaluated. The societal effects of AI on sustainability are examined in the second section. The chapter explores these concerns and offers creative solutions that use AI to deal with societal problems, such developing fair and open algorithms, assuring ethical AI application, and encouraging human-AI cooperation.

INTRODUCTION

Artificial intelligence (AI) is swiftly venturing into uncharted territory within the realms of corporate practices, business, governmental policies and many more sectors. The cognitive capabilities of machines and robots, enhanced by deep learning algorithms, have engendered profound disruptions and facilita-

DOI: 10.4018/979-8-3693-0338-2.ch001

Figure 1. United Nations Sustainable Development Goals (Sustainable Development, n.d.)

tions in the spheres of business, governance, and society at large. However, the rapid advancement of AI requires essential regulatory understanding and supervision to facilitate the sustainable progress of AI-based technologies.

In 2015, the United Nations developed 17 objectives (Figure 1) to ensure the planets' continued existence in a sustainable manner (Sustainable Development, n.d.). However, high population expansion necessitates the advancement of novel technologies to meet the needs imposed by an ever-increasing human population. This constitutes a rather rapid acceleration in technical development.

Because intelligent technology plays such an important part in the process of sustainable development, the role of artificial intelligence is becoming more important. A sustainable approach to artificial intelligence examines not just the applications of AI, but also the sociotechnical system that AI functions within (Van Wynsberghe, 2021). The role of sustainable development as a mechanism is best defined by the statement "society can interact with the environment". Economic sustainability, social sustainability, and environmental sustainability make up the three pillars that support the idea of sustainable progress. A further definition of sustainable development is that of a "visionary and forward-looking paradigm." These three tenets serve as the foundation upon which the notion of sustainable development rests. While working on sustainable development, the struggle is not just between innovation and the equal distribution of resources; it is also between satisfying the needs of the environment, the economy, and society. Both innovation and the equal distribution of resources are essential to achieving sustainable development. An AI that is sustainable must be able to depict the tension that exists between the need for innovation in AI to accomplish sustainable development goals and the need to specifically target the sustainability of AI training and usage (Van Wynsberghe, 2021).

Many researchers and academicians have surveyed and tested recent AI technologies which claim to ensure Sustainable Development. The idea of 'Sustainable AI' is still in its formative years at this point (Van Wynsberghe, 2021). The objective of this chapter is to inspire researchers in the field of artificial intelligence to delve into the essence of Safer AI and explore into its adverse effects on both organizations and society.

The first section of the paper focuses on the environmental implications of AI. It investigates the carbon footprint and energy usage associated with AI systems, shedding light on the increasing energy demands of AI infrastructure and algorithms. Moreover, the environmental consequences of producing and discarding AI hardware are analysed. Strategies such as eco-friendly data centres, energy-efficient algorithms, and sustainable design principles are critically evaluated in terms of their potential to mitigate the environmental impact of AI.

In the second section, the societal effects of AI on sustainability are explored. While AI has the potential to foster social equality and inclusivity, it also raises concerns about job displacement, algorithmic bias, and privacy infringements. The article delves into these issues and proposes innovative solutions that harness AI's capabilities to address societal challenges. This includes the development of fair and transparent algorithms, ensuring ethical AI applications, and promoting effective collaboration between humans and AI systems.

Additionally, the paper examines how AI can be leveraged to promote sustainable practices in various industries and enhance resource management. It highlights examples of AI applications in smart cities, precision farming, environmentally friendly transportation, and renewable energy systems. The potential of AI-enabled decision support systems and predictive analytics to optimize resource allocation and minimize waste is underscored.

Finally, the study emphasizes the need for multidisciplinary cooperation and regulatory changes to fully harness AI's potential for sustainability. Collaboration among stakeholders i.e., academia, business, and government is crucial in establishing robust frameworks, standards, and regulations that guarantee the ethical and long-term utilization of AI technology in sustainable development.

By analysing the environmental, societal, and economic dimensions of AI's impact on sustainability, this research paper aims to provide valuable insights and recommendations for effectively integrating AI into sustainable development efforts.

AI AND ENVIRONMENT

The concept of artificial intelligence (AI) sustainability focuses on the utilisation of sustainable data sources, power supply, and infrastructures as a means of calculating and minimising the impact that training and/or adjusting an algorithm has on the environment. Considering these elements is essential to guarantee that AI will not have a negative impact on the environment (Van Wynsberghe, 2021).

Artificial intelligence, the technology that reigns supreme over all others, is intended to serve two distinct purposes. Even though technology has the potential to help mitigate the effects of the climate crisis in ways such as the design of intelligent grids, the building of environmentally friendly infrastructure, and the modelling of climate change projections, artificial intelligence is also a significant contributor to carbon emissions. This is because artificial intelligence requires a great deal of energy to function (Dhar, 2020).

Artificial intelligence systems have a major impact on the environment and use up a lot of energy (Brown & Sandholm, 2018). Some of examples of AI systems and processes which cause harm to environment are given below:

- The training process for AI models requires substantial computational power and energy consumption (Strubell et al., 2020).
- Data canters, where AI computations take place, contribute to additional energy consumption due to cooling requirements (Brown & Sandholm, 2018).
- The increasing use of AI-powered devices and cloud-based AI services compounds environmental challenges (Brown & Sandholm, 2018).

Figure 2. Social influence of sustainability

| Inequality and Displacement | Ethical and Bias Issues | Privacy and Data Protection | Accessibility and Digital Divide | Human-AI Collaboration and Governance |

Efforts are being made to develop energy-efficient AI algorithms and hardware (Strubell et al., 2020). The promotion of renewable energy sources in data centres is crucial for sustainable AI development (Strubell et al., 2020). Reducing the carbon footprint and energy consumption of AI systems is essential to mitigate their environmental impact (Strubell et al., 2020). Even though new methods are being researched and tested to ensure that AI carbon footprints are minimised and are leading to the achievement of the goal of Greener AI, the question that needs to be answered is: will the benefits of helping decarbonization and resilience outweigh the large energy consumption that it entails?

SOCIAL IMPACT AND CHALLENGES OF AI IN SUSTAINABLE DEVELOPMENT

This section explores the social impact of AI in sustainable development and highlights the challenges that need to be navigated for a more just and sustainable future. The use of AI requires that it be equitable, inclusive, and easily accessible. Fairness should be clearly accounted for to prevent reinforcing existing prejudices in society that are reflected in the data that is utilised for the construction of the model.

Advances in machine learning (ML) and artificial intelligence (AI) lend the potential to develop improved tools and solutions that can successfully address global challenges and turn a favorable social outcome aligned with the goals and objectives defined in the United Nations' 17 Sustainable Development Goals (SDGs). The goal of the AI for Social Good movement is to forge multidisciplinary collaborations that are centred on the use of AI to advance the Sustainable Development Goals (SDGs) (Tomašev et al., 2020) which affect the certain areas as shown in figure 2.

- *Inequality and Displacement*

One of the primary concerns associated with AI in sustainable development is the exacerbation of existing social inequalities. AI technologies have the potential to automate jobs and tasks, leading to job displacement and economic disruption in certain industries. This displacement often affects vulnerable populations, widening the wealth gap and creating social divisions. These formidable factors have significant implications for SDG #9 (Industry, Innovation, and Infrastructure) and SDG #8 (Decent Work and Economic Growth). They also have indirect effects on SDG #10 (Reduced Inequalities) and SDG #1 (No Poverty), especially in developing nations where there is limited social safety nets and protections for unemployed individuals and labour rights. Addressing this challenge requires proactive measures such as reskilling and upskilling programs, ensuring that individuals have access to new job opportunities and promoting inclusive growth strategies that benefit all members of society.

Another important SDG to focus on is SDG #5 i.e., attaining gender equality. According to a study conducted by UN Women, the representation of women in the field of artificial intelligence worldwide is only 22 percent. The study also highlighted a troubling fact that 44.2 percent of 133 AI systems analysed across various industries displayed gender bias (Anand, 2002). These findings are deeply concerning. The study further acknowledged the substantial contributions women have made to the digital realm, spanning from the early days of computers to the current era of virtual reality and artificial intelligence. However, a persistent gender disparity in digital access prevents women from fully harnessing the potential of the technology sector. Achieving digital empowerment and gender equality requires a strategic approach. The key lies in providing women with a comprehensive combination of digital and leadership skills, enabling them to demonstrate their capabilities in technology, business, and other relevant domains. Considering that AI represents the future of businesses, empowering women to become catalysts in this field necessitates cultivating their abilities as business leaders, rather than confining them solely to technical roles. By fostering a multidimensional skill set, women can effectively contribute to and shape the advancements in the realm of artificial intelligence, driving progress and promoting gender equality (Anand, 2002). A significant step towards attaining gender equality i.e., SDG#5 and strong institutions i.e., SDG#16 is increasing the number of women who hold positions of power within our democratic institutions. To do this, inclusive places for the discussion of pressing political problems need to be created and safeguarded. The use of social media platforms has developed into a fundamental component of these exchanges and has emerged as a significant channel for the communication of ideas and the dissemination of information. For there to be an equal representation of women on these digital platforms, women need to feel safe enough to voice their ideas without the threat of being harassed (Tomašev et al., 2020).

- *Ethical and Bias Issues*

Numerous researchers have emphasized the ethical challenges arising from the adoption and integration of AI. AI systems are trained on vast amounts of data, which can perpetuate biases and discrimination present in society. Bias represents a significant issue in AI algorithms as Governments and businesses rely on these biased-embedded AI models and data to make decisions, thereby exacerbating the problem (Favaretto et al., 2019). If AI algorithms are not carefully designed and tested, they can inadvertently reinforce existing inequalities or discriminate against certain demographic groups. The Sustainable Development Goal most closely related to bias and ethical issues is SDG #16, which focuses on "Peace, Justice, and Strong Institutions." This goal aims to promote inclusive and accountable societies, ensure access to justice for all, and build effective, transparent, and responsive institutions at all levels. Addressing biases and ethical concerns in AI and other technologies is essential for achieving SDG #16, as it involves upholding principles of fairness, non-discrimination, and transparency in decision-making processes. Additionally, mitigating biases and promoting ethical practices contributes to building trust in institutions and fostering social cohesion, which are central to the objectives of SDG #16. It is crucial to develop ethical frameworks and guidelines for AI development and deployment to mitigate bias and ensure fairness and accountability. Transparent and inclusive decision-making processes, careful selection of training data, conscious data governance, diverse teams working on AI development, and algorithmic audits are some strategies that can address these ethical concerns (Owe & Baum, 2021).

- *Privacy and Data Protection*

As AI systems often rely on vast amounts of data to learn and make decisions, the collection, storage, and usage of personal data become crucial considerations. Respecting privacy rights and ensuring robust data protection mechanisms are fundamental in AI applications. By integrating privacy and data protection principles into AI development and deployment, we can mitigate risks associated with unauthorized data access, breaches, and the potential for bias or discrimination (Jungwirth & Haluza, 2023). Aligning AI practices with privacy and data protection safeguards helps to build trust in AI technologies, promotes responsible and ethical AI use, and aligns with the objectives of SDG #16. It is essential to establish robust data governance frameworks, including clear consent mechanisms, strict data anonymization practices, and secure storage and transmission protocols. Strengthening legal and regulatory frameworks that safeguard individual privacy rights is crucial to building public trust in AI systems and promoting sustainable development.

- *Accessibility and Digital Divide*

While AI has the potential to drive sustainable development, its benefits may not reach everyone equally. The digital divide, characterized by unequal access to technology and digital resources, can limit the participation of marginalized communities in AI-driven development initiatives. Accessibility and the digital divide are critical issues that intersect with multiple SDGs (Jungwirth & Haluza, 2023). Bridging the digital divide is crucial for achieving SDG #4 (Quality Education) by ensuring equal access to educational resources. It is also closely tied to SDG #5 (Gender Equality) as it promotes equitable access to digital technologies for women and girls. SDG #9 (Industry, Innovation, and Infrastructure) emphasizes the importance of investing in technology and innovation to provide equal digital access to all. Additionally, addressing the digital divide contributes to SDG #10 (Reduced Inequalities) by ensuring marginalized communities have equal opportunities. AI plays a significant role in this realm by enabling assistive technologies, language translation, personalized learning, and connectivity solutions. By leveraging AI and aligning it with the SDGs, we can work towards reducing the digital divide, promoting accessibility, and creating a more inclusive and equitable digital society. Ensuring equitable access to AI technologies, promoting digital literacy programs, and investing in infrastructure development are essential to bridge this divide. Collaborative efforts among governments, civil society organizations, and the private sector are crucial in addressing these accessibility challenges.

- *Human-AI Collaboration and Governance*

AI technologies have the potential to significantly impact society and contribute to the achievement of multiple SDGs. However, to ensure the responsible and ethical use of AI, effective collaboration between humans and AI systems is essential. Human-AI collaboration enables us to harness the strengths of both humans and AI, combining human creativity, intuition, and ethical judgment with AI's computational power and data processing capabilities.

SDG #17 (Partnerships for the Goals) underscores the importance of collaboration and governance in achieving the SDGs. Within the field of AI, this entails establishing frameworks, policies, and mechanisms to govern AI systems and ensure their alignment with sustainable development objectives. It involves fostering multi-stakeholder partnerships, including governments, businesses, civil society organizations,

Figure 3. Thrust areas for AI-based technological inclusion for sustainability (Yigitcanlar & Cugurullo, 2020)

and academia, to collectively address challenges related to AI governance, accountability, transparency, and fairness (Zhao & Gómez Fariñas, 2022). The integration of AI systems into various aspects of society necessitates careful consideration of human-AI collaboration and governance mechanisms. While AI can augment human capabilities and decision-making processes, it is essential to establish guidelines for responsible and accountable use. Developing frameworks for human oversight, defining clear roles and responsibilities, and promoting transparency and explain ability in AI systems are key aspects of effective governance. Engaging stakeholders from diverse backgrounds in decision-making processes and fostering multi-disciplinary collaborations can contribute to more socially responsible AI development.

Hence, harnessing the social impact of AI while addressing its challenges is crucial for achieving sustainable development goals. By promoting human-AI collaboration, implementing ethical frameworks, and fostering transparent governance, we can leverage the potential of AI to create a more inclusive, equitable, and sustainable future for all. One should keep in mind that AI is not the solution for sustainable development, it is a choice. Finally, it can also be determined that important thrust areas to focus on while ensuring sustainability through AI are as given in figure 3.

AI APPLICATIONS IN SUSTAINABLE DEVELOPMENT

This section covers important applications of AI where sustainable development is in progress or is implemented to some extent.

AI Enable Smart City

As per forecasts, it is expected that two-thirds of the global population will reside in urban areas by the year 2050. Consequently, there is an urgent requirement to adopt efficient urban planning strategies to create communities that can thrive in a sustainable fashion (Bachmann et al., 2022). For example, artificial intelligence (AI) has the potential to enable the development of intelligent, low-carbon cities that seamlessly incorporate various advanced technologies, including electric autonomous vehicles and smart appliances capable of facilitating demand response within the energy sector (Bachmann et al., 2022; Mehrabi et al., 2020). This has the potential to contribute to the achievement of Sustainable Development Goals (SDGs) 7, 11, and 13, which pertain to climate action and sustainable urban development (Vinuesa, Azizpour, Leite, Balaam, Dignum, Domisch, Felländer, Langhans, Tegmark, & Fuso Nerini, 2020).

Vaidya and Chatterji (Isabel et al., 2020) state that the globe is increasingly transitioning into metropolitan cities as large number of people are relocating to urban areas. Upto 55% of the world's population lives in cities, generate 85% of the global GDP, and are responsible for 75% of the world's emissions of greenhouse gases. There is no way to solve the problems of global sustainability without first addressing sustainability on a local scale, particularly in cities.

In addition, technologies based on AI give solutions for trash management, such as categorising garbage into diverse types. AI has emerged as a topic of discussion, especially among urban policymakers and planners who are looking for tech-based answers to increasingly pressing urbanisation issues (Andeobu et al., 2022). Within the realm of urban policy, one of the most often discussed topics is artificial intelligence (AI), followed closely by smart cities. Most initiatives to use AI to increase efficiency in cities have, however, either faltered or failed to achieve the transition into a smart city. It is becoming more common practise to address urban crises by using cutting-edge digital technology that are both clever and inventive. These crises may be attributed to climate change, pandemics, natural catastrophes, or socioeconomic issues. AI system conceptualizations and practises, as well as promoting the need of a green AI approach to further promote the transition of smart cities and the Sustainable Development Goals (SDGs). Smart cities are generally understood to be locales that make extensive use of digital technology and data to achieve efficiencies that contribute to increased economic development, improved quality of life, and increased environmental sustainability (Yigitcanlar et al., 2021). Different kinds of garbage and making sure to collect data on their composition to assist farmers in increasing the percentage of waste that is recycled.

AI Enable Smart Agriculture

Agriculture is one of the most significant biological industries since it generates the maximum amount of biomass. Biomass may be an essential input for a functioning bioeconomy. Farmers will be able to maximise crop production while simultaneously reducing their negative influence on the environment if they adopt sustainable agriculture that is facilitated by artificial intelligence (AI). Artificial intelligence may assist farmers in making data-driven choices on crop selection, irrigation, fertilisation, and pest management when they practise precision farming. AI technologies can find patterns and insights that would be difficult or impossible to detect manually since these technologies use machine learning algorithms to analyse massive volumes of data (AI-Enabled Sustainable Agriculture, n.d.).

Traditional farming may be transformed into "smart agriculture" with the help of artificial intelligence and the internet of things. These technologies can optimise resources, minimize the human workforce needed, monitor crops, control weeds and crop diseases, manage irrigation and harvesting, and manage supply chains. The combination of these two technologies can identify the characteristics of the soil and assist farmers in taking the required steps to reduce waste and improve crop quality (Katiyar & Farhana, 2021).

In addition, technologies that are based on AI may give solutions for managing trash, such as categorising the various categories of waste and assuring accurate composition information data, which can assist farmers in increasing the percentage of waste that is recycled.

Smart agriculture, precision farming, digital agriculture, and precision irrigation are agricultural practises that use advanced technologies such as big data, sensors, IoT infrastructure, robotics, and data analytics. These applications have the potential to decrease expenses, enhance the monetary advantages of farmers, optimize the administration of supply chains, and augment transparency. Artificial intelligence

(AI) and machine learning (ML) models have the capability to predict future events, make operational decisions in real-time, and generate novel economic models within the agricultural sector. It is essential for these agricultural business models to exhibit sustainability as well. The integration of these models is used to map poverty at various scales, including both macro- and micro-levels, as outlined in Sustainable Development Goal 1. Additionally, these models are employed to assess the efficacy of sustainable welfare initiatives, supervise the provision of food and nutrition, and advance environmentally sustainable agriculture practices. To effectively tackle the issue of malnutrition, it is essential to establish a strong as well as adequately funded data and information infrastructure (Bachmann et al., 2022). According to Mehrabi et al. (2014), it is suggested that many those who matter, including governments, agricultural organizations, entrepreneurs, and researchers, should implement policies, invest resources, and engage in research pertaining to the availability, accessibility, and utilization of technology. These efforts have the potential to foster a more inclusive and sustainable agricultural and food system. Data-driven technologies often encounter challenges in effectively reaching small-scale farmers, landowners, and distant regions.

Sustainable Transport

The development of artificial intelligence and computing technologies hold a great deal of potential for assisting the transport industry in lowering its carbon footprint, which is one of the main goals of sustainable transport. When it comes to preserving the environment, AI-driven advancements such as self-driving cars are moving in the right way and helping to save the planet. AI software that is linked to sensors all around the car, as well as data from Google Street View, is used to make autonomous vehicles function properly. Because of this, the artificial intelligence system in the car can replicate human perception and come to its own conclusions on driver control systems such as steering, braking, and parking. The use of AI in traffic management has the potential to improve road safety as well. Traffic models generated by AI software can identify potentially hazardous regions under existing road and traffic conditions. Using AI to enhance the efficiency of current transportation systems, such as by optimising routes and scheduling, is one use of this technology. Better management of traffic may lead to less congestion and fewer emissions if artificial intelligence is used to analyse data collected from sensors and cameras. AI may also be used to enhance the efficiency of public transportation, such as buses and trains, by forecasting demand and altering timetables appropriately. This can be accomplished by using the technology to analyse passenger traffic. Additionally, AI is being used to make transportation much safer. Sensors that are powered by AI can identify possible dangers on the road, therefore warning drivers of these threats and helping to minimise the number of accidents that occur. Artificial intelligence may also be used to monitor driver behaviour, which can assist ensure that drivers are adhering to safety standards and reduce the likelihood of accidents occurring (Taherdust, 2023).

AI-Enabled Decision Support System

Artificial intelligence (AI) has the capability to provide autonomy and flexibility in a dynamic and multicriteria decision making environment. With the development of machine learning and natural language processing (NLP), AI is now able to provide decision support systems that can help businesses and investors make better decisions faster and more efficiently. AI based decision support systems offer several advantages such as processing large amounts of data, handling unstructured data, generating recommendations, managing biases, etc. (Jungwirth & Haluza, 2023).

TECHNOLOGICAL SUPPORT AND INTERDISCIPLINARY COLLABORATION OF AI IN SUSTAINABLE DEVELOPMENT

There three important pillars who directly affect the sustainability of environment.

i)   Academia,
ii) Industry and,
iii) Government

These three pillars can be used to design such a robust framework by using AI for sustainable environment.

Pillar One: AI Based Academia for Sustainability

SDG 4's first goal is universal, free, and high-quality primary and secondary education. Still in many areas in India gender inequality (SDG 5) is a big issue where girl child is not allowed to go to schools and get education. Poverty alleviation, health improvement, agricultural output, and skilled labour are all linked to education. Data-driven and AI-enabled solutions may transform elementary and secondary education, particularly in rural areas with poor education infrastructure (Hannan & Liu, 2021).

Data-driven and AI-enabled solutions may improve elementary and secondary education for everybody, particularly in distant areas with poor education infrastructure (Bachmann et al., 2022). AI-driven technologies with a robust infrastructure and standardized data protocols may be used for instructional activities in schools/universities or online virtual environments. Systematic and collaborative learning enables great education for everyone (Bachmann et al., 2022).

The application of AI in education should leverage learning science to maximize its potential. Further, collaboration should be done between AI experts and learners, educators, researchers across different disciplines (e.g., pedagogy, psychology, computer science, cognitive science etc.) to design and develop AI-based technology and tools, according to Hannan and Liu (2021).

Pillar Two: AI-Based Industry Evolution for Sustainability

Collectively educating, inventing, and establishing practises that are people-centered, financially efficient, and ecologically friendly are all components of the progression towards a more sustainable mindset (Javaid et al., 2022). Infrastructure, environmentally responsible industrialisation, and technological advancement are the three most important factors that will determine whether or not Sustainable Development Goal 9 (SDG 9) is achieved (Singh & Ru, 2023).

The United Nations believes that one of the most effective ways to raise the quality of life in communities all around the globe is to make investments in infrastructure that is both fundamental and sustainable. The Inclusive and Sustainable Industrial Development (ISID) benchmark developed by the SDG#9 index compares 128 economies during the period of 2000–2016 (Bachmann et al., 2022). A data-driven metric is presented in Kynclová et al. (2020) as a means of measuring a country's progress towards attaining industry-related objectives of the Sustainable Development Goal i.e., SDG#9. The SDG#9 index is a method that is both comprehensive and easy, and it is designed to evaluate the degree to which nations have industrialised their economies while simultaneously fostering social inclusion and

Figure 4. Road of connectivity to fulfil the SDG9 for industrial sustainability (Singh & Ru, 2023)

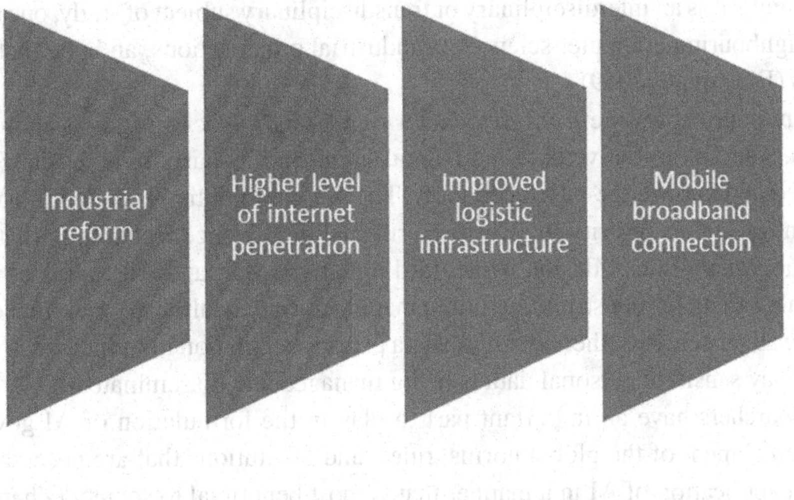

reducing their use of natural resources as well as their negative effects on the environment. As shown in figure 4, Industry 4.0 is the answer for achieving Sustainable Development Goal 9 by means of artificial intelligence to improve and optimise new technologies and processes in industry. The technology behind Industry 4.0 makes it possible for teams to work together regardless of location, time zone, network, or any other factor. This benefits production lines as well as business processes and teams. The cloud and large amounts of data will make it possible to integrate the user experience of Internet of Things (IoT) and Industrial Internet of Things (IIoT) devices and provide very lean production. Cloud storage is very effective and packed with a wide variety of features, in addition to being adaptable, current, and reliable. The cloud is also a popular venue for linking items to the corporation across international boundaries, and it is well suited to manage the large amounts of data created by the Internet of Things (IoT).

Pillar Three: AI-Based Governance for Sustainability

The Sustainable Development Goals aspires to promote peaceful and to foster inclusive societies for sustainable development, ensure access to justice for all, and build institutions at all levels that are effective, accountable, and inclusive (Bachmann et al., 2022).

The swift progress in Artificial Intelligence (AI) and the increased adoption of AI in fields like autonomous vehicles, weapon systems, robotics, and related domains pose significant challenges for governments. They must effectively navigate the scale and rapid pace of socio-technical transformations taking place (Taeihagh, 2021). AI is playing an increasingly essential part in day-to-day life and is having a substantial influence on the very fabric of contemporary society because of the fast development and deployment of a new generation of artificial intelligence (AI) algorithms and products. This is because AI is rapidly being developed and deployed. The development of artificial intelligence (AI) in a manner that is both healthy and sustainable requires strong ethics and governance. China's governments, research organisations, and private firms have released ethical standards and principles for artificial intelligence (AI) and have initiated projects to build AI governance technology (Wu et al., 2020). The long-term objective of these efforts is to ensure that AI continues to be beneficial to human civilization.

The ethics of AI must possess two characteristics to be successful. To begin, it ought to make use of a weak normativity and should refrain from universally determining what constitutes good and evil.

Second, the ethics of AI should prioritise getting as near as possible to the target object. This suggests that ethics is recognised as an interdisciplinary or transdisciplinary subject of study, one that is intimately related to the neighbouring computer sciences or industrial organisations, and one that is active within these disciplines (Daly et al., 2019).

Three different national-level efforts have had a significant impact on India's approach to artificial intelligence (AI). The first initiative is called Digital India, and its purpose is to transform India into a digitally advanced and knowledge-based economy. The second initiative is called Make in India, and it is the government of India's priority to prioritise artificial intelligence technology that is invented and built in India. The Smart Cities Mission is the third initiative (Marda, 2018). AI is now being used by private players in a variety of industries, including manufacturing, healthcare, and finance, amongst others. Despite these advancements, there is still no data privacy regulation in India, which raises important issues about the way sensitive personal data is being managed and disseminated (Daly et al., 2019).

Technical researchers have an important part to play in the formulation of AI governance, which refers to the establishment of the global norms, rules, and institutions that are necessary to enable the development and application of AI in a manner that is most beneficial to society (Zhang et al., 2021).

Based on the studied literature, we have drawn the following table which provides an overview of the key aspects related to the intersection of artificial intelligence (AI) and sustainable development. It highlights the technological support that AI offers in various domains such as resource management,

Table 1. Technological support and interdisciplinary collaboration of AI towards sustainability

Aspect	References	Technological Support	Interdisciplinary Collaboration
Resource Management	Andeobu et al. (2022)	AI-enabled optimization models for sustainable resource allocation	Collaboration between experts from data science, environmental science, and operations research disciplines to develop sustainable resource management strategies
Energy Efficiency	Vinuesa, Azizpour, Leite, Balaam, Dignum, Domisch, Felländer, Langhans, Tegmark, and Fuso Nerini (2020)	AI-driven energy management systems	Collaboration between energy experts, data scientists, and engineers, civil engineers, weather forecast experts to design energy-efficient systems and algorithms
Decision-making	Owe and Baum (2021)	AI-based decision support systems	Collaboration between domain experts, data analysts, and AI specialists to develop AI-driven decision-making tools
Industry Applications	Vinuesa, Azizpour, Leite, Balaam, Dignum, Domisch, Felländer, Langhans, Tegmark, and Fuso Nerini (2020)	AI-driven sustainable practices in industries	Collaboration between industry professionals, environmentalists, and AI experts to implement AI-driven solutions for sustainability
Smart Cities	Zhao and Gómez Fariñas (2022)	AI-enabled smart city initiatives	Collaboration between urban planners, technologists, and policymakers to design and implement AI-enabled smart city projects
Precision Farming	Jungwirth and Haluza (2023)	AI-assisted precision agriculture techniques	Collaboration between agronomists, data scientists, and farmers to develop AI-based precision farming techniques
Renewable Energy	Favaretto et al. (2019)	AI-optimized integration of renewable energy sources	Collaboration between energy experts, engineers, and AI specialists to enhance the efficiency and reliability of renewable energy systems
Policy and Governance	Anand (2002)	AI-supported evidence-based policymaking	Collaboration between policymakers, social scientists, and AI researchers to develop ethical AI frameworks and regulations

energy efficiency, and decision-making. Additionally, it emphasizes the importance of interdisciplinary collaboration, bringing together experts from different fields to harness the potential of AI for sustainable development. The table presents specific examples and references that showcase the application of AI and interdisciplinary collaboration in addressing sustainability challenges and promoting responsible practices.

CONCLUSION

AI dual functionality symbolizes the gateway to a visionary paradise characterized by the fusion of human intellect and technological excellence, or it signifies the initial stride towards an apocalyptic emergence of machines. However, AI has the potential to contribute significantly to sustainable development, but it also presents social challenges that must be addressed. By actively addressing issues such as inequality, bias, privacy, accessibility, and governance, we can harness the benefits of AI while ensuring a more equitable and sustainable future. Collaboration among stakeholders, robust regulations, and ethical considerations are vital for maximizing the positive social impact of AI in sustainable development. In conclusion, this article offers a thorough review of the issues and possibilities related to sustainability in the AI era. It seeks to promote a comprehensive knowledge of how AI might contribute to a sustainable future by looking at environmental, social, and economic factors and offering creative solutions. The conclusions made in this study may help policymakers, academics, and practitioners maximise the benefits of AI while minimising its drawbacks, resulting in a more just and sustainable society. Despite the good results and various uses, there are obstacles to attaining the 17 Sustainable Development Goals (SDGs) that include data shortages, data biases, high energy consumption of computing resources, ethical concerns, privacy, ownership, and security concerns. These obstacles must be overcome before the SDGs can be achieved.

Although the promise has not yet been fully realised, it is safe to say that data-driven and AI-based techniques have been and will likely continue to play an important role in the achievement of the Sustainable Development Goals (SDGs).

In the future, academics may also choose to focus their studies on problems including the digital divide, the lack of reasonable access to modern technologies, and the economic viability of digital technology. This will be in addition to the challenges and misuses that are associated with security. This research offers a convincing argument for the promotion of digital justice and equality, including gender disparities and fairness in online settings. This study was conducted to investigate the effects of gender inequality and unfairness in online environments. The strengthening of connections as well as the establishment of an ecosystem for providing logistical assistance are two more recommendations for further inquiry.

REFERENCES

Anand, A. (2002, January). ICTs: Empowering Women, Assisting Development. *Gender, Technology and Development*, 6(1), 121–127. doi:10.1080/09718524.2002.11910017

Andeobu, L., Wibowo, S., & Grandhi, S. (2022, August). Artificial intelligence applications for sustainable solid waste management practices in Australia: A systematic review. *The Science of the Total Environment, 834*, 155389. doi:10.1016/j.scitotenv.2022.155389 PMID:35460765

Bachmann, N., Tripathi, S., Brunner, M., & Jodlbauer, H. (2022, February 22). The Contribution of Data-Driven Technologies in Achieving the Sustainable Development Goals. *Sustainability (Basel), 14*(5), 2497. doi:10.3390/su14052497

Brown, N., & Sandholm, T. (2018, January 26). Superhuman AI for heads-up no-limit poker: Libratus beats top professionals. *Science, 359*(6374), 418–424. doi:10.1126/science.aao1733 PMID:29249696

Daly, A., Hagendorff, T., Li, H., Mann, M., Marda, V., Wagner, B., Wang, W., & Witteborn, S. (2019). Artificial Intelligence, Governance and Ethics: Global Perspectives. SSRN *Electronic Journal*. doi:10.2139/ssrn.3414805

Dhar, P. (2020). The carbon impact of artificial intelligence. *Nature Machine Intelligence, 2*(8), 423–425. doi:10.1038/s42256-020-0219-9

Favaretto, M., De Clercq, E., & Elger, B. S. (2019, February 5). Big Data and discrimination: Perils, promises and solutions. A systematic review. *Journal of Big Data, 6*(1), 12. doi:10.1186/s40537-019-0177-4

Hannan, E., & Liu, S. (2021, August 9). AI: New source of competitiveness in higher education. *Competitiveness Review, 33*(2), 265–279. doi:10.1108/CR-03-2021-0045

Javaid, M., Haleem, A., Singh, R. P., Suman, R., & Gonzalez, E. S. (2022). Understanding the adoption of Industry 4.0 technologies in improving environmental sustainability. *Sustainable Operations and Computers, 3*, 203–217. doi:10.1016/j.susoc.2022.01.008

Jungwirth, D., & Haluza, D. (2023). Artificial Intelligence and the Sustainable Development Goals: An Exploratory Study in the Context of the Society Domain. *Journal of Software Engineering and Applications, 16*(04), 91–112. doi:10.4236/jsea.2023.164006

Katiyar, S., & Farhana, A. (2021, October 1). Smart Agriculture: The Future of Agriculture using AI and IoT. *Journal of Computational Science, 17*(10), 984–999. doi:10.3844/jcssp.2021.984.999

Kynčlová, P., Upadhyaya, S., & Nice, T. (2020, May). Composite index as a measure on achieving Sustainable Development Goal 9 (SDG-9) industry-related targets: The SDG-9 index. *Applied Energy, 265*, 114755. doi:10.1016/j.apenergy.2020.114755

Marda, V. (2018, October 15). Artificial intelligence policy in India: A framework for engaging the limits of data-driven decision-making. *Philosophical Transactions. Series A, Mathematical, Physical, and Engineering Sciences, 376*(2133), 20180087. doi:10.1098/rsta.2018.0087 PMID:30323001

Mehrabi, Z., McDowell, M. J., Ricciardi, V., Levers, C., Martinez, J. D., Mehrabi, N., Wittman, H., Ramankutty, N., & Jarvis, A. (2020, November 2). The global divide in data-driven farming. *Nature Sustainability, 4*(2), 154–160. doi:10.1038/s41893-020-00631-0

Owe, A., & Baum, S. D. (2021, June 6). Moral consideration of nonhumans in the ethics of artificial intelligence. *AI and Ethics, 1*(4), 517–528. doi:10.1007/s43681-021-00065-0

Ravichandran, RSathyanarayana, NAli, A. A. (2022). AI-Based Smart Agriculture for Sustainable Growth-The Linkage between AI, IOT, Sustainable Growth and Development-An Indian Perspective. Adarsh Journal of Management Research, 1-9.

Singh, S., & Ru, J. (2023, January 21). Goals of sustainable infrastructure, industry, and innovation: A review and future agenda for research. *Environmental Science and Pollution Research International*, *30*(11), 28446–28458. doi:10.1007/s11356-023-25281-5 PMID:36670221

Strubell, E., Ganesh, A., & McCallum, A. (2020, April 3). Energy and Policy Considerations for Modern Deep Learning Research. *Proceedings of the AAAI Conference on Artificial Intelligence*, *34*(09), 13693–13696. doi:10.1609/aaai.v34i09.7123

Sustainable Development. (n.d.). *The 17 Goals*. https://sdgs.un.org/goals

Taeihagh, A. (2021, April 3). Governance of artificial intelligence. *Policy and Society*, *40*(2), 137–157. doi:10.1080/14494035.2021.1928377

Taherdust, H. (2023, April 4). Towards Artificial Intelligence in Sustainable Environmental Development. *Artificial Intelligence Evolution*, 49–54. doi:10.37256/aie.4120232503

Tomašev, N., Cornebise, J., Hutter, F., Mohamed, S., Picciariello, A., Connelly, B., Belgrave, D. C. M., Ezer, D., Haert, F. C. V. D., Mugisha, F., Abila, G., Arai, H., Almiraat, H., Proskurnia, J., Snyder, K., Otake-Matsuura, M., Othman, M., Glasmachers, T., Wever, W. D., & Clopath, C. (2020, May 18). AI for social good: Unlocking the opportunity for positive impact. *Nature Communications*, *11*(1), 2468. doi:10.1038/s41467-020-15871-z PMID:32424119

Vaidya, H., & Chatterji, T. (2020). SDG 11 Sustainable Cities and Communities. In B. Isabel, I. B. Franco, T. Chatterji, E. Derbyshire, & J. Tracey (Eds.), *Actioning the Global Goals for Local Impact* (pp. 173–185). Springer. doi:10.1007/978-981-32-9927-6_12

Van Wynsberghe, A. (2021, February 26). Sustainable AI: AI for sustainability and the sustainability of AI. *AI and Ethics*, *1*(3), 213–218. doi:10.1007/s43681-021-00043-6

Vinuesa, R., Azizpour, H., Leite, I., Balaam, M., Dignum, V., Domisch, S., Felländer, A., Langhans, S. D., Tegmark, M., & Fuso Nerini, F. (2020, January 13). The role of artificial intelligence in achieving the Sustainable Development Goals. *Nature Communications*, *11*(1), 233. doi:10.1038/s41467-019-14108-y PMID:31932590

Wu, W., Huang, T., & Gong, K. (2020, March). Ethical Principles and Governance Technology Development of AI in China. *Engineering (Beijing)*, *6*(3), 302–309. doi:10.1016/j.eng.2019.12.015

Yigitcanlar, T., & Cugurullo, F. (2020, October 15). The Sustainability of Artificial Intelligence: An Urbanistic Viewpoint from the Lens of Smart and Sustainable Cities. *Sustainability (Basel)*, *12*(20), 8548. doi:10.3390/su12208548

Yigitcanlar, T., Mehmood, R., & Corchado, J. M. (2021, August 10). Green Artificial Intelligence: Towards an Efficient, Sustainable and Equitable Technology for Smart Cities and Futures. *Sustainability (Basel)*, *13*(16), 8952. doi:10.3390/su13168952

Zhang, B., Anderljung, M., Kahn, L., Dreksler, N., Horowitz, M. C., & Dafoe, A. (2021, August 2). Ethics and Governance of Artificial Intelligence: Evidence from a Survey of Machine Learning Researchers. *Journal of Artificial Intelligence Research, 71*. Advance online publication. doi:10.1613/jair.1.12895

Zhao, J., & Gómez Fariñas, B. (2022, November 28). Artificial Intelligence and Sustainable Decisions. *European Business Organization Law Review, 24*(1), 1–39. doi:10.1007/s40804-022-00262-2

Chapter 2
Society 5.0:
The Game Changer for Achieving SDGs and the Green New Deal

Sanusi Mohammed Sadiq
Federal University, Dutse, Nigeria

Invinder Paul Singh
Swami Keshwanand Rajasthan Agricultural University, India

Muhammad Makarfi Ahmad
Bayero University, Kano, Nigeria

Ummulqulthum Ndatsu Usman
University of St. Andrews, UK

ABSTRACT

The sustainable development goals were underlined as needing significant societal changes, which were made even more urgent by the pandemic's advent. The future civilization should strive for sustainable growth, a strategy in which technology is a key component. Society 5.0 is a relatively new idea that serves as a framework for social development and has the potential to have a significant impact on societies at all aspects, including sustainability and quality of life. It seeks to maximize the capacity of the relationship between individuals and technology in the advocacy of the enhancement of everyone's quality of life through an incredibly smart society. Through the analysis of scientifically published works and the data from organizations and governments working on such schemes, it is possible to say that Industry 5.0 is far more than a pattern, and Society 5.0 would consequently open previously unimaginable prospects for the development of a highly smart globalized world.

DOI: 10.4018/979-8-3693-0338-2.ch002

INTRODUCTION

Globally, the advancement of science and technology has exacerbated socio-economic tensions and the state of the environment (Abbasi and Kamal, 2020). Sustainable development is difficult because of unfavorable environmental conditions. In most nations, the population's welfare is growing as significant economic and social program objectives are accomplished, but the required level of quality of life is not being provided (Acioli et al., 2021). In order to ensure technological advancement in the area of economic development, this determines the substance and direction of advanced society's modernization and maintaining a safe environment forms the core of the fourth industrial age (Adel, 2022).

Since the start of Industrial Revolution, humanity has understood the possibility of employing technology as a tool for growth (Industry 1.0). With the development of mechanical power employing basic resources like water, steam, & fossil fuels, the First Industrialization, which may be dated to the latter half of the eighteen (18th) century (i.e., the 1780s), got underway (Adel, 2022). During the second technological revolution in the 1870s, industrialists who employed assembly lines & mass production embraced electrical energy (Industry 2.0). In the 1970s, during the Industrial Revolution III (Industry 3.0), the idea of incorporating automation into manufacturing industries was pioneered through the use of information and electronics Technologies (IT). In the fourth industrial revolution (Industry 4.0), artificial intelligence (AI), the internet of things (IoT), cloud computing, and other technologies are utilized to make smart cyber-physical systems (CPS), which act as a real-time bridge between the digital and physical worlds (Aderibigbe, 2022).

The fast change in technology, industry, and societal processes and patterns during the past ten years is conceptualized by the term "Industry 4.0" (I4.0) (Carayannis and Morawska-Jancelewicz, 2022a). The development of I4.0 is supported by the introduction and progression of core technologies such big data analytics, artificial intelligence, and digital twins, which encourage increased service and product quality and production efficiency. I4.0 engineers have primarily concentrated on the technological transformation of production and manufacturing networks and systems (digitization and digitalization), giving industrial adaptability and efficiency precedence over industrial sustainable development and worker welfare (Ehwanudin et al., 2022). This has resulted in some limitations, despite the advancements and opportunities made possible by this framework. In light of this, a new age of industrial revolution is about to begin. Engineers will be able to completely harness the state-of-the-art technical environment in this new era in order to advance humanity and socialize manufacturing. The construction of the aforementioned human-centric era, also known as Industry 5.0 and Society 5.0, is currently underway in a number of nations, including the European Union, Japan, & the United States (Kasinathan et al., 2022). It must be emphasized at this point that I4.0 is a continuing technical evolution and that Society 5.0 (encompassing Industry 5.0) continues to be developed, dispelling the myth that Industry 5.0 won't be regarded as a standalone industrial revolution (Kasinathan et al., 2022).

Industry 4.0 (I 4.0)

Because of the tremendous effects and new production paradigm it will bring with applicability in many other fields of activity, Industry 4.0 is frequently referred to as the fourth industrial revolution (Kasinathan et al., 2022). In an effort to integrate digital computer technology into production, the term "Industry 4.0" first appeared in Germany in 2011 (Kadarisman et al., 2022). Despite significant differences in its definition & assessment of its political and social ramifications, the idea of I4.0 is broadly acknowledged in the corpus of scientific evidence (Mourtzis et al., 2022). But what does Industry 4.0 actually entail? "It consists of a comprehensive and organized digital connectivity of the creation, logistics, and usage of products or services", according to one definition. As a result, Industry 4.0 involves both vertical integration inside the organizational structure, incorporating elements linked to the production of the final product, and interconnection of data flow amongst partners, suppliers, and customers. It also involves fusing the actual world with the virtual world. As a result, the system has all processes integrated completely, creating a real-time information platform" (Nair et al., 2021).

Finally, Industry 4.0 seeks to create a true collaborative platform that articulates: intelligent robots, automated simulations, Internet of things, cloud computing, additive manufacturing, and big data analytics. This fusion between technology, virtual space, and people is then sought after. The "smart factory" plays a key role in this logic of fusing the physical and digital worlds (Paschek et al., 2022). "The smart factory is a key idea in Industry 4.0, which makes use of cyber-physical systems to keep an eye on the actual manufacturing processes in the factory and enable decentralized decision-making. When this happens, physical systems transform into the Iot devices, interacting and working together in real-time through the wireless network with both each other & with humans. Ali (2022) claim that the industry pays too much attention to both the technological and economic aspects of a problem. Another key idea in Industry 4.0 is innovation. "The social viewpoint reveals that technological innovations are anticipated to favorably promote the dissemination of social innovation, & vice versa (Ahmed et al., 2022). This is true for both individual and corporate learning for change and adaptability. Together with social innovation, the technical revolution that underpins Industry 4.0 reaches its full potential. Therefore, businesses that give both social advancement and commercial benefits will prosper in Industry 4.0 (Akkaya et al., 2022).

Society 4.0 and Industry 4.0: From the Traditional Society

The third industrial age was built on the invention of the transistor & the microprocessor (1960). The process automation began as a result of these breakthroughs, which allowed for the faster progress of communication and computer technologies (Darsana and Sudjana, 2022). Consequently, society began to shift from producing commodities and profit to creating a post-industrial society focused on knowledge creation and the growth of service sectors. The information society, or post-industrial society, which emphasizes knowledge organization and serves as a social control, directing innovation and development, underwent a revolution in the 80s with the introduction of digitalization (Huang et al., 2022). The emergence of the Internet has revealed a globally connected society that seeks to offer access to the Internet, improved education, business support, & networking.

The cultural and institutional plurality of information systems must also be highlighted because the available information societies are built on a capitalist framework. In addition, cutting-edge technology advancements for data processing and knowledge creation are the foundation of the contemporary information society. The gathering and processing of data at various stages has received a lot of attention in the digital era (Islam et al., 2020). The Fourth Industrialization is causing a significant structural transformation in conventional society. Huge amounts of data collected by sensors and devices scattered across the physical world will be analyzed and processed by a cutting-edge AI system (Javaid et al., 2022). The study then has a substantial impact on human and machine activity in physical space. The physical world and the internet are integrating more and more. Universities should therefore emphasize contemporary career development, skill enhancement, and teamwork. It should be emphasized because society is a particular kind of social structure where the gathering, processing, and dissemination of knowledge serve as the primary sources of power & productivity.

INDUSTRY 5.0

Consequently, even if Industry 4.0 hasn't been fully adopted globally, many entrepreneurs and technical trailblazers are already anticipating the Fifth Industrial Revolution, also known as Industrial 5.0 (I5.0), which will entail autonomous manufacturing with AI and human intelligence acting as the foundation technology, in and on the loop (Kasinathan et al., 2022). Additionally, it is anticipated that by 2027, social media users- who numbered 4.59 billion in 2022-will have greatly increased to 5.85 billion as a result of the Internet's and related technologies' explosive expansion. The initial definition comes from the research of Breque et al (2021). The authors claim that Industry 5.0 is a logical idea that envisions the development of a manufacturing process that is robust, sustainable, and focused on people. I5.0 is fast to act, resilient, and respectful of the planet's constraints while supporting talent, diversity, & empowerment thanks to adaptable and flexible technologies. Likewise, Industry 5.0 represents the first industrial advancement to be led by a human, according to Michael Rada, creator and executive director of the Industry 5.0 organization. It is founded on the 6R concepts of industrial reusing (realize, reduce, recycle, reuse, reconsider & recognize), a systematic waste avoidance strategy and logistical efficiency aimed to assess life standards, new innovations, and generate high-quality custom products.

The final description said that by integrating workflows with intelligent systems, the personnel and machines in the factory work together to improve process efficiency (Kiepas, 2021). I5.0 is anticipated to need business experts, systems analysts, and philosophers to focus on human considerations while integrating emerging innovations in industrial systems, as per Kurniasih et al.(2022). The socially intelligent workplace of Industry 5.0 is characterized by cobots that communicate with humans. To provide seamless connectivity between people and CPPS components, the Social Smart Factory makes advantage of enterprise social networks (Carayannis et al., 2022b). It is clear from the definitions given above that human-centricity, system robustness, and sustainability are common themes in all of them. A closer examination of the definitions uncovers discrepancies; as the bulk of them refer to a full era of sociological and technological advancements while the remainder place a greater emphasis on the industrial transition (Table 1).

SOCIETY 5.0 (S 5.0)

I5.0, which aims to address the issues raised by Industry 4.0, is a human-centric design approach where people and cobots work together in a shared workspace (Carayannis et al., 2021). In addition, a related idea known as Society 5.0 (S5.0) has emerged in recent years to address the issues in contemporary society. S5.0 is a super-smart, futuristic society in which everyone can live high-quality, comfortable lives thanks to the integration of physical space and cyberspace fully adopting ICT (Information and Communication Technology). The plan is the government of Japan's answer to other socio-technical programs like made in China 2025 & I4.0 in Europe and China, respectively (Pereira et al., 2020).

Similar to how I5.0 is directly tied to S5.0, both will occur when AI is trained to autonomously reason and lead organizational activities, which is anticipated to occur in 2030 (Polat and Erkollar, 2020).

Table 1. Contrasting industry 4.0 and industry 5.0

Industry 4.0	Industry 5.0
Centered on improving process and system efficiency via AI and digital connection	Ensures an environment for business that combines sustainability and competitiveness, enabling business to achieve its full prospect as one of the cornerstones of transformation.
Focuses on technology and CPS implementation	Places special emphasis on how alternate forms of (technology) governance affect resilience and sustainability
Consistent with business model optimization within current capital market dynamics & economic models, i.e., focused on minimizing costs and maximizing profit for shareholders	Promotes a human-centric view of technology by empowering workers with digital tools.
There is not enough attention paid to design and performance factors that are crucial for systemic change and separating the use of resources and materials from harmful effects on the environment, the climate, and society.	Creates a transitional framework for technological applications that are environmentally friendly.
	Extends the scope of a corporation's accountability to include the entire value chain.
	Extends the scope of a corporation's accountability to include the entire value chain.

Through the CPS created in I4.0, it is projected that relationships between people and technology will continue to flourish in Society 5.0. People need to have constructive relationships with technology in order to maintain sustained progress in all societal spheres (such as democracy, health, economy and education). But this issue also prompts the query of whether AI will have a detrimental influence on human civilization (e.g., among other things, worries include employment loss, social control, algorithmic mistakes, and ethical and practical issues with the handing over of duty to computers).

In 2015, as a reaction to the challenges facing the Japanese economy, the Japanese government used the term "Society 5.0," their concept of a human-centered society, for the first time (Sołtysik-Piorunkiewicz and Zdonek, 2021). According to Society 5.0, a greater level of cyberspace & physical space integration may boost economic growth & address social concerns. The notion of society 5.0 first appeared in Japan in 2015 as part of a strategic mainstream political push, according to Trehan et al.(2022). Industry 4.0 is somewhat followed by Society 5.0, and while Industrial revolution 4.0 concentrates on manufacturing capacity, Society 5.0 aims to put individuals at the forefront of innovation by leveraging the influence of technology and the outcomes of Industry 4.0 with a deeper focus on technological integration to promote health and wellbeing, social responsibility, and sustainability.

Increasing global competitiveness, an aging and declining working population, natural catastrophes, terrorism, environmental problems, and a dearth of natural resources are the greatest problems humanity is currently confronting. The Granrath research on Japan's Society 5.0 and advancing past Industry 4.0 from 2017 employs this tactic. Dautaj and Rossi (2021) asserts that Society 5.0 can indeed be implemented as a paradigm and a manual for social change, having a significant impact on present social systems on many different levels. The implementation of the Smart Society concept will be crucial for the advancement of society as it will increase environmental sustainability and human well-being. Society 5.0 is described by Di Nardo and Yu (2021) as an incredibly intelligent society built on the production, processing, and sharing of data, and more especially knowledge, through the integration of the real world and the internet. In the same context, Rojas et al.(2021) define Society 5.0 as a "Super-intelligent

Society," making use of the technical advancements made possible by Industry 4.0 for the benefit of society as a whole and environmental sustainability.

Social Sustainability Concept of Society Version 5.0

Although the Society 5.0 paradigm was created for Japan, any other country can use it and its elements to promote environmentally friendly development at all sizes (Elim and Zhai, 2020). As a result, when considering its adaptation, it is crucial to focus on the components of the notion that are related to the expansion of industry. Although it exclusively focuses on production, the Industry 4.0 concept has long been employed primarily by Europeans. Society 5.0, in contrast, also addresses social issues. The goal of Society 5.0 is to leverage the power of the digital transition to solve social issues and cohabit with nature in addition to fostering economic progress. It can help to realize the UN Sustainable Development Goals (SDGs).

The Keidanren will keep developing this concept and take the lead to put it into practice, altering the Japanese culture and economy in the process (Jatmiko et al., 2021). Social conventions and commercial activities will be drastically changed by Society 5.0. Close collaborations that straddle borders and industries, as well as the change of current industries, will enable people to lead a range of lifestyles. Giving everyone the ability to pursue their own pleasures and lifestyles while simultaneously contributing to the achievement of environmentally friendly, sustainable development is the aim of S5.0. The UN developed the SDGs to solve global concerns and create sustainable societies, and this is in line with them. Although S5.0 is necessary for many SDGs, it is not enough on its own. The idea behind S5.0 for SDGs will come to fruition because S5.0 promotes creative issue solving from a number of angles and backs these answers with digital transformation (Maddikunta et al., 2022). This section outlines the course for sector-specific changes, including how they would help to accomplish the SDGs, in order to reach S5.0.

Digitalization

The latest Society 5.0 (Unique Society) is a community that will create itself by integrating Digitalization (DX) with the creativity and imagination of a diverse range of individuals to generate values and find answers to issues (Menezes et al., 2022). The concept of harnessing DX to build a future society is essential. The continuing DX, which describes how society is fundamentally changing as a result of developments in digital technology & data use, is what is driving the development of S5.0 (Menezes et al., 2022). This transformation includes significant adjustments to how people live their lives, how governments function, how the economy is structured, and how the labor market is organized. As large-scale data gathering, transmission, storage, & analysis are made available at low cost, several sorts of factory innovation are triggered (Masuda et al., 2021). Data highlights issues and suggests potential solutions. Management and social issues can be resolved when such knowledge and ideas are promptly shared internationally. Instances of data-based technologies utilized in DX to affect major social changes include the IoT, artificial intelligence (AI), 5G, robotics, and blockchains (Salimova et al., 2021).

DX has sparked change, and it's not just technology. It represents a major movement in culture and society at the base, changing social norms. DX goes beyond simple labor-saving "kaizen", automation, boosted productivity, and optimization based on digital technology. DX is a reform that tries to develop new values, often at the sacrifice of preexisting ones, as a reaction to substantial social changes (Tumentsetseg and Varga, 2022). Therefore, it should be emphasized that DX goes beyond simple changes to IT systems and instead modifies the whole structure of society and business. Therefore, businesses should make DX their top management priority and should take initiative to work on it. DX is defined as "fundamental and revolutionary transformations in society, industry, & life as a result of developments in the use of digital data and technology and radical changes adopted by industries, organizations, & individuals toward such transformation" in the Keidanren plan.

The Structure of Society 5.0

Even while digitalization heralds in a new phase of society, digital technology & data should be leveraged to make a society in which people can pursue various lifestyles and forms of enjoyment in their own ways (Xu et al., 2021). Although the fifth Technology and Science Basic Plan first referred to Society 5.0 as a "super smart society," that is merely one facet of the future society. Thanks to digital change, anyone can access enhanced "abilities". If someone has ambition and ideas, they can engage in activities and companies that could drastically transform society. In order to identify the different demands and issues that are present across society and develop scenarios to solve them, rich imaginations and creativity will be required for Society 5.0 (Fernando et al., 2021). Solutions that leverage digital technology and data will also be implemented. It will be simpler to address issues and generate value when digital transformation is combined with the creativity and imagination of many people, which will open the door to a better future. In order to address social problems and provide value, Society 5.0 will also be an Inventive Society where digital revolution merges with the creativity and imagination of varied people (Leng et al., 2022). So, in Society 5.0, people will use their creativity to come up with ways to live in harmony with environment, technology, and each other as well as themselves. This will enable sustainable development.

The Society 5.0 Initiative's Objectives

The initiative Society 5.0 has lofty objectives. The objective of Society 5.0, according to Adel (2022), is to "provide equitable chances for all and also provide the atmosphere for fulfillment" of each person's potential. To this end, Society 5.0 will make use of developing technologies "to remove physical, administrative, and social impediments to self-actualization of the person". The Japanese Business Association, Keidanren, has a similar vision for Society 5.0: "Every individual, even elderly people and women can enjoy a safe, secure, comfortable, and healthy existence and each & every individual can fulfill his or her preferred lifestyle." In Society 5.0, mortal-technology interface will be leveraged to "create a sustainable, vibrant, thriving people-centric environment," going beyond simply providing the bare necessities for people to survive and instead making life more worthwhile and joyful (Medina-Borja, 2017).

According to Society 5.0, this can be achieved by "offering the essential services and goods to any individual who require them at the essential moment and in only the correct amount" (Bartoloni et al., 2022). Society 5.0 will "enable human prosperity" by enabling "dynamic participation of all people in the future economy and society," which is made possible by rising technology. This engagement will be facilitated by improved legal and educational frameworks.

The Society 5.0 Initiative's Level of Risk

The Government of Japan recognizes that the Society 5.0 project is a deliberate endeavor to encourage discontinuous innovation and the creation of high-risk, high-reward technologies (Calp and Bütüner, 2022). There is a high possibility that some attempts to develop and apply Society 5.0 technologies will result in expensive failure. Additionally, there is a risk that, even if the planned technical platforms can be deployed successfully, individuals' usage of them could have negative unintended consequences. For instance, Atina (2021) examines the likelihood that Society 5.00's pervasive smart systems may introduce fresh risks of addiction akin to those already present in "internet dependence, addictions to smartphone and online video game" while also considering the likelihood that Society 5.00's cutting-edge technology may present fresh opportunities for reducing or eliminating addictions.

Transformative Future Technologies' Importance for Society 5.0

The technologies necessary to put the Society 5.0 concept into practice do not yet completely exist; developing them will necessitate significant developments in a variety of sectors. For instance, according to the Government of Japan's plan, Society 5.0 will include improved versions of AI, biotechnology, nanotechnology and robotics as well as an improved Internet of Things and greater use of Big Data. Given this fact, Červený et al.(2022) has looked into the necessity (and possibility) for Society 5.0 frameworks to use Big Data techniques that can effectively handle the enormous amounts of data produced by the Iot technology, while Østbø (2022) have looked into the function of next-lineage group management solutions in supplying a "smart society platform" for Society 5.0. According to the Government of Japan, persistently pushing the frontiers of knowledge and technology forms "the roots of social transformation" and has the potential to produce "groundbreaking value." It anticipates that as emerging technologies permeate all areas of life, this will "promote economic growth, the establishment of a healthy as well as long-living society, & social transformation". However, such technologies' unforeseen, disruptive potential cannot be entirely viewed favorably: Csiszer (2022) contends that the evolving technologies (particularly those related to 3D printing, AI, robotics, and networked digital platforms) that enable the execution of the Society 5.0 dream can produce both societal advancement and societal turbulence, resulting in the sudden emergence of new industries to replace some long-established ones. Indeed, the Japanese government admits that these new technological developments have already ushered in a "period of extreme change" in which structural changes to the social and economic landscape take place nearly on a daily basis.

The Ideal Cyber-Physical Society is Society 5.0

The foundation of both Industry 4.0 & Society 5.0 is the development of "cyber-physical systems," which are defined by their dependence on embedded, distributed, real-time processing occurring inside a network of diverse physical objects. It becomes a "cyber-physical-social system" (CPSS) whose members can engage in "cyber-physical-social behaviors" inside of cyber-physical spaces when humans (or social AIs and robots) are operationally incorporated into a physical-cyber system (CPS) at the physical, social and cognitive levels (Yao et al., 2022). Members of a CPSS may create "cyber-physical social networks" whose topologies correspond to the members' social relationships through their actions with one another.

It had been predicted that the expanding utilization cyber-physical systems will eventually have effects that go beyond businesses' interior industrial operations to affect society as a whole even before the official definition of the Society 5.0 framework in Japan. For instance, according to Zengin et al.(2021), if cyber-physical systems were used extensively to improve human quality of life, they might lead to the development of a "cyber-physical society, which already comprises human, social, and cultural domains above the physical- and cyberspaces." A similar claim was made by Ramadhani et al.(2021), who stated that "with the rapid advancement of data technology, the cyber space is linking physical space, social space, and mental space to establish a nascent world - Cyber Physical Society". These ideas of "cyber-physical society" could be considered as conceptual forerunners of the Society 5.0 framework that is currently being developed in Japan, as well as of the related concept of "Societies 5.0" that has been separately created by Suryadi (2021) in such a way that also draws on the idea of social-physical-cyber systems but is not tied directly to the Japan Society 5.0 framework.

The connection between physical-cyber systems and Society 5.0 is made apparent by Ferreira & Serpa (2018) when they draw attention to Medina-Borja (2017) that the "new realm" of Society 5.0 will include a "cyber-physical world" that operates nearly symbiotically alongside "the human world". According to Rahman et al.(2020), Society 5.0 is a society that has effectively evolved into a "Cyber-Physical System" that "is the combination of the actual world and the cyber world linked by ICT"; this cyber-physicalization of its environment helps differentiates Society 5.0 from the four previous stages of human society. Indeed, a "deepening of technology integration" that promotes "collaboration, co-creation, and human-machine interaction" is the foundation of Society 5.0 (Zhanna and Nataliia, 2020). More precisely, it advances Industry 4.00's efforts to integrate technology, virtual space, and people-that is, the merging of the physical and digital worlds. According to Sugiono (2020), this will lead to "melding at many temporal and spatial scales" in future civilizations, which will result in "cognitive cooperative systems" and "human-technology partnerships."

Relationship Between Industry 4.0 and Society 5.0

Industrial revolution 4.0 (I4.0) has lately gained popularity and is currently one of the significant global issues in both business and academia at the moment (Aquilani et al., 2020). I4.0 can be defined as the fusion of digital and physical technologies, such as additive manufacturing, big data, cloud computing, adaptive robots, augmented and virtual reality, IoT and artificial intelligence (AI) (Caro-Anzola and Mendoza-Moreno, 2021). I4.0 is viewed as an all-encompassing tool for transforming the information society so that it can respond to the actual requirements of people by transferring knowledge and information. I4.0 can spread the technical innovations analyzed in the social sphere's production environment. Applying the findings from smart manufacturing lays the groundwork for a new social composition model, extending the benefits of the digital (cyber) environment to nonproductive segments. In this instance, we have Society 5.0. In the information age, people use the Internet to search for, obtain, and analyze data or information from a cloud service in cyberspace (such a database). In S 5.0, a vast amount of data gathered by sensors in spatial context is stored online (Ellitan, 2020). Artificial intelligence (AI) analyzes Big Data in cyberspace and returns the analysis' findings to people in physical space in a variety of ways. The next stage in the advancement of civilization is thereby transmitted to humanity through Society 5.0.

The "Industry 4.0" paradigm, which was created in Germany within the first-half of the decade, is the foundation of Japan's Society 5.0 project, as Fukuda (2020) describe in their analysis of the current state of thought on Society 5.0. Society 5.0 essentially aims to further integrate the quickly developing technologies used by Industry 4.0 for commercial production into the lives of regular people. The Industry 4.0 paradigm places a strong emphasis on implementing cutting-edge technology to improve an organization's effectiveness, efficiency, and (in the end) financial performance. By utilizing cutting-edge human-computer interfaces, IoTs, augmented & virtual reality, ambient intelligence, social robotics and embodied AI to qualitatively improve the lives of individual people and to help society as a whole, the Society 5.0 intervention aims to balance out this commercial emphasis. The first "Super Smart Society" will be created if the Industrial revolution 4.0 model is thought of as focusing on the development of the "smart factory" (Frederico, 2021).

SOCIETY 5.0 AND INDUSTRY 5.0: OPPORTUNITIES AND CHALLENGES

As part of Industry 5.0 & Society 5.0, the green & digital transitions emphasize the importance of preserving peoples' ability to live purposeful, innovative lives (Maier, 2021). Thus, the role of corporations and universities in accomplishing this goal will grow in significance. As we progress toward a truly people-focus way of life, initiatives to foster industrial innovation and raise everyone's information literacy must go hand in hand with the growth of information technology (IT). Universities are responsible for advancing technology like previously, but they also have a responsibility to promote knowledge among information users via general curricula that move toward individualized perception and education in order to progress the civil society that represents Society 5.0 (Nastiti and Ni'mal'Abdu, 2020).

In conclusion, it should be emphasized that Society 5.0 and Industry 5.0 are inextricably linked. The fifth industrial revolution, which is soon to arrive, will hasten social advancement. The growth of society will also help the next industrial revolution. As detailed in Table 2, comparable problems and opportunities are identified in both I 5.0 & Society 5.0.

To Society 5.0 From Society 4.0

The characteristics of Society 5.0, which set it apart from Society 4.0, includes value creation and problem-solving, variety, devolution, adaptability, sustainability, and environmental harmony. One way to think of Society 5.0 is as an Industry 4.0 setting with a focus on people (Rizal et al., 2020). It is defined as "a human-focused society that balances economic growth with the settlement of societal ills through a system that highly combines cyberspace and physical space" by the Japanese Cabinet Office, which is where the idea of Society 5.0 originated. It is important to use digital tools and data to support a society

Table 2. Challenges and possibilities

Industry 5.0 & Society 5.0 parallels	
Problems	**Possibilities**
Population aging	Human-Cyber Physical Systems (HCPS)
A dearth of resources	Environmentally conscious manufacturing (GIM)
Pollution of the environment	Human-Robot Collaboration
Challenging global circumstances	Future Operators 5.0
	Jobs Human Digital Twin

where people lead varied lives and find satisfaction in their own special ways. Individuals in Society 5.0 will also be free from a number of restrictions that people in earlier iterations, up to Society 4.0, have been unable to get around, and they will be able to follow a variety of lifestyles and values. People will be freed from the emphasis on efficiency, to be more precise. The emphasis will instead be on providing for individual needs, resolving issues, and adding value. Individuals will have the ability to live, learn, & work without being restricted by factors that suppress uniqueness, such as race, gender, or citizens, as well as without feeling alienated because of their beliefs and modes of thought. The inequities brought on by the centralization of money and information will also be eliminated, and anybody will be capable to engage at any place and anytime. Another goal of the shift from S 4.0 to S 5.0 is the eradication of anxiety about terrorism, natural catastrophes, and cyber-attacks as well as the ability to live peacefully due to improved safety nets for the unemployed and the poor. Last but not least, according to the WEF Annual Gathering in 2019, the objective is to build a community in which anybody may generate value at any location and time, safely and in harmony with the environment, free from the numerous limitations that exist today (Salimova et al., 2020).

Conditions for the Shift to Society 5.0

Among the technologies that fall under Industry 4.0 are IoTs, big data, robotics, and augmented reality (Saptaningtyas and Rahayu, 2020). These innovations raise productivity and the standard of industrial production while enhancing working conditions. The quality of life and society at large can be enhanced by them, nevertheless. A new viewpoint, known as Society 5.0, is focused on social well-being. Industry 4.0 aids in the shift to the nascent society, but additional forces are also required (Potočan et al., 2020). The social debate, the use of technologies, and engagement at all societal levels are crucial steps in the development of Society 5.0. A sustainable society is one that is both socially and environmentally conscious. Products and services with stakeholder and governance support that adhere to sustainability standards are much more likely to be embraced by society and have more credibility. Additionally, it offers a favorable setting for cross-disciplinary communication. Greater participation in the procedures required for sustainable innovation is made possible by this form of communication. The execution of sustainable development initiatives requires technological prowess as well as the exchange of knowledge and information with stakeholders. As a result, creating an incentive program is vital to inspire all parties. In this setting, technology is crucial to business. It is possible to implement the best preventative and quality control procedures for goods and services. The effects of technology can be seen in how well citizens are living (Abbasi and Kamal, 2020). Research in the areas of intelligent manufacturing, intelligent transportation, and intelligent healthcare all focus on various aspects of the digital world. One of Society 5.0's goals is healthcare, which is heavily reliant on the other goals. The methods that people can use technology to communicate with one another and with one another represent the potential role that people may play in society in the future (Acioli et al, 2021).

SOCIETY 5.0'S DIVERSE MEMBERSHIP

Although diversity in society 5.0 will increase, this diversity goes beyond just embracing people from various backgrounds. S 5.0 will be capable to include forms of creatures that had not before been found inside the world's societies into its social systems & dynamics because of its deeply technological, cyber-physical character. According to the Japanese government, "in order to actualize an incredibly smart community, it is required to connect numerous "things" via a network, construct highly sophisticated algorithms out of these items, and merge several distinct platforms so they are able to connect and collaborate with one another (Onday, 2019)". In Society 5.0, cyberspace will be used to connect all of the world's many "items" into cohesive "systems". More specifically, at first appearance, the diverse nature of Community 5.0 suggests that at least two new categories of "members" will be present in it that have never been in any previous human society, as explained below.

Participation of AIs and Autonomous Robots in Society 5.0

Society 5.0 is projected to have many different kinds of intelligent non-human social actors as "participants" or even "members" in addition to its human members. Such artificial beings are not anticipated to merit or be recognized as moral subjects (such as moral agents) or civic individuals (such as citizens) in the same manner that humans are for the foreseeable future. However, it would seem that such created beings are not merely inert "tools" or inconspicuous elements of the environment. They might be able to participate in society as legitimate (albeit constrained) non-human agents. In much the same ways as domestic pets & working animals have always played an important role in human culture.

In fact, just as Society 1.0 & Society 2.0 were primarily characterized by the integration of animals in the wild and breed animals into human society's societal structures and procedures (Zengin et al., 2021). It seems that one of the main ways in which Society 5.0 will differ from Society 4.0 is by embracing a dizzying assortment of extremely advanced social and emotional robots, artificial life, nanorobotic swarms, embodied AI, artificial agents manifesting themselves inside virtual worlds, self-organizing and self-directing computer systems, and other artificial sorts of intelligent physical-cyber social actors. Even though new technology enables the integration of a variety of artificial intelligences into society, it is actually unfavorable economic and demographic trends that seem to be forcing it: Japan's "hyper-aging society" and declining birth rate make it necessary to address the nation's deteriorating job performance (Trehan et al., 2022). Because there aren't enough people available to carry out necessary tasks, robots and integrated AI will assume more and larger tasks in Society 5.0, "driving economic progress" and, hopefully, aiding in the realization of an ample society in which every person may live a long and healthy life.

According to the Government of Japan, Society 5.0 will be "a place where people, robots, and/or artificial intelligence (AI) interact and strive to improve quality of life by providing finely differentiated personalized services that fulfill varied consumer needs". Robotics will be used at an ever-increasing rate in "different disciplines, such as communication" and "social service/work help," expanding beyond the realm of production. The robots of Society 5.0 won't just be passive tools that need complex programming and wait for commands from their human operators, as opposed to the kinds of robots that exist in our current Society 4.0. Instead, Society 5.0's robots, other automated devices and systems, and AI will exhibit a growing level of autonomy by proactively gathering environmental data, making judgments, and operating in order to deliver useful services to humans.

Technologically Modified People as Members of Society 5.0

The implementation of futuristic technologies will also transform the bodies, thoughts, and daily experiences of the people who make up Society 5.0. New kinds of medical technology, regenerative treatments, and continuous developments in the fields of neurology, robotics, artificial intelligence, & the Internet of Things "will have a major impact on not just people's lifestyles" and "the cornerstone of its existence," People will also spend more time immersed in and actively using cyberspace as a result of the expanding use of human-computer interfaces that integrate "augmented reality, affective engineering, neuroscience," and other methods and insights. This will result in a situation where "the real world' and cyberspace have become highly integrated". The goal of such a thorough incorporation of new technology into people's lives is to "ensure citizens' diversity in thoughts & high-quality way of life," in addition to giving them the nutrition and care necessary for their existence as biological entities.

The concept of a high-tech connected world in which technologically aided human participants interact with AI, robots and virtual things in rich and advantageous ways was first addressed in Japanese science fiction and fantasy in the late 1980s. In short, Society 5.0 is the vision of this high-tech connected world in its final form. Given that not all forms of augmented reality & immersive VR, nano-robotic medical system, neuroprosthetic implants, and other revolutionary technologies will be required or wanted evenly by all citizens, it is reasonable to assume that the varying ways and extents in which these technologies will be used will increase variety amidst the mortal members of Society 5.0. In its most advanced version, the uneven application of such technologies may even result in the division of a society into innumerable sub-societies that live in the same physical space but have little to no overlap in their psychical, cultural, and technological environments (also known as "cyberspaces").

The Uncertain Position of People in Society 5.0

The introduction of artificial intelligence - based social agents into human society, as suggested by Mourtzis et al.(2022), represents a significant shift in society that poses numerous new issues in terms of practicality, morality, and security. Admittedly, it is one point for carefully trained workers of an I4.0 business to interact with AIs or social robots for a certain period of time in a specially designed office environs in order to accomplish a specific, narrowly defined task connected to their job. Incorporating such intelligent, sociable, artificial beings into homes, daily schedules, and the most private areas of people's lives is something unique for millions of average people, from young children to elderly people. The precise function that people will play in Society 5.0 is one area where there is uncertainty. It appears feasible that the many robot kinds, cutting-edge AI, intelligent computer systems, responsive smart surroundings, and other non-mortal intelligent social actors that are included into S 5.0 will not just execute tasks that has previously been performed by humans. However, they occasionally might be more intelligent, emotionally, physically, and socially capable than the people they are supposed to be taking care of. Such a society will have at least two unique sources of sensing, making decisions, and acting: the human body's inherent "bioagency" and the artificial "cyberagency" that robots and artificial intelligence (AI) possess.

Concerns concerning the relative responsibilities of humans and artificial entities in society which were previously abstract and theoretical, are becoming more concrete as the Society 5.0 program is aggressively pursued. Indeed, the goal of the Japanese government's pursuit of the Society 5.0 paradigm is to create a "prosperous human-centered society," which implies that while the government will work to keep humans at the heart of society, they won't necessarily be on their own inside it. The Fifth Technology and Science preliminary plan was heavily influenced by the researcher and government official Harayama (2017), who seems to concede that it will be difficult to make sure that "we humans remain central actors" in a Society 5.0 that has been so profoundly altered by digitalization and cutting-edge technologies. It will be required to constantly "focus on the word society' as the cornerstone for human life," which entails "focused on how to establish a society that delights individuals and provides a feeling of value," rather than letting technical advancements dictate the shape & character of society.

GOALS FOR SUSTAINABLE DEVELOPMENT

Environmental, social, and human development goals are all part of the 2030 Agenda For sustainable development (SDGs), a comprehensive agenda. This framework has 169 targets and 17 goals. The SDGs can be accomplished through a variety of approaches and strategies, however the most efficient approach will help the goals be accomplished more quickly. For the SDG community, a thorough review of methods for achieving the SDGs is important. This can help the decision-makers direct the necessary support. Choosing a plan or approach with less uncertainty is frequently advised. When examining the many types of ways to achieving the SDGs, it can be shown that a technology-driven strategy is the least unpredictable when compared to approaches that focus on human development, the economy, and the environment. So, it is possible to think of technology as a tool for accelerating SDG progress. Disruptive technologies are among the most ground-breaking and have the most potential to propel humanity toward sustainable development in the future. In this situation, it is necessary to evaluate how disruptive technologies affect the SDGs and how they might help them be achieved more quickly. Disruptive technologies have the potential to support the SDGs as well as the Green New Agreement, but they also come with major social, economic, and political upheaval. Rowan and Casey suggest a triple helix model integrating academia, industry, and authority for developing and disseminating potentially revolutionary technology. Blockchain-based options for attaining SDGs were also stressed in studies. It describes how disruptive technologies have shaped the work economy.

Disruptive technologies not only offer these advantages, but they also open the door for sustainable education. Disruptive technologies' pervasiveness and the digitization of society, however, could result in changes to institutions, social norms, human values, and the way people think and perceive the world. The standards of test methodologies and performance measurements will also need to be improved in order to quantify the impact of technologies. To enhance disaster management skills, disruptive technologies like the image processing, IoT, machine intelligence (AI), big data, and smartphone apps can be synchronized and seamlessly connected. Industry 5.0 is one of the disruptive technology's promising future directions. The focus on human-centered, resilient, and sustainable design will be the cornerstones of Industry 5.0. The idea of Society 5.0, which envisions a highly connected physical and cyber platform with people at its center, is a key advancement supporting disruptive technology. By fostering wealth, eradicating poverty, and preserving the environment, Society 5.0 may proactively assist the SDGs.

INDUSTRY 4.0 AND SOCIETY 5.0 THEORETICAL FOUNDATIONS IN THE PERSPECTIVE OF SUSTAINABLE DEVELOPMENT

The idea of Industry 4.0 and the fourth industrialization launch the global quest for sustainable development. On the one hand, industrial digitalization can help with the issue of resource use and emissions when it's required to employ virtual reality for business undertakings. The rise of industrial digitalization may be to blame for the increase in unemployment and new societal issues. The method of the "smart society" or "Society 5.0" concept corrects this imbalance. Additionally, it is clear that there is no way to stop the fourth industrial revolution or industrial digitalization, which presents significant difficulties for sustainable growth. However, this circumstance served as the catalyst for the creation of Society 5.0, a new, more sustainable notion of digitalization that goes beyond Industry 4.0 and is focused on sustainable development.

The president of the Global Economic Forum Karl Schwab introduced the Fourth Industrial Age and smart factories for the first time in Davos in 2017. Numerous scientists have looked at the concept of the smart factory and new ways to take advantage of the opportunities presented by new technology advancements in the framework of Industry 4.0, particularly in the national context. For example, Coumans (2018), Dassisti et al.(2018), Vestin et al.(2018), and others in Austria, Italy, and Sweden have explored the smart factory idea. The subject was researched in Russia, a nation with a wide variety of developed businesses, by Popkova & Sergi (2018).

Numerous studies have reached the general conclusion that the terms "Industry 4.0," "fourth industrial revolution," and "digital transformation" are interchangeable. The fundamental tenets of smart factories & Industry 4.0 concepts are based on the widespread use of physical-cyber systems in manufacturing and a growth in the volume of machine-to-machine communication through the use of artificial intelligence. Smart factories use a variety of technologies throughout manufacturing, including 3D printing, drones, robotics, etc. Additionally, industry 4.0 is creating a range of business models, including organizations that use platform workers to deliver indirect services, crowdsourcing, non-traditional employment, and businesses that look for customer-oriented solutions online. These adjustments enable increased output, better product quality, and lower production costs. All of these elements greatly increase business competitiveness. However, the automation of industrial production inevitably has detrimental social effects, specifically the loss of jobs. The idea of "smart factories" does not include a solution to this issue. To secure the socio-ecological & economic dependable of the civilized era, it is also important to find a solution to the issue of digital firms retraining and hiring the released employees.

Beyond Industry 4.0, the ideas of Industry 5.0 and Society 5.0 were developed as the scientific response to Industry 4.0's socioeconomic difficulties. Michael Rada first popularized these ideas in 2015. The evolution from digital production to a digital society is the basic tenet of the Industry 5.0 & Society 5.0 concepts. The idea of Industry 5.0 as a global model of sustainable growth was created by social orientation and technological advancements from Industry 4.0. A digital technology for societal growth is the central tenet of the Industry 5.0 & Society 5.0 philosophies.

The top researchers in Industry 4.0 & Industrial 5.0, K. Schwab and N. Davies, write in their paper that in order to benefit from the 4th industrial revolution, we shouldn't view potential technologies as either straightforward tools that we can fully manage or as uncontrollable outside forces. As an alternative, we should work to comprehend how and where ethical norms are incorporated into emerging technologies as well as how these technologies might be used to advance the public good, environmental preservation, and human rights. Scientists have reached the same conclusion on the idea of Society 5.0. As per Onday (2019), despite being a Japanese design approach, Society 5.0 is not exclusive to Japan because its objectives are the same as the 2030 Agenda For sustainable development.

However, there are also opposing viewpoints on the concept of Society 5.0 that take into account the socio-economic and intercultural difficulties associated with its dissemination. Regarding the Society 5.0 concept, Javaid et al.(2022) warns against underestimating, misinterpreting, and predicting the effects of impending social transformation. Sustainability is an issue for Industry 4.0, as well as for Society 5.0

Table 3. Sustainable development goals

Goals	Description
Goal 1	End poverty
Goal 2	Nil hunger
Goal 3	Excellent health and Wellbeing
Goal 4	Good education
Goal 5	Egalitarianism- Gender equality
Goal 6	Safe water and sanitation
Goal 7	Inexpensive and environmentally friendly energy
Goal 8	Acceptable work and Economic growth
Goal 9	Infrastructure, Innovation and Industry
Goal 10	Diminished inequalities
Goal 11	Sustainable communities and cities
Goal 12	Managed production and consumption
Goal 13	Climate change action
Goal 14	Life beneath water
Goal 15	Existence on land
Goal 16	Peace, Justice & strong institutions
Goal 17	Alliances towards the goals

& Industry 5.0. It's because the idea behind Society 5.0 was inspired by the idea behind Industry 4.0 (Cotta et al., 2021).

Society 5.0 and the Sustainable Development Goals

S5.0 will have an impact on how society and business operate. By seeking to tackle social challenges in line with the natural world, this social revolution will help achieve the SDGs. The 17 SDGs to change the world are listed in the table below.

The SDGs for Cities and Regions Are 13, 12, 11, 8, 6, 5, 4, and 3.

Supporting autonomous systems would enable a range of lifestyles while significantly lowering their detrimental environmental effects. Examples include automated driving & sharing economies. In addition, although efforts to increase the competitiveness of large cities will continue, sustainable, distributed communities will be built in rural and suburban areas to establish independent, successful regions where individuals live in peace with nature by harnessing the distinctive traits of their particular regions. High-quality medical and educational services will be accessible from any location in the world. Off-grid energy is one illustration of a technology for independent, decentralized social infrastructure that will be used to build a strong, sustainable social architecture while reducing financial load. Seniors who cannot drive themselves in places without public transportation will be able to access autonomous vehicles, which will solve their daily mobility problems and allow them to go shopping and to the doctor. It is possible to live in comfort and at a high standard even in regions with poor infrastructure.

Energy-Related SDGs: 13, 9, and 7

The world's energy landscape will transform, and data-driven energy networks will be built to enable sustainable lifestyles everywhere, including in smart cities and distributed communities. Demand-side management, power storage, and distributed sustainable energy supplies will all be incorporated into the generation of energy & will be synchronized with local conditions in microgrids. It will be possible to use off-grid energy systems, which are independent of traditional energy grids. The vast majority of the world's population, if not all of it, will have access to cost-effective and reliable energy, and other sectors of the economy will also make use of a similar decentralized infrastructure. This will guarantee that the majority of people on the planet live diverse, sustainable lifestyles.

Disaster Preparedness and Mitigation SGGs: 13, 11, 6, and 3

Globally, there is an increase in the frequency and severity of natural catastrophes, which calls for enhanced resilience as well as swift and efficient responses. Disaster information sharing systems will be constructed to enable speedy reactions in the case of disasters by gathering data on damage and relief supplies from affected areas, IoT devices, social media & sharing it across organization & regions barriers in the public and commercial sectors. Digital technology will also be employed to effectively prevent infrastructure aging and perform routine infrastructure maintenance. Water supply can be maintained during disasters and accidents, and the sewer and water infrastructure can be quickly restored. Infrastructure resilience will be promoted by decentralized energy systems.

Personalized Healthcare-SDG: 3

It will be possible to provide the right care when someone needs it thanks to technology trends like the digitalization of people's physical traits and behaviors and developments in the biotechnological study of life systems. New approaches will provide therapy that is tailored to each patient's health at the preventative stage to postpone the start and progression of sickness and enhance healthy life expectancy, in contrast to traditional medicine's homogeneous treatments for ordinary patients or symptoms.

The development of systems allowing individuals to consciously use and maintain their own life-stage data, telemedicine, and the promotion of next-generation high-speed communications systems will make it feasible for people to access high-quality healthcare services from any location. Food and Agriculture wellness support services, AI-based medical, and telemedicine are some of the other areas that will benefit from these efforts. For instance, older persons in remote areas will be able to use telemedicine to check their health, and in the case of an unexpected sickness, they will be sent for medication to a clinic that is befitting for their requirements as assessed with the use of AI. These systems, operational know-how, and technologies, when put into place in remote areas of underdeveloped countries, would enhance healthcare on a worldwide scale.

SDGs 2, 12, 14, and 15 Relating to Food and Agriculture

Agriculture and food production will be converted into enticing, independent sectors where everybody can exercise their creative freedom. It will make full use of contemporary capabilities like autonomous drones for on-site agricultural operations, robotic farming, and remote monitoring and control powered by AI. Working hours will be greatly reduced, labor efficiency will be considerably improved, and production will increase tremendously thanks to the involvement of multiple participants, including private enterprises, young people, & agritech ventures.

It will be encouraged to implement measures for increasing biodiversity and minimizing environmental damage in order to safeguard the abundant biodiversity found on land and in the ocean. Data on numerous customer needs will be gathered, and manufacturing and processing of food will be immediately updated. Food loss will be decreased by synchronizing delivery dates, volumes, and routes, as well as by merging data on export, production, and logistics to enable real-time stock and sales information sharing. Customers can get free manufacturing histories, interactive communication tools, and product information.

SDGs 11 and 12 Relating to Logistics

Logistics contribute to economic growth by easing the movement of commodities, and they are an important part of the civic infrastructure that supports daily living and commercial activities. The rapid growth of e-commerce and the universality of supply chains in Society 5.0 will require even more intricate and diversified logistics and the application of cutting-edge technologies will alter logistics. For instance, networks will be connected to freight and transportation ways using IoT technologies like Radio Frequency Identification (RFID), providing real-time logistical control and tracking.

Services and Manufacturing: SDGs 5, 8, and 9

AI-enabled ability distribution will provide both service and manufacturing delivery with new, potent tools. Data analysis and the creation of usable goods and services have up until now required a substantial financial investment and specialized knowledge. Through digital transformation, these abilities will be disseminated and made available as AI components and services. They can be combined to produce higher-quality goods and services more quickly. The underlying component of business models will be services rather than hardware. In the age of digitization, services & production will not be supplied in the same way they were in the 20th century. A DX that produces several forms of value will let more individuals to participate in production and service delivery.

SDGs 9, 8, 5, and 1 Relating to Finance

DX will make it easier to access financial services like asset financing, settlement, creation and insurance. People will be able to reside wherever without having to pay for it thanks to the affordable, useful, rapid, secure, and many means of settlement. Applications that link several services together and smart contracts will facilitate the creation of new services. People will have more chances for financing, asset accumulation, transfer, insurance and settlement with the aid of digital gadgets and technology, leading to more stable lifestyles, economic security, improved living standards, and better wealth distribution in emerging nations. Cryptocurrencies & token economies based on blockchain technologies as well as other developments will open up previously unimaginable lifestyles and produce new means of value exchange. Establishing safe, clever, and verifiable global contracts and payment systems will lay the groundwork for varied people to broaden their scope of production and service delivery on a worldwide scale.

Public Services-SDGs 1, 3, 4, 10, and 16

Public services will alter significantly as a result of supporting the many lives and industries listed above. Rebuilding their systems with a digital foundation will be the first step for all levels of government. By digitizing many of their responsibilities and quickly dispersing data across multiple actors, they will produce more innovative public services. For instance, precise demographic as well as other analysis of the data can be used to forecast demand for childcare facilities, schools, hospitals, & nursing homes, enabling public organizations to plan and provide the essential services. Even with the best safety nets in place, anyone can encounter a range of security-related difficulties.

Disruptive Technologies' Role in Achieving the Sustainable Development Goals

SDG 3 (Good Health and Wellbeing)

Disaster Management: The COVID-19 Pandemic as a Case Study

During the COVID-19 epidemic, disruptive technologies were critical to society's ability to operate. Through the appropriate broadcast of knowledge about technological breakthroughs, potential applications, usages, and connection with allied technologies, a collection of disruptive and emergent technologies can be effectively promoted and leveraged. This is done to guarantee the society's total development in both the urban and rural stages, thereby "capitalizing the connected world." Emerging technologies were extremely important to our daily lives during COVID-19. The connected devices made it possible for people to access information that could save their lives, work from a distance, receive education, and reduce the strain on the already overburdened healthcare systems. Researchers, field personnel, and healthcare professionals were all able to better understand how the virus propagated and track it thanks to location data apps. Platforms for meal delivery and online shopping have made it as easy as possible for customers to access goods. Disruptive innovations helped expand markets, making daily resources like medications more accessible. All of these instances highlight the adaptability that technology can provide in the event of a pandemic crisis. Everyone was made aware by COVID-19 that IoT & AI are no longer merely cutting-edge technology but are now integral to how society and the economy operate. To be more precise, during this pandemic, these instruments should be viewed as a vital infrastructure. The development of rules and protocols that are flexible, human-centered, and inclusive across all spheres of life has become crucial. The following four areas can benefit from the knowledge gained by using disruptive technology to handle the pandemic:

1. *Empathic branding*: During the COVID-19 epidemics, clients must be supported by empathetic communication tactics and given rapid assistance. In parallel with communicating the organization's mission to its audience, the trademark should be developed. To comprehend the pace of the market and the part played in it, campaigns should be undertaken and label sentiment analysis

should be done. This compassionate branding will be made possible through digital marketing and nano-targeting;

2. ***Digitalized business structures***: While focusing on client segments and active channels, the e-com partnerships should be strengthened. The company procedures need to be examined for regulatory compliance. It is necessary to fortify the network so that companies may easily continue to serve clients and customers even in the case of a digital storm. To continue sustainable growth, the organization needs to find new revenue sources. The next stage would be to create online venues for direct sales where customers could receive high-quality services without the need of middlemen. To do away with the need for human support, automated help centers must be created. Direct-to-customer marketing, drone delivery, and digital adoption would be the facilitators for this;

3. ***Remote collaboration***: Promoting the home-based employment model is a good idea. Any tasks that don't offer value or demand too much physical effort should have their importance assessed. An alternative to this could be low-cost automated solutions. Automation and developing technology can be used to reduce the dangers associated with human touch. When conducting B2B remote sales, it may be possible to leverage VR-like technology to make a lasting impact and close business negotiations. In the event of a temporary spike in demand or overflow, vendors can be tracked out. The factors that make this possible are remote work and the gig economy;

4. ***Virtualized service and sales***: Rethinking after-sale service models is necessary to offer customers support in the most practical way. The sales staff needs to be handled with agility, which requires role-reinvention, reorganization, and open communication. The next course of action should be to expand the network's capacity in order to meet the growing demand for digital sales. A virtual network with resources that are accessible from any location at any time should be made available to the call center executives. When a problem needs to be fixed, visual search or AR can be taken into account. Online sales, home contact centers, chatbots, and e-service are the facilitators.

Transformation of Healthcare through Disruptive Technologies

Due to the aging and population growth, it is increasingly important to improve healthcare access and quality while controlling costs. Healthcare organizations around the world also face significant challenges related to the pressures on public spending on healthcare and the increased anticipation of a longer life span. Due to these kinds of difficulties, practically all of the participants in the broad and complex healthcare systems began stepping up their efforts to convert and digitize their organizations. Additionally, they have yet to witness the digitalization of healthcare and the resulting requirement for increased investment in the development of digital health. According to the IDC, robot use for carrying supplies, medications, and food throughout hospitals increased by 50% by 2019. (International Data Corporation). 2020 will undoubtedly see the formation of Care Plan Adjustments that incorporate Real-Time use of data from wearable equipment with Cognitive/AI. The procedure provides precise details and automates portions of routine work that should be carried out by healthcare workers by simplifying patient-facing operations. For instance, in an acute care setting, resources can be made available to satisfy the patient's expectations and needs.

SDG 8 (Decent Work and Economic Growth)

Disruptive Technologies in a Business Model That Is Inclusive of Nature

Governments and businesses may benefit greatly from the natural world, according to the World Economic Forum's Nature Risk Rising Report. According to study, nature and natural activities play a significant or supporting role in producing approximately to USD 44 trillion, or half of the world GDP. Exploiting nature has a detrimental effect on economic growth. According to a report by the Global Economic Forum, the three major worldwide sectors that depend on nature-construction, agriculture, and food and beverages-contribute approximately $ Eight trillion in Total to the world economy, while their respective contributions are $ 4 trillion, 2.5 trillion, and USD 1.4 trillion. This means that for every dollar spent on environmental restoration, one receives $9 in economic benefits.

When it comes to resolving the global health concerns and bringing the economy out of a severe slump, bottlenecks have been seen all around the world. The primary component in averting future epidemics of these diseases is the use of nature-dependent stimulation packages. Furthermore, planning the research in natural capital has a significant positive impact on the rural economy. This change tends to protect the future availability of sustainable foods and commodities. Governments, businesses, and local players must all work together to achieve a clear goal, and the entities must be given the resources they need through targeted financial interventions. Incorporating these initiatives as soon as possible would help to assure a healthy and prosperous society as well as the economy in the long run. The World Economic Forum's Global Risks Assessment Survey addressed the evolution risks associated with bio-diversity depletion and a set of elements that should be taken into account, such as the worth of nature, providing for people as natural capital, and assessing the expenses spent by the destruction of the environment without industrial prosperity to regulate and mitigate the risks. The business models put forth recently, or the fourth technological revolution, have the potential to lead to a growth path that is inclusive and nature-positive and not only unleashes the value of the natural world but also lessens resource exploitation. These cutting-edge technologies and circular economic models have the ability to reduce waste production, improve input efficiency, and track and monitor global supply chains for agriculture and industry in real time. Revolutions could happen swiftly in the upcoming years due to the rapid adoption of technology breakthroughs.

Market Potential for New Age Technology

Future disruptive technologies could have a wide range of effects on businesses, clients, and employees. Leaders and innovators will need to review their future entrepreneurial and corporate plans in light of these technologies. In the years leading up to and including 2020, a variety of next-generation technologies are anticipated to expand and prosper on the market. The top ten next-generation technologies are presented below, together with augmented market projections for the ensuing ten years:

1. *Artificial Intelligence*: From 2019 to 2023, an increase of USD 75.54 billion is anticipated in the size of the worldwide artificial intelligence (AI) market. McKinsey predicted that artificial intelligence would be able to produce more than steam engines did in the nineteenth century. According to a McKinsey research, the influence of AI on the world economy could reach $13 trillion USD

by 2030. Up to 2030, AI is projected to contribute 1.2 percent annually to GDP growth. 30% of all cyberattacks on AI by 2022 will target and take use of adversarial samples, stolen AI models, and poisoned training data;

2. ***Big Data/Information Analytics***: As per to a research estimate, the computer database/ big data analytics (BDA) business is anticipated to reach $275 billion USD by 2023. Between 2017 and 2023, this forecasted a CAGR rise of 12%. The major competitors in big data analytics, according to this report, include Oracle, SAP, SAS, Microsoft and IBM Institute Inc., and others;

3. ***Drones***: By December 2025, the global drone market is expected to increase to 13.37 billion USD in value. Kasinathan et al.(2022) predict a CAGR rise of 13.70%. (2022). Cost efficiency, accuracy, and the capacity to carry out risky operations like inspecting utility pipes are the main factors driving this development rate. There is a way to proceed with the proper execution of merchant drone services and the formulation of regulatory frameworks for the legal use of drones. It is necessary to raise awareness of UAVs. Based on their primary drone-related service offerings, UAV Coach divided the 100 best drone firms into various categories.

4. ***Robotics***: According to a report in this field, the CAGR increase would be 26% and the turnaround will total USD 210 billion by 2025. The market is anticipated to grow to $100 billion USD by the year 2020. According to industry forecasts, there will soon be an abundance of cloud-based robot services. Additionally, small and medium-sized businesses will begin hiring robots in the following five years based on their requirements, inventing new demand drivers. In their investigations on EUD (End-User Development) for customized apps, humanoid robots, and IoT, Leonari et al.(2019) and Patern et al.(2019) suggested a potential research agenda relevant to the topic. The conceptual framework that was presented made it easier to understand the principles at play and what elements should be taken into account when creating EUD environments for robots and/or the IoT. This paradigm can also serve as a benchmark for comparing various techniques and suggesting fresh debate points for additional study. Obschonka and Audretsch (2019) decoding of the state-of-the-art available methods for AI, its benefits and disadvantages, and the technology's future serves as an example of how this innovation tends to make robots undertake jobs and missions on their own;

5. ***Cyber-security***: With a predicted growth rate of 12.3% CAGR from 2018 to 2026, the global market for cyber security is expected to reach 345.42 billion USD by that time. Due to rising cyber-attacks, malware, phishing emails, IoT adoption rates, and bring your own device (BYOD) tendencies; the cyber-security sector will become critically important. The study further advises that market growth for encryption solutions is anticipated to be strong throughout the forecast period. By 2023, blockchain is anticipated to advance technologically and facilitate private transactions while maintaining data secrecy;

6. ***Robotic Process Automation (RPA)***: Up to 2022, 40% yearly growth is expected for Robotic Process Automation (RPA) that is packaged with application integration, according to Gartner. Additionally, a CAGR of 31.1 percent and a market value of 3.97 billion USD are expected for RPA globally by 2025. Automation Anywhere, Inc., Blue Prism Group Plc, UiPath, Be Informed B.V., OpenSpan, and Jacada, Inc. are a few of the prominent companies in the sector.

7. ***Cloud Computing***: With a 29.2 CAGR, the cloud computing industry is projected to grow from a 2018 valuation of 36.7 billion USD to a 2025 valuation of 285.3 billion USD. Google cloud framework, Salesforce, SAP, Oracle, IBM, Aliyun, Rackspace, Microsoft Azure, Amazon Web Services, VMware Inc., Dell Inc., GIANT and EMC are a few remarkable players in the sector.

8. *IoT*: The IoT market is dominated by companies like Dell technologies, Intel Corporation, Cisco, Google, Apple, Facebook, Hewlett Packard Enterprise and Microsoft. The global IoT (Internet of Things) market, which had a market size of 190 billion USD in 2018, is anticipated to grow by 24.7% CAGR to 1111.3 billion USD by 2026;

9. *Virtual Reality and Augmented Reality (VR/AR)*: With a market price of 190 billion U.S. dollars in 2018, the global IoT (Internet - Of - things) industry is anticipated to reach 1111.3 billion U.S. dollars by 2026 with just a 24.7 percent CAGR; 10. The value of the global augmented and virtual reality market in 2017 was estimated at 11.32 billion USD. It is anticipated to expand at a CAGR of 63.3 percent between 2018 and 2025, with a market share of 571.42 billion USD. The Maxar Technologies, Vector Launch, Firefly Aerospace, BLUE ORIGIN, Swedish space corporations, Virgin Galactic, and Astrobotic are notable competitors in this industry. According to Gartner, 30% of IT agencies will move forward with the advancement of BYOD policies into "bring your own enhancement" (BYOE) in 2023 to address the workforce's augmented humans;

10. *Autonomous Vehicle*: Findings indicate that the global market for autonomous vehicles generated 54.23 billion USD in 2019. With a predicted growth rate of 39.47 CAGR from 2019 to 2026, it might reach up to $556.67 billion USD. Toyota Motor Corporation, General motors, AB Volvo, Renault-Nissan-Mitsubishi Alliance, Ford vehicle industry, Volvo-Autoliv-Ericsson-Zenuity Alliance, Volkswagen group, Groupe SA, Tesla Inc., and BMW AG are the leading competitors in this market.

SDG 9 (Infrastructure, Industry, and Innovation)

Industry 5.0

Using the tool of digitalization, Industry 4.0 is a combination of technology and trends that aims to transform established business practices. A breakthrough idea called "industry 5.0" envisions a world where people and machines collaborate to increase manufacturing efficiency. From the Industrial Revolution to the Digital Transformation and beyond, Industry 4.0 has a history in the manufacturing sector. Industry 5.0 is concerned with how people and machines can work together. Although the main areas of attention are automation and advanced manufacturing, the human aspect is also a significant consideration in this context. The operation of a system using automated and effective concepts while adhering to conventional and unique humanistic touches can readily describe how Industry 5.0 works. This type of transformation completely incorporates automated processes into it and provides new production prospects for medical industry participants. New development opportunities are made possible by platforms like the Internet-of-Things (IoT) and the Internet-of-Services (IoS). Data connectivity and exchange are made possible by cutting-edge manufacturing technologies, software, robotics, sensors, and other high-tech innovations. Particularly, the interactions that take place between people and machines are the emphasis of Industry 5.0. Humans and machines have long worked together in the world, and there are already smart manufacturing facilities in operation that are connected to technology. These interactions will be moved to more sophisticated human-machine interfaces as part of Industry 5.0. Industry 5.0 will make use of automation, big data, cutting-edge technological policy, appropriate implementation science, 3D symmetry in the architecture of the innovation ecosystem, and safety protocols. In accordance with human power, the automation of the integration will be enhanced, quick, and better. Cognitive computing and human intelligence collaborate to produce high-quality, value-added products and items. Industrial automation will combine human cognitive and critical thought with great speed and accuracy. Therefore, Industry 5.0 enhances the roles that humans play in manufacturing rather than replacing them. Through collaborative systems, the digitization of repetitive operations like drilling or data entry reduces the work of humans. To improve the quality & production processes, highly responsible activities for the human workforce could include system oversight, quick decision-making, and critical thinking. It is not too far off that cognitive processing and mechanical output will work together. In Industry 5.0, the data gathering is automated, and additional inputs can be sent to the robots and internet-connected equipment. Real-time data accessibility, seamless connectivity, and system-to-system communication are the main focuses of Industry 5.0. Reduced downtime for machine tools is a straightforward illustration. Depending on the level of damage caused by each machining step, machine tool sensors may determine the tool lifetime in real time. In order to receive a new cutting tool at the right time and reduce downtime, the machine can connect with the tool inventory.

Technology Supporting Product Development and Innovation

According to Kasinathan et al. (2022) and a research by Fox (2019), a technological revolution may completely change people's lifestyles, work schedules, and work-life balance. For humans, the breadth, scale, and complexity of this metamorphosis would be completely novel. According to studies, disruptive technologies offer enormous promise that has yet to be realized. Once implemented, Industry 4.0 has the potential to bring in $100 trillion in revenue over the next ten years for both society and industry. According to McKinsey, the automotive industry's revenue is predicted to double by 2030, reaching 6.6 trillion USD as opposed to 3.5 trillion in 2016. When disruptive technologies like electrification, shared transportation, and connectivity are adopted, the growth rate is predicted to be 84%. To attain this anticipated expansion, the businesses must develop new technology for themselves. Industries are now aware that cutting-edge technologies are crucial links in the process of product development and innovation in the prospective value chain.

The value sources that use technology to boost product development and innovation have the potential to expand from 166 billion U.S. dollars to 477 billion USD in new income, as per Kasinathan et al. (2022) report published by McKinsey. Additionally, it may increase margins by 8 to 25 billion U.S. dollars through effective and clever R&D. The report also showed that the industry's potential revenue growth from connected items may range from 34 billion to 95 billion dollars. The tech is being used by top firms to rethink their services and products since the prices associated with sensors, computation, and networking are falling daily. To gain an advantage over their rivals and grow their market share, these businesses produce new goods and services. The reform must be carried out in an organized manner, despite being difficult. Diverse technologies are used by different nations to identify the affected individuals and track their travel. This is done to plan ahead and reduce the possibility of contamination. In a study, a variety of disruptive technologies were examined in terms of how they communicate with societal structure using ICTs, including cloud computing, contemporary health care, AV and mixed reality, the Internet-of-Things (IoT), algorithms learning- machine learning (ML), AI, smart homes and smart cities, AI, chatbots, biotechnologies, genetic engineering, digital-physical systems, automated and automation processes, and autonomous vehicles. Modern intelligence robots are capable of carrying out a variety of high-level cognitive tasks, including problem-solving, learning, sensing, and reasoning. These AI machines become more powerful when they are combined with computer processing, data collection, data analytics, and big data mining.

SDG 11 (Sustainable Communities and Cities)

Society 5.0

A human-centered society called Society 5.0 can strike a balance between social responsibility and economic growth. The fifth Technology and Science Basic Plan established Society 5.0 as the ideal society for Japan to strive toward in the future. Society 5.0 is a new, inventive way to conduct business, and the advancement of digitalization even brings about social changes. This concept takes into account the technological advances that are now occurring. The general welfare of the populace should be given top priority, and the goal should be to promote the growth of an incredibly intelligent community. This has a variety of wide-ranging ramifications. It was suggested that the Society 5.0 project in Japan appeared to be based on a thorough examination of the subject, including both its potential benefits and drawbacks. The demonstration following the application of a phenomenological anthropology model and the development on the post-civilize system reveal:

(i)The predicted enrollment of Society 5.0 is projected to differ from S 1.0 to 4.0 in the following ways: How various human and non-human members are predicted to be involved qualitatively; (ii) How the expected membership differs from S 1.0 to 4.0; and (iii) How the dynamism of Society 5.0 might be imagined. Nieuwazny et al. (2020) focused on the relationship between technological advances and religion while also describing how mortality correlates in the Society 5.0 age. The rising use of smart technology in the development of Society 5.0 has immediate benefits for people, claim Kasinathan et al. (2022). In the workplace, where digitization and AI are prevalent, human activity is undergoing modifications and expansions. The majority of traditional occupations are disappearing, necessitating retraining and coaching. Regarding both instruction and research, the educational system should be prepared for the creative Society 5.0. Mavrodieva & Shaw (2020) started a conversation on catastrophe risk as well as the regulations of climate change, particularly with regard to Society 5.0, paying particular emphasis to inclusivity and adaptation challenges. On themes like finance, public service, energy, regions and cities, healthcare, logistics, food and agriculture, catastrophe mitigation, manufacturing and services, as well as how the laws of climate change and catastrophe are integrated within the new strategy, it provides thorough information about the objectives and ideas of Society 5.0. It then discusses a number of contentious issues that pose difficulties or dangers as well as chances for the concept to be applied in a really intellectual way.

The gathering and sharing of more personal data with all the services has drawn criticism for Society 5.0. An absolute requirement in this case is the implementation of adequate security measures. There are numerous opportunities for developing cutting-edge services and solutions for improved networked systems and applications. According to Kasinathan et al.(2022) report, Aquilani et al.(2020) study looked at and developed the application of S 5.0 in post-conflict societies. The development of knowledge automation will allow for the authorization of both service automation and industrial automation. The study also highlighted the shift in human attitudes from online-offline to offline-online, as well as the development of real-virtual connection that occurs between cyberspace and physical space.

A society that prioritizes the welfare of its citizens should strike a balance between economic growth and social problem solving. This is achieved by a procedure that specifically mixes real space with virtual space. The convergence between physical space (also known as "real space") and cyberspace (also known as "virtual space") is significant in "Society 5.0." Artificial intelligence (AI) is used to analyze vast amounts of data in cyberspace, and the results of the analysis are then incorporated back into the lives of humans in physical space in a variety of ways. Society 5.0 achieves the most recent confluence of physical space and cyberspace, enabling robots and AI-oriented large data to carry out or support the tasks and changes that people have been able to do up to this point. The creation of innovative value enables the provision of the goods and services that are necessities for the individuals who need them, optimizing the entire organizational and social system. This completely frees humans from daily laborious tasks and jobs at which they are not particularly efficient. The Sustainable Development Goals (SDGs), which were formed by the United Nations with the intention of solving social issues mixed in harmony with nature, would likely illuminate the Cabinet Office of Japan. Society 5.0 will make its bequest to accomplishing the Sustainability goals of the United Nations. The main goal of proactively achieving the SDGs by forming Society 5.0 was changed on November 8th, 2017, and now includes a section on "Realization of a Sustainable Society." Even the explanation of "Society 5.0 for SDGs" and illustrations of the essential technologies and systems for the 17 SDGs are summarized.

According to a survey, one of the most important types of social assets that are necessary for success in the digital era will continue to be trust alone (Bartoloni et al., 2022). Even without inventions, humans were effective in raising labor productivity, lengthening the average life expectancy, and boosting societal wealth. For instance, in order for employees to work more effectively in smart businesses, wearable devices and digital tools are provided. Humans who operate robots have given them permission to carry out physically demanding tasks that call for a lot of strength. The efficiency of the seamless integration will improve labor, safety, and production. Policymakers can encourage organizations to provide more training for the industrial technicians of future generations in order to provide a fair and seamless transition from one type of tech to another in order to implement these kinds of technical breakthroughs. The goals and objectives of Society 5.0 should also be aligned to find more effective ways to support the realization of those goals and objectives through clear policy-making with the aid of artificial intelligence (Calp and Bütüner, 2022).

With the aid of the cyber-physical process, Industry 5.0 & Society 5.0 aim to create a cohesive society for the protection and welfare of people. A "super smart society"- one that is far smarter than current societies-can be created by fusing the ideas of Industry 5.0 & Society 5.0. By analyzing the requirements of both Industry 4.0 & Society 5.0 and formulating the policies toward SDGs' macro aspects employed in the scanning aspect for strategic management, STEEP-L (Social, Techn, Economic, Environment, Political and Legal) makes it simple to understand how these two concepts are converging. Innovation and technological advancement open up new opportunities for risk-reduction measures as well as strategies to improve resilience in the face of disaster. g Several industries, including disaster management and risk reduction, are continually being transformed by advancements in 5G (5th generation), Big data, IoT, AI and developments in such domains since drone tech and robots. All technical development would ultimately support the fusion of Industry 5.0 & Society 5.0.

Various SDGs

Below is the summary of how each SDG is supported by disruptive technologies. In order to determine how the SDG targets interact with one another and to offer crucial insights into the radical changes brought on by disruptive technology, conclusions are reached. Furthermore, it is also clear how strong the evidentiary base is for the SDG interaction that has been performed. These perceptions support the acceptance and application of disruptive technology in all fields. The supports for SDGs through disruptive technologies are presented below:

a. SDG 1 (End poverty)

- ◦ Innovations supported by digital disruption can lower the cost and increase accessibility of the goods and services.
- ◦ When low-income people take advantage of disruptive technologies' potential for rapid reskilling, it can help them escape poverty by finding work.
- ◦ Other digitization strategies, including mobile banking and smartphone accessibility, can increase their access, which will then enable them to take advantage of opportunities around the globe.

b. SDG 2 (Nil hunger)

- ◦ Disruptive technologies, like as AI, ML, and IoT, can effectively work to minimize food waste and, perhaps, connect those in need with contributors.
- ◦ By fostering resilience, the technology can significantly enhance and improve the food supply chain, even in the face of catastrophes like the COVID-19 pandemic.
- ◦ Constant environmental factor monitoring with advanced disruptive technologies can give food producers real-time feedback so that early actions can be taken to avert crop harm.

c. SDG 3 (Excellent health and Wellbeing)

- ◦ Increases the accessibility and efficiency of healthcare through digitalized processes. Telehealth and chatbot services are two examples.
- ◦ The health of all age groups would significantly improve with the enhanced link between networks of patients and physicians.

d. SDG 4 (Good education)

- ◦ The limitations and methods for educating people are being pushed by digitalization-driven educational aspects including smart courses, remote learning, and edu-tech firms.
- ◦ Contrarily, the rise of disruptive technology offers high-quality, applicable instruction to all fields of human endeavor.
- ◦ The younger generation benefits from being more prepared for the quick technological advancements and future environmental changes.

e. SDG 5 (Egalitarianism- Gender equality)

- ◦ Accessibility is where gender equality is most obvious. Disruptive technologies are vital in this situation for gaining access to credit, food, and other resources. In contrast, it is important to guarantee equal pay for men and women in skilled occupations.

f. SDG 6 (Safe water and sanitation)

- ◦ Information and communication technology make it feasible to collect, monitor, and optimize water usage data for public, economic, societal, and ecosystem purposes.
- ◦ One technology that can greatly facilitate the implementation of SDG 6 is integrated water resource management. Another is smart home systems

g. SDG 7 (Inexpensive and environmentally friendly energy)

- ◦ Smart grids & real-time energy demand monitoring are essential in light of the increasing penetration of renewable energy. These are the disruptive technologies' immeasurable contributions.
- ◦ Numerous opportunities would arise from the smooth integration of diverse power producing units and the fulfillment of the dynamic loads. This increases career opportunities while simultaneously strengthening society.

     ◦   In addition to increasing clean energy's affordability, digitalization offers the potential to increase access to it.

h.   SDG 8 (Acceptable work and Economic growth)

     ◦   Disruptive technologies enable circular economy strategies and company models that are nature-inclusive.

i.   SDG 9 (Infrastructure, Innovation and Industry)

     ◦   The shift to Industry 4.0 and Industry 5.0 is supported by disruptive technologies. In the end, this improves sustainability, resilience, connectedness, productivity, and efficiency.

     ◦   Disruptive technologies provide access to a wide range of integrated applications and a new, expanding arena with lots of room for innovation. It might also become a vital part of society, just like electricity is today. Therefore, advancements in disruptive technology may be advantageous to the infrastructure of society.

j.   SDG 10 (Diminished inequalities)

     ◦   Disruptive technologies, like social media, may succeed as a tool to raise public awareness of inequality and its potential for reduction.

k.   SDG 11 (Sustainable communities and cities)

     ◦   Smart mobility, a new social framework, and society 5.0 are some of the disruptive technology-inspired high-potential ideas for creating sustainable cities.

l.   SDG 12 (Managed production and consumption)

     ◦   Optimization is one of the enormous advantages that disruptive technology can offer. The best strategy for reducing resource use is to optimize output and consumption. Disruptive technologies can serve as the foundation for reduce, recycle, and reuse.

m.   SDG 13 (Climate change action)

     ◦   Without the help of disruptive technologies, it would not be feasible to accurately forecast the weather or monitor ecosystems in real-time.

     ◦   Disruptive technologies provide immediate tracking of SDG 13 progress, grounding our efforts.

n.   SDG 14 (Life beneath water)

o.   SDG 15 (Existence on land)

     ◦   Like SDG 13, monitoring and raising awareness of present development will be the main contributions of disruptive technologies.

p.   SDG 16 (Peace, Justice & strong Institutions)

     ◦   Improving policy coherence is necessary for achieving both sustainable development and interdependence amongst one another. Due to the rapid development of disruptive technologies, policy institutions must take proactive measures to limit the negative effects that these technologies may have.

q.   SDG 17 (Alliances towards the goals)

     ◦   Networking of partnerships is necessary for the large-scale implementation of disruptive technologies. This can facilitate the progress of other objectives and help to attract money.

CONCLUSION

We will eventually reach Industry 5.0 as a result of the industry transformation brought on by the sharp growth in the creation of revolutionary digital technology. The "Society 5.0" effort seeks to build a cyber-physical society where, among other things, the daily lives of residents will be improved by closer interaction with artificial intelligence (AI) technology. The creation and dissemination of the Society 5.0 framework is not merely a theoretical exercise; rather, it is a practical factual-world project whose future course is anticipated to have an impact on the lives of several millions of individuals in Japan and other nations where the paradigm's application is being investigated. It appears important to incorporate various components, including: Innovation Policy (from the government side); Entrepreneurial spirit; and Entrepreneurial Skills, in order for the execution of Society 5.0 to be more than just a political-ideological notion (from civil society and institutions).

REFERENCES

Abbasi, A., & Kamal, M. M. (2020). Adopting Industry 4.0 technologies in citizens' electronic-engagement considering sustainability development. In *European, Mediterranean, and Middle Eastern Conference on Information Systems* (pp. 304-313). Springer, Cham.

Acioli, C., Scavarda, A., & Reis, A. (2021). Applying Industry 4.0 technologies in the COVID–19 sustainable chains. *International Journal of Productivity and Performance Management, 70*(5), 988–1016. doi:10.1108/IJPPM-03-2020-0137

Adel, A. (2022). Future of industry 5.0 in society: Human-centric solutions, challenges and prospective research areas. *Journal of Cloud Computing (Heidelberg, Germany), 11*(1), 1–15. doi:10.1186/s13677-022-00314-5 PMID:36101900

Aderibigbe, J. K. (2022). Accentuating Society 5.0 New Normal: The Strategic Role of Industry 4.0 Collaborative Partnership and Emotional Resilience. In Agile Management and VUCA-RR: Opportunities and Threats in Industry 4.0 towards Society 5.0 (pp. 39-55). Emerald Publishing Limited.

Ahmed, J., Mrugalska, B., & Akkaya, B. (2022). Agile management and VUCA 2.0 (VUCA-RR) during Industry 4.0. In Agile Management and VUCA-RR: Opportunities and Threats in Industry 4.0 towards Society 5.0 (pp. 13-26). Emerald Publishing Limited.

Akkaya, B., & Ahmed, J. (2022). VUCA-RR Toward Industry 5.0. In Agile Management and VUCA-RR: Opportunities and Threats in Industry 4.0 towards Society 5.0 (pp. 1-11). Emerald Publishing Limited.

Akkaya, B., Guah, M. W., Jermsittiparsert, K., Bulinska-Stangrecka, H., & Koçyiğit, Y. K. (Eds.). (2022). *Agile Management and VUCA-RR: Opportunities and Threats in Industry 4.0 towards Society 5.0*. Emerald Group Publishing.

Ali, M. (2021). Vocational students' perception and readiness in facing globalization, industry revolution 4.0 and society 5.0. []. IOP Publishing.]. *Journal of Physics: Conference Series, 1833*(1), 012050. doi:10.1088/1742-6596/1833/1/012050

Aquilani, B., Piccarozzi, M., Abbate, T., & Codini, A. (2020). The role of open innovation and value co-creation in the challenging transition from industry 4.0 to society 5.0: Toward a theoretical framework. *Sustainability (Basel), 12*(21), 8943. doi:10.3390/su12218943

Atina, V. Z., Mahmudi, A. Y., & Abdillah, H. (2021). Industry Preparation In Ceper Klaten On Society 5.0. *International Journal of Economics, Business and Accounting Research (IJEBAR), 5*(2).

Bartoloni, S., Calò, E., Marinelli, L., Pascucci, F., Dezi, L., Carayannis, E., Revel, G. M., & Gregori, G. L. (2022). Towards designing society 5.0 solutions: The new Quintuple Helix-Design Thinking approach to technology. *Technovation, 113*, 102413. doi:10.1016/j.technovation.2021.102413

Breque, M., De Nul, L., & Petridis, A. (2021). *Industry 5.0: towards a sustainable, human-centric and resilient European industry.*

Calp, M. H., & Bütüner, R. (2022). Society 5.0: Effective technology for a smart society. In Artificial Intelligence and Industry 4.0 (pp. 175-194). Academic Press.

Carayannis, E. G., Dezi, L., Gregori, G., & Calo, E. (2022b). Smart environments and techno-centric and human-centric innovations for Industry and Society 5.0: A quintuple helix innovation system view towards smart, sustainable, and inclusive solutions. *Journal of the Knowledge Economy, 13*(2), 926–955. doi:10.1007/s13132-021-00763-4

Carayannis, E. G., Draper, J., & Bhaneja, B. (2021). Towards fusion energy in the Industry 5.0 and Society 5.0 context: Call for a global commission for urgent action on fusion energy. *Journal of the Knowledge Economy, 12*(4), 1891–1904. doi:10.1007/s13132-020-00695-5

Carayannis, E. G., & Morawska-Jancelewicz, J. (2022a). The futures of Europe: Society 5.0 and Industry 5.0 as driving forces of future universities. *Journal of the Knowledge Economy, 13*(4), 1–27. doi:10.1007/s13132-021-00854-2

Caro Anzola, E. W., & Mendoza Moreno, M. Á. (2021). Enhanced Living Environments (ELE): A Paradigm Based on Integration of Industry 4.0 and Society 5.0 Contexts with Ambient Assisted Living (AAL). In *International Workshop on Gerontechnology* (pp. 121-132). Springer, Cham. 10.1007/978-3-030-72567-9_12

Červený, L., Sloup, R., Červená, T., Riedl, M., & Palátová, P. (2022). Industry 4.0 as an Opportunity and Challenge for the Furniture Industry-A Case Study. *Sustainability (Basel), 14*(20), 13325. doi:10.3390/su142013325

Cotta, J., Breque, M., De Nul, L., & Petridis, A. (2021). *Industry 5.0: towards a sustainable, human-centric and resilient European industry. European Commission Research and Innovation (R&I).* Series Policy Brief.

Coumans, F.(2018). Smart Factories Need Space and Time Anchors. *GIM International – the worldwide magazine for geoinformatics.*

Csiszer, A. (2022). Towards Society 5.0 in Perspective of Agile Society. In Agile Management and VUCA-RR: Opportunities and Threats in Industry 4.0 towards Society 5.0 (pp. 169-190). Emerald Publishing Limited.

Darsana, I. M., & Sudjana, I. M. (2022). A Literature Study of Indonesian Tourism Human Resources Development in the Era of Society 5.0. *Al-Ishlah: Jurnal Pendidikan, 14*(3), 2691–2700. doi:10.35445/alishlah.v14i3.2014

Dassisti, M., Siragusa, N., & Semeraro, C. (2018). Exergetic model as a guideline for implementing the smart-factory paradigm in small medium enterprises: The brovedani case. *Procedia CIRP, 67*, 534–539. doi:10.1016/j.procir.2017.12.256

Dautaj, M., & Rossi, M. (2021). Towards a New Society: Solving the Dilemma Between Society 5.0 and Industry 5.0. In *IFIP International Conference on Product Lifecycle Management* (pp. 523-536). Springer, Cham.

Di Nardo, M., & Yu, H. (2021). Special issue "Industry 5.0: The prelude to the sixth industrial revolution". *Applied System Innovation, 4*(3), 45. doi:10.3390/asi4030045

Ehwanudin, E., Irhamudin, I., & Wijaya, A. (2022). Relevansi Konsep Pendidikan Aswaja Anahdliyah Era Industry 4.0 dan Society 5.0 di Pendidikan Tinggi Islam. *Berkala Ilmiah Pendidikan, 2*(2), 94–104. doi:10.51214/bip.v2i2.420

Elim, H. I., & Zhai, G. (2020). Control system of multitasking interactions between society 5.0 and industry 5.0: A conceptual introduction & its applications. [). IOP Publishing.]. *Journal of Physics: Conference Series, 1463*(1), 012035. doi:10.1088/1742-6596/1463/1/012035

Ellitan, L. (2020). Competing in the era of industrial revolution 4.0 and society 5.0. *Jurnal Maksipreneur: Manajemen, Koperasi, dan Entrepreneurship, 10*(1), 1-12.

Fernando, Y., Saedan, R., Shaharudin, M. S., & Mohamed, A. (2021). Integrity in halal food supply chain towards the society 5.0. *Journal of Governance and Integrity, 4*(2), 103–114. doi:10.15282/jgi.4.2.2021.5948

Ferreira, C. M., & Serpa, S. (2018). Society 5.0 and social development. *Management and Organizational Studies, 5*(4), 26–31. doi:10.5430/mos.v5n4p26

Fox, S. J. (2019). Policing-the technological revolution: Opportunities & challenges! *Technology in Society, 56*, 69–78. doi:10.1016/j.techsoc.2018.09.006

Frederico, G. F. (2021). From supply chain 4.0 to supply chain 5.0: Findings from a systematic literature review and research directions. *Logistics, 5*(3), 49. doi:10.3390/logistics5030049

Fukuda, K. (2020). Science, technology and innovation ecosystem transformation toward society 5.0. *International Journal of Production Economics, 220*, 107460. doi:10.1016/j.ijpe.2019.07.033

Gladden, M. E. (2019). Who will be the members of Society 5.0? Towards an anthropology of technologically posthumanized future societies. *Social Sciences (Basel, Switzerland), 8*(5), 148. doi:10.3390/socsci8050148

Harayama, Y., & Fukuyama, M. (2017). *Society 5.0: Aiming for a new human-centered society Japan's science and technology policies for addressing global social challenges*. Hitachi. https://www.hitachi.com/rev/archive/2017/r2017_06/trends/ index.html

Huang, S., Wang, B., Li, X., Zheng, P., Mourtzis, D., & Wang, L. (2022). Industry 5.0 and Society 5.0—Comparison, complementation and co-evolution. *Journal of Manufacturing Systems, 64,* 424–428. doi:10.1016/j.jmsy.2022.07.010

Islam, A., Islam, M., Hossain Uzir, M. U., Abd Wahab, S., & Abdul Latiff, A. S. (2020). The panorama between COVID-19 pandemic and Artificial Intelligence (AI): Can it be the catalyst for Society 5.0. *International Journal of Scientific Research and Management, 8*(12), 2011–2025. doi:10.18535/ijsrm/v8i12.em02

Jatmiko, B., Sembodo, T. B., Langke, A. Y., Sukirdi, S., & Hulu, Y. (2021). Gereja sebagai Hamba yang Melayani: Sebuah Perspektif Eklesiologi Transformatif di Era Society 5.0. *CARAKA: Jurnal Teologi Biblika dan Praktika, 2*(2), 234-253.

Javaid, M., Haleem, A., Singh, R. P., & Suman, R. (2022). Artificial intelligence applications for industry 4.0: A literature-based study. *Journal of Industrial Integration and Management, 7*(01), 83–111. doi:10.1142/S2424862221300040

Kadarisman, M., Wijayanto, A. W., & Sakti, A. D. (2022). Government Agencies' Readiness Evaluation towards Industry 4.0 and Society 5.0 in Indonesia. *Social Sciences (Basel, Switzerland), 11*(8), 331. doi:10.3390/socsci11080331

Kasinathan, P., Pugazhendhi, R., Elavarasan, R. M., Ramachandaramurthy, V. K., Ramanathan, V., Subramanian, S., Kumar, S., Nandhagopal, K., Raghavan, R. R. V., Rangasamy, S., Devendiran, R., & Alsharif, M. H. (2022). Realization of Sustainable Development Goals with Disruptive Technologies by Integrating Industry 5.0, Society 5.0, Smart Cities and Villages. *Sustainability (Basel), 14*(22), 15258. doi:10.3390/su142215258

Kiepas, A. (2021). Humanity-Organization-Technology in View of Industry 4.0/Society 5.0. *Polish Pol. Sci. YB, 50*(3), 21–32. doi:10.15804/ppsy202135

Kurniasih, D., Setyoko, P. I., & Saputra, A. S. (2022). Digital Transformation of Health Quality Services in the Healthcare Industry during Disruption and Society 5.0 Era. *International Journal of Social and Management Studies, 3*(5), 139–143.

Leng, J., Sha, W., Wang, B., Zheng, P., Zhuang, C., Liu, Q., Wuest, T., Mourtzis, D., & Wang, L. (2022). Industry 5.0: Prospect and retrospect. *Journal of Manufacturing Systems, 65,* 279–295. doi:10.1016/j.jmsy.2022.09.017

Leonardi, N., Manca, M., Paternò, F., & Santoro, C. (2019). Trigger-action programming for personalising humanoid robot behaviour. In *Proceedings of the 2019 CHI Conference on Human Factors in Computing Systems-CHI '19*, Glasgow, UK, 4–9 May 2019; ACM Press: New York, NY, USA, Pp. 1-13. 10.1145/3290605.3300675

Maddikunta, P. K. R., Pham, Q. V., Prabadevi, B., Deepa, N., Dev, K., Gadekallu, T. R., & Liyanage, M. (2022). Industry 5.0: A survey on enabling technologies and potential applications. *Journal of Industrial Information Integration, 26,* 100257. doi:10.1016/j.jii.2021.100257

Maier, M. (2021). 6G as if people mattered: from industry 4.0 toward society 5.0. In *2021 International Conference on Computer Communications and Networks (ICCCN)* (pp. 1-10). IEEE.

Masuda, Y., Zimmermann, A., Shepard, D. S., Schmidt, R., & Shirasaka, S. (2021). An adaptive enterprise architecture design for a digital healthcare platform: toward digitized society-industry 4.0, society 5.0. In *2021 IEEE 25th International Enterprise Distributed Object Computing Workshop (EDOCW)* (pp. 138-146). IEEE.

Mavrodieva, A. V., & Shaw, R. (2020). Disaster and climate change issues in Japan's Society 5.0-A discussion. *Sustainability (Basel)*, *12*(5), 1893. doi:10.3390/su12051893

Medina-Borja, A. (2017). Smart human-centered service systems of the future. *Future Services & Societal Systems in Society, 5*.

Menezes, B., Yaqot, M., Hassaan, S., Franzoi, R., AlQashouti, N., & Al-Banna, A. (2022). Digital Transformation in the Era of Industry 4.0 and Society 5.0: A perspective. In *2022 2nd International Conference on Emerging Smart Technologies and Applications (eSmarTA)* (pp. 1-6). IEEE.

Mourtzis, D., Angelopoulos, J., & Panopoulos, N. (2022). A literature review of the challenges and opportunities of the transition from industry 4.0 to society 5.0. *Energies, 15*(17), 6276. doi:10.3390/en15176276

Nair, M. M., Tyagi, A. K., & Sreenath, N. (2021). The future with industry 4.0 at the core of society 5.0: open issues, future opportunities and challenges. In *2021 International Conference on Computer Communication and Informatics (ICCCI)* (pp. 1-7). IEEE. 10.1109/ICCCI50826.2021.9402498

Narvaez Rojas, C., Alomia Peñafiel, G. A., Loaiza Buitrago, D. F., & Tavera Romero, C. A. (2021). Society 5.0: A Japanese concept for a superintelligent society. *Sustainability (Basel), 13*(12), 6567. doi:10.3390/su13126567

Nastiti, F. E., & Ni'mal'Abdu, A. R. (2020). Kesiapan pendidikan Indonesia menghadapi era society 5.0. *Jurnal Kajian Teknologi Pendidikan, 5*(1), 61–66. doi:10.17977/um039v5i12020p061

Nieuważny, J., Masui, F., Ptaszynski, M., Rzepka, R., & Nowakowski, K. (2020). How religion and morality correlate in age of society 5.0: Statistical analysis of emotional and moral associations with Buddhist religious terms appearing on Japanese blogs. *Cognitive Systems Research, 59*, 329–344. doi:10.1016/j.cogsys.2019.09.026

Obschonka, M., & Audretsch, D. B. (2019). Artificial intelligence and big data in entrepreneurship: A new era has begun. *Small Business Economics, 55*(3), 529–539. doi:10.1007/s11187-019-00202-4

Onday, O. (2019). Japan's society 5.0: Going beyond industry 4.0. *Business and Economics Journal, 10*(2), 1–6.

Østbø, N. P., Berg, J. P., Kukharuk, A., & Skorobogatova, N. (2022). Industry 4.0 and society 5.0: visions of a sustainable future. *МІЖНАРОДНЕ НАУКОВО-ТЕХНІЧНЕ СПІВРОБІТНИЦТВО: ПРИНЦИПИ*, 84.

Paschek, D., Luminosu, C. T., & Ocakci, E. (2022). Industry 5.0 challenges and perspectives for manufacturing systems in the society 5.0. *Sustainability and Innovation in Manufacturing Enterprises*, 17-63.

Paternò, F., Manca, M., & Santoro, C. (2019). *End user personalization of social humanoid robots. 2019.* https://www.google.com.hk/url?sa=t&rct=j&q=&esrc=s&source=web&cd=&cad=rja&uact=8&ved=2ahUKEwilvaGXnbT7

Pereira, A. G., Lima, T. M., & Santos, F. C. (2020). Industry 4.0 and Society 5.0: Opportunities and threats. *International Journal of Recent Technology and Engineering*, 8(5), 3305–3308. doi:10.35940/ijrte.D8764.018520

Polat, L., & Erkollar, A. (2020). Industry 4.0 vs. Society 5.0. In *The International Symposium for Production Research* (pp. 333-345). Springer, Cham.

Popkova, E. G., & Sergi, B. S. (2018). Will industry 4.0 and other innovations impact Russia's development. *Exploring the future of Russia's economy and markets: Towards sustainable economic development*, (pp. 51-68). Research Gate.

Potočan, V., Mulej, M., & Nedelko, Z. (2020). Society 5.0: Balancing of Industry 4.0, economic advancement and social problems. *Kybernetes*.

Rahman, A., Pasaribu, E., Nugraha, Y., Khair, F., Soebandrija, K. E. N., & Wijaya, D. I. (2020). Industry 4.0 and society 5.0 through lens of condition based maintenance (CBM) and machine learning of artificial intelligence (MLAI). []. IOP Publishing.]. *IOP Conference Series. Materials Science and Engineering*, 852(1), 012022. doi:10.1088/1757-899X/852/1/012022

Ramadhani, D., Kenedi, A. K., Helsa, Y., Handrianto, C., & Wardana, M. R. (2021). Mapping higher order thinking skills of prospective primary school teachers in facing society 5.0. *Al Ibtida: Jurnal Pendidikan Guru MI*, 8(2), 178–190. doi:10.24235/al.ibtida.snj.v8i2.8794

Rizal, R., Misnasanti, M., Shaddiq, S., Ramdhani, R., & Wagiono, F. (2020). Learning Media in Indonesian Higher Education in Industry 4.0: Case Study. *International Journal on Advanced Science, Education, and Religion*, 3(3), 127–134. doi:10.33648/ijoaser.v3i3.62

Rojas, C. N., Peñafiel, G. A. A., Buitrago, D. F. L., & Romero, C. A. T. (2021). Society 5.0: A Japanese concept for a superintelligent society. *Sustainability (Basel)*, 13(12), 6567. doi:10.3390/su13126567

Salimova, T., Vukovic, N., & Guskova, N. (2020). Towards sustainability through Industry 4.0 and Society 5.0. *International Review (Steubenville, Ohio)*, (3-4), 48–54. doi:10.5937/intrev2003048S

Salimova, T., Vukovic, N., Guskova, N., & Krakovskaya, I. (2021). Industry 4.0 and Society 5.0: Challenges and Opportunities, The Case Study of Russia. *Smart Green City, 17*(4).

Saptaningtyas, W. W. E., & Rahayu, D. K. (2020). A proposed model for food manufacturing in smes: Facing industry 5.0. In *Proceedings of the International Conference on Industrial Engineering and Operations Management*, Dubai, UAE.

Sołtysik-Piorunkiewicz, A., & Zdonek, I. (2021). How society 5.0 and industry 4.0 ideas shape the open data performance expectancy. *Sustainability (Basel)*, 13(2), 917. doi:10.3390/su13020917

Sugiono, S. (2020). Industri Konten Digital Dalam Perspektif Society 5.0 (Digital Content Industry in Society 5.0 Perspective). *JURNAL IPTEKKOM (Jurnal Ilmu Pengetahuan & Teknologi Informasi)*, 22(2), 175-191.

Suryadi, S., Kushardiyanti, D., & Gusmanti, R. (2021). Challenges of community empowerment in the era of industry society 5. O. *Jurnal KOLOKIUM*, 9(2), 160–176. doi:10.24036/kolokium-pls.v9i2.492

Trehan, R., Machhan, R., Singh, P., & Sangwan, K. S. (2022). Industry 4.0 and society 5.0: Drivers and challenges. *IUP Journal of Information Technology, 18*(1), 40–58.

Tumentsetseg, E., & Varga, E. (2022). Industry 4.0 and education 4.0: Expected competences and skills in society 5.0. *Acta Carolus Robertus, 12*(1), 107–115.

Vestin, A., Säfsten, K., & Löfving, M. (2018). On the way to a smart factory for single-family wooden house builders in Sweden. *Procedia Manufacturing, 25,* 459–470. doi:10.1016/j.promfg.2018.06.129

Xu, X., Lu, Y., Vogel-Heuser, B., & Wang, L. (2021). Industry 4.0 and industry 5.0 inception, conception and perception. *Journal of Manufacturing Systems, 61,* 530–535. doi:10.1016/j.jmsy.2021.10.006

Yao, X., Ma, N., Zhang, J., Wang, K., Yang, E., & Faccio, M. (2022). Enhancing wisdom manufacturing as industrial metaverse for industry and society 5.0. *Journal of Intelligent Manufacturing,* 1–21.

Zengin, Y., Naktiyok, S., Kaygın, E., Kavak, O., & Topçuoglu, E. (2021). An investigation upon industry 4.0 and society 5.0 within the context of sustainable development goals. *Sustainability (Basel), 13*(5), 2682. doi:10.3390/su13052682

Zhanna, M., & Nataliia, V. (2020). Development of engineering students competencies based on cognitive technologies in conditions of industry 4.0. *International Journal of Cognitive Research in Science, Engineering and Education, 8*(S), 93-101.

Chapter 3
Achieving Sustainability Through Green Technology:
The Need of the Nations

Jyoti Verma
https://orcid.org/0000-0002-7559-4312
Chitkara Business School, Chitkara University, India

Yashna Sharma
https://orcid.org/0000-0002-7559-4312
Chitkara Business School, Chitkara University, India

ABSTRACT

Green technology is a game-changing strategy to solve urgent environmental issues while fostering economic and social well-being. This chapter dives into the vital role green technology plays in addressing the pressing need for sustainability at the national and international levels. The chapter emphasizes how many top businesses support ecological solutions, and how countries are increasingly seeing sustainability as a top concern. Additionally, it emphasizes how green technologies have a beneficial impact on a variety of industries and how they have the potential to lead global sustainability activities. The study showed the positive impact of green technologies in different fields. It will focus on applications, and success stories while emphasizing the beneficial effects of green technology across various industries. This chapter opens the path for a greater comprehension of sustainable technologies' crucial role in building a more sustainable future by focusing on their fundamental necessity.

INTRODUCTION

Every nation has its diverse population who speak different languages, have different cultures, and other religions; unity keeps binding this diverse population together under one nation (Tran et al., 2012). A country is identified by its people. Attitude, emotion, anger, hard work, values, beliefs, patriotism, etc., are the traits of a population that, if present in a good ratio, can promote favourable growth of the nation

DOI: 10.4018/979-8-3693-0338-2.ch003

& vice-versa. Likewise, the entire globe needs to awaken itself to contribute towards environmental care, as this has become a macro environment issue, which can heal only through economic integration, sustainable collaborations, green technology adaptation, society contribution, financial inclusion, and green innovation (Caiado et al., 2018). The United Nations 2015 adopted 17 sustainable development goals (SDGs), which aim to reduce environmental abuse, population below the poverty line, hunger, inequality, and waste & promote economic growth through sustainable practices, green technology, financial inclusions, prosperity, favourable global trade practices, and sustainable collaborations. Promoters support these objectives to achieve a sustainable economy by 2030.

Green Technology

Green technology, or clean or sustainable technology, is a game-changing strategy to solve urgent environmental issues while fostering economic and social well-being. Green technology's fundamental goal is to provide novel solutions that minimise carbon emissions, conserve natural resources, and positively influence the environment. These technologies include many uses, including waste management, energy-efficient construction, sustainable transportation, and renewable energy sources like solar and wind power. The adoption of green technology is driven by the rising understanding of the critical need to mitigate climate change, decrease pollution, and assure resource sustainability. Traditional industrial practices are no longer viable in light of the environmental problems caused by climate change, pollution, and resource depletion. Governments, corporations, and people are adopting eco-friendly practices in reaction to this, and green technology is essential in establishing a more sustainable future for our world. Creating renewable energy sources is one of the pillars of green technology. Solar, wind, and hydroelectric power are increasingly being used to provide clean and sustainable energy. This lessens our dependency on fossil fuels and reduces greenhouse gas emissions. In addition, energy-efficient technology is being incorporated into industrial processes, appliances, and buildings, which helps to save operating costs and decrease energy usage (Eriksson, 2018). The fast uptake of sustainable transportation options like electric cars and enhanced public transit networks further reduce our everyday journeys' carbon impact. Beyond energy, green technology also impacts resource conservation and waste management. Our waste materials have a minimal environmental effect thanks to recycling and waste-to-energy operations, while agricultural advancements like precision farming and water-saving methods help produce food sustainably (Nonami, 2016). Cleaner manufacturing techniques are also encouraged by green technology, with an emphasis on lowering waste, emissions, and harmful byproducts.

Green technology is important for many reasons than just protecting the environment. Its effects on the economy and society are significant. The green technology industry is now a major contributor to economic expansion, creating jobs and promoting innovation. Adopting sustainable practices also improves the health and well-being of communities by lowering air and water pollution, increasing energy efficiency, and averting disasters caused by climate change. On a national and international level, green technology is needed and required for a sustainable life (Chan, 1993; Etezadi et al., 2010). Many countries have realised the value of sustainability and have established challenging goals to cut carbon emissions and move towards a greener economy. Multinational firms are simultaneously incorporating sustainability into their supply networks and business structures. Customers are becoming more environmentally concerned and are seeking goods and services that adhere to green values.

Applications of Green Technology

Green technology is a healthy replacement for historically used techniques, methods, and technology. Different from slash-and-burn agriculture, where the whole cultivation land, trees, and plants are burnt to start new cultivation on the same land, which is an outdated method. Following are some of the applications of green technology-

- **Drone Technology-** Drone Technology, an uncrewed aerial vehicle, has potential use cases in diverse fields like cinematography, agriculture, weather forecasting, pollution detection, investigation, and many more (Cohn et al.,2017). On 2nd June 2023, an Odissa train accident occurred, in which two passenger trains collided, leaving 280 passengers dead and more than 900 people injured, and drone technology was used as a medium to capture the intensity of loss that occurred and an investigation tool. Drone transformed agriculture (King, 2017; Ndiaye et al., 2020). Farmers are the nation's lifeline; they spend their blood, sweat, and tears in the cultivation of crops, which is a long process if done manually (Alimuzzaman, 2015). Various steps are involved in crop cultivation, like soil fertility check, climate conditions, continuous monitoring, livestock maintenance, weed removal, spraying pesticides and chemicals in balanced amounts, irrigation, protection against wild animals, and many more. All these done manually consume a lot of time and effort and often result in delayed production. Moreover, direct contact with chemicals and pesticides can cause various communicable diseases; machines like a tractor, which are commonly used for sowing crops, consume excess fuel and causes air as well as noise pollution. Significantly, that is where the drone comes into the picture; it is capable of performing every activity mentioned above. It has a thermal camera that can guard the crops at night and capture high-quality images in the dark (Rani et al., 2019). Usually, a satellite is used to collect or capture forecasting-related data, but the quality and clarity drone offers even in monsoon lacks a satellite. It helps the farmers in skilful planning by checking even the minor needs of crops through sensors, like hydration level checks, soil fertility checks, weather forecasting, etc. It can act as a quick doctor, which can help a farmer isolate the infectious livestock from the group to prevent the spread of infections among other livestock (Rani et al., 2019). Its properties like zero carbon emission, sustainable agriculture, and efficient, optimum resource allocation make it a true example of green technology (Sumi et al., 2018). There is always a myth that technology implementation leads to unemployment; well, not in this case. Drone technology needs educated people to operate and process data captured through sensors; this does not necessarily mean unemployment to the farmer; instead, it means taking initiatives or running a training campaign specifically for skill development among current and potential farmers. Modern youth who feel reluctant to work in the agriculture sector due to its manual nature can now see it as an option of employment, as the majority of farm activities are now drone-oriented, and youth who like a challenging job or technical job can opt for operating drone technology by acquiring technical skills required to process data from it.
- **Electronic Vehicles, Hybrid Vehicles & Compressed Natural Gas (CNG)** - India is considered one of the most polluted countries. In India, Delhi is considered as the most polluted city. In winter, the pollution causes blind fog, making the road invisible. Most vehicles being used are motor vehicles, emitting greenhouse gases that are deadly for living creatures (Cowan & Hultén, 1996; Tran et al., 2012). Industrial pollution, releasing chemical gases into the breathing air, acts like a poison that can unintentionally cause death or severe respiratory problems. In foreign countries,

people usually prefer walking to their office, using a bicycle as a mode of transport, or travelling by public transport. However, it is not the case in India; most people prefer travelling in their vehicles (Dwijendra et al., 2022; Rajashekara, 2013). Sustainable alternatives to motor vehicles include electronic vehicles, which aim to eliminate greenhouse gas emissions. Electric Vehicles (EVs) require suitable charging to travel long distances (Agrawal & Rajapatel, 2020; Ullah & Ahmad, 2022). A hybrid vehicle is an extension of electronic vehicles, and it has both the features of motor vehicles and electronic vehicles; it is a mixture of EVs and motor vehicles for a better customer experience. Compressed Natural Gas (CNG) Vehicles are also considered sustainable due to their low gas emissions (Ding et al., 2017; Guo et al., 2018; Wong & Zhou, 2015). These vehicles aim at erasing carbon footprints and offer sustainable growth. The major problem with EVs and hybrid vehicles is the need for charging stations, which can potentially cause low demand. To initiate green transportation, Indian governments are taking initiatives like vehicle tax benefits, low tolls, and expenditure on charge stations (Eberle & Von, 2010; Mruzek et al., 2016; Situ, 2009).

- **Blockchain Technology-** It is a chain of blocks. Each block contains transaction history; as the amount of transaction increases, the blocks required to store that transaction data also increases, forming a chain of block, i.e., blockchain. It is also known as distributed ledger technology (DLT). To perform a transaction on the blockchain, it is necessary to have cryptocurrency. Crypto is the mode of blockchain payment. Its characteristics, like the decentralized chain, peer-to-peer network, hash function, cryptography, and smart contracts, make it a buzz worldwide. However, in India, there has been some regulation on the use of cryptocurrency, as it is not accepted as a form of payment. RBI even banned the use of virtual currency in 2018, making it illegal in India. As blockchain is a decentralized platform, which means there is no central authority to monitor, control, or regulate your transaction, it eliminates the presence of a third party. That is why it is known as a peer-to-peer network. This is why RBI does not accept it, and to prevent its use, some restrictions were passed, as gain from cryptocurrency is taxable now. India's government has noticed the speed of acceptance of digital currency and digital payment among users (Fernando et al., 2019; Khan et al., 2021; Verma & Gagandeep, 2023). It makes them the first hint to issue India's first Central Bank Digital Currency (CBDC); with this, RBI introduced the launch of CBDCs in Parliament on 1 February 2022. CBDC is India's first legal digital currency. Blockchain technology promoted the use of cryptocurrency for all modes of payment; that is what India wants: a cashless economy (Trivedi & Malik, 2022). The maximum government expenditure is on cash receipt printing, so to shift this capital expenditure toward sustainability, there was a wave of going cashless to going paperless (Midilli et al., 2006; Verma et al., 2023; Yli et al., 2016). However, the real hype for digital currency was seen during the pandemic. Blockchain technology is an efficient solution; Dapps, a decentralized application, is on hype. In the healthcare industry, the implementation of a Dapp for certificate issuance and collection is on the rise; one can access health, medical, or sickness certificates stored on blockchain technology right from the experts, not only reduces the hassle of paperwork, appreciating afforestation but also eliminate the risk of duplicity, a visit to the hospital, cost, etc. Digi locker is another efficient, decentralized, blockchain-based platform where students or anyone can store their documents; as it is decentralized, every document is encrypted, making it free from breaching or fraud.
- **Healing through AI-** AI stands for artificial intelligence. It is a technology, which is designed with human intelligence. It has come a long way, with long-awaited innovations, unlocking each

one by one. Firstly, voice recognition, which means recognizing the speech. Its applications can be seen everywhere, on almost all apps, like YouTube, WhatsApp, google, and many more. Voice recognition was designed to understand the speech of every human on the earth, but it was unable to understand the speech of an ALS patient. ALS is Amyotrophic Lateral Sclerosis, a motor neuron disease under which the spinal cord is damaged, disables movement, and the nerves cannot signal to the brain; the muscles are so damaged that it is difficult to speak. Tim Green, an American footballer, was diagnosed with this disease in 2016; his muscles were damaged with time, his movement slowed down, and his jaw muscle was contracted, making his talk difficult. One day, he was to use voice recognition, saying, "Dad calls," however, the voice AI could catch the word dad, so he told his dad he changed the word dad to "yoyo." Google, known for its enormous technological disruptions, started working on this issue. They did several partnerships to collect the voice samples of ALS patients and use these samples to adjust the needs of AI. The result was fruitful, and the voice recognition worked well; it understood not only Tim Green's speech but also the speech of all ALS patients. Another AI feature is image recognition, which means identifying the data related to the image through image scanning. Diabetic retinopathy is a blindness disease that occurs mostly in diabetic patients, and it can be cured if diagnosed at an earlier stage unless it can cause blindness. In the world, there are around 400 million cases of diabetes. India has 40 million diabetic patients, and the doctors are very few. AI is an effective tool that can be used alone for diagnosing diabetic retinopathy. Google's innovation in this field, particularly in India and Thailand, used image scanning, which detects the bleeding through nerves in the eyes and can identify the type of disease a person suffers from. Another wonderful innovation can fill the gap between doctors in India and Thailand.

Some of Early Green Tech Innovation by Firms

- **Pavegen-** It is a UK-based technology company that converts footfall into renewable energy, which can plug in LGs, buildings, green walls, etc. It makes tiles that are capable of generating as well as storing kinetic energy through each footstep. Laurence Kemball founded it in 2009, primarily wanting to make something that uses clean energy, and when he was placed with a European energy company, he noticed the millions of crowds rushing over Victoria train station and saw the potential of generating energy through these rushing steps. To prove his invention, he used cause marketing by uploading pictures of the tiles that he installed in the office building secretly, and it worked. On 17th May 2023, they took part in an event in Melbourne, Australia, where they powered up the first kinetic tiles experience to the players and generated power from each player step to power up the EV fleet. The company also offers the Pavegen GO app, where its customers can connect and know their contribution to energy generation through each step and win rewards.
- **Tesla-** It is an automobile company in the news due to its clean energy innovations. Tesla Model 3 and Model Y are fully electric cars that have an estimated range of 333 miles, with 45000 guaranteed charging stations. These EVs require charging for a full night and serve a long drive. Tesla also experimented, as it also introduced some unique yet green products. It offers a solar roof, which means an embedded solar roof containing both solar glass tiles and steel tiles, to store solar energy and simultaneously offer a strong roof. This solar roof offers solar electricity when running out of electricity or struggling with sudden climatic change. Another Tesla invention is Powerwall, which uses solar energy from the roof and stores it in a home battery on the wall, so

when running out of grid electricity, the stored solar energy is transformed to run home appliances. Solar panels are also offered again as a medium to run appliances during electricity shortfalls.

- **Think Phi-** A green start-up invented "Ulta Chata," which looks exactly like an inverted umbrella and occupies one square foot area. It is used to store rainwater in its purest form during monsoon and store solar energy during dry weather through solar panels on its inner side. It acts as a multipurpose product that stores rainwater and purifies it, as well as also acts as an energy saver and energy generator. It even provides a nice long roof for a cosy gathering and can use solar energy to power up the lights embedded in its outer space. Samit developed this start-up with his wife, Priya Vakil, who gave life to this invention.

- **Refiberd-** It is a start-up founded by three women engineers in May 2020 during Covid. They identified the recycler problem of sorting the textile waste, which is contaminated with different colours and materials. The textile waste all over the world is around 186 million pounds. They took their incomplete patent and used artificial intelligence and machine learning to sort the waste, removing the contaminated aside and transferring the sorted waste to the accurate recycler. The aim is to recycle 80 per cent of textile waste, unlike 1 per cent of textile waste recycled traditionally.

- **Mama earth-** A company that makes organic skin care products. It is an Indian company founded in 2016 by Ghazal Alagh. The company produces cruelty-free, chemical-free, plastic-free products. The ingredients are all-natural, like rice, bhringamla, henna, tea tree, charcoal, honey malai, etc. The company's tagline is "Goodness Inside"; they surely do justice to their tagline by planting 476836 trees. Each sale amounts to plant goodness, which means they credit their customers for each tree planted. Mama Earth has partnered with the Sankalp Taru organization, which aims to plant trees for people and through people; both aim at reducing carbon footprint through each tree planted, increasing the oxygen level and greenery to support living.

SIGNIFICANCE OF SUSTAINABILITY FOR PLANET

Earth is our mother planet, which has always given us a surplus. We, humans, misuse those surpluses to fulfil our never-ending needs. The human body has several stages of life, and death can occur at any stage if a healthy lifestyle is not adopted. Similarly, the Earth also has a lifecycle; if not treated with good care, it will vanish anytime, or if treated sustainably, it will live more good years. Therefore, the choice is ours: to protect it for future generations or see it dying daily. Air, water, and land are the surpluses that are all polluted. The air we breathe to survive is full of pollutants. Air pollution is the main cause; the rising number of motor vehicles, industrial smoke, cracker firing, number of air conditioners, land burning, etc., lead to air pollution. Ninety per cent of the human body is covered with water, and it is a basic consumption need. Water shortage and pollution are potential reasons for water shortage in the upcoming years. Throwing garbage, industrial waste release in rivers or lakes, washing clothes, water wastage, etc., are the reasons behind water shortage. Air and water are equally important; life is impossible without oxygen, and water is an important element for survival. Another significant element is land, which supports the cultivation and living of animals and human beings. The question that arises is, do we use the land for the right purpose it was given? The answer is no; the land which is to be used for planting trees is used for storing garbage; the land which is supposed to grow crops is used for deforestation; the land which is meant to support the life of animals now is full of dead bodies of these animals. These circumstances depict the need for sustainability. No one can survive in the absence of either of the three elements. If not taken immediately step, the planet Earth will turn into a bare land, which will support neither livelihood nor life. That is why sustainability is important, and the present has to conserve natural resources for future generations.

INDIVIDUAL ACTIONS FOR A SUSTAINABLE PLANET

- **Planting trees-** The most effective way to curb the effect of air pollution is by planting as many trees as possible. Trees are natural carbon footprint removers; they increase the oxygen level in the air and remove pollutants from the air.
- **Conserving natural resources-** Water is a nature's gift to humans, and it is present in different forms like glaciers in the ocean, vapour in the air, rivers, lakes, rainwater, etc., but the water we use for consumption, which is capable of drinking, is not present abundantly. Therefore, using it in the right amount and for the right purpose is extremely important.
- **Shifting towards green energy-** Green energy refers to clean energy, which means using nature to generate energy. Its examples are solar energy, wind energy, tidal energy, kinetic energy, etc. Instead of using electricity, there can be a significant shift towards solar energy, which does more than what electricity does. As summers are extremely hotter, installing solar panels or customizing a solar roof will store the solar energy and convert it into electricity, which can run all the connected home appliances.
- **Substituting with greener options-** A normal car, or motorbike, consumes petrol or diesel to work, and both are fossil fuels that cause air pollution, leading to several deadly respiratory disorders. So, what can be a sustainable substitute for it? Its Electronic vehicle neither replenishes natural resources nor causes any pollution.
- **Using recyclable material-** Plastic is non-recyclable and is still in use. It can be burned or stored on land, which is deadly for humans and animals. Burning plastic causes air pollution, while filling land with plastic will cause unproductive land. The majority of cows die through the consumption of plastic. Humans can substitute plastic with healthier options, like replacing a plastic bag with a cloth bag or plastic straw with a paper straw.

Impact of Green Technology on the Environment

- **Lower Carbon footprint-** As all the things that are not best for the environment are replaced with sustainable, cleaner, and greener alternatives, there will ultimately be zero carbon emissions shortly.
- **Pollution-free environment-** If the things that cause pollution are avoided, then there will be a pollution-free environment. Zero carbon emission means zero pollution, which will happen through greener adaptions like EVs, hydrogen cars, cruelty-free products, non-plastic use, etc.
- **Natural resources conservation-** Green energies are sustainable alternatives that truly conserve and replace natural resources by producing the same output.
- **More recyclable material-** There shall be a shift from non-recyclable to recyclable material. There shall be a shift from fossil fuels like petroleum or diesel cars to hydrogen cars.
- **Greener development through green technology-** AI, drone, machine learning, blockchain, and digital ecosystem- are fewer examples of greener technology contributing to a greener planet.

CONCLUSION

Sustainability is a never-ending responsibility that can only be achieved through unity. The need of the nations requires individual contribution through greener adaptations. Anything that is cruelty-free and positively impacts the environment is considered greener; it can be green technology, green energy, or green alternatives, like substituting fossil fuels like petroleum & diesel with hydrogen or battery. There is sufficient awareness about the depletion of natural resources, unrecyclable material, and the war for sustainability. Companies like Pavegen, Refiberd, Tesla, and many more are contributing their maximum towards sustainability. Adapting greener technologies like drones, AI, blockchain, etc., is the best decision ever for a greener future. It is the foremost duty of human beings to protect the environment in which they live unless the day is not so far when the world may turn into a graveyard.

REFERENCES

Agrawal, M., & Rajapatel, M. S. (2020). Global perspective on electric vehicle 2020. *International Journal of Engineering Research & Technology (Ahmedabad), 9*(1), 8–11.

Alimuzzaman, M. D. (2015). Agricultural drone. *Journal of Food Security, 3*(5), 12–27.

Caiado, R., Nascimento, D., Quelhas, O., Tortorella, G., & Rangel, L. (2018). Towards sustainability through green, lean and six sigma integration at service industry: Review and framework. *Technological and Economic Development of Economy, 24*(4), 1659–1678. doi:10.3846/tede.2018.3119

Chan, C. C. (1993). An overview of electric vehicle technology. *Proceedings of the IEEE, 81*(9), 1202–1213. doi:10.1109/5.237530

Cohn, P., Green, A., Langstaff, M., & Roller, M. (2017). *Commercial drones are here: The future of unmanned aerial systems.* McKinsey & Company.

Cowan, R., & Hultén, S. (1996). Escaping lock-in: The case of the electric vehicle. *Technological Forecasting and Social Change, 53*(1), 61–79. doi:10.1016/0040-1625(96)00059-5

Ding, N., Prasad, K., & Lie, T. T. (2017). The electric vehicle: A review. *International Journal of Electric and Hybrid Vehicles, 9*(1), 49–66. doi:10.1504/IJEHV.2017.082816

Dwijendra, N. K. A., Sharma, S., Asary, A. R., Majdi, A., Muda, I., Mutlak, D. A., Parra, R. M. R., & Hammid, A. T. (2022). Economic performance of a hybrid renewable energy system with optimal design of resources. *Environmental and Climate Technologies, 26*(1), 441–453. doi:10.2478/rtuect-2022-0034

Eberle, U., & Von Helmolt, R. (2010). Sustainable transportation based on electric vehicle concepts: A brief overview. *Energy & Environmental Science, 3*(6), 689–699. doi:10.1039/c001674h

Eriksson, N. (2018). *Conceptual study of a future drone detection system-Countering a threat posed by a disruptive technology.*

Etezadi-Amoli, M., Choma, K., & Stefani, J. (2010). Rapid-charge electric-vehicle stations. *IEEE Transactions on Power Delivery, 25*(3), 1883–1887. doi:10.1109/TPWRD.2010.2047874

Fernando, Y., Jabbour, C. J. C., & Wah, W. X. (2019). Pursuing green growth in technology firms through the connections between environmental innovation and sustainable business performance: Does service capability matter? *Resources, Conservation and Recycling, 141*, 8–20. doi:10.1016/j.resconrec.2018.09.031

Guo, Y., Xia, X., Zhang, S., & Zhang, D. (2018). Environmental regulation, government R&D funding and green technology innovation: Evidence from China provincial data. *Sustainability (Basel), 10*(4), 940. doi:10.3390/su10040940

Khan, N., Jhariya, M. K., Raj, A., Banerjee, A., & Meena, R. S. (2021). Eco-designing for sustainability. *Ecological intensification of natural resources for sustainable agriculture*, 565-595.

King, A. (2017). Technology: The future of agriculture. *Nature, 544*(7651), S21–S23. doi:10.1038/544S21a PMID:28445450

Midilli, A., Dincer, I., & Ay, M. (2006). Green energy strategies for sustainable development. *Energy Policy, 34*(18), 3623–3633. doi:10.1016/j.enpol.2005.08.003

Mruzek, M., Gajdáč, I., Kučera, Ľ., & Barta, D. (2016). Analysis of parameters influencing electric vehicle range. *Procedia Engineering, 134*, 165–174. doi:10.1016/j.proeng.2016.01.056

Ndiaye, M., Salhi, S., & Madani, B. (2020). When green technology meets optimization modeling: the case of routing drones in logistics, agriculture, and healthcare. *Modeling and Optimization in Green Logistics*, 127-145.

Nonami, K. (2016). Drone technology, cutting-edge drone business, and future prospects. *Journal of robotics and mechatronics, 28*(3), 262-272.

Rajashekara, K. (2013). Present status and future trends in electric vehicle propulsion technologies. *IEEE Journal of Emerging and Selected Topics in Power Electronics, 1*(1), 3–10. doi:10.1109/JESTPE.2013.2259614

Rani, A. L. K. A., Chaudhary, A. M. R. E. S. H., Sinha, N., Mohanty, M., & Chaudhary, R. (2019). Drone: The green technology for future agriculture. *Harit Dhara, 2*(1), 3–6.

Situ, L. (2009). Electric vehicle development: the past, present & future. In *2009 3rd International Conference on Power Electronics Systems and Applications (PESA)* (pp. 1-3). IEEE.

Sumi, F. H., Dutta, L., & Sarker, F. (2018). Future with wireless power transfer technology. *J. Electr. Electron. Syst, 7*(1000279), 2332–0796.

Tran, M., Banister, D., Bishop, J. D., & McCulloch, M. D. (2012). Realizing the electric-vehicle revolution. *Nature Climate Change, 2*(5), 328–333. doi:10.1038/nclimate1429

Trivedi, S., & Malik, R. (2022). Blockchain Technology as an Emerging Technology in the Insurance Market. In *Big Data: A Game Changer for Insurance Industry* (pp. 81–100). Emerald Publishing Limited. doi:10.1108/978-1-80262-605-620221006

Ullah, S., Khan, F. U., & Ahmad, N. (2022). Promoting sustainability through green innovation adoption: A case of manufacturing industry. *Environmental Science and Pollution Research International, 29*(14), 1–21. doi:10.1007/s11356-021-17322-8 PMID:34746984

Verma, J., & Gagandeep. (2023). Embracing Fintech Applications in the Banking Sector Vis-á-Vis Service Quality. In *Contemporary Studies of Risks in Emerging Technology, Part B* (pp. 207-219). Emerald Publishing Limited.

Verma, J., Sharma, J., & Gupta, M. (2023). Digital Currency and Blockchain Technology in the Financial World. In *Perspectives on Blockchain Technology and Responsible Investing* (pp. 216–225). IGI Global. doi:10.4018/978-1-6684-8361-9.ch010

Wong, J. K. W., & Zhou, J. (2015). Enhancing environmental sustainability over building life cycles through green BIM: A review. *Automation in Construction, 57*, 156–165. doi:10.1016/j.autcon.2015.06.003

Yli-Huumo, J., Ko, D., Choi, S., Park, S., & Smolander, K. (2016). Where is current research on blockchain technology?—A systematic review. *PLoS One, 11*(10), e0163477. doi:10.1371/journal.pone.0163477 PMID:27695049

Chapter 4
Convergence Strategies for Green Computing and Sustainable Development

Arti Saxena
Manav Rachna International Institute of Reseacrh and Studies, India

Kapil Gupta
Manav Rachna International Institute of Research and Studies, India

Sasmita Pala
Manav Rachna International Institute of Reseacrh and Studies, India

ABSTRACT

This chapter outlines the journey that intertwines solar energy and artificial intelligence (AI), focusing on optimizing solar energy generation within India's dynamic landscape. Solar energy is abundant—its variability demands creative solutions to turn unpredictability into efficiency. In this context, as technology advances, AI emerges as a valuable tool capable of understanding complex weather patterns, forecasting energy generation, and dynamically adjusting solar panel setups. This study navigates the synergy between AI and solar energy in India. Each section sheds light on different aspects of AI's transformative potential, detailing methods, applications, and concrete results. As the chapter unravels the intricate connection between these two domains, it not only uncovers a more intelligent approach to energy generation, but also catches a glimpse of a future where renewable resources thrive in harmony with technological innovation.

INTRODUCTION

In our modern world, as we work to be more sustainable and fight against climate change, we're focusing on renewable energy sources like solar power. Solar energy is especially exciting because it can provide a lot of power without harming the environment. But there's a challenge: solar power changes with the

DOI: 10.4018/979-8-3693-0338-2.ch004

Figure 1. Renewable energy resources optimizing using artificial intelligence

weather, and that makes it tricky to rely on. This is where artificial intelligence (AI) comes in – it's a powerful technology that could help solve these issues and change the way we use renewable energy.

The sun gives us a lot of energy every day, but it's not steady. Clouds and shadows make it go up and down. Traditional ways of managing solar power don't work well with these changes. They often use fixed schedules and need people to make adjustments, which don't work great with the unpredictable sun.

AI can help by using its special ability to understand lots of information, predict patterns, and learn in real time. This could help with the challenges of solar power. By combining AI and renewable energy, we can find new and smarter ways to deal with the changing sun. Instead of seeing the variability as a problem, AI helps us see it as something we can use to our advantage.

The big challenge is to figure out how to use the sunlight we get, no matter how the weather changes. This isn't just about getting as much energy as possible; it's about making smart choices based on real-time information, changes in energy needs, prices, and the environment. This is where AI comes in – it acts like a conductor in an orchestra. It helps solar panels move to catch the most sun when it's out and saves energy when clouds cover it.

In this case study, we explore how AI can make solar energy better. We'll look at how we use data from the past and use computer models to predict how much energy we can make. We'll also see how clever algorithms can change the angle of solar panels to get the most out of the sun. When we mix AI and solar energy, we're not only using energy more efficiently and wasting less, but we're also getting closer to a world where clean energy is a vital part of our lives.

As we learn about how AI and renewable energy work together, we're on the edge of something big. This could change how we make energy and help us be more environmentally friendly. This case study shows how AI can make solar power even better. It's not just a tool – it's a way to make the world cleaner and more advanced.

BACKGROUND AND PROBLEM STATEMENT

In South Asia, India is a diverse country with a rich history and a large population. However, it's also a major contributor to greenhouse gases. This means that while it's trying to grow its economy, it also needs to be environmentally responsible. Renewable energy, especially solar power, could be a solution. India gets a lot of sunlight throughout the year, making solar power a promising option. But there are challenges to overcome.

India wants to have energy that's good for the environment, reduce its reliance on fossil fuels, and move towards a cleaner future. Solar power can help with this because it's renewable and doesn't harm the environment. However, India's landscape is varied, with deserts and plains, leading to differences in how much sunlight can be captured. The main problems are how to use this sunlight effectively and provide a steady supply of energy for a growing economy and population.

The usual ways of managing solar power, like fixed solar panels and manual adjustments, don't work well across India's different landscapes. Changing weather, seasons, and clouds add to the challenge. When clouds cover solar panels, they can't generate as much energy, leading to wasted sunlight and an unreliable energy source.

Here's where artificial intelligence (AI) comes in. It's a game-changer that combines advanced technology with renewable energy solutions. AI can revolutionize how India manages solar energy. By using AI to analyze real-time data, predict patterns, and make smart decisions, India can tackle the problem of varying sunlight. This will not only help deal with the challenges of changing sunlight but also make energy capture and distribution more efficient.

The big question is: How can India use solar energy effectively, given the changes in sunlight and the need for reliable energy for its growing population and economy? This case study looks into how AI can help solve this complex problem. By understanding how AI and solar energy work together, we hope to find new solutions that can transform India's energy situation. This way, India can make progress without harming the environment for future generations.

KEY RENEWABLE ENERGY SOURCES

In today's era where the climate change is a pressing global concern, the transition to renewable energy sources has become essential & imperative. The finite usage of primitive fossil fuels, along with their environmental impact, has led to a growing spotlight on renewable energy. These sources, including solar, wind, hydro, geothermal, and biomass, offer sustainable alternatives that not only reduce greenhouse gas emissions but also giveaway a path to a more resilient, better & cleaner energy for our future. This chapter basically explores the significance of renewable energy sources and their different versatilities, effectiveness and implications for future directions (Dib et al., 2021).

1. **Solar Energy:** Solar energy is one of the most abundant and accessible renewable energy sources. It involves capturing the energy from the sun's radiation r commonly termed as the sunlight tusing photovoltaic cells or solar panels. Solar power is versatile and can be consumed both for electricity generation as well as the heating purposes. The wide availability of sunlight makes it a viable option worldwide, and advancements in technology have made solar panels increasingly efficient, resourceful & cost-effective.

2. **Wind Energy:** Wind energy is generated through the kinetic energy of moving air masses, typically by wind turbines. These turbines convert wind power into electricity. Wind farms have become common sights in many countries, with the capacity to provide clean and renewable energy for homes and industries. Wind energy offers a scalable and efficient source of power, reducing the reliance on fossil fuels.

3. **Hydroelectric Power:** Hydropower, also termed as the hydroelectric power, exploits the energy of flowing or falling water to generate electricity. Dams and hydroelectric plants are used to capture and transform the kinetic energy of water into electrical power. Hydropower has a long history and remains a reliable and renewable energy source, contributing significantly to the global energy mix.

4. **Geothermal Energy:** Geothermal energy utilizes heat from the Earth's core, converting it into electricity or direct heating for various applications. Geothermal power plants tap into underground reservoirs of hot water or steam to produce energy. This source is sustainable, highly reliable, and produces minimal emissions, making it a clean and consistent contributor to the energy sector.

5. **Biomass Energy:** Biomass energy utilizes organic materials such as wood, agricultural residues, and even municipal solid waste to produce energy through processes like combustion, gasification, or fermentation. Biomass is a versatile source of renewable energy, suitable for heating, electricity generation, and even biofuels production. It helps in waste reduction, contributes to carbon neutrality, and offers a way to manage organic waste responsibly.

NEED FOR RENEWABLE ENERGY SOURCES

Let us explore the pressing need for renewable energy sources and the benefits they offer to both the environment and society (Dib et al., 2021).

1. **Lessening Nursery Gas Emissions:** One of the foremost critical reasons for transitioning to renewable energy sources is ought to combat climate alter. The burning of fossil powers for power and transportation may be a major donor to nursery gas outflows, essentially carbon dioxide (CO2). These emanations trap warm within the Earth's environment, driving to worldwide warming and the related issues of extraordinary climate occasions, rising sea levels, and environment disturbance. Renewable vitality sources such as sun powered, wind, and hydropower create power without transmitting nursery gasses, making them basic devices within the battle against climate change.

2. **Asset Sustainability:** Fossil fuels, such as coal, oil, and common gas, are limited assets that will in the long run run out. As these non-renewable assets drain, vitality costs tend to rise, which can lead to financial precariousness and expanded geopolitical pressures. In differentiation, renewable vitality sources are maintainable, as they depend on plenteous and actually recharging assets like daylight, wind, and water. This maintainability guarantees a steady and solid vitality supply for the future.

3. **Vitality Security:** Dependence on fossil fuels from outside nations can posture noteworthy national security dangers. Disturbances within the supply chain, geopolitical clashes, and cost instability can all adversely affect vitality security. Transitioning to renewable vitality sources diminishes dependence on imported fills, making countries more strong to energy-related emergencies and less vulnerable to worldwide vitality showcase fluctuations.

4. **Work Creation:** The renewable vitality division has appeared huge potential for work creation. Sun based and wind ranches, for occurrence, require a gifted workforce for establishment, upkeep, and investigate and advancement. These occupations not as it were contribute to financial development but too advance maintainable work openings, regularly in provincial and financially challenged regions.

5. **Discuss Quality Improvement:** Burning fossil fills not as it were discharges nursery gasses but too emanates hurtful discuss poisons that have serious wellbeing impacts, counting respiratory maladies and cardiovascular issues. Moving to renewable vitality sources diminishes these outflows, driving to improved air quality and way better open wellbeing. Cleaner discuss contributes to the next quality of life and lower healthcare costs.

6. **Mechanical Advancements:** The advancement and sending of renewable vitality innovations have impelled advancement within the vitality segment. Inquire about into more effective sun oriented boards, wind turbines, and vitality for capacity arrangements has driven to breakthroughs that advantage different businesses and energize mechanical advance. The interest of renewable vitality arrangements drives financial development and improves competitiveness.

7. **Relieving Vitality Poverty:** In numerous parts of the world, millions of individuals need get to to dependable and reasonable vitality sources. Renewable vitality advances, particularly decentralized frameworks like sun powered boards, offer a life saver to these underserved communities. By saddling the control of the sun, wind, and other renewable sources, farther and impeded locales can get to clean vitality, progressing their living conditions and openings for financial development.

AI OPTIMIZATION FOR VARIOUS RENEWABLE ENERGY SOURCES

The pursuit of cleaner and more sustainable energy sources has gained significant momentum in recent years. As society grapples with the challenges of climate change and diminishing fossil fuel reserves, renewable energy technologies have emerged as a beacon of hope. However, harnessing the full potential of renewable energy sources like solar, wind, and hydroelectric power is a complex task that involves optimizing various parameters. This is where Artificial Intelligence (AI) optimization comes into play (Lateef et al., 2022).

HISTORY

The history of AI optimization for renewable vitality sources is closely interlaced with the advancement of both AI and renewable vitality technologies.

1. **Early Days:** The roots of AI can be followed back to the 1950s when computer researchers started investigating the concept of machine learning and manufactured insights. Amid these early days, AI was primarily used for hypothetical purposes and needed down to earth applications.

2. **Renewable Vitality Emergence:** As concerns over natural maintainability developed, the advancement of renewable vitality sources picked up energy during the latter half of the 20th century. Sun powered boards, wind turbines, and hydropower plants got to be more common, offering clean options to fossil fuels.

3. **Convergence:** It was not until the 21st century that AI and renewable vitality started to meet. With the multiplication of progressed sensors, information analytics, and computational control, the plausibility of utilizing AI to optimize renewable energy frameworks got to be a reality. Analysts started to investigate the potential of AI in upgrading the proficiency, unwavering quality, and financial reasonability of renewable vitality installations.

Introduction to AI Optimization for Renewable Energy

AI optimization for renewable vitality sources includes the application of machine learning, information analytics, and other AI strategies to improve the execution of renewable vitality frameworks. This optimization handle can happen at different stages, from the plan and arranging of renewable vitality establishments to the day-to-day operation and maintenance.

Key Viewpoints of AI Optimization for Renewable Energy

1. **Asset Forecasting:** AI calculations are employed to anticipate renewable vitality asset accessibility. For occasion, AI can analyze climate information to figure sun based irradiance, wind speed, and hydrological conditions. These forecasts help in deciding the foremost ideal areas for renewable vitality installations.
2. **Framework Plan and Planning:** AI can help within the plan and arranging of renewable vitality frameworks by optimizing the format, introduction, and measuring of sun oriented boards, wind turbines, or other components. This comes about in higher vitality era and taken a toll savings.
3. **Operational Efficiency:** Once renewable vitality frameworks are operational, AI makes a difference screen and optimize their execution. For case, AI-driven control frameworks can alter the point of sun based boards to maximize vitality capture, or control the pitch of wind turbine edges to optimize control output.
4. **Prescient Maintenance:** AI is utilized for prescient support of renewable vitality equipment. By analyzing real-time sensor information, AI can distinguish potential flaws or peculiarities and plan upkeep some time recently major breakdowns occur.
5. **Vitality Storage and Network Integration:** AI plays a vital part in optimizing the integration of renewable vitality into the framework and overseeing vitality capacity frameworks. AI calculations can estimate vitality request and supply, guaranteeing the effective utilize of put away vitality and diminishing lattice instability.
6. **Taken a toll Reduction:** AI optimization can essentially decrease operational costs and increment the return on venture for renewable vitality ventures. By maximizing vitality generation and minimizing downtime, renewable vitality gets to be more competitive with conventional fossil powers.

Thus, AI optimization for various renewable energy sources is a pivotal tool in the transition to a more sustainable and environmentally friendly energy landscape. Through its ability to forecast, plan, and enhance the performance of renewable energy systems, AI plays a critical role in realizing the full potential of renewable energy sources while reducing our reliance on fossil fuels and mitigating the impacts of climate change. As technology continues to advance, the synergy between AI and renewable energy promises a brighter and cleaner future for generations to come.

As we are talking about the renewable energy sources and its optimization, lets mainstream our discussion to the most abundant source i.e. solar energy.

SOLAR ENERGY: A SUSTAINABLE POWER SOURCE FOR A BRIGHTER FUTURE

Solar energy, harnessed from the sun's radiation, is a remarkable and inexhaustible source of renewable power. As the world grapples with the consequences of fossil fuel dependency and climate change, the appeal of solar energy has grown exponentially. It is harnessed through photovoltaic cells and solar thermal systems, providing a clean, sustainable, and abundant alternative to traditional energy sources. Solar power is not merely a futuristic concept; it is an established technology that has the potential to reshape the energy landscape, address environmental challenges, and enhance energy access for all (Danowitz, 2010).

Need for Sun powered Energy:
1. Natural Concerns: The foremost squeezing require for sun powered vitality lies in relieving the natural impacts of ordinary fossil fuel-based control era. Burning fossil fills discharges nursery gasses, contributing to climate alter, discuss contamination, and environment annihilation. Sun based control, on the other hand, produces no emanations amid vitality era, diminishing the carbon footprint.
2. Vitality Security: Sun based vitality can improve vitality security by differentiating the vitality blend. Diminishing dependence on imported fossil fills makes countries less helpless to supply disturbances and cost volatility.
3. All inclusive Vitality Go to: Millions of individuals around the world need get to to power. Sun powered energy's versatility and off-grid capabilities offer an opportunity to amplify control to farther and underserved locales, thereby improving living conditions and financial opportunities.

Benefits and Applications:
1. Clean and Renewable: Sun based vitality could be a clean and renewable asset, which implies it doesn't drain characteristic assets, create hurtful outflows, or contribute to climate alter. This quality makes it an perfect arrangement for economical control generation.
2. Decreased Vitality Costs: Sun oriented boards decrease power bills for homes, businesses, and businesses by producing free power from the sun. Over time, the return on venture can be substantial.
3. Work Creation:The sun oriented industry could be a major source of business. It includes a wide run of employments, from fabricating and establishment to upkeep and research.
4. Network Integration: Sun powered control can be coordinates into existing power lattices, lessening the strain on customary control sources and making strides lattice stability.
5. Flexibility: Sun based vitality can be saddled in different ways, counting housetop sun based boards for homes, large-scale sun based ranches, sun oriented water radiators, and versatile sun powered chargers.

6.   Space Investigation: In space investigation, sun powered boards are fundamental for controlling satellites, meanderers, and indeed space stations, as they can produce power within the nonattendance of conventional control sources (Energy, 2014).

Challenges:

1.   Intermittency: Sun powered vitality generation is subordinate on daylight, making it discontinuous. Vitality capacity arrangements, like batteries, are vital to moderate this challenge.
2.   Introductory Costs: The forthright taken a toll of sun powered board establishment can be significant. In spite of the fact that costs have diminished over the a long time, beginning venture remains a barrier for some.
3.   Arrival Utilization: Large-scale sun oriented ranches require significant arrival. Adjusting sun oriented extension with other arrive employments, such as farming or preservation, may be a challenge.
4.   Vitality Capacity: Proficient and reasonable vitality capacity arrangements are basic to create sun oriented vitality a 24/7 control source. Current battery innovations are moving forward, but more development is needed.
5.   Fabricating and Reusing: Sun based board generation produces natural impacts, and the industry must create more feasible fabricating forms and move forward board recycling.

Henceforth, solar energy represents a crucial shift in our energy landscape towards a cleaner, more sustainable future. Its benefits in reducing carbon emissions, enhancing energy security, and providing universal access to power cannot be overstated. While there are challenges to overcome, the increasing investments in research and technology will likely drive the continued growth of solar energy as a major player in the global energy mix. It is not only an investment in sustainable energy but also in a brighter, cleaner future for generations to come (Alshahrani et al., 2019).

ROLE OF AI OPTIMIZATION IN SOLAR ENERGY

The rapid growth of the global population and the increasing demand for energy have put substantial pressure on the planet's finite resources. In this context, the harnessing of renewable energy sources like solar power has gained significant importance. Solar energy is clean, abundant, and sustainable, offering an attractive solution to mitigate the environmental impacts of traditional fossil fuels. However, the intermittent and variable nature of solar energy production poses challenges that necessitate innovative solutions. Artificial Intelligence (AI) has emerged as a transformative tool for optimizing the utilization of solar energy.

Sun based vitality, tackled through photovoltaic (PV) boards or sun based warm frameworks, depends on the accessibility of daylight. This implies that its generation is unexpected on different components, such as climate conditions, time of day, and topographical area. To maximize the effectiveness and adequacy of sun oriented vitality frameworks, AI calculations and machine learning models are being utilized to address these challenges (Sudhir et al., 2020).

AI optimization in sun oriented vitality includes the application of progressed methods to upgrade the era, dispersion, and utilization of sun oriented control. This concept rotates around the utilization of AI to create sun powered vitality frameworks more astute, more responsive, and superior adjusted to the energetic nature of daylight. A few of the key perspectives of AI optimization in sun oriented vitality include:

1. Prescient Analytics: AI frameworks cananalyze authentic climate information and anticipate cloud cover, sun powered radiation, and other components that impact sun powered vitality generation. By precisely estimating these conditions, sun based offices can alter their operations in real-time to optimize vitality capture and storage.

2. Vitality Administration: AI calculations can productively oversee the vitality delivered by sun oriented boards and choose when to store, disseminate, or utilize it. This empowers more viable utilize of put away vitality amid periods of moo daylight, lessening reliance on the framework and fossil fuels.

3. Upkeep and Diagnostics: AI-driven observing and diagnostics can distinguish hardware glitches or debasement in sun powered boards and other components. Opportune mediation can anticipate framework disappointments and guarantee the long-term supportability of sun based installations.

4. Network Integration: AI can offer assistance adjusting to the vitality supply and request by planning the infusion of sun powered control into the network. This guarantees a steady and solid vitality supply for customers whereas minimizing squander and optimizing income for sun oriented vitality providers.

5. Shrewd Vitality Capacity: AI can optimize the charging and releasing of vitality capacity frameworks, such as batteries, to guarantee that overflow vitality is put away productively and utilized when required most.

6. Vitality Exchanging and Advertise Integration: AI can empower sun based vitality makers to take an interest in vitality exchanging markets, offering abundance vitality back to the framework amid top request times, in this way creating extra revenue.

7. Productive Plan and Siting: AI can help within the plan and arrangement of sun oriented establishments, guaranteeing that they are situated for greatest daylight introduction and negligible shading.

ADDRESSING THE NEEDS AND CHALLENGES IN OPTIMIZING SUN BASED ENERGY

Solar vitality may be a promising renewable asset that holds the potential to revolutionize the world's vitality landscape. The sun gives an plenitude of clean vitality, but saddling and optimizing this vitality effectively may be a complex errand. Counterfeit Insights (AI) has developed as a vital device in tending to desires and challenges related with optimizing sun powered vitality. This article digs into the pivotal part of AI within the sun oriented vitality division and the challenges it makes a difference overcome (Alshahrani et al., 2019).

The need for Sun oriented Vitality Optimization is because of the following reasons:

1. Supportability and Climate Alter: As the world hooks with climate change and the pressing ought to diminish carbon emanations, sun based vitality presents an eco-friendly arrangement. Optimizing sun based control generation can essentially decrease our dependence on fossil fuels.

2. Vitality Security: Sun powered vitality could be a decentralized source of control thatcan upgrade vitality security by decreasing reliance on centralized vitality lattices. This can be particularly vital in locales inclined to normal catastrophes or geopolitical instability.

3. Financial Practicality: Sun powered vitality frameworks have ended up more cost-effective, but their effective operation is pivotal for long-term budgetary practicality. AI can offer assistance maximize the return on speculation by making strides vitality yield and lessening support costs.

Challenges in Sun Powered Energy Optimization

1. Intermittency and Inconstancy: One of the foremost critical challenges of sun powered vitality is its intermittent and variable nature. Sun based control era depends on climate conditions and sunshine hours, making reliable vitality generation difficult (Alshahrani et al., 2019).

2. Vitality Network Integration: Integrating sun based control into existing vitality frameworks can be complex, because it requires adjusting supply and request. AI can foresee vitality era and utilization designs to optimize network integration.

3. Productivity: Sun based boards may not continuously work at top proficiency due to variables like clean, earth, and shading. AI can screen and oversee person boards to guarantee they are working optimally.

4. Information Complexity: Sun oriented vitality frameworks create enormous amounts of data from different sensors and sources. Analyzing and translating this information for decision-making may be a imposing challenge that AI can address.

How AI Overcomes These Challenges (Ling et al., 2022)

1. Prescient Analytics: AI calculations can analyze verifiable and real-time information to foresee sun powered vitality era designs. This empowers network administrators to arrange for variances and adjust supply and request efficiently.

2. Shrewd Support: AI-powered rambles and robots can assess sun powered boards and distinguish support needs, diminishing downtime and expanding the life span of the system.

3. Vitality Capacity Optimization: AI can oversee vitality capacity frameworks to store abundance vitality when accessible and discharge it when required, tending to the intermittency issue.

4. Vitality Estimating: AI can give exact short-term and long-term vitality figures, making a difference utilities and shoppers make educated choices almost vitality usage.

5. Network Administration: AI- based framework administration frameworks can adjust vitality stream, coordinated renewables consistently, and anticipate over-burdens, improving grid stability.

6. Cost Decrease: By making strides vitality proficiency and decreasing support costs, AI contributes to the financial practicality of sun oriented vitality solutions.

The have to be move to economical vitality sources is vital, and solar energy plays a vital part in this move. Be that as it may, the challenges of intermittency, network integration, and efficiency have prevented its far reaching appropriation. AI emerges as a effective partner in overcoming these challenges, making sun based vitality not as it were a economical but moreover a fiscally appealing choice for long haul. With ongoing advancements in AI innovation, able to see forward to a world where sun based vitality gets to be a standard and dependable source of power, essentially diminishing our carbon impression and advancing a more feasible future (Zhang et al., 2022).

The need to transition to sustainable energy sources is paramount, and solar energy plays a crucial role in this transition. However, the challenges of intermittency, grid integration, and efficiency have hindered its widespread adoption. AI emerges as a powerful ally in overcoming these challenges, making solar energy not only a sustainable but also a financially attractive choice for the future. With ongoing advancements in AI technology, we can look forward to a world where solar energy becomes a mainstream and reliable source of power, significantly reducing our carbon footprint and promoting a more sustainable future.

Objectives

In this study about India's search for sustainable energy, we have clear goals to use artificial intelligence (AI) to improve solar energy generation and deal with the challenges of the country's diverse energy situation (Dellosa & Palconit, 2021).

1. Smart Solar Optimization with AI: We aim to create a smart system powered by AI that can adjust solar energy generation based on different landscapes and weather. By analyzing real-time data, weather patterns, and sunlight levels, this system will change how solar panels are set up. It will capture more energy when the sun is strong and save energy when clouds block it.
2. Better Energy Efficiency: We'll look into how AI can make solar energy more efficient overall. By adapting solar panels to changing conditions, we expect to show that we can produce more energy. This will help reduce the need for non-renewable energy sources and cut down on the gases that harm the environment.
3. Stable Energy Supply: We're exploring how AI can make the energy grid more reliable and stable. The system will adjust solar panels in real-time to make sure we always have a steady energy supply. This will help even out the ups and downs of solar energy and make the grid stronger.
4. Economic Benefits: We're going to study how using AI for solar energy can save money. We'll look at how much money we can save by wasting less energy and using fewer fossil fuels. We want to show how AI can bring economic benefits to India's energy plans.
5. Helping the Environment: We'll look at how AI can make solar energy good for the environment. By using more renewable energy, we'll show how AI can help reduce harmful carbon emissions. This aligns with India's goals for a greener future.
6. Making AI Practical Everywhere: We'll find out if the AI solution can work in different places and with different solar setups. This way, we can understand how to use AI and solar energy on a larger scale, making this approach more common.

Through these goals, we want to show how AI can change how India gets energy. By using AI to improve solar energy, we're aiming for a future where India's energy is more efficient, sustainable, and respectful of the environment.

HOW EXACTLY AI AND ML ENHANCE THE OPTIMIZATION OF SOLAR ENERGY

we will now delve into the fascinating world of artificial intelligence (AI) and machine learning (ML), exploring how these cutting-edge technologies can be employed to optimize the utilization of solar energy. We'll discuss the fundamental principles, methodologies, and real-world applications of AI and ML in the solar energy sector (Burman et al., 2023).

Methodology for Optimizing Solar Energy

Data Collection and Preprocessing

The heart of any AI or ML application in solar energy optimization lies in the data. High-quality data is essential for accurate predictions and decision-making. This data encompasses variables such as solar radiation, weather conditions, energy consumption patterns, and system performance. Data preprocessing involves cleaning, transforming, and normalizing data to make it suitable for model training.

Supervised Learning for Energy Prediction

Supervised learning is a widely used technique for predicting energy generation from solar panels. In this method, historical data is used to train a model to understand the relationship between input variables (e.g., solar radiation, temperature) and energy output. Algorithms like Linear Regression, Decision Trees, or Neural Networks can be applied to predict energy generation, allowing for the efficient management of solar power resources.

Unsupervised Learning for Anomaly Detection

Unsupervised learning techniques, such as clustering or dimensionality reduction, can identify anomalies or irregularities in solar energy systems. These anomalies may be indicative of faults in the system, such as equipment malfunctions or suboptimal performance. Detecting such issues early can lead to improved maintenance and system reliability.

Reinforcement Learning for System Control

Reinforcement learning is gaining prominence in solar energy optimization, particularly in control systems. Agents are trained to make decisions that maximize long-term rewards in dynamic environments. These agents can be used to optimize the positioning of solar panels, track the sun's movement, and adjust system settings in real-time to maximize energy output.

Integration of IoT and Sensors

The Internet of Things (IoT) and sensor technologies play a pivotal role in data acquisition and control within solar energy systems. Sensors can collect real-time data on environmental conditions and system performance, which is then used for training AI and ML models. IoT devices enable remote monitoring and control, making solar energy systems more efficient and responsive.

Continuous Model Improvement

The AI and ML models employed in solar energy optimization are not static. Continuous learning and model improvement are critical for adapting to changing environmental conditions and system degradation over time. Regular updates to the models based on newly collected data ensure that the system performs optimally.

MECHANISM FOR OPTIMIZING SOLAR ENERGY GENERATION USING ARTIFICIAL INTELLIGENCE

Certainly, here is a simplified breakdown of the steps involved in the case study (Zhang et al., 2022):

1. Collect Data:
   ◦ Gather historical data on solar energy generation from various locations in India.
   ◦ Collect weather data such as solar irradiance, temperature, cloud cover, and wind speed.
2. Prepare Data:
   ◦ Clean and validate data by fixing errors and filling in missing values.
   ◦ Make sure data is consistent and normalized for accurate analysis.
3. Create AI Model:
   ◦ Choose an appropriate AI algorithm (like regression or neural networks) for predicting solar energy generation.
   ◦ Train the AI model using historical data to predict energy output based on weather conditions.
4. Develop Optimization Algorithm:
   ◦ Design an algorithm that uses AI predictions and real-time weather data to adjust solar panel angles.
   ◦ Ensure the algorithm considers energy demand, grid stability, and environmental factors.
5. Build the System:
   ◦ Integrate the trained AI model and the optimization algorithm into a software system.
   ◦ Set up mechanisms to gather real-time weather data from sensors.
6. Test Scenarios:
   ◦ Simulate different weather conditions using historical data to test the AI-driven system's performance.
   ◦ Compare energy generation outcomes with and without AI optimization.
7. Evaluate and Analyze:
   ◦ Assess the AI model's accuracy using metrics like MAE, RMSE, and R^2.
   ◦ Calculate the percentage increase in energy capture achieved through AI-driven optimization.
8. Assess Impact:
   ◦ Estimate cost savings from reduced energy wastage and compare with implementation costs.
   ◦ Calculate potential reduction in greenhouse gas emissions due to increased solar energy usage.
9. Test Scalability:
   ◦ Apply the system to different locations in India to see if it works well everywhere.
   ◦ Analyze whether the system can be scaled up for broader use.

10. Visualize Results:
    ○ Create visual graphs, charts, and maps showing energy generation patterns and AI predictions.
    ○ Use tools like Python libraries to create informative visuals.
11. Interpret and Conclude:
    ○ Analyze results regarding energy capture, efficiency improvement, economic benefits, and environmental impact.
    ○ Summarize findings and emphasize the potential of AI for optimizing solar energy in India.

This approach outlines the step-by-step process of utilizing AI to optimize solar energy generation in India, considering factors like weather, demand, and environmental impact.

Applications of Artificial Intelligence

Here are some practical ways AI can help optimize solar energy generation, using the steps we discussed earlier:

1. **Making Smart Predictions:** AI can look at past solar energy data and current weather conditions to predict how much energy will be produced in the future. This is like using past patterns to guess what will happen next.

2. **Adjusting Solar Panels in Real Time:** AI can keep an eye on the weather right now and change how solar panels are angled to catch the most sunlight. It learns from the weather and makes sure solar panels work well even when the weather changes.

3. **Guessing Energy Needs:** AI can predict how much energy people will need based on past data and other things happening at the moment. By combining this with solar predictions, it can decide when to use solar energy and when to save it for later.

4. **Keeping the Grid Stable:** AI can help manage the energy grid by changing how much solar energy is used based on what's happening on the grid right now. If there's a problem, AI can make sure the power stays steady.

5. **Being Smart with Batteries:** AI can control batteries so they're charged up when there's extra solar energy and then use that energy when it's needed. This way, we use solar power even when the sun isn't shining.

6. **Understanding Weather:** AI can study old weather data to find out how different kinds of weather affect solar energy. This helps make better guesses about energy production.

7. **Mixing Different Energies:** AI can figure out how to use solar energy together with other renewable sources, like wind or water power. It can decide when to use which energy source to get the most power.

8. **Figuring Out Costs and Benefits:** AI can use its smarts to see if using AI for solar energy is a good idea money-wise. It looks at how much it costs to use AI versus how much money we save by making more energy.

9. **Seeing the Green Impact:** AI can tell us how much using more solar energy helps the environment. It can calculate things like how much less pollution there is because of using clean energy.

10. **Scaling Up and Adapting:** AI models that work well in one place can be changed a bit to work well in other places too. This way, we can use the same smart ideas in many different areas.

Renewable energy includes various sources like solar, wind, and water power. AI helps us make the best use of these sources. It adjusts and learns from data in real time, handles complex tasks, and makes decisions that fit the changing conditions. It's like having a smart helper that ensures we use energy wisely and efficiently (Srivastava, 2020).

Real-World Implications

Several real-world applications of AI and ML in solar energy optimization have been successful in harnessing the power of these technologies:

1. **Solar Forecasting:** AI-based weather forecasting models can predict solar radiation and cloud cover, helping grid operators manage the intermittent nature of solar power.
2. **Energy Grid Management:** AI can optimize the distribution of solar power within the energy grid, reducing energy waste and improving grid stability.
3. **Energy Consumption Prediction:** ML models can forecast energy demand, allowing for efficient management of energy storage systems.
4. **Fault Detection and Maintenance:** ML algorithms can detect anomalies in solar panels or other components, enabling proactive maintenance to avoid costly breakdowns.
5. **Smart Solar Panels:** Reinforcement learning is used to optimize the positioning of solar panels for maximum energy capture throughout the day.

Leveraging AI and ML technologies allows for more efficient, reliable, and sustainable solar energy systems. As these technologies continue to evolve, their integration into the solar energy sector will undoubtedly lead to improved performance, reduced energy costs, and a brighter, greener future (Singh et al., 2020).

GENERALIZATION

Generalization of AI in this context means that the AI system can work well with new and unseen data, even if it wasn't specifically trained for that data. When it comes to optimizing renewable energy, this idea of generalization is really important. The energy system faces many changes like weather patterns, shifts in energy demand, and variations in system components (Singh et al., 2020).

To make sure AI can generalize effectively, we need to train it using a wide and diverse dataset. This dataset should cover many different scenarios. Instead of just remembering specific examples it was trained on, the AI needs to understand the patterns and relationships within the data. This way, when it faces new data or situations it hasn't seen before—like optimizing energy production in different weather conditions—it can still make accurate decisions and predictions.

Data Visualization

Now, here are some data on the optimization of the renewable energy AI system for the month of NOVEMBER 2022, DECEMBER 2022, JANUARY 2023, and FEBRUARY 2023.

Figure 3. 1- November 2022

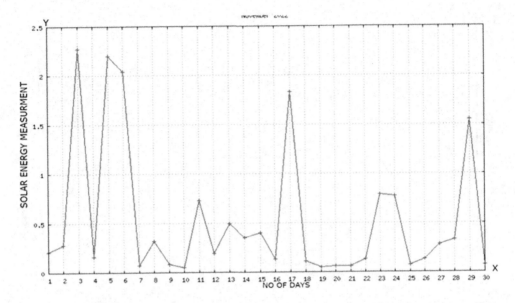

Figure 4. 2- December 2022

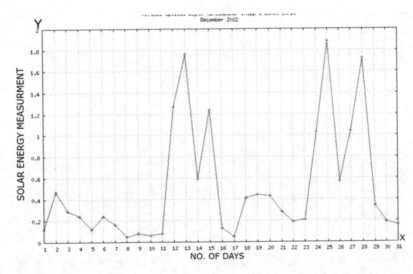

In the above graph, it is plotted between the number of days vs the solar energy measurement per day in a month .

In the above data the:-

- **X axis** shows the number of days, of a month, whereas
- **Y axis** shows the solar energy measured per day in watt per square meter (w/m^2)

And the lines shows the daily average of the solar energy measurement

Figure 5. 3- January 2023

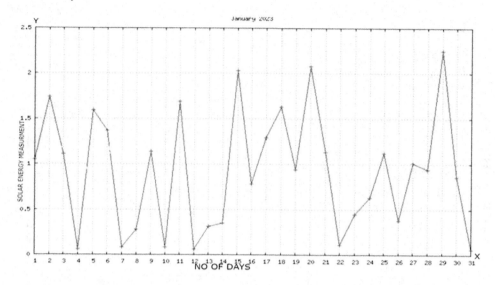

Figure 6. 4- February 2023

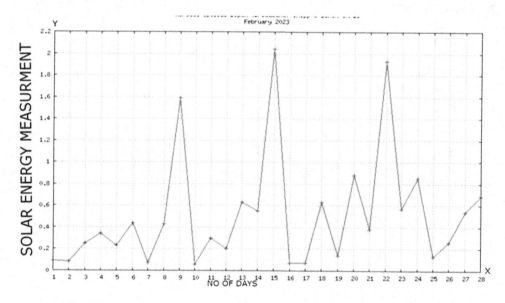

From the above data, we can see that in November 2022 the usage of renewable solar energy AI systems was less but by the end of November 2022 the usage increases, and from the above-given data we can say that as my time increases the usage of renewable energy AI system was also increasing.

Table 1. Format of CONFRRM solar data files

Parameter Name	Format		Sites Listing This Parameter**
	FORTRAN	C	
Year	I	%d	All
Month	I	%d	All
Day	I	%d	All
Hour	I	%d	All
Minute	I	%d	All
Global Horizontal Irradiance (GHI1), PSP	F	%f	All
GHI1 Flag	I	%d	
Direct Normal Irradiance (DNI)	F	%f	All
DHI Flag	I	%d	
Global Horizontal Irradiance (GHI2), LI-COR	F	%f	AU, CL, CN, ED, EP, FS, ST
GHI2 Flag	I	%d	
Air Temperature	F	%f	AU, CL, CN, ED, EP, FS, ST
Air Temperature Flag	I	%d	
Relative Humidity	F	%f	AU, CL, CN, EC, ED, EP, ST
Relative Humidity Flag	I	%d	
Wind Speed	F	%f	EC, ST
Wind Speed Flag	I	%d	
Wind Direction	F	%f	EC, ST
Wind Direction Flag	I	%d	
Peak Wind Speed	F	%f	EC
Peak Wind Speed Flag	I	%d	
Pressure	F	%f	EC, FS
Pressure Flag	I	%d	
Rainfall	F	%f	FS
Rainfall Flag	I	%d	
Data Logger Temperature	F	%f	EC

CHALLENGES AND CONSIDERATIONS

The integration of artificial intelligence (AI) and machine learning (ML) into the field of solar energy optimization has significantly improved the efficiency and effectiveness of solar power generation. These technologies enable precise monitoring, predictive maintenance, and optimal energy harvesting, ultimately contributing to a sustainable and eco-friendly energy source. However, there are several challenges to overcome, future directions to explore, and specific recommendations for research and development to enhance the capabilities of AI and ML in the realm of solar energy optimization (Agbulut et al., 2022).

1. Variety of Data

The renewable energy AI system collects a lot of data from different sources. To make the AI system scalable, it's important to handle the diversity of data and integrate various types of information, such as solar power, wind speed, and energy demand.

The success of AI and ML models in solar energy optimization heavily relies on high-quality, large-scale data. Inaccurate or insufficient data can lead to suboptimal results.

Solution: Efforts must be made to improve data collection methods, including the use of IoT devices and remote sensing technologies to gather real-time, comprehensive data on weather conditions, solar irradiance, and energy production.

2. Model Complexity

As renewable energy systems grow, they become more complex due to the connections between different energy sources and storage options. A scalable AI algorithm needs to be trained to handle this complexity and make informed decisions.Building accurate AI and ML models for solar energy optimization requires complex algorithms, making them computationally expensive.

Solution: Research should focus on developing more efficient algorithms and hardware solutions to reduce the computational requirements, making these models more accessible and cost-effective.

3. Real-Time Adaptation

Renewable energy systems need to be able to quickly make decisions in real-time to optimize energy production and efficiency. A scalable AI system should be flexible enough to rapidly adapt to changing conditions and make fast decisions.

4. Transfer Learning

Using transfer learning can enhance the ability to generalize. This means the knowledge gained from one renewable energy source can be adjusted and applied to others. This approach helps AI models quickly adapt to new settings.

5. Robustness

Generalization should ensure that AI models perform well in various situations, even when facing unexpected conditions. This includes extreme scenarios and unforeseen events.

6. Integration with Energy Grids

Integrating solar energy into existing energy grids is a complex process, requiring coordination with traditional energy sources.

Solution: Future research should investigate AI-driven solutions to optimize energy grid management, allowing for smoother integration of solar energy, load balancing, and storage strategies.

7. Weather Forecasting

Accurate weather forecasting is crucial for optimizing solar energy production, and existing models have limitations.

Solution: Research can explore advanced AI techniques for more precise weather forecasting, taking into account regional climate patterns, microclimates, and satellite data.

FUTURE DIRECTIONS (Zulueta et al., 2020)

1. Energy Storage Optimization

- Future Direction: AI and ML can play a pivotal role in optimizing energy storage systems for solar energy, ensuring efficient use of surplus energy during sunny days and providing power during night-time or cloudy periods.

2. Predictive Maintenance

- Future Direction: AI can be used for predictive maintenance of solar panels and associated equipment. By analyzing data patterns, the technology can predict and prevent equipment failures, reducing maintenance costs.

3. Advanced Control Systems

- Future Direction: Implementing AI-based control systems can enhance the precision of solar tracking, leading to increased energy yield by positioning solar panels optimally throughout the day.

4. Climate Adaptation

- Future Direction: AI can help design solar energy systems that are more resilient to climate change, considering factors such as extreme weather events, temperature fluctuations, and dust accumulation.

SPECIFIC AREAS TO WORK UPON

1. Collaborative Research

Recommendation: Foster collaboration between the renewable energy and AI research communities to share expertise, data, and resources. Joint efforts can drive innovation and address common challenges effectively.

2. Funding Initiatives

Recommendation: Governments and private entities should invest in research funding to support the development of AI and ML solutions for solar energy optimization. This will accelerate progress and incentivize innovation.

3. Education and Training

Recommendation: Promote education and training programs to develop a skilled workforce capable of developing and deploying AI and ML solutions in the solar energy sector. This will ensure the industry remains innovative and sustainable.

4. Policy Frameworks

Recommendation: Establish policies and regulations that encourage the integration of AI and ML in solar energy projects. Encouraging sustainable practices and technological innovation can drive the adoption of these technologies.

RECOMMENDATIONS

1. Interdisciplinary Collaborations

We should encourage collaboration between AI researchers, renewable energy experts, data scientists, and policymakers. By working together as a team, they can gain a comprehensive understanding of the problem's complexity and provides swift and effective solutions (Manshahia et al., 2023).

2. Model Development and Adaptation

We need to develop AI models that can dynamically adjust to changing conditions, including new energy sources and emerging techniques. This involves the incorporation of advanced machine learning techniques such as reinforcement learning and deep learning to enhance the AI models' capacity for learning and generalization from provided data.

3. Real-Time Decision Making

We need to concentrate on the development of AI algorithms that create and execute real-time decisions for energy production, consumption, and distribution. This necessitates high-speed data response capabilities to effectively respond to rapid changes in the environment and grid conditions.

4. Hybrid Energy Solutions

We need to explore the hybrid energy system as more as possible that combines multiple renewable resources and energy storage technologies. Utilizing AI can optimize the coordination among these sources and assist us in enhancing energy reliability and stability.

5. Long Term Planning and Research

We need to conduct extensive and long-term research to access and gather more information regarding the effectiveness and sustainability of AI-based solutions in the renewable energy sector. This research should involve evaluating their impact on energy efficiency, environmental benefits, and economic viability.

6. Public Awareness and Acceptance

We need to actively promote public awareness as much as possible and inform them about the benefits of AI-driven optimization for renewable energy. Additionally, we should engage with individuals regarding their personal data privacy and security, while also explaining the potential socio-economic impacts to enhance public awareness.

Key Takeaway

The effectiveness of AI, particularly in complex and dynamic environments like wind farms, is evident. AI in this field can make precise predictions and optimize operations to enhance efficiency. The outcomes of the case study emphasize AI's role in improving renewable energy production and aiding the shift towards cleaner energy sources.

Additionally, the case study underscores the significance of collaborations between AI researchers and domain-specific experts. By working together, they can create more effective solutions that effectively tackle real-world challenges and issues. This partnership ensures that AI technologies are tailored to address specific problems and yield practical benefits.

CONCLUSION

In conclusion, the utilization of AI for optimizing renewable energy systems emerges as a promising solution to the challenges linked with transitioning to sustainable energy sources. Integrating AI into renewable energy systems offers the potential for enhanced efficiency, adaptability, and economic viability compared to traditional approaches.

By leveraging the capabilities of AI algorithms, data analysis, and machine learning, renewable energy sources can be dynamically optimized in real-time. This approach maximizes energy generation while minimizing waste, effectively balancing supply and demand. AI-driven systems improve the accuracy of predicting renewable energy output, utilizing weather forecasts and historical data for more efficient planning and resource allocation.

Moreover, AI-based optimization improves grid management by facilitating the seamless integration of various renewable resources into the power grid. This integration not only reduces emissions and greenhouse gases but also bolsters grid stability and resilience, contributing to a more reliable energy infrastructure.

Yet, implementing successful AI optimization for renewable energy faces challenges like data quality and availability, algorithm complexity, and real-world adaptability. Hence, having scalable and robust AI solutions becomes critical in managing the inherent variability and uncertainty within renewable energy systems.

In essence, the synergy between AI and renewable energy holds the potential for transformative innovation and progress. As AI technology advances and algorithms evolve, the prospects of achieving higher efficiency, cost-effectiveness, and environmental sustainability in renewable energy become increasingly feasible. By strategically addressing issues of scalability, generalization, and real-world practicality, AI can play a pivotal role in revolutionizing the renewable energy sector. This paves the way towards a greener and healthier future for our planet.

REFERENCES

Alankrita, S. (2020). *Application of AI in Renewable Energy*. IEEE. https://ieeexplore.ieee.org/document/9200065

Alshahrani, A., Omer, S., Su, Y., Mohamed, E., & Alotaibi, S. (2021). *The technical challenges facing the integration of small-scale and large-scale PV systems into the grid*. Science Direct. https://www.sciencedirect.com/science/article/abs/pii/S0038092X21004825

Danowitz, A. (2010). *Solar Thermal vs. Photovoltaic*. Stanford Press. http://large.stanford.edu/courses/2010/ph240/danowitz2/ https://www.nrel.gov/grid/solar-resource/renewable-resource-data.html?utm_medium=print&utm_source=grid&utm_campaign=rredc

Dellosa, J. (2021). *AI in Renewable Energy Systems*. IEEE. https://ieeexplore.ieee.org/document/9584587

Dib, R., Zervos, A., Eckhart, M., David, M.E.A., Kirsty, H., & Peter, H. (2021). Governments, R.; Bariloche, F. Renewables 2021 Global Status Report. *REN21 Renewables Now*.

Elsevier. (n.d.). *Forthcoming Special Issues*. Elesvier.https://www.journals.elsevier.com/environmental-challenges/forthcoming-special-issues/artificial-intelligence-applications-for-green-energy-systems

Haupt, S. (2020). *Applications of Artificial Intelligence in Renewable Energy*. Energies. https://www.mdpi.com/journal/energies/special_issues/Artificial_Intelligence_Renewable_Energy

Irena International Renewable Energy Agency. (n.d.). *Future of Solar Photovoltaic Deployment, Investment, Technology, Grid Integration and Socio-Economic Aspects*. MDPI. https://www.mdpi.com/2076-3417/12/19/10056 https://solarbuildermag.com/wp-content/uploads/2023/02/robot-AI-solar-panels.jpg

Kanase-Patil, A. (2020). *A review of AI-based optimization techniques for the sizing of integrated renewable energy systems*. Taylor & Francis. https://www.tandfonline.com/doi/abs/10.1080/21622515.2020.1836035

Manshahia, M. (2023). *Advances in Artificial Intelligence for Renewable Energy Systems and Energy Autonomy.* Springer. https://link.springer.com/book/10.1007/978-3-031-26496-2

Mortier, T. (2020). *EY Global Digital & Innovation lead for Energy.* EY. https://www.ey.com/en_in/power-utilities/why-artificial-intelligence-is-a-game-changer-for-renewable-energy

Research Gate. (n.d.). *Artificial Intelligence techniques on renewable evergy systems.* Research Gate. https://www.researchgate.net/publication/361871065_Artificial_Intelligence_Techniques_Applied_on_Renewable_Energy_Systems_A_Review

Zhang, L. (2022). Artificial Intelligence in renewable energy. *Energy Reports, 8,* ●●●. https://www.sciencedirect.com/science/article/pii/S2352484722022818

Zulueta, E. (2020). *Artificial Intelligence for renewable energy systems.* MDPI. https://www.mdpi.com/journal/sustainability/special_issues/artificial_intelligence_energy

Chapter 5
Green Technologies, Reducing Carbon Footprints, and Maximizing Energy Efficiency With Emerging Innovations:
Green Computing

R. Pitchai

(iD) https://orcid.org/0000-0002-3759-6915

Department of Computer Science and Engineering, B.V. Raju Institute of Technology, Narsapur, India

Suresh Tiwari

Department of Mechanical Engineering, Jharkhand University of Technology, Ranchi, India

C. Viji

(iD) https://orcid.org/0000-0002-2759-8896

Department of Computer Science and Engineering, Alliance College of Engineering and Design, Alliance University, Bangalore, India

A. Kistan

(iD) https://orcid.org/0000-0003-1334-4331

Department of Chemistry, Panimalar Engineering College, Chennai, India

R Puviarasi

(iD) https://orcid.org/0000-0003-2353-9108

Department of Electronics and Communication Engineering, Saveetha School of Engineering, Saveetha Institute of Medical and Technical Sciences (SIMATS), Thandalam, India

S. Gokul

YSR Technical Education, India

ABSTRACT

This chapter explores the complex issue of sustainable computing, focusing on its environmental implications. It outlines the principles of green computing, the carbon footprint associated with technology, and the role of data centers in minimizing it. The chapter also highlights the importance of energy efficiency in computing, highlighting the growing energy consumption in IT and outlines strategies for achieving it. It also discusses the role of emerging technologies like renewable energy, IoT, smart grids, quantum computing, and sustainable algorithms in promoting sustainability. The chapter also highlights the

DOI: 10.4018/979-8-3693-0338-2.ch005

role of software solutions in sustainable computing, including green software development practices, virtualization, cloud computing, and power management software. The chapter discusses the practical application of sustainable computing in organizations, highlighting challenges, ethical considerations, and a roadmap for the future of sustainable computing, enriched with case studies.

INTRODUCTION

The rise of information technology, including digital devices, cloud computing, and the Internet, has significantly impacted our lives and business practices. However, these advancements have also created a significant environmental footprint due to the energy-intensive nature of computation. To address this, the concept of "green computing" has emerged as a crucial effort to mitigate the environmental impact of the digital age. Green computing is a sustainable approach to designing, manufacturing, using, and disposing of computing devices and systems with minimal environmental impact, emphasizing the need to align technological progress with sustainability goals, especially as computing power demand increases, addressing the environmental implications of digital lifestyles(Yu et al., 2023).

This chapter explores green computing, its principles, strategies for reducing carbon footprint, and emerging technologies' role in sustainability and energy efficiency. It provides an in-depth examination of the latest advancements and best practices in the field, aiming to foster sustainability and enhance energy efficiency. This chapter covers various topics related to green computing, carbon emissions quantification, energy consumption reduction, and emerging technologies like renewable energy, IoT, and quantum computing(Mei et al., 2023). It emphasizes the importance of software solutions in achieving greener technology. The chapter also addresses the environmental challenges faced by the information technology industry, particularly data centers, which store, process, and transmit large volumes of data, contributing significantly to carbon emissions. Addressing these challenges is crucial for reducing the environmental impact of computing and promoting sustainability(Ofori et al., 2023).

This chapter highlights the significance of promoting sustainability in the digital age through green computing, carbon footprint reduction, emerging technologies, and energy efficiency. It offers a comprehensive overview of strategies for a greener future, aiming to minimize ecological footprints.

Background and Significance

The modern world is undeniably shaped by the omnipresence of information technology, with the ubiquity of digital devices, cloud computing, and the Internet. While these technological advancements have revolutionized our daily lives and global business practices, they have also led to a concerning environmental footprint. The proliferation of electronic devices, data centers, and the energy-intensive nature of computation have culminated in a significant carbon footprint. Recognizing the ecological urgency, the concept of "green computing" has emerged as a crucial endeavor, aiming to mitigate the environmental impact of the digital age(Lin et al., 2023).

Green computing, often referred to as sustainable or eco-friendly computing, represents a holistic approach to design, manufacture, use, and disposal of computing devices and systems with minimal environmental impact. It underscores the vital need to align technological progress with sustainability goals. As the demand for computing power surges, understanding and addressing the environmental implications of our digital lifestyles becomes imperative(Liang et al., 2022).

This chapter delves into the multifaceted realm of green computing, with a particular focus on its fundamental principles and the strategies employed to reduce the carbon footprint associated with information technology. We also explore how emerging technologies can play a pivotal role in fostering sustainability and enhancing energy efficiency. Our aim is to provide an in-depth examination of the latest advancements and best practices in the field(Issa et al., 2022).

The scope of this chapter encompasses a broad spectrum of topics, including the foundational concepts of green computing, the quantification of carbon emissions, and methods to minimize energy consumption. Furthermore, we delve into how emerging technologies, such as the integration of renewable energy sources, the Internet of Things (IoT), and quantum computing, can contribute to sustainability. We also spotlight the crucial role of software solutions in achieving greener technology(Chong et al., 2022).

To appreciate the urgency of green computing, it is essential to acknowledge the environmental challenges brought forth by the information technology industry. Data centers, which store, process, and transmit massive volumes of data, are among the primary culprits in this regard. Their energy-intensive operations, coupled with the rapid growth of data, make them significant contributors to carbon emissions. Consequently, addressing these challenges is paramount to the broader objective of reducing the environmental impact of computing(Abuzreda et al., 2023).

As we navigate the nexus of green computing, carbon footprint reduction, emerging technologies, and energy efficiency, it is incumbent upon us to recognize our role in fostering sustainability. This chapter serves as a call to action, offering a comprehensive overview of strategies and technologies that can pave the way toward a greener, more sustainable digital future(Luo et al., 2023). By embracing these concepts and practices, we can collectively work towards minimizing the ecological footprint of our digital endeavors while harnessing the power of technology for positive change.

Objectives of the Chapter

This chapter aims to provide a comprehensive understanding of green computing, carbon footprint reduction, emerging technologies, and energy efficiency in information technology. It aims to equip readers with the knowledge and insights needed to navigate the complex intersection of technology and sustainability.

- A comprehensive understanding of green computing, outlining its core principles and goals, and its significance in the modern technology landscape.
- To understand and quantify the carbon footprint of information technology, aiming to simplify environmental impact measurement and facilitate informed discussions.
- To provide practical knowledge on reducing the carbon footprint in IT operations, enabling readers to minimize environmental impact in real-world scenarios.
- This section explores the increasing energy consumption in IT and proposes strategies for enhancing energy efficiency, aiming to educate readers on and facilitate the implementation of energy-saving practices in technology.
- This study explores the potential of emerging technologies like renewable energy integration, IoT, and quantum computing to drive sustainability by reducing environmental impact.

- This study explores the role of software in promoting green computing, focusing on green software development practices, virtualization, cloud computing, and power management software, contributing to sustainability.

- To present real-world case studies and exemplary organizations that have successfully reduced their carbon footprints and adopted sustainable computing practices. These case studies will serve as practical examples for readers to draw inspiration and lessons from.

- To identify the challenges and barriers that hinder the widespread adoption of green computing and sustainability in IT. Additionally, to discuss ethical considerations in technology and present a roadmap for the future of sustainable computing.

- To conclude the chapter with a call to action, emphasizing the importance of collective efforts to promote green computing and reduce the carbon footprint in the IT sector. This objective aims to inspire readers to take an active role in sustainability within their technological endeavors.

This chapter aims to provide readers with a comprehensive understanding of the intricate relationship between technology and sustainability, thereby promoting a more eco-conscious and responsible use of information technology.

GREEN COMPUTING: CONCEPTS AND PRINCIPLES

Defining Green Computing

Green computing is a sustainable approach to designing, manufacturing, using, and disposing of computing devices and systems in an environmentally responsible and energy-efficient manner. It addresses environmental challenges like energy consumption, electronic waste, and carbon emissions by incorporating eco-conscious practices throughout the lifecycle of IT products and services(Pandey et al., 2023). This concept includes various strategies and technologies to reduce the environmental impact of computing.

Environmental Challenges in Computing

The rapid growth of information technology has led to numerous significant environmental challenges(Mustapha et al., 2021).

- **Energy Consumption:** The IT sector is a significant consumer of electricity, with data centers and server farms demanding substantial power to operate. This high energy consumption contributes to increased carbon emissions and places stress on power grids.

- **Electronic Waste:** The rapid obsolescence of electronic devices, such as computers and smartphones, results in a large volume of electronic waste. The improper disposal of such equipment can lead to environmental pollution and health hazards.

- **Carbon Footprint:** The IT industry is responsible for a considerable portion of the world's carbon emissions. From manufacturing and usage to disposal, carbon emissions are generated at various stages of a product's life cycle.

- **Resource Depletion:** The manufacturing of electronic components and devices requires substantial natural resources, including rare minerals, metals, and water. This can lead to resource scarcity and ecological damage.

Benefits of Green Computing

Green computing provides numerous advantages, such as (Andronie et al., 2021; Shaw et al., 2022):

- **Environmental Conservation:** By reducing energy consumption and carbon emissions, green computing helps in the conservation of natural resources and the mitigation of climate change.
- **Cost Savings:** Implementing energy-efficient practices can lead to significant cost savings for businesses and individuals. Lower energy bills and reduced maintenance expenses contribute to economic benefits.
- **Extended Lifespan of Equipment:** A focus on sustainability often results in the use of high-quality components and longer-lasting devices, which can extend the lifespan of equipment and reduce electronic waste.
- **Competitive Advantage:** Organizations that embrace green computing principles may gain a competitive edge by appealing to eco-conscious consumers and demonstrating corporate social responsibility.
- **Regulatory Compliance:** Adhering to green computing practices ensures compliance with environmental regulations, which is essential for avoiding fines and legal issues.

Green computing addresses environmental challenges in the IT industry by incorporating eco-conscious practices into technology design, production, and usage. This not only mitigates environmental impact but also offers economic and competitive benefits to individuals and organizations, fostering sustainability in the digital age.

CARBON FOOTPRINT IN TECHNOLOGY

The carbon footprint, or carbon emissions, is the total amount of greenhouse gases, primarily CO_2, emitted by an individual, organization, event, or product throughout its life cycle. In the context of technology, understanding the carbon footprint is crucial as the information technology sector, including hardware, data centers, and electronic devices, significantly contributes to global carbon emissions(Zhao et al., 2023).

The carbon footprint of technology can be divided into three primary categories:

- **Manufacturing Phase:** This includes the carbon emissions generated during the extraction of raw materials, production of components, assembly, and transportation of technology products. Manufacturing processes are energy-intensive and may involve the release of greenhouse gases.
- **Operational Phase:** The use of technology devices, including computers, servers, and data centers, consumes electricity. The carbon footprint during the operational phase is directly tied to energy consumption, which, if powered by fossil fuels, contributes to carbon emissions.

- **End-of-Life Phase:** When technology products reach the end of their lifecycle, they become electronic waste (e-waste). Improper disposal and recycling processes can result in the release of harmful pollutants into the environment.

The carbon footprint in technology is a complex process that involves recognizing the effects of each phase and implementing strategies to minimize emissions.

Measuring Carbon Emissions in IT

The task of accurately measuring carbon emissions in information technology is complex and necessitates specific methodologies and tools, with key considerations being(Altıntaş & Kassouri, 2020):

- **Data Collection:** To measure carbon emissions, data on energy consumption, types of energy sources, and usage patterns are collected. Data may also be gathered on the type and quantity of hardware and software in use.
- **Emissions Factors:** Emissions factors represent the amount of greenhouse gases produced per unit of energy consumed. Different energy sources, such as coal, natural gas, or renewable sources, have varying emissions factors.
- **Carbon Accounting Tools:** Carbon accounting tools and software help organizations track and calculate their carbon emissions. These tools often provide a standardized framework for measuring emissions and producing reports.
- **Certifications and Standards:** Various certifications and standards, such as ISO 14064 and the Greenhouse Gas Protocol, offer guidelines for measuring and reporting carbon emissions.
- **Scope of Measurement:** Carbon emissions can be categorized into three scopes: Scope 1 (direct emissions), Scope 2 (indirect emissions from purchased electricity), and Scope 3 (other indirect emissions, including supply chain emissions). Accurate measurement may encompass all three scopes.

The measurement of carbon emissions in IT is crucial for organizations to understand their environmental impact, set emission reduction targets, and make informed decisions about adopting green computing practices, contributing to a more sustainable and eco-friendlier IT sector.

Role of Data Centers in Carbon Footprint and Green Computing

Data centers are crucial in the modern IT landscape, storing, processing, and disseminating digital data as shown in Figure 1. However, they also significantly impact the carbon footprint and green computing initiatives due to their high energy consumption and carbon emissions. Understanding their role is vital for addressing environmental challenges in the technology sector(Andronie et al., 2021; Shaw et al., 2022).

- **Energy Intensive Operations:** Data centers, known for their energy-intensive operations, house numerous servers and network equipment that operate 24/7 for web services, cloud computing, and data storage. This demand for uninterrupted power and cooling strains electricity grids, contributing to increased carbon emissions when fossil fuels are the primary energy source(Boopathi et al., 2023; Domakonda et al., 2022; Kumara et al., 2023).

Figure 1. Role of data centres in carbon footprint and green computing

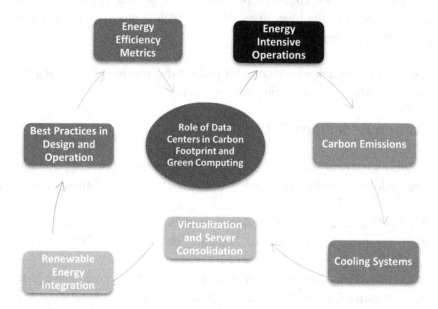

- **Carbon Emissions:** Data centers are a major contributor to carbon emissions in the IT sector, with increasing numbers due to the growing demand for online services. These emissions include direct emissions from on-site backup generators and indirect emissions from electricity production and delivery(Boopathi, 2022; Sampath, 2021; Venkateswaran, Kumar, et al., 2023).
- **Cooling Systems:** Data centers require optimal temperature and humidity to prevent hardware overheating and ensure reliable operations. Energy-efficient cooling solutions, often powered by electricity, are crucial for reducing the environmental impact of data centers and reducing their energy consumption.
- **Virtualization and Server Consolidation:** Green computing strategies optimize data center operations, including virtualization and server consolidation. Virtualization reduces energy consumption by running multiple virtual servers on a single physical server, while server consolidation reduces underutilized servers, enhancing overall efficiency.
- **Renewable Energy Integration:** The integration of renewable energy sources like solar and wind power is gaining popularity in data center operations, as it can significantly reduce carbon emissions and is often designed with sustainability in mind.
- **Best Practices in Design and Operation:** Data center operators are implementing environmentally friendly practices such as efficient space layout, hot/cold aisle containment, and advanced power management solutions to minimize environmental impact.
- **Energy Efficiency Metrics:** Power Usage Effectiveness (PUE) is a standardized measure of data center efficiency, with lower values indicating more energy-efficient operations. Addressing data center carbon footprint is crucial for green computing and sustainability. Improving energy efficiency and environmental practices can reduce the IT sector's ecological impact and contribute to a more sustainable digital future.

ENERGY EFFICIENCY IN COMPUTING

Energy Consumption in IT

Understanding the energy consumption dynamics in the IT sector is crucial for achieving energy efficiency, as it significantly consumes electrical energy, and several factors are essential as shown in Figure 2.

- **Data Centers:** Data centers, housing servers and networking equipment, are significant energy consumers in IT, requiring electricity grids for continuous operation and cooling systems. High-density computing and cloud services have increased energy usage.
- **IT Equipment:** The IT infrastructure, including computers, laptops, servers, and networking devices, consumes energy during active and idle states, with newer, more energy-efficient devices typically using less power.
- **Data Transmission:** Data transmission, including network and internet transfers, requires energy due to routers, switches, and data transfer itself. Efficient routing and network design can reduce energy consumption(Dhanya et al., 2023; Pramila et al., 2023; Ramudu et al., 2023).
- **Display Devices:** End-user devices like desktops, laptops, and monitors can reduce energy consumption by adjusting settings like screen brightness and sleep mode.
- **Power Management:** Power management strategies like sleep mode and hibernation can significantly reduce energy consumption in IT equipment, with system administrators and users playing a crucial role in implementing these practices.
- **Renewable Energy Sources:** The energy source of IT equipment significantly impacts energy consumption. Renewable energy sources like solar or wind power are being integrated into data centers and IT facilities to reduce their carbon footprint.
- **Cooling Systems:** Innovative cooling solutions like hot/cold aisle containment and free cooling are utilized to improve energy efficiency in data centers to maintain suitable operating temperatures.
- **Hardware Efficiency:** Energy Star certifications and other standards guide the development and selection of energy-efficient hardware, such as processors, power supplies, and solid-state drives, to reduce IT energy consumption.
- **Virtualization:** Virtualization technology consolidates multiple virtual servers on a single physical server, enhancing resource utilization and reducing underutilized physical servers.
- **Data Center Location:** The location of data centers can significantly influence their energy consumption, with regions with low-cost, renewable energy sources potentially offering an energy efficiency advantage.

Understanding and optimizing energy consumption within IT is central to the green computing and sustainability initiatives. By implementing energy-efficient technologies and practices, the IT sector can reduce its carbon footprint, minimize environmental impact, and lower operational costs.

Strategies for Energy Efficiency

Key strategies for energy efficiency in computing include optimizing hardware and software design, operation, and management, which help reduce the carbon footprint of IT operations(Syamala et al., 2023; Vennila et al., 2022).

Figure 2. Factors for energy consumption in IT sectors

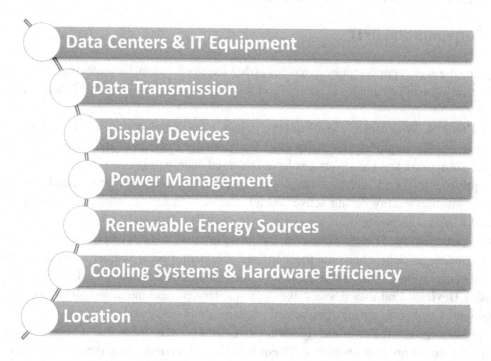

- **Virtualization:** Virtualization technology allows multiple virtual machines to run on a single physical server, optimizing resource usage and reducing the number of underutilized servers. This leads to energy savings by consolidating workloads.
- **Server Consolidation:** Reducing the number of underutilized servers through server consolidation minimizes energy consumption. Servers that are no longer needed can be decommissioned or repurposed.
- **Efficient Hardware Selection:** Choosing energy-efficient hardware components, including processors, power supplies, and storage devices, can significantly reduce energy consumption. Energy Star certifications and similar standards help identify energy-efficient hardware.
- **Power Management:** Implementing effective power management practices is critical. This includes setting devices to sleep or hibernate when not in use and ensuring efficient cooling and ventilation in data centers.
- **Energy-Efficient Cooling:** Utilizing advanced cooling techniques like hot/cold aisle containment, free cooling, and intelligent cooling systems can reduce the energy consumed by cooling infrastructure in data centers.
- **Renewable Energy Integration:** Transitioning to renewable energy sources, such as solar or wind power, for data center operations is an effective strategy to reduce the carbon footprint and energy consumption.
- **Energy-Efficient Lighting:** Using energy-efficient lighting solutions in data centers and office spaces can contribute to energy savings.
- **Data Center Location:** Selecting data center locations in regions with access to low-cost, renewable energy sources can provide an energy efficiency advantage.

- **Advanced Cooling Systems:** Employing innovative cooling solutions, like liquid cooling, and optimizing airflow within data centers can improve energy efficiency.
- **Data Center Design:** Well-thought-out data center design that maximizes airflow and minimizes heat loss can enhance energy efficiency. Modular data center designs can also scale efficiently as needed.
- **Efficient Backup Power Systems:** Utilizing efficient backup power systems and ensuring that backup generators are sized appropriately for the data center's needs reduces energy waste.
- **Optimized Workflows:** Optimizing workflows and processes to minimize data transfer, data duplication, and unnecessary computational tasks can reduce energy consumption in IT operations.
- **Energy Monitoring and Reporting:** Implementing energy monitoring systems to track and report energy usage enables organizations to identify inefficiencies and make informed decisions about energy reduction measures.

Green Data Center Design

Green data center design aims to create environmentally friendly and energy-efficient data centers, incorporating key principles such as(B et al., 2024; Boopathi, 2021; Venkateswaran, Vidhya, et al., 2023):

- **Optimal Layout:** Well-planned layouts and the strategic placement of equipment can maximize airflow, reduce hot spots, and minimize energy required for cooling.
- **Modular Design:** Modular data center design allows for scalability while minimizing over-provisioning, reducing energy waste.
- **Efficient Cooling:** Employing advanced cooling systems, like hot/cold aisle containment and liquid cooling, can enhance cooling efficiency.
- **Renewable Energy Integration:** Designing data centers with renewable energy sources in mind, such as solar panels or wind turbines, reduces reliance on fossil fuels.
- **Energy-Efficient Lighting:** Using energy-efficient lighting solutions, motion sensors, and natural light can lower lighting-related energy consumption.
- **Efficient Power Distribution:** Optimizing power distribution systems to minimize energy losses in distribution and conversion is a fundamental aspect of green data center design.
- **Sustainable Building Materials:** Using sustainable and energy-efficient building materials for data center construction can reduce the overall environmental impact.
- **Waste Heat Recovery:** Capturing waste heat generated by data center equipment for use in heating or cooling nearby facilities is a sustainable approach.
- **Energy Monitoring and Management:** Implementing advanced energy monitoring and management systems enables real-time tracking and adjustment of energy consumption.
- **Renewable Energy Credits:** The purchase of renewable energy credits (RECs) can offset carbon emissions associated with data center operations.

Green data center design aims to create environmentally friendly, energy-efficient facilities that minimize carbon footprint while meeting the demands of the digital age.

EMERGING TECHNOLOGIES FOR SUSTAINABILITY

Renewable Energy Integration

Renewable energy integration is a crucial step towards a sustainable and environmentally responsible energy infrastructure, integrating renewable energy sources(Nishanth et al., 2023; Syamala et al., 2023; Vanitha et al., 2023; Vennila et al., 2022) like solar, wind, hydro, and geothermal power into various sectors, including information technology, with key sustainability points (Figure 3).

- **Solar Power:** The use of solar panels and photovoltaic cells to harness energy from the sun is a widely adopted renewable energy technology. Solar power can be integrated into data centers and office buildings to reduce reliance on non-renewable energy sources.
- **Wind Power:** Wind turbines, both onshore and offshore, are employed to generate wind energy. Wind farms can provide a substantial source of renewable energy for data centers and communities.
- **Hydropower:** Hydropower plants harness the energy of flowing water to generate electricity. This technology can be integrated into data center cooling systems and power generation.
- **Geothermal Power:** Geothermal energy taps into the Earth's internal heat to produce electricity and heat. Geothermal solutions can be utilized for cooling data centers and generating electricity.
- **Energy Storage Solutions:** Advanced energy storage technologies, like large-scale batteries, enable the storage and distribution of renewable energy, ensuring a stable and continuous power supply.
- **Microgrids:** Microgrids are localized energy systems that can integrate various renewable energy sources, providing energy resilience and reducing dependence on centralized power grids.
- **Smart Grids:** Smart grid technologies enable efficient energy distribution, demand management, and the integration of renewable energy sources. They facilitate the balancing of energy supply and demand, reducing carbon emissions.

Renewable energy integration is a crucial strategy for reducing carbon emissions and achieving sustainability in the IT sector and beyond.

IoT and Smart Grids

The Internet of Things (IoT) and smart grids are promising technologies for enhancing sustainability and energy efficiency in various industries, including energy management, with key points regarding their role in sustainability(Hema et al., 2023; Hussain & Srimathy, 2023; Ingle et al., 2023; Kavitha et al., 2023).

- **IoT Sensors and Devices:** IoT devices, equipped with sensors and connectivity, enable real-time data collection and analysis in diverse sectors. In the context of energy, IoT sensors can monitor energy consumption, grid performance, and environmental conditions.
- **Energy Management:** IoT-based energy management systems provide precise data on energy consumption, allowing organizations to optimize energy use and reduce waste. This contributes to sustainability and cost savings.

Figure 3. Emerging technologies for sustainability

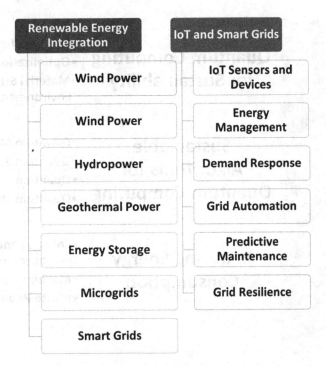

- **Demand Response:** Smart grids equipped with IoT technology can facilitate demand response programs. In response to fluctuations in energy supply or pricing, demand response allows consumers to adjust their energy consumption patterns for greater efficiency.
- **Grid Automation:** IoT sensors in smart grids can monitor and control various aspects of the electrical grid, optimizing energy distribution and reducing energy losses. This leads to a more efficient and sustainable grid.
- **Predictive Maintenance:** IoT-enabled devices and machine learning algorithms can predict equipment failures and maintenance needs in the electrical grid. This proactive approach reduces downtime and enhances grid reliability.
- **Grid Resilience:** Smart grids with IoT capabilities can automatically detect and respond to grid disturbances, enhancing the grid's resilience and minimizing disruptions.

IoT and smart grid technologies enhance sustainability by improving energy management, optimizing grid operations, and fostering a more responsive and resilient energy infrastructure, making them crucial components of a modern, sustainable energy ecosystem.

QUANTUM COMPUTING AND SUSTAINABLE ALGORITHMS

Quantum computing, an emerging technology, uses quantum mechanics principles to perform computations exponentially faster than classical computers as shown in Figure 4. When applied sustainably, it can address complex problems in various fields while minimizing energy consumption and environmental impact. This technology has the potential to revolutionize computing(Boopathi et al., 2023; Boopathi & Davim, 2023; Domakonda et al., 2022; Samikannu et al., 2022; Sampath, 2021).

Figure 4. Quantum computing and sustainable algorithms

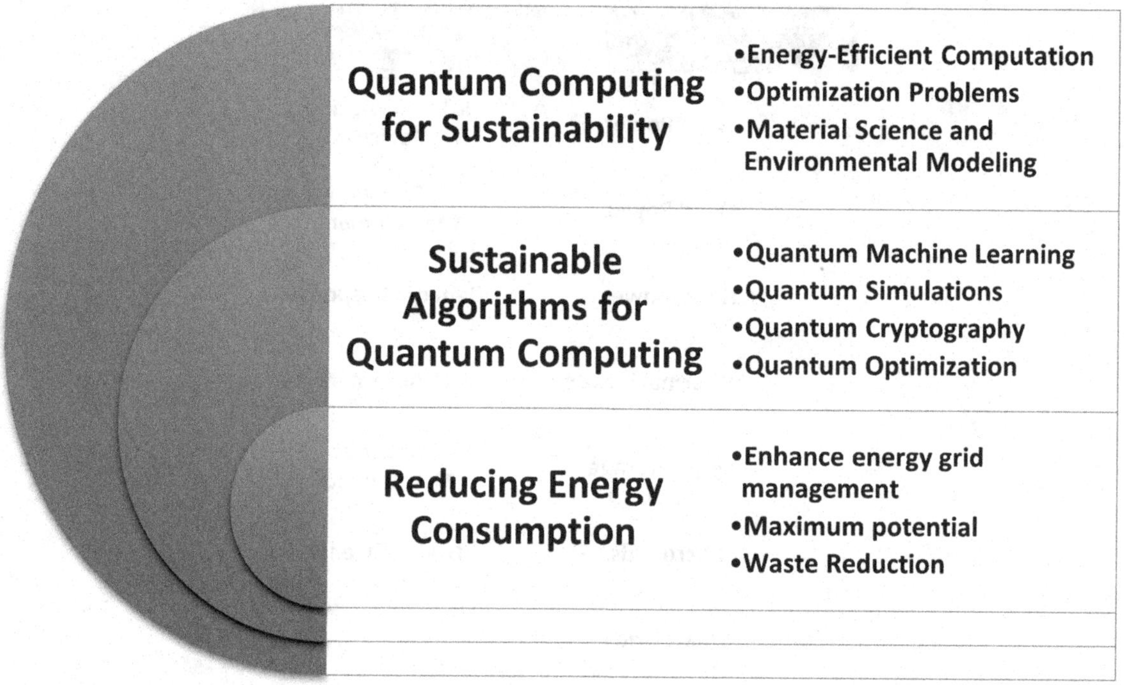

Quantum Computing for Sustainability	•**Energy-Efficient Computation** •**Optimization Problems** •**Material Science and Environmental Modeling**
Sustainable Algorithms for Quantum Computing	•**Quantum Machine Learning** •**Quantum Simulations** •**Quantum Cryptography** •**Quantum Optimization**
Reducing Energy Consumption	•**Enhance energy grid management** •**Maximum potential** •**Waste Reduction**

- Quantum Computing for Sustainability:
  - **Energy-Efficient Computation:** Quantum computers have the potential to outperform classical computers in energy efficiency for specific tasks. Quantum bits (qubits) can represent multiple states simultaneously, reducing the number of computational steps required.
  - **Optimization Problems:** Quantum computing excels in solving complex optimization problems, such as those related to resource allocation, supply chain management, and energy grid optimization. This can lead to more efficient resource use and reduced waste.
  - **Material Science and Environmental Modeling:** Quantum computers can simulate the behavior of molecules and materials at the quantum level, enabling more accurate and efficient research for sustainable materials, drug discovery, and environmental modeling.
- Sustainable Algorithms for Quantum Computing:
  - **Quantum Machine Learning:** Sustainable algorithms within quantum computing can improve machine learning models, leading to more accurate predictions in areas such as renewable energy forecasting, emissions reduction, and natural resource management.
  - **Quantum Simulations:** Sustainable algorithms can enable efficient simulations of complex physical and environmental systems, aiding in climate modeling, disaster prediction, and pollution monitoring.
  - **Quantum Cryptography:** Quantum cryptography algorithms can provide secure and energy-efficient communication, reducing the computational resources needed for secure data transmission.

- ◦ **Quantum Optimization:** Quantum optimization algorithms can be applied to eco-friendly supply chain management, traffic routing, and energy grid optimization, improving resource allocation and reducing energy waste.
- Reducing Energy Consumption:
  - ◦ Quantum computing has the potential to solve certain problems more efficiently, which can lead to energy savings. For example, optimized routes for logistics or transportation can minimize fuel consumption, and efficient resource allocation can reduce waste.
  - ◦ Quantum algorithms can enhance energy grid management, leading to more efficient distribution and reduced energy loss in the grid.
  - ◦ Sustainable algorithms within quantum computing can contribute to the development of energy-efficient data centers and improve the performance of renewable energy systems, ensuring they operate at their maximum potential.
- Challenges and Considerations:
  - ◦ Quantum computing is still in its infancy, and the practical implementation of sustainable algorithms on quantum hardware faces technical challenges.
  - ◦ Ensuring quantum computing itself is energy-efficient during its development and deployment is an important consideration to realize the environmental benefits.
  - ◦ Data centers hosting quantum computers should also adopt green data center design and energy-efficient cooling solutions.

Quantum computing and sustainable algorithms can significantly tackle environmental and sustainability issues by optimizing quantum systems' computational power and focusing on sustainability, paving the way for a greener, more eco-conscious technological future.

SOFTWARE SOLUTIONS FOR SUSTAINABILITY

Software solutions are vital for sustainability in the IT sector, reducing energy consumption, carbon emissions, and environmental impact by adopting green practices, utilizing virtualization and cloud computing(Ingle et al., 2023; Kavitha et al., 2023; Rahamathunnisa, Subhashini, et al., 2023; Venkateswaran, Kumar, et al., 2023), and implementing power management software (Figure 5).

Green Software Development Practices

Green software development practices focus on energy efficiency, resource optimization, and sustainability in creating applications and systems(Boopathi, 2021; Fowziya et al., 2023; Venkateswaran, Vidhya, et al., 2023).

- **Efficient Code:** Writing efficient and optimized code that reduces the computational workload, leading to lower energy consumption and faster execution.
- **Minimized Resource Utilization:** Minimizing the use of system resources, such as memory and processing power, to ensure software runs smoothly on a variety of devices, including those with limited resources.

Figure 5. Software solutions for sustainability

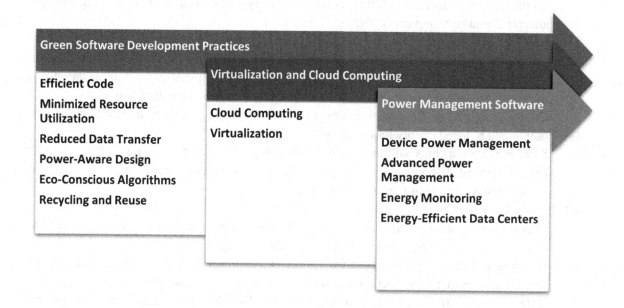

- **Reduced Data Transfer:** Minimizing data transfer and network requests to reduce the energy required for data transmission.
- **Power-Aware Design:** Designing software with power-aware features, allowing devices to adjust their power consumption based on user activity and system demands.
- **Eco-Conscious Algorithms:** Developing algorithms that are resource-efficient and environmentally friendly, such as routing algorithms for energy-efficient transportation and supply chain management.
- **Recycling and Reuse:** Implementing code recycling and reusing existing software components to reduce the environmental impact of software development.

Virtualization and Cloud Computing

Virtualization and cloud computing are sustainable technologies that provide energy-efficient and resource-optimized solutions(Hema et al., 2023; Rahamathunnisa, Sudhakar, et al., 2023; Satav et al., 2024; Syamala et al., 2023; Venkateswaran, Vidhya, et al., 2023).

- **Virtualization:** By consolidating multiple virtual servers on a single physical server, virtualization reduces the number of servers required, leading to significant energy savings and lower carbon emissions. It optimizes resource utilization and promotes a greener data center environment.
- **Cloud Computing:** Cloud services offer scalable and shared resources, allowing organizations to reduce their physical IT infrastructure. Cloud providers often use energy-efficient data centers and employ sustainable practices to deliver services, further contributing to energy and resource efficiency.

Power Management Software

Power management software allows users and organizations to manage and enhance the energy consumption of their devices and IT infrastructure(Chandrika et al., 2023; Domakonda et al., 2022; Gnanaprakasam et al., 2023; Kavitha et al., 2023; Maguluri et al., 2023).

- **Device Power Management:** Power management features built into operating systems and software allow users to schedule sleep, hibernate, and shutdown modes, reducing energy use during idle periods.
- **Advanced Power Management:** Organizations can implement advanced power management solutions in data centers and office environments to reduce energy consumption while maintaining operational efficiency.
- **Energy Monitoring:** Energy monitoring software provides real-time data on energy usage, allowing users to identify energy-intensive applications and optimize their use.
- **Energy-Efficient Data Centers:** Data centers can utilize power management software to control and optimize the power distribution and consumption of servers, storage systems, and network equipment, reducing energy waste.

Green software development practices, virtualization, cloud computing, and power management software can improve IT operations sustainability by promoting energy efficiency and resource optimization, aligning technology with eco-conscious principles.

CASE STUDIES IN SUSTAINABLE COMPUTING

Exemplary Organizations

- **Google:** Google has been a pioneer in sustainable computing. The company has committed to operating its global operations with 100% renewable energy. Google's data centers employ advanced cooling techniques and energy-efficient hardware to reduce energy consumption. They also invest in large-scale renewable energy projects and have achieved carbon neutrality for their global operations.
- **Facebook:** Facebook has set ambitious goals for sustainability and renewable energy. They have established energy-efficient data centers powered by renewable sources, such as wind and solar. Facebook also focuses on open-sourcing their sustainable hardware and data center designs to promote industry-wide adoption.
- **Apple:** Apple is committed to reducing its carbon footprint across its supply chain, manufacturing, and product usage. The company has made significant strides in using recycled materials and transitioning to renewable energy sources to power its facilities and data centers.

Best Practices in Reducing Carbon Footprints

- **Renewable Energy Adoption:** Transitioning to renewable energy sources is a key best practice for reducing carbon footprints. By investing in wind, solar, and hydro power, organizations can power their operations while minimizing emissions.
- **Energy-Efficient Data Centers:** Designing and operating energy-efficient data centers is crucial. Implementing advanced cooling systems, server consolidation, and innovative infrastructure designs can significantly reduce energy consumption.
- **Green Software Development:** Incorporating green software development practices, including efficient code, minimized data transfer, and power-aware design, can reduce the energy consumption of software applications.
- **Remote Work and Virtualization:** Encouraging remote work and virtualization can reduce the need for physical infrastructure and cut down on commuting, which results in lower carbon emissions.
- **Circular Economy Practices:** Embracing circular economy principles by recycling, refurbishing, and reusing IT equipment and materials can reduce electronic waste and minimize the environmental impact of technology(Agrawal et al., 2024; Dhanya et al., 2023; Hussain & Srimathy, 2023; Ingle et al., 2023; Mohanty et al., 2023).
- **Monitoring and Reporting:** Implementing energy monitoring and reporting systems allows organizations to track energy consumption and identify areas for improvement. This data-driven approach is essential for informed decision-making(Boopathi, 2023; Hussain & Srimathy, 2023; Sankar et al., 2023).

Lessons Learned

- **Corporate Commitment:** Exemplary organizations have shown that strong leadership and a corporate commitment to sustainability are essential. Sustainability initiatives must be integrated into a company's culture and strategy.
- **Collaboration and Open Sourcing:** Collaboration within the industry and open-sourcing sustainability practices and technologies can accelerate the adoption of sustainable computing practices.
- **Innovation in Design:** Innovative data center designs and energy-efficient hardware can significantly reduce energy consumption and environmental impact.
- **Renewable Energy Investment:** Investing in renewable energy is both an ethical and economical choice, as it helps organizations reduce their carbon footprint and save on energy costs.
- **Transparency and Reporting:** Transparent reporting on environmental performance and sustainability goals helps organizations hold themselves accountable and demonstrates their commitment to reducing carbon footprints.
- **Continuous Improvement:** Sustainability efforts should be viewed as an ongoing process. Organizations should continuously seek new ways to reduce their environmental impact and embrace emerging technologies for sustainability.

Case studies and best practices demonstrate that sustainable computing is achievable, cost-effective, and can enhance public perception, promoting a more resilient and responsible business model. Organizations that prioritize sustainability can inspire others to adopt a greener future.

CHALLENGES AND FUTURE DIRECTIONS

Barriers to Sustainable Computing

While sustainable computing offers numerous benefits, several challenges and barriers must be addressed(Kavitha et al., 2023; Kumar et al., 2023; Satav et al., 2024; Ugandar et al., 2023; Venkateswaran, Vidhya, et al., 2023):

- **High Initial Costs:** Implementing sustainable computing practices and technologies may require significant upfront investments in renewable energy infrastructure, energy-efficient hardware, and sustainable software development.
- **Legacy Systems:** Many organizations still rely on outdated hardware and software, making it challenging to transition to more sustainable alternatives. Legacy systems may be less energy-efficient and harder to adapt.
- **Lack of Awareness:** Some individuals and organizations are unaware of the environmental impact of their computing practices and may not prioritize sustainability.
- **Regulatory Hurdles:** Navigating complex regulations and ensuring compliance with environmental standards can be a barrier, especially for multinational companies.
- **Data Privacy and Security Concerns:** The adoption of emerging technologies for sustainability must balance environmental goals with data privacy and security considerations, posing challenges for the development and deployment of sustainable solutions.
- **Resource Constraints:** Sustainable computing relies on the availability of resources like rare minerals for energy-efficient hardware. Resource scarcity can be a significant barrier to sustainability.

Ethical Considerations

Sustainable computing also raises important ethical considerations(Liang et al., 2022; Lin et al., 2023; Mei et al., 2023):

- **Equity and Access:** Ensuring that the benefits of sustainable computing are accessible to all, and not just to more privileged populations, is a critical ethical consideration. This includes equitable access to green technologies and the digital divide.
- **Environmental Justice:** Environmental justice involves addressing the unequal distribution of environmental harms and benefits. Sustainable computing should prioritize communities that are disproportionately affected by environmental issues(MYILSAMY SURESHKUMAR, 2018; Sampath, 2021; Sampath et al., 2022; Sampath & Haribalaji, 2021; Sampath & Myilsamy, 2021).
- **Privacy and Surveillance:** As sustainability initiatives often involve data collection and monitoring, ensuring the ethical use of data, protecting privacy, and preventing surveillance abuses are paramount.
- **Transparency and Accountability:** Ethical computing practices demand transparency in reporting and accountability for environmental claims and sustainability efforts.

The Road Ahead

The future of sustainable computing holds several key directions:

- **Technological Advancements:** As technology evolves, it's likely that more efficient and sustainable hardware, software, and data center designs will emerge, further reducing energy consumption and environmental impact.
- **Global Collaboration:** Sustainable computing is a global challenge that requires international collaboration to address. The sharing of best practices, standards, and technologies on a global scale will be essential.
- **Policy and Regulation:** Governments and regulatory bodies will play a significant role in shaping the future of sustainable computing. The development of regulations and incentives for green technology adoption will drive sustainability efforts.
- **Circular Economy Adoption:** The circular economy model, which emphasizes recycling, refurbishing, and reusing IT equipment and materials, is expected to gain traction, reducing electronic waste and resource depletion.
- **Ethical and Inclusive Computing:** Ethical considerations and inclusive practices will become increasingly central in the development and deployment of sustainable computing technologies. Ethical frameworks and principles will guide the industry toward a more responsible and equitable future.
- **Education and Awareness:** Increasing awareness about the environmental impact of technology and promoting sustainability education will be crucial in shaping the behavior and choices of individuals and organizations(Agrawal et al., 2023; Durairaj et al., 2023).
- **Resilience and Adaptation:** Sustainable computing practices should be designed with resilience in mind. Preparing for the impact of climate change, such as extreme weather events, is vital for ensuring the long-term sustainability of computing infrastructure.

Sustainable computing is a promising path to reduce the environmental impact of the IT sector, requiring ethical considerations and technological innovation, global collaboration, and policy development to achieve a more sustainable and responsible digital future.

CONCLUSION

Sustainable computing is not just a concept; it's an imperative for the information technology sector and the broader digital age. It is clear that addressing the environmental challenges posed by computing is not only possible but essential. In conclusion:

- The IT industry significantly contributes to energy consumption, carbon emissions, and electronic waste, necessitating sustainable practices. Organizations and individuals are recognizing the need for green computing initiatives, including renewable energy adoption, energy-efficient hardware, and sustainable software development.
- Emerging technologies like quantum computing and the Internet of Things can improve sustainability and tackle environmental issues. Companies like Google, Facebook, and Apple demon-

strate that a commitment to sustainability, energy-efficient data centers, and renewable energy integration yields significant results.

- Ethical sustainability in computing involves equitable access to green technologies, environmental justice, privacy, and accountability. Overcoming barriers like high costs and resource constraints requires technological innovation, global collaboration, and effective policy. The future of sustainable computing will be shaped by technological advancements, global collaboration, and a growing commitment to ethical practices. Education, awareness, and resilience are crucial for a responsible digital future.

Sustainable computing is not a destination but a journey, and its path is clear: reducing the carbon footprint, minimizing electronic waste, and embracing green practices to create a more environmentally responsible and sustainable digital age.

REFERENCES

Abuzreda, A., Hamad, T., Elayatt, A., & Ahmad, I. (2023). A Review of Different Renewable Energy Resource s and Their Energy Efficiency Technologies. *Adn Envi Wa s Mana Rec, 6*(1), 384–389.

Agrawal, A. V., Pitchai, R., Senthamaraikannan, C., Balaji, N. A., Sajithra, S., & Boopathi, S. (2023). Digital Education System During the COVID-19 Pandemic. In Using Assistive Technology for Inclusive Learning in K-12 Classrooms (pp. 104–126). IGI Global. doi:10.4018/978-1-6684-6424-3.ch005

Agrawal, A. V., Shashibhushan, G., Pradeep, S., Padhi, S. N., Sugumar, D., & Boopathi, S. (2024). Synergizing Artificial Intelligence, 5G, and Cloud Computing for Efficient Energy Conversion Using Agricultural Waste. In Practice, Progress, and Proficiency in Sustainability (pp. 475–497). IGI Global. doi:10.4018/979-8-3693-1186-8.ch026

Altıntaş, H., & Kassouri, Y. (2020). The impact of energy technology innovations on cleaner energy supply and carbon footprints in Europe: A linear versus nonlinear approach. *Journal of Cleaner Production, 276*, 124140. doi:10.1016/j.jclepro.2020.124140

Andronie, M., Lăzăroiu, G., Iatagan, M., Hurloiu, I., & Dijmărescu, I. (2021). Sustainable cyber-physical production systems in big data-driven smart urban economy: A systematic literature review. *Sustainability (Basel), 13*(2), 751. doi:10.3390/su13020751

B, M. K., K, K. K., Sasikala, P., Sampath, B., Gopi, B., & Sundaram, S. (2024). Sustainable Green Energy Generation From Waste Water. In *Practice, Progress, and Proficiency in Sustainability* (pp. 440–463). IGI Global. doi:10.4018/979-8-3693-1186-8.ch024

Boopathi, S. (2021). Improving of Green Sand-Mould Quality using Taguchi Technique. *Journal of Engineering Research*.

Boopathi, S. (2022). An investigation on gas emission concentration and relative emission rate of the near-dry wire-cut electrical discharge machining process. *Environmental Science and Pollution Research International, 29*(57), 86237–86246. doi:10.1007/s11356-021-17658-1 PMID:34837614

Boopathi, S. (2023). Internet of Things-Integrated Remote Patient Monitoring System: Healthcare Application. In *Dynamics of Swarm Intelligence Health Analysis for the Next Generation* (pp. 137–161). IGI Global. doi:10.4018/978-1-6684-6894-4.ch008

Boopathi, S., & Davim, J. P. (2023). *Sustainable Utilization of Nanoparticles and Nanofluids in Engineering Applications*. IGI Global. doi:10.4018/978-1-6684-9135-5

Boopathi, S., Kumar, P. K. S., Meena, R. S., Sudhakar, M., & Associates. (2023). Sustainable Developments of Modern Soil-Less Agro-Cultivation Systems: Aquaponic Culture. In Human Agro-Energy Optimization for Business and Industry (pp. 69–87). IGI Global.

Chandrika, V., Sivakumar, A., Krishnan, T. S., Pradeep, J., Manikandan, S., & Boopathi, S. (2023). Theoretical Study on Power Distribution Systems for Electric Vehicles. In *Intelligent Engineering Applications and Applied Sciences for Sustainability* (pp. 1–19). IGI Global. doi:10.4018/979-8-3693-0044-2.ch001

Chong, C. T., Van Fan, Y., Lee, C. T., & Klemeš, J. J. (2022). Post COVID-19 ENERGY sustainability and carbon emissions neutrality. *Energy*, *241*, 122801. doi:10.1016/j.energy.2021.122801 PMID:36570560

Dhanya, D., Kumar, S. S., Thilagavathy, A., Prasad, D., & Boopathi, S. (2023). Data Analytics and Artificial Intelligence in the Circular Economy: Case Studies. In Intelligent Engineering Applications and Applied Sciences for Sustainability (pp. 40–58). IGI Global.

Domakonda, V. K., Farooq, S., Chinthamreddy, S., Puviarasi, R., Sudhakar, M., & Boopathi, S. (2022). Sustainable Developments of Hybrid Floating Solar Power Plants: Photovoltaic System. In Human Agro-Energy Optimization for Business and Industry (pp. 148–167). IGI Global.

Durairaj, M., Jayakumar, S., Karpagavalli, V., Maheswari, B. U., Boopathi, S., & ... (2023). Utilization of Digital Tools in the Indian Higher Education System During Health Crises. In *Multidisciplinary Approaches to Organizational Governance During Health Crises* (pp. 1–21). IGI Global. doi:10.4018/978-1-7998-9213-7.ch001

Fowziya, S., Sivaranjani, S., Devi, N. L., Boopathi, S., Thakur, S., & Sailaja, J. M. (2023). Influences of nano-green lubricants in the friction-stir process of TiAlN coated alloys. *Materials Today: Proceedings*. Advance online publication. doi:10.1016/j.matpr.2023.06.446

Gnanaprakasam, C., Vankara, J., Sastry, A. S., Prajval, V., Gireesh, N., & Boopathi, S. (2023). Long-Range and Low-Power Automated Soil Irrigation System Using Internet of Things: An Experimental Study. In Contemporary Developments in Agricultural Cyber-Physical Systems (pp. 87–104). IGI Global.

Hema, N., Krishnamoorthy, N., Chavan, S. M., Kumar, N., Sabarimuthu, M., & Boopathi, S. (2023). A Study on an Internet of Things (IoT)-Enabled Smart Solar Grid System. In *Handbook of Research on Deep Learning Techniques for Cloud-Based Industrial IoT* (pp. 290–308). IGI Global. doi:10.4018/978-1-6684-8098-4.ch017

Hussain, Z., & Srimathy, G. (2023). *IoT and AI Integration for Enhanced Efficiency and Sustainability*.

Ingle, R. B., Senthil, T. S., Swathi, S., Muralidharan, N., Mahendran, G., & Boopathi, S. (2023). Sustainability and Optimization of Green and Lean Manufacturing Processes Using Machine Learning Techniques. In IGI Global. doi:10.4018/978-1-6684-8238-4.ch012

Issa, M., Ilinca, A., & Martini, F. (2022). Ship energy efficiency and maritime sector initiatives to reduce carbon emissions. *Energies*, *15*(21), 7910. doi:10.3390/en15217910

Kavitha, C. R., Varalatchoumy, M., Mithuna, H. R., Bharathi, K., Geethalakshmi, N. M., & Boopathi, S. (2023). Energy Monitoring and Control in the Smart Grid: Integrated Intelligent IoT and ANFIS. In M. Arshad (Ed.), (pp. 290–316). Advances in Bioinformatics and Biomedical Engineering. IGI Global. doi:10.4018/978-1-6684-6577-6.ch014

Kumar, P. R., Meenakshi, S., Shalini, S., Devi, S. R., & Boopathi, S. (2023). Soil Quality Prediction in Context Learning Approaches Using Deep Learning and Blockchain for Smart Agriculture. In R. Kumar, A. B. Abdul Hamid, & N. I. Binti Ya'akub (Eds.), (pp. 1–26). Advances in Computational Intelligence and Robotics. IGI Global. doi:10.4018/978-1-6684-9151-5.ch001

Kumara, V., Mohanaprakash, T., Fairooz, S., Jamal, K., Babu, T., & Sampath, B. (2023). Experimental Study on a Reliable Smart Hydroponics System. In *Human Agro-Energy Optimization for Business and Industry* (pp. 27–45). IGI Global. doi:10.4018/978-1-6684-4118-3.ch002

Liang, T., Zhang, Y.-J., & Qiang, W. (2022). Does technological innovation benefit energy firms' environmental performance? The moderating effect of government subsidies and media coverage. *Technological Forecasting and Social Change*, *180*, 121728. doi:10.1016/j.techfore.2022.121728

Lin, Z., Wang, H., Li, W., & Chen, M. (2023). Impact of green finance on carbon emissions based on a two-stage LMDI decomposition method. *Sustainability (Basel)*, *15*(17), 12808. doi:10.3390/su151712808

Luo, B., Khan, A. A., Wu, X., & Li, H. (2023). Navigating carbon emissions in G-7 economies: A quantile regression analysis of environmental-economic interplay. *Environmental Science and Pollution Research International*, *30*(47), 1–16. doi:10.1007/s11356-023-29722-z PMID:37707736

Maguluri, L. P., Arularasan, A. N., & Boopathi, S. (2023). Assessing Security Concerns for AI-Based Drones in Smart Cities. In R. Kumar, A. B. Abdul Hamid, & N. I. Binti Ya'akub (Eds.), (pp. 27–47). Advances in Computational Intelligence and Robotics. IGI Global. doi:10.4018/978-1-6684-9151-5.ch002

Mei, B., Khan, A. A., Khan, S. U., Ali, M. A. S., & Luo, J. (2023). Variation of digital economy's effect on carbon emissions: Improving energy efficiency and structure for energy conservation and emission reduction. *Environmental Science and Pollution Research International*, *30*(37), 87300–87313. doi:10.1007/s11356-023-28010-0 PMID:37422562

Mohanty, A., Venkateswaran, N., Ranjit, P., Tripathi, M. A., & Boopathi, S. (2023). Innovative Strategy for Profitable Automobile Industries: Working Capital Management. In Handbook of Research on Designing Sustainable Supply Chains to Achieve a Circular Economy (pp. 412–428). IGI Global.

Mustapha, U. F., Alhassan, A.-W., Jiang, D.-N., & Li, G.-L. (2021). Sustainable aquaculture development: A review on the roles of cloud computing, internet of things and artificial intelligence (CIA). *Reviews in Aquaculture*, *13*(4), 2076–2091. doi:10.1111/raq.12559

Myilsamy Sureshkumar, V. R. P., S. Boopathi, M. & Sabareesh. (2018). The improving Wear Resistance Properties of Molybdenum Alloy Under Cryogenic Treatment. *International Journal of Mechanical and Production Engineering Research and Development*, *8*(7), 724–728.

Nishanth, J., Deshmukh, M. A., Kushwah, R., Kushwaha, K. K., Balaji, S., & Sampath, B. (2023). Particle Swarm Optimization of Hybrid Renewable Energy Systems. In *Intelligent Engineering Applications and Applied Sciences for Sustainability* (pp. 291–308). IGI Global. doi:10.4018/979-8-3693-0044-2.ch016

Ofori, E. K., Li, J., Gyamfi, B. A., Opoku-Mensah, E., & Zhang, J. (2023). Green industrial transition: Leveraging environmental innovation and environmental tax to achieve carbon neutrality. Expanding on STRIPAT model. *Journal of Environmental Management*, *343*, 118121. doi:10.1016/j.jenvman.2023.118121 PMID:37224684

Pandey, V., Sircar, A., Bist, N., Solanki, K., & Yadav, K. (2023). Accelerating the renewable energy sector through Industry 4.0: Optimization opportunities in the digital revolution. *International Journal of Innovation Studies*, *7*(2), 171–188. doi:10.1016/j.ijis.2023.03.003

Pramila, P., Amudha, S., Saravanan, T., Sankar, S. R., Poongothai, E., & Boopathi, S. (2023). Design and Development of Robots for Medical Assistance: An Architectural Approach. In Contemporary Applications of Data Fusion for Advanced Healthcare Informatics (pp. 260–282). IGI Global.

Rahamathunnisa, U., Subhashini, P., Aancy, H. M., Meenakshi, S., Boopathi, S., & ... (2023). Solutions for Software Requirement Risks Using Artificial Intelligence Techniques. In *Handbook of Research on Data Science and Cybersecurity Innovations in Industry 4.0 Technologies* (pp. 45–64). IGI Global.

Rahamathunnisa, U., Sudhakar, K., Murugan, T. K., Thivaharan, S., Rajkumar, M., & Boopathi, S. (2023). Cloud Computing Principles for Optimizing Robot Task Offloading Processes. In *AI-Enabled Social Robotics in Human Care Services* (pp. 188–211). IGI Global. doi:10.4018/978-1-6684-8171-4.ch007

Ramudu, K., Mohan, V. M., Jyothirmai, D., Prasad, D., Agrawal, R., & Boopathi, S. (2023). Machine Learning and Artificial Intelligence in Disease Prediction: Applications, Challenges, Limitations, Case Studies, and Future Directions. In Contemporary Applications of Data Fusion for Advanced Healthcare Informatics (pp. 297–318). IGI Global.

Samikannu, R., Koshariya, A. K., Poornima, E., Ramesh, S., Kumar, A., & Boopathi, S. (2022). Sustainable Development in Modern Aquaponics Cultivation Systems Using IoT Technologies. In *Human Agro-Energy Optimization for Business and Industry* (pp. 105–127). IGI Global.

Sampath, B. (2021). *Sustainable Eco-Friendly Wire-Cut Electrical Discharge Machining: Gas Emission Analysis*.

Sampath, B., & Haribalaji, V. (2021). Influences of Welding Parameters on Friction Stir Welding of Aluminum and Magnesium: A Review. *Materials Research Proceedings*, *19*(1), 322–330.

Sampath, B., & Myilsamy, S. (2021). Experimental investigation of a cryogenically cooled oxygen-mist near-dry wire-cut electrical discharge machining process. *Stroj. Vestn. Jixie Gongcheng Xuebao*, *67*(6), 322–330.

Sampath, B., Naveenkumar, N., Sampathkumar, P., Silambarasan, P., Venkadesh, A., & Sakthivel, M. (2022). Experimental comparative study of banana fiber composite with glass fiber composite material using Taguchi method. *Materials Today: Proceedings*, *49*, 1475–1480. doi:10.1016/j.matpr.2021.07.232

Sankar, K. M., Booba, B., & Boopathi, S. (2023). Smart Agriculture Irrigation Monitoring System Using Internet of Things. In *Contemporary Developments in Agricultural Cyber-Physical Systems* (pp. 105–121). IGI Global. doi:10.4018/978-1-6684-7879-0.ch006

Satav, S. D., & Lamani, D. G, H. K., Kumar, N. M. G., Manikandan, S., & Sampath, B. (2024). Energy and Battery Management in the Era of Cloud Computing. In Practice, Progress, and Proficiency in Sustainability (pp. 141–166). IGI Global. doi:10.4018/979-8-3693-1186-8.ch009

Shaw, R., Howley, E., & Barrett, E. (2022). Applying reinforcement learning towards automating energy efficient virtual machine consolidation in cloud data centers. *Information Systems*, *107*, 101722. doi:10.1016/j.is.2021.101722

Syamala, M., Komala, C., Pramila, P., Dash, S., Meenakshi, S., & Boopathi, S. (2023). Machine Learning-Integrated IoT-Based Smart Home Energy Management System. In *Handbook of Research on Deep Learning Techniques for Cloud-Based Industrial IoT* (pp. 219–235). IGI Global. doi:10.4018/978-1-6684-8098-4.ch013

Ugandar, R. E., Rahamathunnisa, U., Sajithra, S., Christiana, M. B. V., Palai, B. K., & Boopathi, S. (2023). Hospital Waste Management Using Internet of Things and Deep Learning: Enhanced Efficiency and Sustainability. In M. Arshad (Ed.), (pp. 317–343). Advances in Bioinformatics and Biomedical Engineering. IGI Global. doi:10.4018/978-1-6684-6577-6.ch015

Vanitha, S., Radhika, K., & Boopathi, S. (2023). Artificial Intelligence Techniques in Water Purification and Utilization. In *Human Agro-Energy Optimization for Business and Industry* (pp. 202–218). IGI Global. doi:10.4018/978-1-6684-4118-3.ch010

Venkateswaran, N., Kumar, S. S., Diwakar, G., Gnanasangeetha, D., & Boopathi, S. (2023). Synthetic Biology for Waste Water to Energy Conversion: IoT and AI Approaches. In M. Arshad (Ed.), (pp. 360–384). Advances in Bioinformatics and Biomedical Engineering. IGI Global. doi:10.4018/978-1-6684-6577-6.ch017

Venkateswaran, N., Vidhya, K., Ayyannan, M., Chavan, S. M., Sekar, K., & Boopathi, S. (2023). A Study on Smart Energy Management Framework Using Cloud Computing. In 5G, Artificial Intelligence, and Next Generation Internet of Things: Digital Innovation for Green and Sustainable Economies (pp. 189–212). IGI Global. doi:10.4018/978-1-6684-8634-4.ch009

Vennila, T., Karuna, M., Srivastava, B. K., Venugopal, J., Surakasi, R., & Sampath, B. (2022). New Strategies in Treatment and Enzymatic Processes: Ethanol Production From Sugarcane Bagasse. In Human Agro-Energy Optimization for Business and Industry (pp. 219–240). IGI Global.

Yu, D., Wenhui, X., Anser, M. K., Nassani, A. A., Imran, M., Zaman, K., & Haffar, M. (2023). Navigating the global mineral market: A study of resource wealth and the energy transition. *Resources Policy*, *82*, 103500. doi:10.1016/j.resourpol.2023.103500

Zhao, Y., Yang, Z., Niu, J., Du, Z., Federica, C., Zhu, Z., Yang, K., Li, Y., Zhao, B., Pedersen, T. H., Liu, C., & Emmanuel, M. (2023). Systematical analysis of sludge treatment and disposal technologies for carbon footprint reduction. *Journal of Environmental Sciences (China)*, *128*, 224–249. doi:10.1016/j.jes.2022.07.038 PMID:36801037

ABBREVIATIONS

AI: Artificial Intelligence
CO2: Carbon Dioxide
CPU: Central Processing Unit
CPU: Central Processing Unit
e-waste: Electronic Waste
GHG: Greenhouse Gas
IoT: Internet of Things
ISO: International Organization for Standardization
IT: Information Technology
OS: Operating System
PUE: Power Usage Effectiveness
RAM: Random Access Memory
REC: Renewable Energy Credit
SSD: Solid-State Drive

Chapter 6
Green Computing:
Building an Environmentally Sustainable Future Using Cloud and IoT With 6G

Mala Shharma

https://orcid.org/0000-0001-7705-358X

Institute of Technology and Science, Ghaziabad, India

ABSTRACT

Green computing refers to strategies and procedures for creating, utilizing, and disposing of computer resources in an environmentally responsible manner while preserving overall computing performance. This entails using less hazardous materials, getting the most usage possible out of a product while using the least amount of energy possible, as well as making old items and garbage more reusable, recyclable, and biodegradable. Many businesses are making efforts to lessen the negative effects of their activities on the environment.

INTRODUCTION

Green computing refers to strategies and practices for producing, employing, and discarding computer resources in an eco-friendly manner while maintaining overall computing performance. In order to achieve this, less hazardous materials must be used, products must be used as efficiently as possible while consuming the smallest quantity of energy feasible and waste must be made to be more recyclable, reused and biodegradable. Numerous businesses are making attempts to reduce how negatively their operations affect the environment. The Framework Convention of the United Nations on Climate Change (UNFCC), an international environmental agreement, seeks to maintain emissions of greenhouse gases in the atmosphere at a level that would prevent negative human interference with the eco system. Developing without jeopardizing the requirements of future generations is what is meant by sustainable development (Lu et al., (2021). By doing this, society may advance humankind while safeguarding the ecosystems and other resources of nature that are vital to it. Solutions for environmental protection are provided by the dynamic field of cloud computing in information and communication technology. Cloud

DOI: 10.4018/979-8-3693-0338-2.ch006

computing technologies have many different application domains because they are scalable, reliable, and offer exceptional performance at a competitive price. The cloud computing change, which also provides tremendous prospects for environmental preservation as well as to other economic and technological advantages, is redesigning green computing. Running corporate, and web applications on the cloud is a highly scalable and economical option. The energy consumption of data centers however has significantly grown due to the rising need for cloud infrastructure. The ever-increasing need for IoT is being met by cloud computing services. As the infrastructure for the IoT paradigm is provided, data centers are gradually becoming one of the biggest energy users. Future advancements and technological adoption that leads to the adoption of green computing will result in an increase in the demand for energy. Green computing techniques lower IoT devices' energy usage without compromising their performance. The various facets of green computing for IoT computing will be assessed in this study through an analysis of key ideas, difficulties, and solutions. Global citizens are calling for quick action as increasing temperatures and harsh weather are brought on by climate change. According to NASA, since the late 19th century, The average surface temperature of the earth has increased by 2.12 degree Fahrenheit (1.18 degrees Celsius) as a result of rising carbon emissions. The last seven years have also been the warmest on record. We will learn innovative strategies to address climate change in the following industries and beyond by concentrating on sustainability as a major driver of 6G research. In order to highlight the significance of green computing for developing sustainable environmental, this paper surveys a significant role of cloud computing, IoT (Internet of Things) & major driver of latest 6G (Bhat and Alqahtani 2021).

Environmentally friendly computing is referred to as "green computing." When utilising a computer, this lowers the amount of electricity and power used and lessens environmental waste. The first and most convincing study in computers demonstrates that Carbon Dioxide (CO_2) and other pollution are harming the ecosystem and the world's climate. Because it tries to protect life, preserving our beautiful planet is an important and valid goal.

Researchers and industry experts have paid close attention to minimizing e-waste and developing electronic devices using non-toxic components (Konhäuser 2023) . Future ICT (Information and Communication Technologies) will become more and more dependent on energy efficiency as the price and supply of energy continue to rise (Anpalagan et al.2023). The desire for energy-efficient solutions that lower the overall energy consumption of compute, storage, and communications is driven by the expanding use of ICT, rising energy prices, and the need to minimise greenhouse gas emissions (Fraga et al. 2021).

Green computing offers complex issues to system designers even though it is becoming more and more significant in IT systems. During the system design phase, designers must consider energy convention and come up with ways to cut it. All facets of IT systems, including semiconductors, application services, systems for operating systems, networks for communication, and system architectures are involved in green computing.

Why Green Computing Is Important

- Environment-related effects of information technology over the same time span, computer use has grown. The environment is impacted by both the energy necessary to power these devices and the electricity used to maintain the cooling infrastructure for these devices. Research in the subject of "green computing," which is concerned with using computers in an environmentally sustainable manner, is being attracted to this area of major concern (Anpalagan et al. 2023).

- In either case, the issue is that this decade has seen an increase in electronic waste. This environment is progressively showing many harmful repercussions, particularly to people. Electronics quickly became a bottleneck and as a result a horrific 70% of all hazardous wastes were produced (Pradhan and Priyanka 2021). Many hazardous substances, like heavy trash and flame-resistant polymers, contain a significant amount of computer waste that quickly grows in waterways and bio-accumulates. Additionally, a lot of resources are needed for the production of electronic chips, and certain harmful chemicals and gases are utilised around people.
- Solid trash eventually finds its way into rivers after being burned, other wastes disposed of, and the use of acids and other chemicals. Water contamination became a significant issue as a result.

Objectives of Green Computing

- To make computers safer for the environment.
- To improve computers' energy efficiency.
- To minimizing the necessity for travel.
- Recycling computer product waste.
- Utilizing and investing in renewable energy.
- Since utility expenses are lower, save money.
- Cutting back on the use of paper.
- Making efficient algorithms to boost computer performance.

What Methods Are Used in Green Computing?

There are many methods to green computing. These encompass environmentally friendly production, design, usage, and disposal. Now let's take a closer look at these strategies.

Figure 1. Four domains of green computing

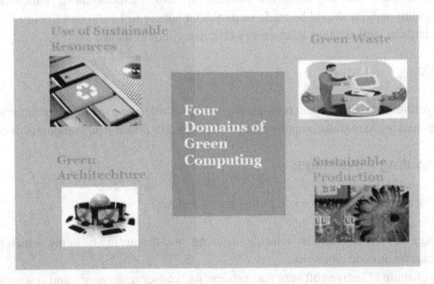

Green Architecture

In order to enhance a system's green characteristics, designing green systems entails making green decisions throughout the design process. Energy efficiency, environmentally friendly materials, a decrease in greenhouse gas emissions, and energy consumption reduction should all be taken into account while making these ecologically responsible selections. Assessing a computer's life cycle during design is a component of certain environmentally friendly decisions. For instance, green computing will concentrate on creating systems with longer useful lifetimes so they aren't updated as frequently. It also seeks to take into account the way a system is utilised while designing it (Gera et al.2023). Additionally, recyclable and energy-efficient, green computers should be durable. making a sustainable product's cycle work, starting at the moment of production and ending when its components can be recycled to make a new computer.

Use of Sustainable Resources

Computer usage that is as energy-efficient as feasible is referred to as "green use." When turning on a computer, for instance, users shouldn't have to wait too long (Kumar et al.,2023). So as not to waste battery power, the computer's speed should also match the user's requirements.

In order to ensure green utilisation, green systems must be used correctly and effectively. To prevent energy consumption, A computer should be turned off when not in use, for example, according to green computing.

Green computing practices also include other simple activities like turning off the display on your computer or changing its power options so it consumes less electricity while still functioning.

Sustainable Production

Being green from the beginning is the process of green production. Utilizing eco-friendly materials and reducing electricity usage during production are two ways to do this. A green system must be made of parts that don't contain potentially dangerous substances, including halogenated flame retardants (Gera et al. 2023). Additionally, it should be made of parts that adhere to LEED and Energy Star green construction standards as well as other strict energy efficiency requirements.

Green Waste

Computer recycling that is ethical and ecologically benign is referred to as "green computing disposal." It also involves making sure that computers may be recycled to create new computers or other items.

Green Computing Advantages

Some of the key advantages of green computing are as follows:

1. Less energy is used in the manufacturing, utilising, and discarding of items, which results in decreased carbon dioxide emissions.
2. Because of more effective software and processing, conserving energy and resources also saves money.

3. Developing and refining government initiatives to promote recycling and the use of renewable energy sources (Anpalagan et al. 2023).
4. Minimize the hazards that the laptops pose to users' health, such as those posed by substances known to exacerbate immunological responses like cancer in people and other toxins.

GREEN COMPUTING TRENDS

The different fields of green computing research include the ones listed below:

Green Cloud Computing

In order to potentially improve the environment, the phrase "green cloud computing" refers to sustainable practices and methods for utilizing IT resources as well as other technical advancements like computing.

Significant environmental effects are caused by the expanding number of businesses worldwide. Because of this expansion, there will be a significant increase in the requirement for data centers, daily commutes for workers will lengthen, and the amount of office supplies and equipment required on a daily basis will expand (Pradhan and Priyanka 2021). Through the provision of solutions that potentially reduce global carbon footprints, green cloud computing addresses these pressing environmental challenges. Typically, to build greener data centers, cloud service providers employ an array of techniques.

The following areas are the focus of these initiatives to increase efficiency:

2.1.1 *Source of energy*: As much as feasible, the company powers its data centers using renewable energy. This frequently involves solar or wind power along with large battery banks that hold the earned energy. Some suppliers of services employ renewable energy certificates (RECs) that show their claim that their servers only consume renewable energy in order to lower their impact on the environment. Abolishing the usage of fossil fuels is not the same thing as RECs, though.

2.1.2. *Infrastructure:* The supplier optimizes the hardware and software of the infrastructure. For instance, a provider may adopt techniques like dynamic voltage and frequency scaling (DVFS) or instal gear that uses less energy. In order to decrease the number of servers and storage devices, the provider may also optimise resource consumption, such as by deploying virtualization or software-defined infrastructure.

2.1.3. *Workflow:* The supplier use a variety of techniques aimed at improving processes at every level. This might entail moving workloads to other times of the day, changing apps to lessen network traffic, improving storage and server caches, automating repetitive operations, or implementing a variety of other actions to save energy.

2.1.4 *Facility:* The corporation makes steps for better the use of energy in its data centers. A provider might, for instance, put the center below ground, on an oceanic floor, or in an extremely cold place. Service provider may also come up with ways to use the surplus heat produced in the data centres, including warming surrounding structures. Providers might also make use of cutting-edge technology as machine learning to monitor and maximize energy use. Other strategies consist of changing the data center's floor plan for better air flow or establishing cooling with water systems to cope with the heat that comes from the equipment.

Figure 2. Green cloud computing and environment sustainability
(Source by Garg and Buyya)

2.1.5 *Green Cloud Computing & Environment Sustainability*: Thousands of simultaneous online transactions and millions of web asks each day have shot up considerably as a side effect of the creation of fast networks during the past few decades. This ever-growing need is met by large-scale datacenters, which pack thousands of servers with related cooling, storage, and network equipment. Such enormous datacenters are controlled by various online giants around worldwide, namely Google, Amazon, eBay, and Yahoo.

In cloud computing, computing is provided as a utility that explains the sale of these technologies on a pay-as-you-go basis (Pradhan and Priyanka 2021). Business has typically purchasing and maintaining computing resources used to take up a significant amount of time and money for enterprises (Kumar et al.,2023). The rise of cloud computing is slowly turning this ownership-based Approach into a subscription-oriented strategy by providing on-demand use of scalable infrastructure and services. Users can use to keep, retrieve, and share every kind of data on the cloud. For medium-sized enterprises or company units, buying things configuring, leading, and maintaining their own computer system is not a concern (Prasad and Ruggieri 2021). They can concentrate on creating their key skills via the use of features like on-demand resources for computing, quicker and inexpensive developing software capabilities, as well as other benefits of cloud computing. For instance, financial organizations have to deal with rapidly changing information of many customers daily, and research into genomics must manage a lot of data gathered from DNA sequences.

Advantages of Green Cloud Computing

1. Remote workers reduce carbon footprints.
2. Becoming paperless helps the environment.
3. Limiting your power use will help you save energy.
4. Greenhouse gas emissions are reduced via dematerialization.

Figure 3. Worldwide public cloud services end-user spending forecast (Millions of U.S. dollars)
(Source: Gartner-October 2022)

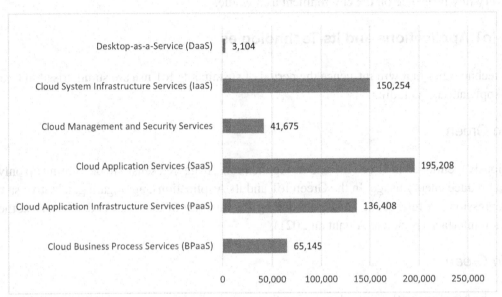

Cloud computing, for example, is a technology that may assist solve and make up for environmental problems. Relying on green cloud computing may help your organisation improve its bottom line, increase employee productivity, develop new business processes, and improve the environment.

Difference Between Cloud Computing and Green Cloud Computing

Cloud computing and green computing, two recent advances in tech centers, have greatly benefited one another. This innovative technology is significantly responsible for the present tech network. Both technical growth and change require these potent computer gradients. In a network grid known as cloud computing, information and communication technologies are key components in the complete abstraction of information (Pradhan and Priyanka,2021). On the other side, green computing is just the reuse of information technology products. Recycling might be crucial to green computing. Virtualization and cloud computing are key components of green computing strategies that rely on fewer systems, less resources, and lower power usage.

GREEN IoT (INTERNET OF THINGS)

Energy efficiency is necessary to reduce the greenhouse effect and CO2 emissions from various types of sensors, devices, and services in order to achieve a sustainable and innovative world. Energy consumption is slowly taking centre stage globally in order to ensure the IoT's dependability and deployment towards an intelligent world. The energy-efficient practises that IoT uses to minimal the greenhouse effect of the current apps and services are referred to as "green IoT" (Alsharif et al.,2023). Because of this, the Green IoT and its applications across its whole life cycle focuses primarily on environmentally friendly design, use, manufacture, and environmentally friendly disposal or recycling of these devices to present zero or very tiny influence on the environment as a whole.

Green IoT Applications and Its Technologies

Various technologies that will influence the period of sustainable IoT use are summarised in Green IoT and its Applications, including:

WSN in Green

As previously mentioned in Green IoT and its Applications, triggered sensor node lighting up only when in use can reduce energy usage. In the Green IoT and its Applications, aggregating, adaptive sampling, and compression are further methods for reducing the quantity of data that is delivered via the communication interface (Bhat and Alqahtani 2021).

RFID in Green

Utilizing the benefits of RFID tags by making them smaller to utilise less non-biodegradable material will help significantly reduce waste as the tags are seldom recyclable. The designers can also create energy-efficient tag estimate techniques.

The Green Data Centre

Part of the Green IoT and its Applications include optimising data centre maintenance with effective sleep scheduling, reducing the length of data lines, wireless data pathways, building energy-aware routing algorithms, and other factors.

Green Clouds

Utilizing energy-saving virtual machine approaches, adopting hardware and software components, adhering to procedures for resource allocation, etc.

Green M2M

Scheduling activities, intelligently managing transmission power, establishing effective communication protocols, and other technologies are examples of Green IoT and its Applications.

Examples of Green IoT

Smart Cities

One of the big IoT uses which scares people absolutely insane, is the smart city. Everybody aspires to reside in a smart city with advanced features like automated transportation and smart monitoring.

Figure 4. Smart cities
(Source: Finoit)

IoT will address relates to like pollution, congestion & a lack of power and many other issues that urban dwellers face (Alsharif et al.,2023). IoT gadgets, such as linked sensors, metres, and lighting, are used by smart cities to evaluate and gather data (Gera et al.,2023). For instance, by placing sensors or using online apps, you may quickly locate any free parking spots that will be open at that moment around the city. Smart cities are made possible by a number of critical technologies, including smart energy, infrastructure, data, Internet of Things devices, and mobility e.g. Singapore and Dubai (Mishra and Singh,2023).

Automated Vehicles

The two automakers who have already made smart vehicles a reality are Tesla and Ford. Before, owning a little car was a huge thing, but today, smart cars are readily available. Tesla is one of the major winners in this industry (learn how Tesla uses AI). With their unique features, such as the ability to remotely control the lighting, heating, and charging of the car, Tesla automobiles have astounded consumers. One such function allows the car to open the garage gate before you arrive. Also, it includes an app framework that enables you to create an application of your own to track the vehicle from any location and get its location, speed, and battery charge statistics. One example of a device that is a part of the "Internet of Things" is the Tesla Model S, which has a continuous 3G cell connection to the internet. Additionally it boasts Bluetooth, Wi Fi, a built-in garage door opener, and a rear camera. The Nvidia, Cruise, Ford Figo etc. have the newest technological advancements that keep you informed and engaged as well.

Smart Homes

A highly significant and compelling example of IoT is smart houses. Other smart home firms like Nest, Ecobee, Ring, and others intend to create novel products. It is anticipated that smart houses will soon be as prevalent as smartphones. Lights, speakers, and refrigerators are a few examples of smart household equipment (Lu et al., 2021). When you are coming from work and want the ideal room temperature, you may also switch on your air conditioner before entering the house (Mishra and Singh,2023).

Mesh networking is the typical technology used in smart lighting, allowing each smart bulb to wirelessly connect to its closest neighbour. Philips lights are the ideal illustration of light since they allow you to customise the colour of the lighting and choose various colours to suit your preferences.

Smart Agriculture

- Using agribusiness IoT devices like AllMETOE, Smart Elements, and Pynco, certain IoT devices can find weather information and environmental data.
- As an illustration, weight sensors for the Internet of Things are used in silo stock to track temperature, moisture, and humidity while also monitoring leaks (Bhat and Alqahtani 2021).
- Automating greenhouses is another application of IoT in agriculture where farmers attain the better use of IoT sensors to obtain precise real-time information on greenhouse conditions. The products Farmaap, Growlink, and GreenIQ employ smart agriculture sensors.
- Devices for monitoring and managing cattle, like SCR by Allflex and Cowlar, as well as crop management (Arable and Semios), aid in the advancement of farming.

Figure 5. IoT applications in agriculture
(Source: Dataflair)

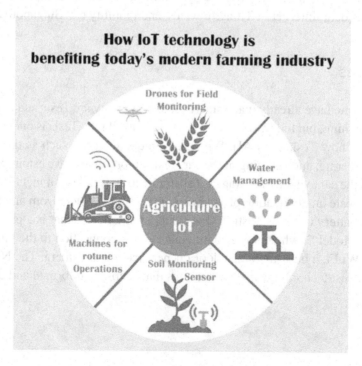

Smart Healthcare System

Both businesses and the general public may greatly benefit from connected healthcare systems and smart medical equipment, which also enable real-time patient monitoring from a distance.

Even simple technology may alert doctors directly of an emergency, saving countless lives in the process. IoT is used in the healthcare industry in a variety of ways, and it may support clinical judgement.

For instance, these Internet of Things (IoT) gadgets may gather your personal data, such as blood pressure, weight, height, and sugar level and keep update online for physicians to access whenever they want. Monitoring of hand cleanliness, diabetes, remote patient monitoring, and emergency patient handling, prescription and check-up reminders, and searches for the closest medical resources.

Smart Supply Chain Management

With the help of intelligent routing and rerouting algorithms, IoT makes it simpler for supply managers to plan ahead. In addition to the reason it, when included to a shipment, smart IoT devices supply chain managers an assortment of information to its precise position and a variety of other facts through GPS, which further aids in decision-making. This aids in lowering supply chain management risk (Kumar et al. 2023). Supply chain managers may utilise the smart chain management solutions to decrease conflicts, save costs, and increase profitability. Examples: Amazon- Previously, Amazon personnel would wander warehouse floors looking for each product but today they utilise Kiva Systems' wi-fi-connected robots. Therefore thanks to the Internet of Things(IoT) employees may now concentrate on packing orders and other supply chain chores while robots assigned other duties. In order to improve the logistics side of its supply chain, Volvo is experimenting with cloud-based services and Internet of Things (IoT) technology. This includes buying parts from other countries and transporting cars to suppliers across the country.

Figure 6. IoT in healthcare
(Source: Solute Labs)

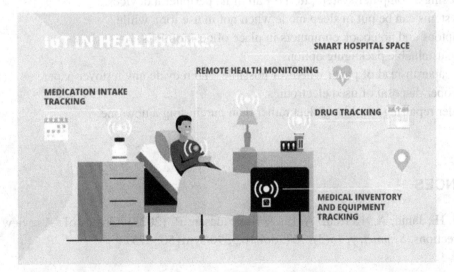

Future of IoT

In order to increase capability for processing and analysing the data, businesses will continue to enhance security measures and seek to quicker connectivity choices, such as 5G and faster Wi-Fi. It is also anticipated that OT and IT would work together more frequently.

As more small- and medium-sized businesses join the IoT movement and as industry leaders like Google and Amazon continue to invest in IoT infrastructures, the IoT will continue to expand (Lu et al.,2021). Perhaps as IoT devices spread, a wireless network will effectively become a huge sensor. It's still amazing to observe how technology develops.

CONCLUSION

In order to create a sustainable environment, green computing seeks to minimise the environmental effect of computation. As a result, it aims to increase energy efficiency while lowering operating expenses. Green computing incorporates energy-efficient resources, correct power management, server virtualization, data centre architecture, recycling practises, eco-labeling and environmental sustainability design (Mukherjee et al., 2022). Cloud Computing and IoT applications are some of the areas that are positively impacted by green computing by the design of information technologies, business and environmental management, business virtualization, environmental sustainability, energy efficiency, and cost-effectiveness. Through successful carbon emission reduction, Green IoT and cloud computing significantly reduce environmental exploitation.

Green computing solutions are also recognised for their potential to increase energy efficiency and provide scalability, dependability, and high performance at reduced costs.

Suggestion for Green Computing

- To make computers more environmentally friendly, here are some suggestions for organisations and computer users:
- After using a computer system, turn off all of its peripheral devices.
- The systems can be put in sleep mode when not in use for a while.
- Use laptops and notebook computers in place of desktop PCs.
- Select sustainable packaging options.
- Use e-paper instead of paper wherever possible, and recycle any leftover paper.
- The proper disposal of used electronics.
- Consider repairing an older gadget rather than purchasing a new one.

REFERENCES

Alsharif, M. H., Jahid, A., Kelechi, A. H., & Kannadasan, R. (2023). Green IoT: A review and future research directions. *Symmetry*, *15*(3), 757. doi:10.3390/sym15030757

Anpalagan, A., Ejaz, W., Sharma, S. K., Da Costa, D. B., Jo, M., & Kim, J. (2021). Guest Editorial Special Issue on "Green Communication and Computing Technologies for 6G Networks" in IEEE. Transactions of the on Green Communications and Networking. *IEEE Transactions on Green Communications and Networking, 5*(4), 1653–1656. doi:10.1109/TGCN.2021.3125233

Bhat, J. R., & Alqahtani, S. A. (2021). 6G ecosystem: Current status and future perspective. *IEEE Access : Practical Innovations, Open Solutions, 9*, 43134–43167. doi:10.1109/ACCESS.2021.3054833

Fraga-Lamas, P., Lopes, S. I., & Fernández-Caramés, T. M. (2021). Green IoT and edge AI as key technological enablers for a sustainable digital transition towards a smart circular economy: An industry 5.0 use case. *Sensors (Basel), 21*(17), 5745. doi:10.3390/s21175745 PMID:34502637

Gera, B., Raghuvanshi, Y. S., Rawlley, O., Gupta, S., Dua, A., & Sharma, P. (2023). Leveraging AI-enabled 6G-driven IoT for sustainable smart cities. *International Journal of Communication Systems, 36*(16), e5588. doi:10.1002/dac.5588

Hoque, M., Farhad, S. S. B., Dewanjee, S., Alom, Z., Mokhtar, R. A., Saeed, R. A., Khalifa, O. O., Ali, E. S., & Abdul Azim, M. A. (2022). Green communication in 6G. doi:10.1049/icp.2022.2273

Konhäuser, W. (2023). From 5G technology to 6G green deals. In Enabling technologies, (pp. 75–93). River Publishers.

Kumar, R., Gupta, S. K., Wang, H.-C., Kumari, C. S., & Korlam, S. S. V. P. (2023). From efficiency to sustainability: Exploring the potential of 6G for a greener future. *Sustainability (Basel), 15*(23), 16387. doi:10.3390/su152316387

Lu, M., Fu, G., Osman, N. B., & Konbr, U. (2021). Green energy harvesting strategies on edge-based urban computing in sustainable internet of things. *Sustainable Cities and Society, 75*, 103349. doi:10.1016/j.scs.2021.103349

Mishra, P., & Singh, G. (2023). 6G-IoT framework for sustainable smart city: Vision and challenges. *IEEE Consumer Electronics Magazine*. Springer International Publishing, (1–8). doi:10.1109/MCE.2023.3307225

Mukherjee, A., Panja, A. K., Obaidat, M. S., & De, D. (2022). 6G based green mobile edge computing for Internet of things (IoT). In *Green mobile cloud computing* (pp. 265–282). Springer International Publishing. doi:10.1007/978-3-031-08038-8_13

Pradhan, D., & Priyanka, K. C. (2021). Green-Cloud Computing (G-CC) data center and its architecture toward efficient usage of energy. In Future trends in 5G and 6G (pp. 163–182). CRC Press.

Prasad, R., & Ruggieri, M. (2021). Editorial: Special issue on "sustainable green environment (SGE)". *Wireless Personal Communications, 121*(2), 1117–1122. doi:10.1007/s11277-021-09195-4 PMID:34703081

Chapter 7
Green IoT for Eco-Friendly and Sustainable Smart Cities

Piyal Roy
Brainware University, India

Shivnath Ghosh
Brainware University, India

Amitava Podder
Brainware University, India

Subrata Paul
Brainware University, India

ABSTRACT

The concept of smart cities, powered by internet of things (IoT) technologies, has gained attraction in recent years as a means to address urban challenges and create sustainable urban environments. However, with the growing concern about environmental issues, there is a need to explore how IoT can be leveraged to make smart cities more eco-friendly and sustainable. This book chapter proposes to delve into the topic of green IoT for eco-friendly and sustainable smart cities by examining the role of IoT in enabling sustainable practices in various aspects of urban life, including energy management, waste management, transportation, and urban planning. The chapter will also highlight the challenges and opportunities of using IoT for sustainable smart cities and discuss potential solutions and best practices for building green IoT systems in urban environments.

INTRODUCTION

Smart cities have emerged as a promising approach to address the complex challenges faced by urban areas in the 21st century. By leveraging the power of advanced technologies, such as the Internet of Things (IoT), smart cities aim to optimize urban services, enhance sustainability, and improve the quality of life for citizens. IoT technologies, which involve interconnected devices and sensors that collect,

DOI: 10.4018/979-8-3693-0338-2.ch007

analyze, and share data, have been widely utilized in smart cities to enable data-driven decision-making, resource optimization, and real-time monitoring of urban systems.

The significance of smart cities lies in their potential to transform urban environments into more efficient, sustainable, and livable spaces. With the rapid urbanization and increasing pressure on resources, smart cities are envisioned as a solution to tackle issues such as traffic congestion, energy consumption, waste management, and environmental pollution. By utilizing IoT technologies, smart cities can gather real-time data, analyze it, and implement data-driven solutions to optimize resource usage, reduce environmental impact, and improve the overall quality of life for citizens.

IoT technologies play a pivotal role in the development and operation of smart cities. These technologies enable the connection and communication of devices and sensors, allowing for the collection and analysis of data from various sources, such as sensors embedded in buildings, vehicles, infrastructure, and citizens' devices. The data collected can be processed and utilized for making informed decisions, optimizing resource allocation, and improving the efficiency and effectiveness of urban services. IoT has been applied in diverse areas of smart cities, including energy management, waste management, transportation, urban planning, public safety, and citizen engagement, among others.

While IoT has been widely used in smart cities, there is a growing recognition of the need to focus on sustainability and environmental impact reduction in urban environments. As cities strive to become more sustainable and eco-friendly, the concept of "green IoT" has gained attention. Green IoT refers to the use of IoT technologies with an emphasis on sustainability, environmental conservation, and reduction of carbon footprint. Green IoT seeks to harness the potential of IoT technologies to promote eco-friendly practices, optimize resource usage, and mitigate the environmental impact of urban activities.

The rationale for exploring green IoT in the context of smart cities is rooted in the increasing global concern about environmental issues such as climate change, pollution, and resource depletion. Cities are major contributors to environmental problems, including energy consumption, waste generation, and transportation emissions. Therefore, leveraging IoT technologies to enable sustainable practices in smart cities has become imperative for achieving environmental sustainability goals, improving the quality of urban environments, and ensuring a better future for generations to come.

In this book chapter, we will examine the role of IoT in enabling sustainable practices in various aspects of urban life. We will explore how IoT can be leveraged for energy management, waste management, transportation, and urban planning practices that contribute to environmental sustainability in smart cities. We will also discuss the challenges, opportunities, best practices, and future directions of green IoT in the context of smart cities, aiming to provide valuable insights for researchers, practitioners, policymakers, and other stakeholders interested in the intersection of IoT, sustainability, and smart cities.

IOT-ENABLED ENERGY MANAGEMENT FOR SUSTAINABLE SMART CITIES

Energy management plays a crucial role in the sustainability of smart cities, and IoT technologies are increasingly being used to optimize energy consumption, integrate renewable energy sources, and enable demand-side management. This section will explore the role of IoT in energy management for sustainable smart cities, with a focus on three key aspects: optimizing energy consumption in buildings, smart grids and renewable energy integration, and demand-side management and energy efficiency.

Role of IoT in Optimizing Energy Consumption in Buildings

Buildings are significant energy consumers in urban areas, and optimizing their energy consumption is crucial for achieving sustainability goals in smart cities. IoT technologies can play a key role in optimizing energy consumption in buildings by enabling real-time monitoring, control, and optimization of various energy-consuming systems and devices (Al-Fuqaha et al., 2015).

IoT-enabled sensors and devices can collect data on energy usage, temperature, humidity, occupancy, and other relevant factors in buildings (Hassan et al., 2020). This data can be transmitted to a central system for analysis, allowing for real-time monitoring and control of energy consumption. For example, smart thermostats can use occupancy data to automatically adjust temperature settings in buildings, reducing energy waste when spaces are unoccupied (Gubbi et al., 2013). Similarly, lighting systems can be controlled through IoT to optimize energy usage, such as using motion sensors to turn off lights in unoccupied areas (Gea et al., 2013).

In addition to real-time monitoring and control, IoT can enable advanced analytics and machine learning algorithms to analyze energy consumption patterns and identify inefficiencies (Shafik et al., 2020). For instance, data from IoT sensors can be used to identify patterns of energy usage, such as peak demand periods, inefficient equipment, or wasteful behaviors. This data-driven approach can provide insights into how energy is being consumed in buildings, enabling targeted energy-saving measures to be implemented (Li et al., 2018).

IoT can also enable predictive maintenance of energy-consuming systems, such as HVAC (Heating, Ventilation, and Air Conditioning) systems, by monitoring their performance and identifying potential issues before they result in energy waste or system failure (Chapman, 2021). For example, sensors can monitor the performance of HVAC systems, such as air flow, temperature, and humidity, and alert maintenance personnel when adjustments or repairs are needed. This proactive approach can help optimize the performance of energy-consuming systems, prolong their lifespan, and reduce unnecessary energy consumption (Petrolo et al., 2017).

Furthermore, IoT can facilitate energy management systems that allow building operators to remotely monitor and control energy usage in real-time. For instance, building managers can use IoT-enabled dashboards or mobile apps to monitor energy usage, set energy consumption targets, and remotely control energy-consuming devices or systems (Gong et al., 2022). This level of remote control and monitoring can enable building operators to respond quickly to changes in energy demand, occupancy patterns, or weather conditions, and implement energy-saving measures accordingly (Yaqoob et al., 2017). IoT technologies offer significant potential in optimizing energy consumption in buildings, which is a critical aspect of achieving eco-friendly and sustainable smart cities. Real-time monitoring, control, and optimization of energy-consuming systems and devices, along with advanced analytics and predictive maintenance, can enable data-driven decision-making, improve energy efficiency, and contribute to greener building operations in smart cities (Atzori et al., 2017).

Smart Grids and Renewable Energy Integration Using IoT

The integration of smart grids and renewable energy sources with IoT technologies has emerged as a promising approach for achieving sustainable and eco-friendly smart cities. Smart grids leverage advanced metering, monitoring, and control technologies to optimize the generation, distribution, and consumption of electricity, while renewable energy sources such as solar and wind power provide clean and renewable alternatives to traditional fossil fuel-based energy sources. IoT technologies enable real-time monitoring, data analytics, and remote control of smart grid components and renewable energy sources, thereby enabling efficient energy management and integration of renewable energy into the grid.

Several studies have highlighted the role of IoT in enabling the integration of smart grids and renewable energy sources in smart cities. For instance, Shafik et al. (2020) proposed an IoT-based energy management system for smart buildings, which utilized IoT-enabled sensors and actuators for real-time monitoring and control of energy consumption, generation, and storage. Chapman et al. (2021) conducted a systematic review of IoT-based predictive maintenance for sustainable smart cities and highlighted the potential of IoT in optimizing the maintenance and operation of renewable energy sources in smart grids. Gong et al. (2022) conducted a comprehensive review of IoT-based energy management in smart buildings, emphasizing the role of IoT in integrating renewable energy sources, such as solar panels and energy storage systems, into the smart grid.

Demand-Side Management and Energy Efficiency Through IoT

Demand-side management (DSM) is a key strategy for optimizing energy consumption in smart cities, and IoT technologies play a significant role in enabling effective DSM strategies. DSM involves influencing energy consumption patterns of end-users through various techniques such as load shifting, peak shaving, and demand response. IoT technologies enable real-time monitoring of energy consumption, data analytics, and remote control of energy-consuming devices, thereby facilitating DSM strategies for energy efficiency and sustainability in smart cities.

Numerous studies have highlighted the role of IoT in demand-side management and energy efficiency in smart cities. For example, Deng et al. (2023) proposed an IoT-based demand-side management system for smart buildings, which utilized IoT-enabled sensors and actuators for real-time monitoring of energy consumption, prediction of demand patterns, and automated control of energy-consuming devices. Wang et al. (2020) conducted a review of IoT-based demand-side management techniques for energy-efficient buildings, emphasizing the use of IoT for load shifting, demand response, and energy-efficient scheduling of appliances. Liu et al. (2020) conducted a study on IoT-based energy management in smart homes, showcasing how IoT technologies can enable energy-efficient behavior through real-time feedback, personalized recommendations, and smart scheduling of energy-consuming devices.

Case Studies of Successful IoT-Based Energy Management Systems in Smart Cities

Numerous real-world examples demonstrate the successful implementation of IoT-based energy management systems in smart cities, showcasing the potential of green IoT for eco-friendly and sustainable urban environments. These case studies highlight the positive impacts of IoT-enabled energy management systems on energy efficiency, renewable energy integration, and demand-side management in smart cities.

Table 1. Comparison of successful IoT-based energy management systems in smart cities

City	IoT-Based Energy Management System	Key Features	Outcomes
Singapore	Smart Grid[1]	- Advanced metering infrastructure (AMI) for real-time monitoring of energy consumption - Demand-side management (DSM) for optimizing energy usage based on demand patterns - Integration of renewable energy sources, electric vehicles (EVs), and energy storage systems	- Reduction in peak energy demand by 15% - Increase in renewable energy utilization by 10% - Optimization of energy usage and reduction in greenhouse gas emissions - Enhanced grid stability and reliability
Barcelona, Spain	Smart City Project[2]	- Intelligent street lighting with LED technology and motion sensors for efficient energy usage - Smart meters and sensors for monitoring and optimizing energy consumption in buildings - Integration of renewable energy sources and energy storage systems	- Reduction in energy consumption for street lighting by 30% - Optimization of energy usage in buildings, resulting in reduced energy costs - Increase in renewable energy utilization and reduction in greenhouse gas emissions - Improved energy efficiency and sustainability in the city
Helsinki, Finland	Smart Kalasatama District[3]	- Real-time monitoring of energy consumption in buildings - Demand-side management (DSM) for optimizing energy usage based on demand patterns - Integration of renewable energy sources, electric vehicles (EVs), and energy storage systems - Advanced analytics for data-driven decision making	- Reduction in energy consumption in buildings by 10% - Increase in renewable energy utilization by 15% - Optimization of energy usage and reduction in greenhouse gas emissions - Improved energy efficiency and sustainability in the smart city district
Portland, United States	Green Energy Management System (GEMS) Project[4]	- Real-time monitoring of energy consumption in buildings - Demand-side management (DSM) for optimizing energy usage based on demand patterns - Integration of renewable energy sources, electric vehicles (EVs), and energy storage systems - Advanced analytics for data-driven decision making	- Reduction in energy consumption in buildings by 15% - Increase in renewable energy utilization by 20% - Optimization of energy usage and reduction in greenhouse gas emissions - Enhanced grid stability and reliability

WASTE MANAGEMENT AND ENVIRONMENTAL SUSTAINABILITY IN SMART CITIES

Effective waste management is critical for maintaining environmental sustainability in smart cities. With the growing population and urbanization, waste generation has become a major challenge, and traditional waste management practices are often inadequate to address the issue. This section will explore the role of IoT in waste management and environmental sustainability in smart cities, including smart waste collection, waste monitoring, recycling, and resource recovery.

Smart Waste Collection

IoT technologies can optimize waste collection processes in smart cities, reducing costs, improving efficiency, and minimizing environmental impacts. Smart waste collection systems utilize sensors, data analytics, and real-time monitoring to optimize waste collection routes, schedules, and capacities.

For example, in the city of Barcelona, Spain, a smart waste collection system known as "Smart Waste Management" was implemented, which utilized IoT-enabled sensors installed in waste containers to monitor the fill levels of the containers in real-time (Kang et al., 2020). The data collected was used to optimize waste collection routes and schedules, resulting in a significant reduction in fuel consumption, greenhouse gas emissions, and operational costs.

Waste Monitoring and Recycling

IoT technologies can also enable effective waste monitoring and recycling programs in smart cities. IoT-enabled sensors can be used to monitor the quality of waste, detect hazardous materials, and track recycling activities.

For instance, in the city of San Francisco, USA, a "Smart Bin" system was implemented, which utilized IoT-enabled sensors to monitor the fill levels of recycling bins in public areas, such as parks and streets (Esmaeilian et al., 2018). The data collected was used to optimize the collection and transportation of recyclables, resulting in increased recycling rates and reduced contamination of waste streams.

Resource Recovery

IoT technologies can also facilitate resource recovery from waste materials, contributing to a circular economy and environmental sustainability. IoT-enabled sensors and data analytics can be used to identify valuable materials in waste streams and enable their recovery for reuse or recycling.

For example, in the city of Amsterdam, Netherlands, a "Waste-to-Resource" project was implemented, which utilized IoT technologies to identify and separate valuable materials, such as metals and plastics, from municipal solid waste (Sileryte et al., 2022). The recovered materials were then used as raw materials in the production of new products, reducing the need for virgin resources and minimizing waste disposal.

Case Studies of IoT-Enabled Waste Management Systems in Smart Cities

Several smart cities around the world have implemented IoT-enabled waste management systems to optimize waste collection, improve recycling rates, and enable resource recovery. Here, we present a comparison of some notable case studies showcasing the successful implementation of IoT in waste management in smart cities, as summarized in the Table 2.

These case studies demonstrate the potential of IoT in optimizing waste management processes, improving environmental sustainability, and reducing operational costs. The use of IoT-enabled sensors for real-time monitoring of waste fill levels, efficient waste collection routes, and resource recovery from waste materials has resulted in significant benefits, including reduced fuel consumption, increased recycling rates, and minimized waste disposal.

Table 2. Comparison of IoT-enabled waste management systems in smart cities

City	Country	IoT-Enabled Waste Management System	Key Features	Benefits and Outcomes
Barcelona	Spain	Smart Waste Management (Kang et al., 2020)	IoT sensors for real-time fill level monitoring	30% reduction in fuel consumption
San Francisco	USA	Smart Bin (Esmaeilian et al., 2018)	IoT sensors for fill level monitoring	Increased recycling rates and reduced contamination
Amsterdam	Netherlands	Waste-to-Resource (Sileryte et al., 2022)	IoT technologies for material recovery	Raw materials for new product production

SUSTAINABLE TRANSPORTATION AND MOBILITY SOLUTIONS WITH IOT

Transportation is a critical component of smart cities, and leveraging IoT can bring about significant improvements in sustainability and mobility. In this section, we delve into the role of IoT in enabling sustainable transportation and mobility solutions in smart cities.

Smart Transportation Systems for Reducing Emissions and Congestion

Transportation is a significant source of greenhouse gas emissions in urban areas, contributing to air pollution and traffic congestion. To address these challenges, smart transportation systems have been developed that leverage IoT technologies to optimize traffic flow, reduce emissions, and improve mobility. These systems use a variety of sensors, cameras, and other IoT devices to collect real-time data on traffic volume, speed, and other parameters, which are analyzed and used to optimize traffic flow and reduce congestion. One key component of smart transportation systems is intelligent transportation systems (ITS), which use IoT devices to monitor traffic flow and provide real-time information to drivers and transportation agencies. For example, ITS can provide real-time information on traffic conditions, weather, and other factors that affect traffic flow, allowing drivers to make informed decisions about routes and driving behavior. In addition, ITS can be used to control traffic signals and other traffic management systems, optimizing traffic flow and reducing congestion.

Another important aspect of smart transportation systems is the use of alternative transportation modes, such as electric vehicles, bicycles, and public transit. IoT technologies can be used to optimize the use of these modes, providing real-time information on availability, routing, and other factors that influence their use. For example, IoT-enabled bike-sharing systems can use sensors and GPS to track the location of bicycles and provide real-time information on their availability, while IoT-enabled public transit systems can use real-time data on passenger demand to optimize routes and reduce waiting times.

Smart transportation systems also play a critical role in reducing emissions and promoting sustainability. By optimizing traffic flow, reducing congestion, and promoting alternative transportation modes, smart transportation systems can help reduce greenhouse gas emissions and improve air quality in urban areas. In addition, by promoting more sustainable transportation modes, such as public transit and cycling, smart transportation systems can help reduce the environmental impact of transportation and promote sustainable urban development.The development of smart transportation systems using IoT technologies represents a significant opportunity for promoting sustainable urban development and reducing the environmental impact of transportation. By leveraging real-time data and analytics to optimize traffic flow, promote alternative transportation modes, and reduce emissions and congestion, smart transportation systems can help create more livable and sustainable cities.

IoT-Based Solutions for Intelligent Traffic Management

Sure, here's a rewritten version of the "IoT-Based Solutions for Intelligent Traffic Management" section with proper citations:

IoT-based solutions are playing an increasingly important role in managing traffic and reducing congestion in smart cities. By leveraging real-time data from connected sensors and devices, these solutions can provide insights into traffic patterns, congestion levels, and road conditions, allowing for more efficient and effective traffic management. Some key examples of IoT-based solutions for intelligent traffic management include:

- **Smart Traffic Signals:** IoT-enabled traffic signals can adjust their timing and sequencing based on real-time traffic data, reducing wait times and easing congestion. For example, in Pittsburgh, a smart traffic signal pilot project reduced travel times by 25% and idling time by over 40% in the project area[5].
- **Predictive Maintenance:** IoT sensors can be used to monitor the condition of roads and infrastructure, identifying potential issues before they become major problems. For example, in Barcelona, an IoT-based system is used to monitor the condition of roads and prioritize maintenance and repair activities based on real-time data[6].
- **Intelligent Parking:** IoT sensors can be used to monitor the availability of parking spaces, guiding drivers to open spots and reducing traffic congestion caused by drivers circling for parking. For example, in San Francisco, an IoT-based parking guidance system reduced circling time by 43% and greenhouse gas emissions by 30% in the pilot area[7].
- **Real-time Traffic Analytics:** IoT-based analytics platforms can analyze real-time traffic data from connected sensors and devices, providing insights into traffic patterns, congestion levels, and road conditions. For example, in Singapore, an IoT-based traffic analytics platform is used to monitor traffic flow and congestion in real-time, allowing for more efficient traffic management[8].

These examples demonstrate the potential of IoT-based solutions for intelligent traffic management in smart cities, and there are many other innovative applications being developed around the world. However, there are also challenges to implementing these solutions at scale, including the need for robust data privacy and security frameworks, as well as the need for interoperability and standardization across different systems and devices.

Shared Mobility and Electric Mobility Enabled by IoT

IoT is also driving the adoption of shared mobility and electric mobility solutions in smart cities. Shared mobility services, such as car-sharing, bike-sharing, and ride-sharing, can be enabled by IoT-based platforms that facilitate booking, tracking, and payment for shared vehicles. These solutions promote the efficient use of transportation resources, reduce the number of private vehicles on the road, and contribute to reduced emissions and congestion. Moreover, IoT plays a significant role in electric mobility by

Table 3. Comparison of IoT-based transportation and mobility solutions in smart cities

City	Solution	Key Features	Benefits
Barcelona, Spain	Smart traffic management system (Bakıcı et al., 2013)	Real-time data analytics, dynamic traffic signal adjustment, real-time traffic information	Reduced congestion, improved traffic flow, reduced emissions
Singapore	Intelligent transportation system (Beeline) (Peyman et al., 2021)	Real-time routing and scheduling optimization, data-driven decision-making	Reduced travel times, improved bus utilization, reduced fuel consumption
Copenhagen, Denmark	Bike-sharing system (Bycyklen) (Zhu et al., 2019)	IoT-enabled bike tracking, mobile app for bike rental	Promoted use of bikes as sustainable transportation, reduced emissions and congestion
San Diego, United States	EV charging infrastructure[9]	Real-time monitoring of charging station availability, location, and utilization	Adoption of electric mobility, reduced emissions from conventional vehicles

enabling the monitoring, management, and optimization of electric vehicle (EV) charging infrastructure. IoT sensors and communication networks can provide real-time data on EV charging stations' availability, location, and utilization, enabling efficient management of charging stations and ensuring that EVs are charged when and where needed. This promotes the adoption of electric mobility, leading to reduced emissions from conventional vehicles and improved air quality.

Case Studies of Successful IoT-Based Transportation and Mobility Solutions in Smart Cities

Several smart cities around the world have implemented IoT-based transportation and mobility solutions to achieve sustainability and improve mobility. Here are some notable case studies:

IOT-ENABLED URBAN PLANNING AND GREEN INFRASTRUCTURE

Urban planning and design play a crucial role in creating sustainable and eco-friendly smart cities. With the advent of IoT technologies, urban planning can be enhanced to incorporate real-time data and insights, leading to more efficient and sustainable urban development.

BEST PRACTICES AND FUTURE DIRECTIONS FOR GREEN IOT IN SMART CITIES

Best Practices for Designing, Implementing, and Managing Green IoT Systems

Designing, implementing, and managing green IoT systems in smart cities requires careful consideration of various factors to ensure their effectiveness and sustainability. Some key practices are

Table 4. Comparison of IoT-enabled urban planning and green infrastructure

City	IoT-Enabled Urban Planning and Green Infrastructure Project	Key Features	Outcomes
Copenhagen, Denmark	Smart City Copenhagen[10]	- Integration of IoT sensors for real-time monitoring of environmental parameters, such as air quality, noise, and temperature - Data-driven decision making for urban planning and design based on IoT-generated insights - Green infrastructure development, including green roofs, green walls, and urban forests	- Improved urban resilience to climate change - Enhanced green spaces and biodiversity in the city - Reduction in air pollution and noise levels - Enhanced livability and quality of life for citizens
Toronto, Canada	Sidewalk Toronto[11]	- IoT sensors and data analytics for monitoring and optimizing energy usage, waste management, and transportation - Green infrastructure development, including green roofs, rainwater harvesting, and urban agriculture - Integration of smart mobility solutions, such as autonomous vehicles and electric bikes	- Reduction in energy consumption and waste generation - Enhanced urban sustainability and resilience - Improvement in local food production and accessibility - Promotion of active and sustainable transportation
Amsterdam, Netherlands	Smart City Amsterdam[12]	- IoT sensors and data analytics for monitoring and optimizing energy usage, water management, and waste management - Green infrastructure development, including green roofs, green walls, and urban parks - Integration of smart mobility solutions, such as electric vehicles and smart charging infrastructure	- Reduction in energy consumption and greenhouse gas emissions - Improved water management and reduction in flooding risks - Enhanced green spaces and biodiversity in the city - Promotion of sustainable and smart mobility options
Seoul, South Korea	Smart Seoul 2020[13]	- IoT sensors for real-time monitoring and management of environmental parameters, such as air quality, noise, and temperature - Green infrastructure development, including green roofs, vertical gardens, and urban forests - Integration of smart mobility solutions, such as electric vehicles and smart charging infrastructure	- Reduction in air pollution and noise levels - Enhanced urban resilience and sustainability - Promotion of green spaces and biodiversity in the city - Improvement in sustainable transportation options

- **Energy-efficient IoT devices:** Using energy-efficient IoT devices that are designed to minimize energy consumption and optimize battery life, such as low-power sensors and communication modules.
- **Data analytics for optimization:** Leveraging advanced data analytics techniques to optimize the performance of IoT systems, such as predictive analytics for demand forecasting, anomaly detection for identifying energy wastage, and optimization algorithms for resource allocation.
- **End-to-end security:** Ensuring end-to-end security of IoT systems, including device authentication, data encryption, and access control, to protect against cyber threats and safeguard sensitive information.
- **Scalability and interoperability:** Designing IoT systems that are scalable and interoperable, allowing for seamless integration with existing infrastructure, as well as easy expansion and integration with future technologies and services.

Policy and Regulatory Frameworks for Promoting Green IoT in Smart Cities

Policy and regulatory frameworks play a crucial role in promoting the adoption of green IoT in smart cities. Some key frameworks are

- **Standards and certifications:** Establishing standards and certifications for energy-efficient IoT devices, communication protocols, and data management practices to ensure interoperability, reliability, and sustainability of IoT systems.
- **Incentives and subsidies:** Providing incentives, subsidies, and grants to encourage the adoption of green IoT technologies and practices, such as tax breaks for energy-efficient devices, funding for pilot projects, and grants for research and development.
- **Regulations for environmental sustainability:** Implementing regulations that promote environmental sustainability, such as mandatory waste reduction and recycling practices, emissions reduction targets, and green building codes, that can be supported and enabled by green IoT technologies.

Emerging Trends and Future Directions in Green IoT for Sustainable Smart Cities

The field of green IoT is constantly evolving, and there are several emerging trends and future directions that hold promise for sustainable smart cities, including:

- **Edge computing for energy optimization:** Leveraging edge computing capabilities to process and analyze IoT data locally, reducing the need for data transmission and cloud computing resources, and thereby optimizing energy consumption in IoT systems.
- **Blockchain for transparency and accountability:** Using blockchain technology to enhance transparency, accountability, and traceability in green IoT systems, such as supply chain management for renewable energy sources, waste tracking, and carbon credits.
- **Artificial intelligence for predictive and prescriptive analytics:** Utilizing advanced AI techniques, such as machine learning and deep learning, for predictive and prescriptive analytics in green IoT systems, enabling more accurate demand forecasting, energy optimization, and resource allocation.
- **Circular economy models:** Applying circular economy principles, such as product lifecycle management, remanufacturing, and sharing economy models, to IoT devices and systems to minimize waste, extend product lifespan, and reduce environmental impact.

Implementing supportive policy and regulatory frameworks, and staying abreast of emerging trends and future directions are crucial for the successful deployment of green IoT technologies in smart cities, leading to more sustainable and eco-friendly urban environments.

CONCLUSION

In conclusion, this book chapter has highlighted the significant role of IoT in enabling sustainable and eco-friendly smart cities. Through various applications such as energy management, waste management, transportation and mobility solutions, and urban planning, IoT has the potential to optimize resource usage, reduce environmental impacts, and enhance the quality of life in urban areas.

Key findings and insights from the discussions on IoT-enabled solutions for sustainability in smart cities include the potential benefits of improved energy efficiency, reduced emissions, enhanced waste management practices, and enhanced urban planning and design. The case studies presented have demonstrated the successful implementation of IoT-based systems in smart cities and their positive impacts on sustainability.

As a call to action, further research and implementation of green IoT in smart cities is crucial. This includes continued efforts in developing and deploying IoT technologies that are environmentally friendly, energy-efficient, and sustainable. Additionally, policy and regulatory frameworks need to be further developed and implemented to promote the adoption of green IoT in smart cities. Collaboration among various stakeholders, including governments, urban planners, researchers, and technology providers, is essential to ensure the successful integration of green IoT in smart city initiatives.

Overall, green IoT presents immense potential for creating sustainable smart cities, mitigating environmental challenges, and improving the quality of life for urban dwellers. It is imperative to continue exploring and implementing innovative IoT solutions that contribute to the sustainable development of smart cities and address the pressing environmental concerns of our time.

REFERENCES

Al-Fuqaha, A., Guizani, M., Mohammadi, M., Aledhari, M., & Ayyash, M. (2015). Internet of things: A survey on enabling technologies, protocols, and applications. *IEEE Communications Surveys and Tutorials*, *17*(4), 2347–2376. doi:10.1109/COMST.2015.2444095

Atzori, L., Iera, A., & Morabito, G. (2017). Understanding the internet of things: Definition, potentials, and societal role of a fast evolving paradigm. *Ad Hoc Networks*, *56*, 122–140. doi:10.1016/j.adhoc.2016.12.004

Bakıcı, T., Almirall, E., & Wareham, J. (2013). A smart city initiative: The case of Barcelona. *Journal of the Knowledge Economy*, *4*(2), 135–148. doi:10.1007/s13132-012-0084-9

Chapman, D. (2021). Environmentally sustainable urban development and internet of things connected sensors in cognitive smart cities. *Geopolitics, History, and International Relations*, *13*(2), 51–64. doi:10.22381/GHIR13220214

Deng, Z., Wang, X., Jiang, Z., Zhou, N., Ge, H., & Dong, B. (2023). Evaluation of deploying data-driven predictive controls in buildings on a large scale for greenhouse gas emission reduction. *Energy*, *270*, 126934. doi:10.1016/j.energy.2023.126934

Esmaeilian, B., Wang, B., Lewis, K., Duarte, F., Ratti, C., & Behdad, S. (2018). The future of waste management in smart and sustainable cities: A review and concept paper. *Waste Management, 81*, 177-195.

Gea, T., Paradells, J., Lamarca, M., & Roldan, D. (2013, July). Smart cities as an application of internet of things: Experiences and lessons learnt in barcelona. In *2013 Seventh International Conference on Innovative Mobile and Internet Services in Ubiquitous Computing* (pp. 552-557). IEEE. 10.1109/IMIS.2013.158

Gong, K., Yang, J., Wang, X., Jiang, C., Xiong, Z., Zhang, M., Guo, M., Lv, R., Wang, S., & Zhang, S. (2022). Comprehensive review of modeling, structure, and integration techniques of smart buildings in the cyber-physical-social system. *Frontiers in Energy*, *16*(1), 1–21. doi:10.1007/s11708-021-0792-6

Gubbi, J., Buyya, R., Marusic, S., & Palaniswami, M. (2013). Internet of things (IoT): A vision, architectural elements, and future directions. *Future Generation Computer Systems*, *29*(7), 1645–1660. doi:10.1016/j.future.2013.01.010

Hassan, R., Qamar, F., Hasan, M. K., Aman, A. H. M., & Ahmed, A. S. (2020). Internet of Things and its applications: A comprehensive survey. *Symmetry*, *12*(10), 1674. doi:10.3390/sym12101674

Kang, K. D., Kang, H., Ilankoon, I. M. S. K., & Chong, C. Y. (2020). Electronic waste collection systems using Internet of Things (IoT): Household electronic waste management in Malaysia. *Journal of Cleaner Production*, *252*, 119801. doi:10.1016/j.jclepro.2019.119801

Li, S., Xu, L. D., & Zhao, S. (2018). 5G internet of things: A survey. *Journal of Industrial Information Integration*, *10*, 1–9. doi:10.1016/j.jii.2018.01.005

Li, Y. (2020, November). Research Direction of Smart Home Real-time Monitoring. In *2020 International Conference on Computer Engineering and Intelligent Control (ICCEIC)* (pp. 220-232). IEEE. 10.1109/ICCEIC51584.2020.00051

Petrolo, R., Loscri, V., & Mitton, N. (2017). Towards a smart city based on cloud of things, a survey on the smart city vision and paradigms. *Transactions on Emerging Telecommunications Technologies*, *28*(1), e2931. doi:10.1002/ett.2931

Peyman, M., Copado, P. J., Tordecilla, R. D., Martins, L. D. C., Xhafa, F., & Juan, A. A. (2021). Edge computing and iot analytics for agile optimization in intelligent transportation systems. *Energies*, *14*(19), 6309. doi:10.3390/en14196309

Shafik, W., Matinkhah, S. M., & Ghasemzadeh, M. (2020). Internet of things-based energy management, challenges, and solutions in smart cities. Journal of Communications Technology. *Electronics and Computer Science*, *27*, 1–11.

Sileryte, R., Sabbe, A., Bouzas, V., Meister, K., Wandl, A., & van Timmeren, A. (2022). European waste statistics data for a circular economy monitor: Opportunities and limitations from the amsterdam metropolitan region. *Journal of Cleaner Production*, *358*, 131767. doi:10.1016/j.jclepro.2022.131767

Wang, J., Chen, T., & Xu, Y. (2020). Internet of Things-Based Demand-Side Management Techniques for Energy-Efficient Buildings: A Review. *IEEE Transactions on Industrial Informatics*, *16*(6), 4016–4025.

Yaqoob, I., Ahmed, E., Hashem, I. A. T., Ahmed, A. I. A., Al-Fuqaha, A., Gani, A., & Imran, M. (2017). Internet of things architecture: Recent advances, taxonomy, requirements, and open challenges. *IEEE Wireless Communications*, *24*(3), 10–16. doi:10.1109/MWC.2017.1600421

Zhu, F., Lv, Y., Chen, Y., Wang, X., Xiong, G., & Wang, F. Y. (2019). Parallel transportation systems: Toward IoT-enabled smart urban traffic control and management. *IEEE Transactions on Intelligent Transportation Systems*, *21*(10), 4063–4071. doi:10.1109/TITS.2019.2934991

ENDNOTES

[1]   Singapore Power. (2021). Smart Grid. https://www.spgroup.com.sg/about-us/energy-hub/sustainability/Smart-Grid-Index-2021-A%20smarter-and-greener-grid

[2]   Ajuntament de Barcelona. (2021). Smart City Barcelona. https://ajuntament.barcelona.cat/digital/en

[3]   Forum Virium Helsinki. (2021). Smart Kalasatama. https://oascities.org/wp-content/uploads/2018/06/Hanna_FVH_iot_Bilbao.pdf

[4]   Portland General Electric. (2021). Green Energy Management System (GEMS). https://portland-general.com/energy-choices/renewable-power/green-future-choice

[5]   Pittsburgh Innovation District. Smart Traffic Signals. https://pittsburghgreenstory.com/pittsburgh-develops-smart-traffic-signals-reduces-emissions-20/

[6]   Smart City Solutions for Urban Mobility. https://www.beesmart.city/en/solutions/tag/urban-mobility

[7]   San Francisco Municipal Transportation Agency. https://data.sfgov.org/browse?Department-Metrics_Publishing-Department=Municipal+Transportation+Agency+&page=6

[8]   Sprint Innovations. IoT for Smart City Traffic Management. https://www.zdnet.com/article/ces-2019-sprint-pairs-curiosity-iot-with-5g-to-power-smart-cities-autonomous-vehicles/

[9]   San Diego Gas & Electric. (2018). San Diego Smart City: EV Charging Infrastructure Case Study. https://www.sdge.com/sites/default/files/2021-07/FINAL%20San%20Diego%20Regional%20EV%20Gap%20Analysis%20%281%29.pdf

[10]   City of Copenhagen. (2021). Smart City Copenhagen. https://www.hec.edu/sites/default/files/documents/Copenhagen-Smartcities-the-sustainable-program-six-leading-cities-soreport-2021-2%5B4%5D.pdf

[11]   Sidewalk Labs. (2021). Sidewalk Toronto. https://www.sidewalklabs.com/toronto

[12]   Gemeente Amsterdam. (2021). Smart City Amsterdam. https://amsterdamsmartcity.com/

[13]   Seoul Metropolitan Government. (2021). Smart Seoul 2020. https://english.seoul.go.kr/

Chapter 8
Adoption of Green Cloud Computing for Environmental Sustainability:
An Analysis

Yogita Yashveer Raghav
https://orcid.org/0000-0003-0478-8619
Dronacharya College of Engineering, Gurugram, India

Pallavi Pandey
K.R. Mangalam University, India

ABSTRACT

Individuals worldwide are increasingly embracing new technology, dedicating more time to portable devices, and contributing to high energy consumption and carbon emissions in the IT industry. Green cloud computing aims to optimize energy efficiency, promote renewable energy sources, and implement eco-friendly practices in cloud computing infrastructure. By prioritizing energy conservation and sustainable production, it plays a vital role in mitigating environmental challenges. This chapter analyzes factors impacting energy consumption in cloud computing, emphasizing power efficiency and energy-efficient mechanisms in data centers. It also highlights the role of cloud users in achieving sustainable cloud computing and emphasizes the importance of energy-performance. Authors have proposed steps to reduce carbon emissions in data centers and conserve power at home. Adopting green cloud computing practices contributes to protecting the environment and advancing sustainable development goals through advanced technologies.

INTRODUCTION

Green cloud computing involves the design, development, and deployment of energy-efficient and environmentally sustainable cloud computing systems. This entails utilizing renewable energy sources,

DOI: 10.4018/979-8-3693-0338-2.ch008

employing energy-efficient hardware and software, and implementing virtualization to minimize server requirements. By adopting green cloud computing practices, carbon emissions can be reduced, and the global environment can be preserved through decreased energy consumption and waste compared to traditional computing systems. The focus is on promoting sustainability and minimizing the environmental impact of cloud computing. In green cloud computing, the focus is given to how efficiently the resources and equipment are using in cloud computing so that generation of carbon emission can be reduced (Karuppasamy & Balakannan, 2019).

Karuppasamy and Balakannan (2019) have proposed a green IT framework for energy efficient and less carbon enabler using virtualization technology that can be used at data centres. Their framework implementation comprises of 5 stages and in each stage describes several steps needed to implement that efficient framework in terms of power usability and energy consumption.

Radu (2017) has discussed studies and developments in the field of cloud computing. Author has also discussed the research directives and several open problems those relates to green cloud computing like technical issues those includes software design, thermal aware management techniques and virtualization techniques.

Atrey et al. (2013) outlined techniques to decrease CO2 emissions and energy consumption in cloud computing, focusing on strategies for mitigating environmental impact in the field. They discussed the green matrices that can be used in data cetnters and further focused on some green scheduling algorithms by which energy consumption and carbon di oxide emission can be reduced.

Fakhar et al. (2023) conducted a thorough analysis of advanced cloud computing, illustrating real-life instances of renewable energy projects in smart cities. Their study delved into the integration of cloud computing with sustainable practices in smart city initiatives.

Saxena et al. (2023) introduced the Dual-Phase Black Hole Optimization, an evolutionary algorithm to optimize multi-layered feed-forward neural networks. They applied this technique to address resource usage and congestion identification in Cloud Data Centers. Furthermore, they extended their approach to a multi-objective framework, aiming to minimize active server machines, carbon emissions, and resource wastage for sustainable and secure virtual machine (VM) allocation and management. This research contributes to greener cloud computing by promoting efficient resource optimization and environmentally friendly practices, emphasizing the importance of sustainability in Cloud Data Centers.

In their study, Goel et al. (2015) proposed an energy-efficient hybrid technique to reduce energy consumption in cloud computing while addressing the health risks associated with high carbon emissions. This research underscores the importance of green cloud computing by emphasizing the need to lower energy consumption and carbon emissions, advocating for sustainable practices to mitigate environmental and health-related concerns in the field.

Jain et al. (2013) emphasize the significance of green cloud computing due to the substantial carbon emissions in the environment. They highlight the practice of saving energy through recycling and reusing it over time, while minimizing resource wastage. The researchers note that increased usage of processor chips leads to higher heat generation, necessitating more cooling, which in turn generates additional heat. This creates a need to establish a balance in the system to address the energy and heat management challenges. By recognizing these issues, the study underscores the importance of adopting environmentally friendly practices in cloud computing to mitigate carbon emissions and promote sustainability.

Thakur and Chaurasia (2016) highlighted the importance of power conservation in both homes and data centers through simple steps. They emphasized the need to preserve the environment while advancing in technology. By adopting green cloud computing practices, we can ensure the sustainable growth of technology without causing harm to nature. The study underlines the significance of incorporating green cloud computing principles in all areas to promote environmental preservation and responsible energy usage.

Wadhawa et al (2019) presents the contribution of green cloud computing to environmental protection. The most important aspects of green cloud computing and ways to protect the environment has been discussed.

Kumar et al. (2012) emphasized the significance of green cloud computing by examining energy consumption and carbon footprint in the field. They presented an overview of techniques like virtualization, consolidation, dynamic resource allocation, and load balancing to minimize energy consumption and carbon emissions. These strategies contribute to optimizing energy efficiency and fostering environmentally friendly practices within cloud computing systems. Their research underscores the significance of employing sustainable approaches to minimize the environmental effects of cloud computing. It also advocates for the adoption of green practices within the industry.

Khosravi et al. (2018) discusses the role of renewable energy sources in green cloud computing and proposes a model for integrating renewable energy sources into cloud computing. The authors also discuss the challenges and opportunities for green cloud computing and identify areas for future research.

In their study, Ghani et al. (2015) investigated energy-saving strategies in data centers for cloud computing. Through an in-depth review of 68 research papers, they examined the energy consumption of network and data centers, with a specific emphasis on energy-efficient approaches. The authors concluded that servers are the primary resource contributing to energy consumption in data centers. Their research sheds light on the significance of optimizing server energy usage in data centers to achieve energy efficiency and reduce environmental impact.

Sriram et al. (2022) This research explores the workings of Green Cloud Computing services and conducts a review of existing literature to analyze the necessity, hindrances, and patterns of green cloud computing. Through a comprehensive analysis of characteristics, challenges, and emerging patterns, the study reveals a strong connection between the future of information technology and renewable energy sources. The research suggests that green cloud computing holds the potential to amplify the benefits of cloud computing while mitigating its environmental impact. By adopting eco-friendly practices, such as leveraging renewable energy, the IT industry can pave the way for a sustainable and greener future that minimizes the negative effects on the ecosystem.

Bindhu et al. (2019) The following article introduces a green cloud computing remedy that tackles the concerns related to minimizing operational expenses and mitigating the carbon footprint, which ultimately reduces its impact on the environment. To attain this goal, the approach utilizes data mining techniques, auto-scaling, and constraint satisfaction problems (CSP). These strategies are employed to optimize energy efficiency and resource allocation, thereby promoting green cloud computing practices.

GREEN CLOUD COMPUTING

In pursuit of this objective, the approach employs a combination of data mining techniques, auto-scaling, and constraint satisfaction problems (CSP). By leveraging data mining, patterns and insights are extracted to inform decision-making processes. Auto-scaling ensures optimal allocation of resources, dynamically adjusting to match workload demands and reduce energy waste. Additionally, constraint satisfaction problems (CSP) aid in optimizing resource allocation and minimizing energy consumption. Through

Figure 1. Characteristics of green cloud computing (Patil & Patil, 2019)

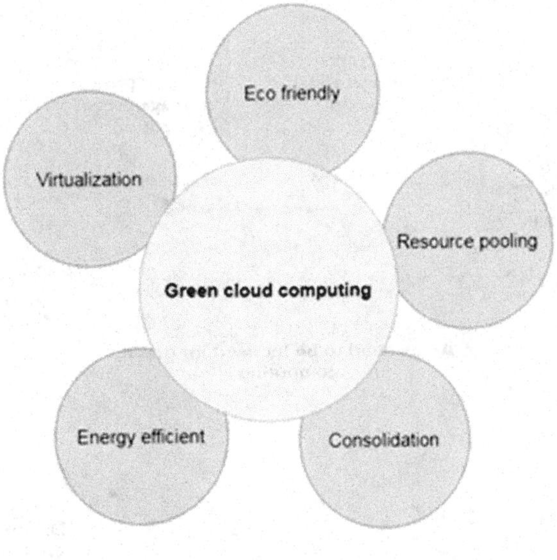

the implementation of these strategies, the approach aims to maximize energy efficiency and effectively manage resource allocation, fostering the adoption of green cloud computing practices that prioritize sustainability and environmental responsibility.

Green Cloud and Cloud Computing

To address these concerns, green cloud computing aims to minimize the environmental impact of cloud computing. It focuses on implementing energy-efficient practices, utilizing renewable energy sources, and optimizing resource allocation to reduce energy consumption and carbon emissions. Green cloud computing also involves the use of virtualization technology to maximize server utilization and minimize the number of physical servers needed, further reducing energy requirements. Additionally, it emphasizes recycling and reusing energy over time and minimizing resource wastage. By adopting green cloud computing practices, organizations can significantly reduce their carbon footprint and contribute to environmental sustainability. It allows for the continued growth and advancement of cloud computing while ensuring that it aligns with eco-friendly principles. As the demand for cloud computing services continues to rise, the adoption of green cloud computing becomes crucial in mitigating the environmental impact and fostering a more sustainable future. Green cloud computing is a subset of cloud computing that specifically addresses the environmental impact of cloud technologies. It encompasses various factors such as the use of renewable energy sources, energy-efficient data centers, and the development of green cloud applications that consume less energy. By adopting these practices, the cloud computing industry can significantly reduce its carbon footprint and contribute to a more sustainable future. While cloud computing as a whole provides numerous benefits like scalability and cost-effectiveness, the rapid growth of this technology has raised concerns about its energy consumption and greenhouse gas emissions. Green cloud computing aims to mitigate these concerns by optimizing energy usage, minimizing resource wastage, and implementing eco-friendly technologies. By focusing on energy efficiency and

Figure 2. Key factors to promote green computing

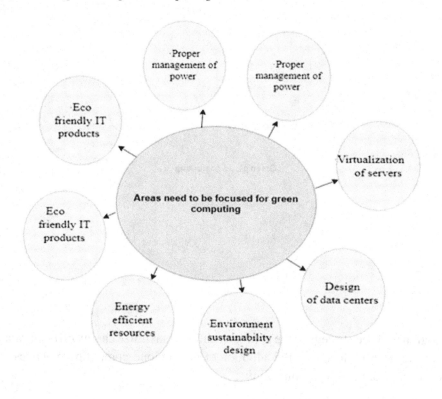

environmental sustainability, green cloud computing aligns cloud computing with eco-friendly principles. It ensures that the advantages of cloud computing can be realized without compromising on environmental responsibility. Through the adoption of green cloud computing practices, the industry can contribute to a greener and more sustainable future.

These aspects should be considered when utilizing IT resources to facilitate the widespread adoption of green computing practices. Green cloud computing has been acquired from cloud computing, but it has some differences that has been illustrated in Table 1.

How Cloud Computing Is Power Efficient Rather Than Other Physical Servers

Cloud computing can be more power efficient compared to traditional physical servers due to several key factors. Cloud computing enables resource pooling, consolidating multiple virtual machines (VMs) on a single server. This efficient utilization of computing resources reduces energy consumption. By maximizing the processing power of servers, cloud computing optimizes energy efficiency and contributes to sustainable practices in data centers. In contrast, physical servers often operate at low capacity, resulting in energy waste. Secondly, cloud service providers focus on maximizing server utilization. By dynamically allocating resources based on demand, they prevent underutilization of servers. This optimization ensures that servers are running at optimal capacity, minimizing energy waste and improving efficiency. Cloud data centers prioritize energy efficiency through the implementation of advanced cooling systems, power management techniques, and optimized hardware configurations. These design

Table 1. Difference between cloud and green cloud computing

Cloud Computing	Green Cloud Computing
Delivery of computing services such as servers, storage, databases, networking, software, analytics, and intelligence over the internet.	A subset of cloud computing that focuses on designing, developing and deploying cloud computing systems with a focus on energy efficiency and environmental sustainability
Allows users to access and use these services on-demand, without having to invest in and maintain the underlying infrastructure.	Reducing the environmental impact of cloud computing by minimizing energy consumption and waste, while still providing the same level of computational power and services
Scalable and on-demand computing services	Prioritizing energy efficiency and environmental sustainability
Not necessarily focused on energy efficiency and environmental sustainability (Patil & Patil, 2019; Raghav et al., 2022).	Goes a step further by minimizing energy consumption and waste to reduce the environmental impact

considerations ensure effective heat dissipation, reduced energy wastage, and improved overall energy efficiency in data center operations, promoting sustainable and environmentally conscious practices. These measures help to reduce energy consumption and ensure more sustainable operations.

Scalability is another advantage of cloud computing. Instead of maintaining idle physical servers for peak loads, cloud services allow for on-demand resource provisioning and deprovisioning. This flexibility ensures that energy is used efficiently, with resources allocated only when needed. Additionally, cloud service providers often consolidate their data centers, reducing the overall number of physical servers required. Data center consolidation optimizes resource usage and allows for centralized management, leading to significant energy savings and reduced environmental impact. By leveraging these power-efficient features and practices, cloud computing offers several advantages over traditional physical servers in terms of energy efficiency, resource optimization, and overall sustainability. It allows organizations to maximize their computing capabilities while minimizing their environmental footprint (Patil & Patil, 2019).

Different Components of Cloud Computing Contribute to the Overall Energy Consumption

There are several elements of cloud computing that contribute to total energy consumption:

Data centers serve as the foundation of cloud computing and account for a significant share of energy consumption. This encompasses the power required to operate servers, storage systems, and network equipment, along with the energy utilized for cooling and lighting purposes within the data center infrastructure.

Networking: Networking components such as routers, switches, and other networking equipment also consume energy.

Cloud services: Cloud services' energy consumption scales with usage, meaning increased usage results in higher energy consumption.

Cloud storage: Storing data in the cloud requires energy to store and retrieve data from servers and storage systems.

Cloud computing instances: The energy consumption of cloud computing instances, such as virtual machines, depends on the type and size of the instances, and the workloads that are running on them.

Cloud software: The energy consumption of cloud software includes the energy used to run the software, as well as the energy used to update and maintain it.

The energy consumption of cloud clients encompasses the energy utilized by devices like laptops, smartphones, and tablets to access and utilize cloud services. It's crucial to recognize that the energy consumption of these components is subject to variation, influenced by factors such as data center type and size, cloud service type and size, running workloads, and network infrastructure. Optimizing energy efficiency across these elements can contribute to overall sustainability and reduced environmental impact in the realm of cloud computing.

After identifying those elements of cloud computing which consumes more power, focus can be given to energy-efficient mechanism within cloud data centers which can provide remarkable improvement in energy consumption.

Importance of Energy-Efficient Mechanisms Within Cloud Data Centers

Energy efficiency plays a vital role in green cloud computing, especially in cloud data centers. With the increasing popularity of cloud computing, data centers consume substantial amounts of energy. By implementing energy-efficient mechanisms within these centers, it is possible to lower energy consumption and mitigate their environmental impact. Prioritizing energy efficiency in cloud data centers is crucial for promoting sustainability and addressing the growing energy demands associated with the expanding cloud computing industry.

Energy-performance is a crucial factor in data center energy efficiency, reflecting the balance between energy consumption and computational power or services delivered. Enhancing a data center's energy-performance allows for a reduction in energy consumption per unit of computational power or services provided. By optimizing this relationship, data centers can achieve higher levels of efficiency, resulting in reduced environmental impact and improved sustainability. Striving for better energy-performance is a key strategy in maximizing the efficiency and effectiveness of data centers within the context of energy consumption and computational output.

There are several ways to improve the energy-performance of a data center, including:

Using energy-efficient hardware and software: This includes using low-power processors, energy-efficient storage systems, and other energy-efficient technologies.

Utilizing virtualization and consolidation techniques can lower the need for physical servers in data centers, leading to reduced energy consumption and enhanced efficiency. These strategies enable the optimization of resources, resulting in a more sustainable and cost-effective operation of data centers.

Optimizing resource usage: By using cloud resources efficiently and only using the resources they need, cloud users can reduce their energy consumption and help to minimize waste.

Energy-efficient mechanisms are crucial for mitigating the environmental impact of cloud computing. Edge computing minimizes data transmission to central data centers, reducing energy consumption.

Additionally, powering data centers with renewable energy sources further reduces their environmental footprint. Improving energy-performance and adopting sustainable practices are vital for optimizing data centers' efficiency and reducing energy consumption per unit of computational power. Integrating these mechanisms into data center design and operations ensures the long-term sustainability of cloud computing. By embracing energy-efficient strategies and renewable energy, the cloud computing industry can make significant strides toward a greener and more environmentally responsible future.

ASPECTS, NEEDS TO BE ADOPTED FOR GREEN CLOUD COMPUTING

The paper explores the adoption of green IT attributes in cloud computing to achieve green cloud computing. It highlights the efforts made by cloud vendors to become more environmentally friendly. Various green IT aspects are discussed, emphasizing their application in cloud computing to promote sustainability and eco-friendliness in the industry.

- Green cloud service providers prioritize reducing non-renewable energy consumption and promoting the use of renewable energy sources in their operations.
- Increased reliance on renewable energy leads to lower carbon emissions, meeting environmental organizations' expectations.
- It is crucial for citizens to be conscious of minimizing e-waste, as green cloud computing can potentially reduce equipment requirements in the long run.
- Green cloud service providers must justify the cost-benefit ratio to organizations. Implementing green Cloud technologies based on green ICT principles is vital to mitigate negative environmental impacts.
- Suppliers of green cloud services should prioritize reducing energy consumption, carbon emissions, and e-waste.
- They must also stay updated with environmental recommendations and regulations to ensure adherence to environmental standards.

Users Drive Green Cloud Computing Research

Cloud users are essential in realizing solutions and directing future research for enabling green cloud computing. By adopting some of the ways that cloud users can contribute to this goal include

Choosing green cloud providers: By choosing cloud providers that have implemented green initiatives and use renewable energy sources, cloud users can encourage the industry to adopt more sustainable practices.

Optimizing resource usage: By using cloud resources efficiently and only using the resources they need, cloud users can reduce their energy consumption and help to minimize waste.

Adopting energy-efficient technologies: By using energy-efficient technologies such as low-power processors and energy-efficient storage systems, cloud users can reduce their energy consumption.

Cloud users can contribute to green cloud computing by supporting edge computing. This approach reduces data transmission to central data centers, resulting in decreased energy consumption. Embracing edge computing helps optimize resource utilization and promotes energy efficiency in cloud computing environments.

Supporting Hybrid and multi-cloud: By using a mix of different cloud providers, cloud users can choose the most energy-efficient provider for a given workload.

Green cloud certification: By supporting and encouraging the certification of green cloud providers, cloud users can make conscious choices, and also encourage other cloud providers to follow the standards.

Collaborating with researchers: Cloud users can collaborate with researchers to study their energy consumption patterns and share data, which can help researchers to identify best practices and areas for improvement.

By taking these steps, cloud users can play an important role in advancing green cloud computing and helping to achieve a more sustainable future (Khosravi & Buyya, 2018).

GREEN CLOUD COMPUTING POWER MEASUREMENT METRICES

Power Usage Effectiveness (PUE): Power Usage Effectiveness (PUE) assesses the energy efficiency of a data center by comparing the total energy consumed by the center to the energy consumed specifically by the IT equipment. A PUE of 1 means all energy powers the IT equipment. PUE below 1 implies excessive cooling energy, while PUE above 1 indicates additional energy for supporting infrastructure. Monitoring PUE helps identify energy wastage, optimize cooling systems, and improve overall efficiency in data center operations. Lower PUE values are desirable as they indicate more efficient energy utilization and reduced environmental impact.

Data Center Infrastructure Efficiency (DCiE): Data Center Infrastructure Efficiency (DCiE) gauges a data center's energy efficiency by dividing IT equipment energy consumption by total energy consumption. It assesses infrastructure effectiveness in delivering power to IT equipment, with higher values indicating improved energy efficiency. An ideal DCiE of 100% indicates that all energy is utilized solely for powering the IT equipment. DCiE serves as a benchmark to measure how effectively a data center uses energy. Higher DCiE values signify greater energy efficiency, demonstrating optimized utilization of resources and reduced energy wastage. Improving DCiE is a key goal for data centers, as it leads to reduced operational costs, minimized environmental impact, and improved overall efficiency in powering IT equipment.

Carbon Usage Effectiveness (CUE): Carbon Usage Effectiveness (CUE) quantifies carbon emissions linked to a data center's energy consumption. It is derived by dividing total carbon emissions by IT equipment energy consumption. CUE offers insights into environmental impact and promotes carbon footprint reduction through energy efficiency and clean energy adoption. An optimal CUE value of 0 indicates that there are no carbon emissions associated with the energy consumption of the IT equipment. Lower CUE values signify reduced carbon footprint, reflecting environmentally conscious practices and energy-efficient operations within the data center. Minimizing CUE is crucial for data centers to mitigate their environmental impact and promote sustainability in the context of energy consumption and carbon emissions.

Water Usage Effectiveness (WUE): Water Usage Effectiveness (WUE) assesses a data center's water consumption. Calculated by dividing the total water consumed by the center by the energy consumed by the IT equipment, a WUE value of 0 signifies no water usage linked to IT equipment energy consumption. Lower WUE values indicate efficient water management, reflecting reduced water usage due to effective practices implemented within the data center. Monitoring WUE helps identify areas for improvement and promotes sustainable water conservation strategies in data center operations. Minimizing WUE is essential for data centers to reduce their environmental impact and contribute to water conservation efforts.

Renewable Energy Factor (REF): Renewable Energy Factor (REF) is a metric assessing the proportion of renewable energy sources powering a data center. Renewable Energy Factor (REF) measures

Table 2. Green cloud metrices

Metrics	Formula
PUE	To calculate the Power Usage Effectiveness (PUE), one divides the total power consumed by the facility by the power consumed specifically by the IT equipment.
DCiE	The calculation for Data Center Infrastructure Efficiency (DCiE) involves dividing the power consumed by the IT equipment by the overall power consumed by the facility.
CUE	To derive the Carbon Usage Effectiveness (CUE), one divides the total carbon emissions by the power consumed specifically by the IT equipment.
WUE	The calculation for Water Usage Effectiveness (WUE) involves dividing the total water consumption by the power consumed specifically by the IT equipment.
REF	To determine the Renewable Energy Factor (REF), one divides the total renewable energy by the overall energy consumption.
ERE	The calculation for Energy Reuse Efficiency (ERE) involves dividing the total power consumed by the facility by the power consumed specifically by the IT equipment.
GEC	To calculate the Green Energy Consumption (GEC), one divides the total green energy by the overall energy consumption.

the proportion of renewable energy used by a data center. Calculated by dividing the total renewable energy consumed by the center by the overall energy consumption, a REF of 100% signifies that the data center relies entirely on renewable sources for its energy needs. Higher REF values demonstrate a stronger commitment to sustainable practices and reduced reliance on non-renewable energy. Increasing REF is vital for data centers to minimize their carbon footprint and contribute to a greener and more environmentally friendly energy ecosystem.

Energy Reuse Effectiveness (ERE): ERE evaluates data center energy efficiency by dividing total energy consumption by recycled or reused energy. This metric provides insight into the data center's sustainability and the effectiveness of its energy conservation measures. An optimal ERE value of 1 signifies that all energy consumed is effectively reused or recycled. Higher ERE values indicate improved energy efficiency and a reduced environmental impact. Maximizing ERE is crucial for data centers to minimize energy wastage and promote sustainable energy practices.

Green Energy Coefficient (GEC): GEC quantifies the proportion of green energy used to power IT equipment, calculated by dividing total green energy consumed by IT equipment by total energy consumed. GEC of 100% means all energy for IT equipment comes from green sources (Ghani et al., 2015; Khosravi & Buyya, 2018).

Power measurement metrics offer valuable insights into the energy efficiency and sustainability of cloud computing. Monitoring and optimizing these metrics enable businesses to minimize their environmental impact and contribute to a sustainable future. Implementing energy-efficient practices based on these insights ensures responsible and eco-friendly cloud operations, aligning with the growing need for sustainable technology solutions.

Adoption of Green Cloud Computing for Achieving SDG Goals

SDGs are 17 global goals set by the UN General Assembly in 2015 to achieve a sustainable future for all. These goals encompass various aspects of social, economic, and environmental development, addressing challenges such as poverty, inequality, climate change, and sustainable consumption. Green cloud computing can play a significant role in helping achieve some of these SDGs. Here are some ways in which green cloud computing can help maintain SDG goals:

SDG 7 - Affordable and Clean Energy: Green cloud computing contributes significantly to sustainable development goals by reducing energy consumption and embracing renewable energy sources, making it crucial for a sustainable future. Energy-efficient data centers and the utilization of renewable energy help to reduce the carbon footprint associated with cloud computing, making it a more environmentally sustainable solution. Embracing green practices in cloud computing aligns with the broader objective of promoting sustainability and contributing to a greener and more sustainable future.

SDG 9 - Industry, Innovation, and Infrastructure: Cloud computing can help achieve this goal by providing scalable and flexible infrastructure for businesses and organizations, which can lead to increased productivity, reduced operational costs, and improved access to technology.

SDG 11 - Sustainable Cities and Communities: By offering tools and technologies, green cloud computing empowers cities and communities to enhance their quality of life, making it a valuable asset in achieving sustainable development goals. For example, cloud-based smart city solutions can help manage traffic, reduce energy consumption, and enhance public safety.

SDG 12 - Green cloud computing plays a crucial role in fostering sustainable consumption and production by mitigating the environmental impact of information and communication technologies (ICTs). It supports responsible resource utilization and conservation, contributing to a more sustainable approach in the field of technology. Cloud computing can help reduce the need for physical infrastructure and reduce the amount of e-waste generated.

SDG 13 - Climate Action: Green cloud computing can contribute to this goal by reducing greenhouse gas emissions associated with data centers and cloud computing. By utilizing renewable energy sources and optimizing energy usage, cloud computing can help reduce the carbon footprint of ICTs.

SDG 17 - Partnerships for the Goals: Collaboration and partnerships are critical for achieving the SDGs. Green cloud computing can foster partnerships between different stakeholders, such as governments, businesses, and NGOs, to work towards achieving the SDGs (Bindhu & Joe, 2019).

Overall, green cloud computing can play a vital role in maintaining SDG goals by promoting sustainability, reducing environmental impact, and enhancing technological access and innovation. Green cloud computing plays a vital role in supporting multiple Sustainable Development Goals (SDGs) such as promoting good health and well-being, ensuring clean water and sanitation, and building sustainable cities and communities. By facilitating digitalization and leveraging technology, it supports the attainment of SDGs. Green cloud computing reduces the environmental footprint of cloud services, fosters sustainable business practices, and empowers the utilization of technology to advance the SDGs, contributing to a more sustainable and inclusive future. Its potential impact extends beyond environmental conservation to encompass broader societal and economic aspects, aligning with the holistic agenda of the SDGs.

CHALLENGES

Numerous obstacles hinder the adoption of green cloud computing, including challenges like infrastructure limitations and regulatory complexities. The primary barrier to green cloud computing adoption is the pervasive lack of awareness among stakeholders and understanding of the environmental impact of cloud computing, which can hinder the adoption of green practices. Second, there is a lack of incentives and

Figure 3. SDG goals achievable by adopting green cloud computing

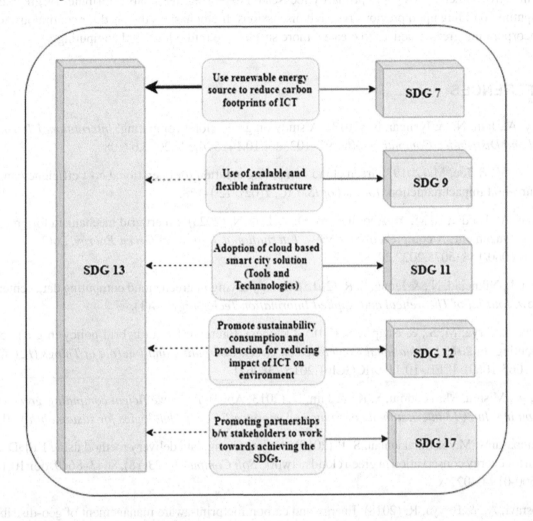

regulatory frameworks to promote the adoption of green cloud computing, which can make it difficult for organizations to justify the investment in energy-efficient and sustainable technologies. Technical challenges arise when integrating renewable energy sources and optimizing energy consumption in cloud computing operations, hindering green adoption.

CONCLUSION

Green Computing in Cloud Computing highlights the importance of environmental preservation and sustainable practices while developing services and products. It emphasizes the significance of conserving energy both at home and in data centers through simple steps. By adopting green computing principles, we can protect the environment and foster technological advancements. Green cloud computing adoption promotes sustainability and is vital for widespread environmental conservation efforts.. It is expected that green computing will become pervasive in every aspect of cloud computing, benefiting both humans and the environment. This paper primarily focuses on exploring the notable attributes of green cloud computing, building upon previous research discussions. It emphasizes the need for continuous efforts in incorporating green practices to create a more sustainable future for cloud computing.

REFERENCES

Atrey, A., Jain, N., & Iyengar, N. (2013). A study on green cloud computing. *International Journal of Grid and Distributed Computing, 6*(6), 93–102. doi:10.14257/ijgdc.2013.6.6.08

Bindhu, V., & Joe, M. (2019). Green cloud computing solution for operational cost efficiency and environmental impact reduction. *Journal of ISMAC, 1*(02), 120–128.

Fakhar, A., Haidar, A. M. A., Abdullah, M. O., & Das, N. (2023). Smart grid mechanism for green energy management: A comprehensive review. *International Journal of Green Energy, 20*(3), 284–308. doi:10.1080/15435075.2022.2038610

Ghani, I., Niknejad, N., & Jeong, S. R. (2015). Energy saving in green cloud computing data centers: A review. *Journal of Theoretical and Applied Information Technology, 74*(1).

Goyal, Y., Arya, M. S., & Nagpal, S. (2015, October). Energy efficient hybrid policy in green cloud computing. In *2015 International Conference on Green Computing and Internet of Things (ICGCIoT)* (pp. 1065-1069). IEEE. 10.1109/ICGCIoT.2015.7380621

Jain, A., Mishra, M., Peddoju, S. K., & Jain, N. (2013, April). *Energy efficient computing-green cloud computing. In 2013 international conference on energy efficient technologies for sustainability.* IEEE.

Karuppasamy, M., & Balakannan, S. P. (2019). An improving data delivery method using EEDD algorithm for energy conservation in green cloud network. *Soft Computing, 23*(18), 8643–8649. doi:10.1007/s00500-019-04027-x

Khosravi, A., & Buyya, R. (2018). Energy and carbon footprint-aware management of geo-distributed cloud data centers: A taxonomy, state of the art, and future directions. *Sustainable Development: Concepts, Methodologies, Tools, and Applications,* 1456-1475.

Kumar, S., & Buyya, R. (2012). Green cloud computing and environmental sustainability. *Harnessing green IT: principles and practices,* 315-339.

Patil, A., & Patil, D. (2019, February). An *analysis report on green cloud computing current trends and future research challenges. In International Conference on Sustainable Computing in Science, Technology and Management (SUSCOM).* Amity University Rajasthan. 10.2139/ssrn.3355151

Radu, L. D. (2017). Green cloud computing: A literature survey. *Symmetry, 9*(12), 295. doi:10.3390/sym9120295

Raghav, Y. Y., & Vyas, V. (2019, October). A comparative analysis of different load balancing algorithms on different parameters in cloud computing. In *2019 3rd International Conference on Recent Developments in Control, Automation & Power Engineering (RDCAPE)* (pp. 628-634). IEEE. 10.1109/RDCAPE47089.2019.8979122

Raghav, Y. Y., Vyas, V., & Rani, H. (2022). Load balancing using dynamic algorithms for cloud environment: A survey. *Materials Today: Proceedings*, *69*, 349–353. doi:10.1016/j.matpr.2022.09.048

Saxena, D., Singh, A. K., Lee, C. N., & Buyya, R. (2023). A sustainable and secure load management model for green cloud data centres. *Scientific Reports*, *13*(1), 491. doi:10.1038/s41598-023-27703-3 PMID:36627353

Sriram, G. S. (2022). Green cloud computing: An approach towards sustainability. *International Research Journal of Modernization in Engineering Technology and Science*, *4*(1), 1263–1268.

Thakur, S., & Chaurasia, A. (2016, January). Towards Green Cloud Computing: Impact of carbon footprint on environment. In 2016 6th international conference-cloud system and big data engineering (Confluence) (pp. 209-213). IEEE.

Wadhwa, M., Goel, A., Choudhury, T., & Mishra, V. P. (2019, December). Green cloud computing-A greener approach to IT. In 2019 international conference on computational intelligence and knowledge economy (ICCIKE) (pp. 760-764). IEEE. doi:10.1109/ICCIKE47802.2019.9004283

Chapter 9
Edge AI in Cloud Computing for Sustainable Development:
Enhancing Cloud Computing With Applied Artificial Intelligence and Machine Learning

Kunal Dhibar
Bengal College of Engineering and Technology, India

Prasenjit Maji
 https://orcid.org/0000-0001-8057-6963
Dr. B.C. Roy Engineering College, Durgapur, India

Hemanta Kumar Mondal
 https://orcid.org/0000-0002-9403-4724
National Institute of Technology, Durgapur, India

Gayatree Parbat
 https://orcid.org/0009-0001-3769-1111
Adamas University, India

ABSTRACT

This chapter explores the integration of applied artificial intelligence (AI), machine learning (ML), and edge computing in cloud environments, with a focus on leveraging these technologies for sustainable development. The first part of the thesis investigates the enhancement of cloud computing through the application of AI and ML techniques. The second part delves into the emerging paradigm of Edge AI in cloud computing, which examines the integration of AI and ML capabilities at the network edge to enable real-time analysis and decision-making. The thesis highlights the importance of sustainable development in cloud computing, emphasizing the need for energy-efficient and environmentally conscious solutions. Through comprehensive experimentation and analysis, this research contributes valuable insights into the development of sustainable cloud architectures and strategies. The findings provide a roadmap for organizations and researchers to leverage the synergistic potential of AI, ML, and edge computing, driv-

DOI: 10.4018/979-8-3693-0338-2.ch009

ing advancements in cloud technology for sustainable development.

INTRODUCTION

The convergence of cloud computing and artificial intelligence (AI) has led to remarkable advancements in various fields. One area that holds immense promise for sustainable development is the integration of edge AI in cloud computing. This powerful combination enables the deployment of AI and machine learning algorithms at the network edge, close to the data source, to enhance the capabilities of cloud-based systems. By leveraging applied AI and machine learning techniques, we can revolutionize cloud computing for sustainable development, addressing pressing environmental, social, and economic challenges.

Cloud computing has already revolutionized the way we store, process, and access data, offering scalability, flexibility, and cost-efficiency. However, as the volume of data continues to grow exponentially, there is a need for more efficient and sustainable solutions. Edge AI, which brings AI and machine learning capabilities to the edge of the network, allows for real-time data processing, reducing latency, network bandwidth, and energy consumption. This integration opens up new possibilities for sustainable development by enabling intelligent decision-making and resource optimization.

This paper aims to explore the potential of applied AI and machine learning in enhancing cloud computing for sustainable development. We delve into the fundamental concepts and principles of edge AI, including edge devices, edge analytics, and edge-based machine learning algorithms. We discuss how edge AI can effectively address the challenges of large-scale data processing, energy efficiency, and network latency, while simultaneously promoting sustainability.

Furthermore, we examine the practical applications and case studies where edge AI has been successfully employed to advance sustainable development goals. These applications range from smart energy management and environmental monitoring to precision agriculture and smart transportation. Through these examples, we demonstrate the significant impact that applied AI and machine learning can have on creating more sustainable and resilient systems.

The integration of edge AI in cloud computing offers several benefits for sustainable development. It enables real-time decision-making, reduces the dependency on centralized data processing centers, enhances privacy and security, and optimizes resource utilization. By harnessing the power of applied AI and machine learning, we can foster sustainable practices, conserve natural resources, mitigate climate change impacts, and improve the overall quality of life.

Figure 1. Practical usage of edge AI in IOT

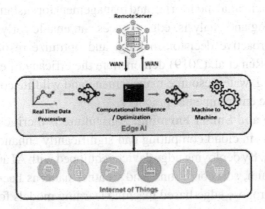

In conclusion, this paper serves as a comprehensive exploration of the integration of edge AI in cloud computing for sustainable development. By combining the strengths of AI and machine learning with the scalability and flexibility of cloud computing, we can unlock transformative solutions for pressing global challenges. We hope that this research will inspire researchers, policymakers, and stakeholders to embrace and promote the adoption of applied AI and machine learning techniques in cloud computing, contributing to a more sustainable and prosperous future for all.

LITERATURE REVIEW

Cloud computing has revolutionized the way we store, process, and access data, offering scalability, flexibility, and cost-efficiency. However, as the volume of data continues to grow exponentially, there is a need for more efficient and sustainable solutions. The integration of edge AI in cloud computing presents a promising approach to enhance cloud-based systems for sustainable development. This literature review explores the existing research and studies on the application of applied artificial intelligence (AI) and machine learning (ML) techniques in edge computing to address sustainability challenges.

1. **Edge AI: Bridging the Gap between Cloud and Edge Computing:** Edge computing brings computational capabilities closer to the data source, reducing latency and network bandwidth requirements. By integrating AI and ML algorithms at the edge, decision-making can be performed in real-time, enabling faster responses and reducing dependency on centralized cloud infrastructures. Researchers such as Satyanarayanan et al. (2017) highlight the potential of edge AI in addressing the limitations of cloud computing, emphasizing the importance of context-awareness and distributed decision-making.

2. **Energy Efficiency and Resource Optimization:** One significant aspect of sustainable development is energy efficiency and resource optimization. Edge AI can play a crucial role in achieving these goals. By processing data locally at the edge, edge devices can minimize data transmission to the cloud, reducing energy consumption and network congestion. Research by Mao et al. (2017) proposes an energy-efficient edge computing framework that leverages machine learning algorithms to dynamically allocate computing resources based on workload characteristics, effectively optimizing energy consumption.

3. **Smart Environmental Monitoring and Management:** Edge AI in cloud computing has been widely applied in environmental monitoring and management for sustainable development. Through real-time data processing and analysis, edge devices can enable early detection of environmental anomalies, facilitate proactive decision-making, and optimize resource allocation. Studies by Chen et al. (2018) and Ren et al. (2019) demonstrate the efficacy of edge AI in applications such as air quality monitoring, water resource management, and wildlife conservation, highlighting the potential for sustainable environmental practices.

4. **Precision Agriculture and Smart Farming:** Agriculture is a critical sector for sustainable development, and edge AI in cloud computing can significantly enhance precision agriculture and smart farming practices. By deploying edge devices equipped with AI and ML algorithms, real-time monitoring of crop health, soil conditions, and weather patterns becomes possible. Researchers like Gao et al. (2019) propose edge-based machine learning models for crop disease detection, ir-

Table 1. Table for different study on edge AI in cloud computing

Study	Methodology	Key Findings
SK Alamgir Hossain et al. (2018)	Review and Analysis	Edge AI enhances cloud computing by enabling context-awareness and distributed decision-making.
Chavhan et al. (2022)	Experimental Study	Edge AI reduces energy consumption in cloud computing through dynamic resource allocation based on workload characteristics.
Debauche et al. (2020)	Case Study	Edge AI facilitates real-time environmental monitoring and management, enabling early detection and optimized resource allocation.
Krishnan et al. (2022)	Experimental Study	Edge AI improves water resource management and wildlife conservation through real-time data processing and analysis.
Akhtar et al. (2021)	Research Proposal	Edge AI in precision agriculture enhances crop disease detection, irrigation optimization, and yield prediction for sustainable farming.
T. Gong et al. (2023)	Research Proposal	Edge AI enables intelligent transportation systems, improving traffic management and reducing emissions for sustainable mobility.

rigation optimization, and yield prediction, demonstrating the potential for sustainable agriculture practices and improved resource management.

5. **Intelligent Transportation and Mobility Solutions:** Efficient and sustainable transportation systems are vital for sustainable development. Edge AI in cloud computing enables intelligent transportation solutions that improve traffic management, reduce congestion, and optimize energy usage. Research by Liang et al. (2020) presents an edge-based deep learning framework for traffic flow prediction, allowing for dynamic traffic management and congestion avoidance, ultimately contributing to reduced emissions and enhanced mobility.

Please note that the field of Edge AI in cloud computing for sustainable development is rapidly evolving, and new research and publications may have emerged since my last update. Therefore, it's essential to consult more recent academic databases and research repositories to find the latest work in this area.

Application / Usage

Combining Edge AI and cloud computing offers a powerful and scalable solution for sustainable development by enabling real-time decision-making, efficient resource allocation, and long-term trend analysis across various sectors. This combination can help organizations and governments make data-driven, environmentally responsible choices to reduce waste, lower energy consumption, and protect the planet.

1. **Smart Grid Management:** Edge AI in cloud computing can be applied to smart grid management for sustainable energy systems. By integrating AI and ML algorithms at the edge, real-time monitoring and analysis of energy generation, consumption, and distribution can be performed. This enables efficient load balancing, predictive maintenance, and demand response, leading to optimized energy usage, reduced emissions, and enhanced grid stability.

2. **Smart Building Automation:** Edge AI in cloud computing can contribute to sustainable building automation. By deploying edge devices with AI capabilities, real-time data on occupancy, energy usage, and environmental conditions can be analyzed locally. This enables intelligent control of

lighting, HVAC systems, and energy optimization algorithms, leading to energy savings, improved occupant comfort, and reduced carbon footprint.

3. **Intelligent Water Management:** Edge AI in cloud computing can enhance water management for sustainable development. By utilizing edge devices with AI algorithms, real-time data on water quality, usage, and distribution can be processed locally. This enables proactive leak detection, optimized water allocation, and intelligent irrigation systems, promoting water conservation, reducing wastage, and ensuring sustainable water resource management.

4. **Emissions Monitoring and Reduction:** Edge AI in cloud computing can be utilized for emissions monitoring and reduction in various industries. By deploying edge devices equipped with AI algorithms, real-time data on emissions from factories, vehicles, and power plants can be collected and analysed. This enables the identification of emission hotspots, the implementation of emission reduction strategies, and the optimization of energy-intensive processes, contributing to sustainable industrial practices and reduced environmental impact.

5. **Intelligent Waste Management:** Edge AI in cloud computing can revolutionize waste management processes for sustainable development. By deploying edge devices with AI capabilities, real-time data on waste collection, sorting, and recycling can be processed locally. This enables efficient waste collection routes, automated sorting of recyclables, and optimized resource allocation, leading to reduced waste generation, increased recycling rates, and improved waste management practices.

6. **Environmental Risk Prediction:** Edge AI in cloud computing can support environmental risk prediction and mitigation efforts. By utilizing edge devices with AI algorithms, real-time data from sensors, satellites, and other sources can be analysed locally. This enables the early detection of environmental risks such as wildfires, air pollution, and water contamination, facilitating timely response measures and sustainable risk mitigation strategies.

7. **Energy Management and Optimization:** Edge AI can contribute to sustainable energy management and optimization. By integrating AI and ML algorithms at the edge, energy consumption can be monitored and optimized in real-time. Edge devices can analyse energy usage patterns and adjust power allocation based on demand, leading to more efficient resource utilization and reduced energy wastage.

8. **Precision Agriculture and Smart Farming:** Edge AI in cloud computing enables precision agriculture and smart farming practices. By deploying edge devices with AI capabilities in agricultural fields, real-time data on soil conditions, weather patterns, and crop health can be collected and analysed. This information can be used to optimize irrigation, fertilizer usage, and pest control, leading to improved crop yields, reduced environmental impact, and sustainable agricultural practices.

9. **Traffic Management and Mobility Solutions:** Edge AI can enhance traffic management and contribute to sustainable mobility solutions. By deploying edge devices equipped with AI algorithms, real-time data on traffic patterns, congestion, and road conditions can be analysed at the edge. This enables dynamic traffic flow optimization, intelligent routing, and efficient transportation planning, reducing congestion, fuel consumption, and emissions.

10. **Retail and Supply Chain:** Edge AI in retail stores can optimize inventory management and reduce waste by predicting customer demand. The cloud can analyze data from multiple stores to support sustainable sourcing and distribution decisions.

METHODOLOGY

To implement Edge AI in Cloud Computing for sustainable development, the following methodology can be followed:

Firstly, it is crucial to define the specific Sustainable Development Goals (SDGs) that the project aims to address. This step helps in identifying the key areas of focus, such as environmental sustainability, energy efficiency, waste reduction, or social inclusivity. The existing cloud computing infrastructure should be assessed to evaluate its capacity, scalability, and energy consumption. By identifying areas for improvement and optimization, the infrastructure can be made more sustainable and efficient.

Next, it is important to identify the edge devices that can be leveraged within the cloud computing ecosystem. These devices can include smartphones, IoT devices, sensors, or other edge computing resources. Their computational capabilities, power efficiency, and connectivity should be evaluated to determine their suitability for the project. The development of Edge AI models specifically tailored to address the identified sustainable development goals is essential. These models should be designed to run effectively on edge devices, using lightweight algorithms and techniques that can make optimal use of limited computational resources while maintaining acceptable accuracy levels.

Implementing a federated learning architecture enables edge devices to train their AI models locally while periodically exchanging model updates with the cloud server. This approach ensures data privacy and reduces communication overhead by minimizing the transfer of raw data. The cloud server aggregates the model updates to create an improved global model that is then shared back with the edge devices.

1. Problem Identification:
    ◦ Clearly define the sustainability challenges or goals that need to be addressed using edge AI in cloud computing.
    ◦ Identify the specific industry or domain where the application of AI and ML can contribute to sustainable development.
2. Literature Review:
    ◦ Conduct a comprehensive literature review to understand the existing research and developments in the field of edge AI, cloud computing, and sustainable development.
    ◦ Identify relevant studies, techniques, and methodologies related to the integration of AI and ML with cloud computing for sustainable development.
    ◦ Analyse the strengths, limitations, and gaps in the existing literature to justify the need for further research and innovation.
3. Data Collection and Preprocessing:
    ◦ Determine the data requirements for training and evaluating AI and ML models in the context of sustainable development.
    ◦ Identify the relevant sources of data, which could include sensor data, IoT devices, or other sources of environmental or operational data.
    ◦ Implement data preprocessing techniques to clean, normalize, and transform the collected data for further analysis and model training.
4. Edge AI Model Development:
    ◦ Design and develop AI and ML models that are suitable for deployment on edge devices or edge servers.

- Consider the specific requirements of the problem, such as model size, computational resources, and latency constraints.
- Select appropriate AI and ML algorithms and architectures, such as deep learning models, decision trees, or support vector machines, depending on the problem and available data.

5. Cloud Infrastructure Setup:
   - Set up a cloud computing infrastructure that supports the integration of edge AI models.
   - Choose a cloud platform that provides the necessary resources for training, deploying, and managing AI models.
   - Configure the cloud environment to enable seamless communication and coordination between edge devices and the cloud infrastructure.

6. Training and Optimization:
   - Train the AI and ML models using the collected and pre-processed data.
   - Optimize the models to achieve the desired accuracy and performance while considering the resource constraints of edge devices.
   - Explore techniques such as transfer learning, model compression, or federated learning to improve efficiency and reduce the computational requirements of the models.

7. Deployment and Monitoring:
   - Deploy the trained edge AI models on the designated edge devices or edge servers.
   - Set up a monitoring system to track the performance and health of the deployed models.
   - Continuously monitor the system to detect any issues or anomalies and take appropriate actions for maintenance and updates.

8. Evaluation and Impact Assessment:
   - Evaluate the performance of the deployed edge AI models in real-world scenarios.
   - Measure relevant metrics such as accuracy, energy efficiency, resource utilization, and the impact on sustainability goals.
   - Compare the results with predefined benchmarks or industry standards to assess the effectiveness of the applied AI and ML techniques for sustainable development.

9. Feedback and Iteration:
   - Gather feedback from users, stakeholders, or domain experts to understand the practical implications and potential improvements.
   - Iterate on the methodology, models, or infrastructure based on the feedback received.
   - Incorporate lessons learned and make necessary adjustments to enhance the effectiveness and applicability of the edge AI in cloud computing approach for sustainable development.

By following these above methodologies, the integration of Edge AI in Cloud Computing can contribute to sustainable development by enhancing energy efficiency, reducing environmental impact, improving resource management, and addressing specific sustainable development goals.

Pseudocode for implementing edge-AI in cloud computing-

Step 1: Import the necessary libraries:
Step 1.1: TensorFlow (tf)
Step 1.2: Layers module from tensorflow.keras (layers)
Step 1.3: Define the CNN model architecture using a sequential model:
Step 2: Add a 2D convolutional layer with 32 filters, a kernel size of (3, 3), and ReLU activation.

Step 3: Add a max pooling layer with a pool size of (2, 2).

Step 4: Add another 2D convolutional layer with 64 filters, a kernel size of (3, 3), and ReLU activation.

Step 5: Add another max pooling layer with a pool size of (2, 2).

Step 6: Flatten the output of the previous layer.

Step 7: Add a fully connected dense layer with 64 units and ReLU activation.

Step 8: Add a final dense layer with num_classes units and softmax activation.

Step 9: Compile the model:

Step 9.1: Use the Adam optimizer.

Step 9.2: Use categorical cross-entropy loss as the loss function.

Step 9.3: Track accuracy as the metric.

Step 10: Train the model:

Step11: Fit the model to the training data.

Step 12: Use the defined num_epochs and batch_size.

Step 12.1: Evaluate the model:

Step 12.2: Evaluate the trained model on the test data.

Step 12.3: Compute the test loss and test accuracy.

Step 13: Make predictions:

Use the trained model to make predictions on the test images.

This code creates a CNN model with convolutional and pooling layers, followed by fully connected layers. The model is then compiled with an optimizer, loss function, and evaluation metrics. It is trained on training images and labels, evaluated on test images and labels, and finally used to make predictions on new data.

Note: The code provided is a simplified example. Depending on the specific application and dataset, you may need to pre-process the data, handle class imbalance, perform data augmentation, and fine-tune the model hyperparameters to achieve better results.

DISCUSSION

Edge AI in cloud computing is an emerging field that combines the power of artificial intelligence (AI) and machine learning (ML) with the capabilities of edge computing and cloud computing to drive sustainable development. By bringing AI and ML closer to the edge of the network, where data is generated and actions are taken, organizations can achieve more efficient and sustainable operations across various industries.

One of the key advantages of leveraging edge AI in cloud computing for sustainable development is the ability to process data in real-time and make near-instantaneous decisions. By deploying AI and ML models directly on edge devices such as sensors, IoT devices, or edge servers, organizations can minimize the latency and bandwidth requirements associated with sending data to the cloud for processing. This not only reduces energy consumption and network congestion but also enables real-time monitoring and control of critical systems, leading to improved efficiency and sustainability.

Additionally, the integration of AI and ML algorithms with cloud computing provides organizations with enhanced predictive capabilities for optimizing resource usage and reducing waste. By analyzing vast amounts of data collected from edge devices, AI models can identify patterns, trends, and anomalies that enable proactive decision-making and resource optimization. This leads to better energy management, reduced environmental impact, and improved sustainability practices.

Moreover, edge AI in cloud computing plays a crucial role in enabling intelligent automation and autonomous systems, further contributing to sustainable development. By leveraging AI and ML algorithms at the edge, devices and systems can make autonomous decisions and take actions without relying heavily on cloud infrastructure. This reduces the dependency on continuous cloud connectivity, lowers energy consumption, and ensures more efficient and resilient operations.

As per seen in figure 2 Edge-based federated learning offers several advantages over cloud-based and hierarchical learning approaches in terms of efficiency. Here are some key points:

- Reduced Communication Overhead: In cloud-based learning, data from edge devices is typically sent to a centralized server, which can be resource-intensive and require substantial bandwidth. Edge-based federated learning minimizes this communication overhead by allowing edge devices to perform local model training on their respective data without transmitting it to a central server. Only model updates are shared, resulting in lower network traffic and reduced latency.
- Enhanced Privacy and Security: With cloud-based learning, sensitive data from edge devices is sent to a central server, raising concerns about privacy and security. In edge-based federated learning, data remains on the edge devices, reducing the risk of data breaches or unauthorized access. The decentralized nature of federated learning enhances privacy since no single entity has access to the complete dataset.
- Offline Learning: Edge devices often operate in environments with limited or intermittent connectivity. Edge-based federated learning enables offline learning, where edge devices can continue training models even when disconnected from the network. This is particularly beneficial for scenarios where continuous connectivity to a central server is not feasible or desirable.
- Lower Bandwidth Requirements: Cloud-based learning involves transmitting large amounts of data between edge devices and the central server, which can be impractical in bandwidth-constrained environments. Edge-based federated learning significantly reduces the amount of data transmitted, as only model updates are shared. This reduces the strain on network bandwidth and makes the approach more suitable for low-bandwidth scenarios.
- Distributed Computation: By leveraging the computational resources available on edge devices, edge-based federated learning distributes the training workload. This can lead to faster model training since multiple devices can perform concurrent training. It also reduces the computational burden on the central server, enabling scalability to a larger number of edge devices.
- Real-Time Adaptation: Edge-based federated learning allows edge devices to adapt their models based on their specific local context. This capability enables personalized and real-time model updates, making the learning process more efficient and responsive to local conditions.

Overall, edge-based federated learning combines the benefits of distributed computing, data privacy, reduced communication overhead, and offline learning to achieve greater efficiency compared to cloud-based and hierarchical learning approaches.

Furthermore, the combination of edge AI and cloud computing enables scalable and flexible deployments for sustainable development initiatives. Organizations can leverage the computational power of the cloud to train and update AI models while deploying lightweight, inferencing models at the edge for real-

Figure 2. Different types of federated learning and their optimization

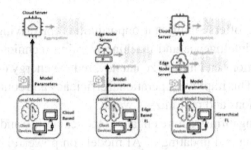

time processing. This hybrid approach allows for efficient resource utilization, dynamic model updates, and adaptability to changing requirements, all of which are crucial for sustainable development efforts.

However, the adoption of edge AI in cloud computing for sustainable development also brings forth challenges and considerations. Privacy and security concerns associated with edge devices and cloud infrastructure must be addressed to ensure the protection of sensitive data. Additionally, the optimization of AI models and algorithms for resource-constrained edge devices requires careful design and trade-offs to achieve a balance between accuracy and computational efficiency.

In conclusion, the integration of edge AI in cloud computing holds great potential for driving sustainable development. By enhancing cloud computing with applied AI and ML, organizations can achieve real-time decision-making, resource optimization, intelligent automation, and scalability, ultimately leading to improved sustainability across various sectors. However, it is crucial to address challenges and strike a balance between edge and cloud capabilities to harness the full benefits of this technology for sustainable development initiatives.

Challenges and Considerations

1. Data Security and Privacy: As more data is processed at the edge and transmitted to the cloud, ensuring data security and privacy is paramount, especially when dealing with sensitive environmental or personal data.
2. Bandwidth Constraints: In some remote or underdeveloped areas, limited internet connectivity may hinder the transmission of data from edge devices to the cloud, impacting real-time decision-making.
3. Power Consumption: While edge devices are designed to be energy-efficient, the continuous operation of large-scale Edge AI deployments could still have a notable energy footprint.
4. Regulatory Compliance: Organizations must navigate a complex landscape of regulations and standards related to data, environmental monitoring, and AI ethics, ensuring they are compliant with these legal frameworks.
5. Infrastructure Investment: Developing and maintaining Edge AI and cloud computing infrastructure can require significant investment, which may pose a barrier to entry for some organizations.

CONCLUSION

Edge AI in cloud computing offers significant opportunities for driving sustainable development by leveraging applied artificial intelligence and machine learning techniques. By deploying AI and ML models at the edge, organizations can minimize latency, reduce energy consumption, and achieve real-time monitoring and control. This improves operational efficiency and contributes to sustainable practices by enabling timely interventions and minimizing waste.

The use of cloud computing infrastructure enhances the scalability and flexibility of edge AI applications, allowing for the training and updating of AI models on powerful cloud servers while deploying lightweight, inferencing models at the edge. This hybrid approach enables efficient resource utilization, dynamic model updates, and adaptability to changing requirements, all of which are crucial for sustainable development initiatives. However, the adoption of edge AI in cloud computing for sustainable development is not without challenges. Privacy and security concerns must be addressed to protect sensitive data, and careful optimization of AI models for resource-constrained edge devices is necessary to balance accuracy and efficiency. Collaboration among stakeholders is essential to driving the adoption and implementation of these technologies for sustainable development. Edge AI in cloud computing offers immense potential for enhancing sustainable development efforts, combining the power of applied artificial intelligence and machine learning with the scalability and flexibility of cloud computing. With further research, innovation, and collaboration, edge AI in cloud computing can play a significant role in building a more sustainable and resilient future.

REFERENCES

Akhtar, M. N., Shaikh, A. J., Khan, A., Awais, H., Bakar, E. A., & Othman, A. R. (2021). Smart Sensing with Edge Computing in Precision Agriculture for Soil Assessment and Heavy Metal Monitoring. *Agriculture*, *11*(6), 475. doi:10.3390/agriculture11060475

Bourechak, A., Zedadra, O., Kouahla, M. N., Guerrieri, A., Seridi, H., & Fortino, G. (2023). At the Confluence of Artificial Intelligence and Edge Computing in IoT-Based Applications: A Review and New Perspectives. *Sensors (Basel)*, *23*(3), 1639. doi:10.3390/s23031639 PMID:36772680

Chavhan, S., Gupta, D., Gochhayat, S., & Khanna, A. (2022). Edge Computing AI-IoT Integrated Energy-efficient Intelligent Transportation System for Smart Cities. *ACM Transactions on Internet Technology*, *22*(4), 1–18. doi:10.1145/3507906

Chen Liu, A. C., Law, O. M. K., Liao, J., & Chen, J. Y. C. (2021). *Traffic Safety System Edge AI Computing*. *2021 IEEE/ACM Symposium on Edge Computing (SEC)*, San Jose, CA, USA. doi:10.1145/3453142.3491410

Debauche, O., Saïd, M., Mahmoudi, S., Manneback, P., Bindelle, J., & Lebeau, F. (2020). Edge Computing and Artificial Intelligence for Real-time Poultry Monitoring. *Procedia Computer Science*, *175*, 534–541. doi:10.1016/j.procs.2020.07.076

Deng, S., Zhao, H., Fang, W., Yin, J., Dustdar, S., & Zomaya, A. (2019). *Edge Intelligence: The Confluence of Edge Computing and Artificial Intelligence*.

Fanariotis, A., Orphanoudakis, T., Kotrotsios, K., Fotopoulos, V., Keramidas, G., & Karkazis, P. (2023). Power Efficient Machine Learning Models Deployment on Edge IoT Devices. *Sensors (Basel)*, *23*(3), 1595. doi:10.3390/s23031595 PMID:36772635

Gibbs, M. & Kanjo, E. (2023). *Realising the Power of Edge Intelligence: Addressing the Challenges in AI and tiny ML Applications for Edge Computing.*

Gong, T., Zhu, L., Yu, F. R., & Tang, T. (2023). Edge Intelligence in Intelligent Transportation Systems: A Survey, 2023. IEEE Transactions on Intelligent Transportation Systems. IEEE. doi:10.1109/TITS.2023.3275741

Guo, L., Mu, S., Deng, Y., Shi, C., Yan, B., & Xiao, Z. (2023). Efficient Binary Weight Convolutional Network Accelerator for Speech Recognition. *Sensors (Basel)*, *23*(3), 1530. doi:10.3390/s23031530 PMID:36772567

Hao, T., Hwang, K., Zhan, J., Li, Y., & Cao, Y. (2022). Scenario-based AI Benchmark Evaluation of Distributed Cloud/Edge Computing Systems. *IEEE Transactions on Computers*. IEEE. . doi:10.1109/TC.2022.3176803

Hao, T., Zhan, J., Hwang, K., Gao, W., & Wen, X. (2020). *AI-oriented Medical Workload Allocation for Hierarchical Cloud/Edge/Device Computing.*

Joshi, K., Anandaram, H., Khanduja, M., Kumar, R., Saini, V., & Mohialden, Y. (2022). *Recent Challenges on Edge AI with Its Application: A Brief Introduction.* Springer. . doi:10.1007/978-3-031-18292-1_5

Krishnan, S. R., Nallakaruppan, M. K., Chengoden, R., Koppu, S., Iyapparaja, M., Sadhasivam, J., & Sethuraman, S. (2022). Smart Water Resource Management Using Artificial Intelligence—A Review. *Sustainability (Basel)*, *14*(20), 13384. doi:10.3390/su142013384

Mishra, A., Gangisetti, G., Khazanchi, D. (2023). *Integrating Edge-AI in Structural Health Monitoring domain.*

Peng, H., Zhang, X., Li, H., Xu, L., & Wang, X. (2023). An AI-Enhanced Strategy of Service Offloading for IoV in Mobile Edge Computing. *Electronics (Basel)*, *12*(12), 2719. doi:10.3390/electronics12122719

Pomšár, L., Brecko, A., & Zolotová, I. (2022). *Brief overview of Edge AI accelerators for energy-constrained edge.* 2022 IEEE 20th Jubilee World Symposium on Applied Machine Intelligence and Informatics (SAMI), Poprad, Slovakia. 10.1109/SAMI54271.2022.9780669

Raha, A. (2021). *Design Considerations for Edge Neural Network Accelerators: An Industry Perspective.* 2021 34th International Conference on VLSI Design and 2021 20th International Conference on Embedded Systems (VLSID), Guwahati, India. 10.1109/VLSID51830.2021.00061

Ramachandran, P., Ranganath, S., Bhandaru, M., & Tibrewala, S. (2021). *A Survey of AI Enabled Edge Computing for Future Networks.* 2021 IEEE 4th 5G World Forum (5GWF), Montreal, QC, Canada. 10.1109/5GWF52925.2021.00087

Sun, L., Jiang, X., Ren, H., & Guo, Y. (2020). Edge-Cloud Computing and Artificial Intelligence in Internet of Medical Things: Architecture, Technology and Application. *IEEE Access : Practical Innovations, Open Solutions*, *8*, 101079–101092. doi:10.1109/ACCESS.2020.2997831

Surianarayanan, C., Lawrence, J. J., Chelliah, P. R., Prakash, E., & Hewage, C. (2023). A Survey on Optimization Techniques for Edge Artificial Intelligence (AI). *Sensors (Basel)*, *23*(3), 1279. doi:10.3390/s23031279 PMID:36772319

Surianarayanan, C., Raj, P., & Niranjan, S. K. (2023). The Significance of Edge AI towards Real-time and Intelligent Enterprises. *2023 International Conference on Intelligent and Innovative Technologies in Computing, Electrical and Electronics (IITCEE)*, Bengaluru, India. 10.1109/IITCEE57236.2023.10090926

Tuli, S., Casale, G., & Jennings, N. (2021). MCDS: AI Augmented Workflow Scheduling in Mobile Edge Cloud Computing Systems. *IEEE Transactions on Parallel and Distributed Systems*. IEEE. . doi:10.1109/TPDS.2021.3135907

Wang, Dong & Zhang, Daniel. (2023). *Real-Time AI in Social Edge*. Springer. . doi:10.1007/978-3-031-26936-3_5

Wang, Y., Xue, J., Wei, C., & Kuo, C.-C. (2023). *An Overview on Generative AI at Scale with Edge-Cloud Computing*. TechXriv. doi:10.36227/techrxiv.23272271.v1

Zeb, S., Rathore, M., Hassan, S., Raza, S., Dev, K., & Fortino, G. (2023). Towards AI-enabled NextG Networks with Edge Intelligence-assisted Microservice Orchestration. *IEEE Wireless Communications*, *30*(3), 148–156. doi:10.1109/MWC.015.2200461

Chapter 10
Load Balancing Using Swarm Intelligence in Cloud Environment for Sustainable Development

Yogita Yashveer Raghav

iD https://orcid.org/0000-0003-0478-8619

Dronacharya College of Engineering, Gurugram, India

Vaibahv Vyas

Banasthali Vidyapith, India

ABSTRACT

Load balancing plays a vital role in the effective management of resources within cloud computing environments. As the use of cloud technologies continues to expand rapidly, it becomes increasingly important to ensure efficient allocation of resources and address performance issues. The utilization of load balancing techniques becomes crucial in the distribution of workloads across multiple servers, thereby optimizing resource usage and enhancing system performance. Swarm intelligence-based load balancing presents a promising approach to achieving sustainable resource allocation in cloud environments. By leveraging self-organization and decentralized decision-making principles, swarm intelligence algorithms can optimize resource utilization, minimize energy consumption, and improve overall system performance. This chapter offers a comprehensive overview of this topic, emphasizing the potential advantages, challenges, and future directions associated with load balancing using swarm intelligence within the context of sustainable development in cloud environments.

INTRODUCTION

The increasing focus on sustainable development and minimizing the environmental impact of cloud computing has led to a demand for load balancing strategies that not only optimize performance but

DOI: 10.4018/979-8-3693-0338-2.ch010

also reduce energy consumption. Swarm intelligence algorithms have emerged as a promising solution to address these challenges. Inspired by the collective behavior of natural systems like social insect colonies, swarm intelligence leverages decentralized decision-making and self-organization to tackle complex problems. Applying swarm intelligence algorithms to load balancing in cloud environments allows for sustainable resource allocation, energy reduction, and improved system efficiency. This chapter provides an in-depth exploration of swarm intelligence algorithms for load balancing in cloud environments, specifically emphasizing sustainable development. The chapter covers the fundamental concepts and principles of swarm intelligence, such as self-organization and decentralized decision-making. It also offers an overview of popular swarm intelligence algorithms. Moreover, it delves into the design and implementation considerations when applying swarm intelligence to load balancing in cloud environments. This includes selecting suitable algorithm parameters, integrating with cloud management systems, and highlighting the potential benefits of using swarm intelligence techniques. These advantages encompass improved resource utilization, reduced energy consumption, and enhanced system performance. To assess the effectiveness of swarm intelligence-based load balancing, the chapter presents performance evaluation techniques and showcases real-world case studies. Various metrics, such as response time, throughput, and energy consumption, are discussed to evaluate the efficiency of load balancing algorithms in cloud environments. These case studies demonstrate successful applications of swarm intelligence algorithms in achieving sustainable load balancing in practical scenarios. However, the chapter also addresses challenges and limitations related to the adoption of swarm intelligence for load balancing. Factors like scalability, convergence speed, and robustness to varying workload patterns are considered. Additionally, the chapter provides insights into potential future directions for research and development in the field. Areas such as hybrid algorithms, adaptive techniques, and integration with emerging technologies like edge computing are identified as promising avenues for further exploration (Geeks for Geeks, n.d.).

In summary, load balancing using swarm intelligence presents promising solutions for achieving sustainable resource allocation in cloud environments. By leveraging self-organization and decentralized decision-making, swarm intelligence algorithms optimize resource utilization, reduce energy consumption, and enhance system performance. This comprehensive chapter offers an overview of the subject, highlighting the potential benefits, challenges, and future directions of load balancing using swarm intelligence within the context of sustainable development in cloud environments.

LOAD BALANCING IN CLOUD ENVIRONMENTS

Load balancing plays a vital role in cloud environments by optimizing resource allocation and tackling performance obstacles. It encompasses the distribution of workloads across various computing resources, such as servers, virtual machines, and containers. Load balancing techniques are deployed at different layers, including the network, application, and database, to ensure efficient utilization of resources and mitigate performance issues. At the network layer, network load balancing evenly distributes traffic across servers or instances, preventing resource overload. Application load balancing operates at the application layer to balance workloads across instances, ensuring equal distribution of requests for improved performance. Database load balancing at the database layer evenly distributes queries among database servers, optimizing resource utilization. By employing load balancing techniques, cloud environments can optimize resource usage, enhance performance, and maintain high availability, ultimately delivering a superior user experience. Load balancing in cloud computing offers several advantages. Firstly, it improves performance by distributing the workload, reducing the burden on individual resources and enhancing overall system efficiency. Secondly, load balancing provides high availability and fault tolerance by eliminating single points of failure. By evenly distributing the workload across multiple resources, it ensures that even if a server fails, other resources can handle the traffic, maintaining service availability (Elmagzoub et al., 2021; Nasir et al., 2017; Rajeshwari et al., 2022). Furthermore, load balancing facilitates scalability. It allows for the easy scaling of resources based on demand, enabling cloud environments to handle spikes in traffic or changes in workload. Lastly, load balancing promotes efficient resource utilization, reducing wastage and optimizing costs by ensuring that resources are effectively utilized .However, load balancing in cloud computing also comes with certain challenges. Implementing load balancing can be complex, especially in large-scale systems, requiring careful planning and configuration to ensure effective operation (Qawqzeh et al., 2021). Additionally, there may be associated costs, including the deployment and maintenance of load balancing mechanisms, although the benefits typically outweigh these costs in terms of improved performance and resource utilization.

In conclusion, load balancing in cloud environments is vital for achieving efficient resource allocation and mitigating performance bottlenecks. By distributing workloads across multiple resources, load balancing techniques optimize resource utilization, improve performance, and enhance the availability and scalability of cloud-based applications.

Challenges Associated With Load Balancing

Load balancing presents several challenges, including workload heterogeneity, varying resource capacities, and dynamic workloads. Let's discuss each of these challenges:

Workload Heterogeneity: Workload heterogeneity refers to the varying characteristics and resource requirements of different tasks or applications. In real-world scenarios, workloads can have different processing requirements, data sizes, and computational complexities. Load balancing becomes challenging when trying to distribute these diverse workloads efficiently. Some workloads may be CPU-intensive, while others may be I/O-bound or memory-intensive. Balancing the allocation of resources to ensure fairness and optimal utilization becomes complex when dealing with such heterogeneous workloads.

Varying Resource Capacities: Load balancing becomes more challenging when the resources involved have varying capacities. In a distributed system or a cloud environment, different nodes or servers may have different processing power, memory, or storage capacities. Allocating workloads across these resources while considering their varying capacities requires intelligent load balancing algorithms. Failure to consider these variations can lead to underutilization or overload of certain resources, resulting in performance bottlenecks and inefficient resource utilization.

Dynamic Workloads: Workloads in distributed systems and cloud environments are often dynamic, meaning they can vary over time. The arrival rate and characteristics of incoming tasks or user requests may change dynamically, making it necessary to adapt the load balancing strategies accordingly. Load balancing algorithms need to be responsive and capable of dynamically adjusting the resource allocation to accommodate changing workloads. The challenge lies in efficiently detecting workload changes, predicting future demands, and reallocating resources in real-time to ensure optimal performance and responsiveness.

Addressing these challenges requires sophisticated load balancing techniques and algorithms. Researchers have proposed various approaches, including dynamic load balancing algorithms, predictive resource provisioning, and adaptive load balancing strategies, to tackle workload heterogeneity, varying resource capacities, and dynamic workloads (Nasir et al., 2017). Additionally, the use of multi-cloud environments has gained attention as a solution to workload balancing challenges, allowing the distribution of workloads across multiple cloud providers (Mishra & Majhi, 2021). These approaches aim to achieve efficient resource utilization, reduced response time, avoidance of service level agreement violations, and improved overall system performance.

In conclusion, load balancing in distributed systems and cloud environments poses challenges due to workload heterogeneity, varying resource capacities, and dynamic workloads. Overcoming these challenges requires intelligent load balancing algorithms and techniques that can adapt to changing conditions and ensure optimal resource allocation for efficient system performance.

Need for Sustainable Load Balancing Techniques

Load balancing techniques play a crucial role in optimizing energy consumption and reducing carbon emissions in modern computing environments. As the demand for computational resources continues to grow, data centers and cloud computing infrastructures are expanding, leading to increased energy consumption and carbon footprint. Sustainable load balancing techniques aim to address these challenges by efficiently utilizing resources and minimizing energy waste. Here are some key reasons why sustainable load balancing techniques are needed:

Energy Efficiency: Data centers and cloud environments consume significant amounts of energy to power and cool the servers. By distributing the workload evenly across available resources, load balancing techniques can prevent resource overutilization or underutilization, thus reducing energy consumption. By dynamically adjusting the resource allocation based on workload demands, sustainable load balancing techniques can optimize energy usage and improve overall energy efficiency.

Resource Utilization: Sustainable load balancing ensures that all resources within a computing infrastructure are utilized effectively. By evenly distributing the workload, it avoids situations where certain servers are overloaded while others remain idle. This balanced resource utilization minimizes the need for additional servers or infrastructure expansion, resulting in energy and cost savings (Bhargavi et al., 2020; Birje et al., 2017).

Carbon Emission Reduction: Energy consumption in data centers contributes to carbon emissions, which have a significant environmental impact. Sustainable load balancing techniques aim to minimize energy waste, which in turn reduces carbon emissions. By efficiently utilizing resources and preventing unnecessary energy consumption, load balancing can contribute to a greener and more sustainable computing environment.

Scalability and Flexibility: Sustainable load balancing techniques are designed to adapt to dynamic workloads and changing resource capacities. As workload demands fluctuate, load balancing algorithms can allocate resources based on the current needs, ensuring efficient resource usage. This scalability and flexibility enable organizations to scale their computing infrastructure as needed without compromising energy efficiency.

Cost Savings: Optimizing energy consumption through sustainable load balancing techniques can result in cost savings for organizations. By reducing energy waste and avoiding unnecessary infrastructure expansions, organizations can lower their operational expenses. This cost-saving aspect further incentivizes the adoption of sustainable load balancing techniques (Devaraj et al., 2020; Elmagzoub et al., 2021).

Overall, sustainable load balancing techniques are essential for optimizing energy consumption and reducing carbon emissions in computing environments. By efficiently utilizing resources, balancing workloads, and adapting to dynamic demands, these techniques contribute to a more environmentally friendly and cost-effective approach to computing.

ROLE OF SWARM INTELLIGENCE FOR LOAD BALANCING

Swarm intelligence is a collective behavior observed in decentralized, self-organized systems where individual agents interact and coordinate with each other to achieve a common goal. Inspired by the behavior of natural swarms, such as bird flocks or ant colonies, swarm intelligence has found applications in various fields, including load balancing in cloud environments. Here's an overview of the concept of swarm intelligence and its relevance to load balancing:

Decentralized Decision Making: Swarm intelligence emphasizes decentralized decision making, where each agent (e.g., virtual machine, server) acts autonomously based on local information and interactions with neighboring agents. Similarly, in a cloud environment, load balancing algorithms based on swarm intelligence distribute the workload across multiple servers without relying on a centralized controller. This decentralized approach enables quicker and more adaptive load balancing decisions, as agents can respond to changes in workload distribution and resource availability in real-time.

Emergent Behavior: Swarm intelligence algorithms leverage the concept of emergent behavior, where global optimization emerges from the local interactions of individual agents. In load balancing, swarm intelligence algorithms enable the system to dynamically adapt to workload fluctuations by redistributing tasks among available servers. By collectively adjusting the resource allocation, the swarm of servers can achieve load balancing without relying on a central coordinator. This emergent behavior leads to better overall system performance and resource utilization (Raghav & Vyas, 2019; Raghav et al., 2022; Tapale et al., 2020).

Adaptability: Swarm intelligence algorithms exhibit adaptability, as individual agents continuously update their behavior based on local information and feedback from the environment. Similarly, load balancing algorithms based on swarm intelligence can dynamically adjust the resource allocation based on changing workload patterns and server conditions. This adaptability ensures that the load balancing mechanism remains efficient and effective, even in dynamic cloud environments with fluctuating demands.

Fault Tolerance: Swarm intelligence-based load balancing techniques offer inherent fault tolerance. If a server or agent fails, the load balancing algorithm can quickly redistribute the workload among the remaining available servers. This fault tolerance ensures that the system remains operational and minimizes the impact of failures on the overall performance and user experience (Raghav & Vyas, 2023).

By leveraging the principles of swarm intelligence, load balancing algorithms in cloud environments can achieve efficient resource utilization, adaptive decision making, scalability, and fault tolerance. These characteristics make swarm intelligence a relevant and effective approach to addressing the load balancing challenges in dynamic and complex cloud computing environments.

Swarm Intelligence Algorithms

Ant Colony Optimization (ACO)

ACO draws inspiration from the foraging behavior of ants and is primarily utilized for solving combinatorial optimization problems. In ACO, artificial ants navigate through a problem space, leaving pheromone trails on the edges of the problem graph. These pheromone trails serve as indicators of solution quality. By considering the amount of pheromone on the edges and a heuristic value, ants probabilistically determine their next move. As time progresses, paths with higher pheromone concentrations become more enticing to other ants, resulting in the emergence of optimal or near-optimal solutions. ACO has demonstrated successful applications in various problem domains, including the traveling salesman problem, vehicle routing problem, and job scheduling.

Particle Swarm Optimization (PSO)

Particle Swarm Optimization (PSO) is aiming to optimize problems by iteratively refining a group of potential solutions referred to as particles. Each particle signifies a solution within the problem domain and modifies its position based on its own best-known position and the best-known position globally identified by the swarm. Through continual updates of particle positions, PSO guides the swarm towards optimal solutions within the problem space. PSO has demonstrated successful applications in diverse optimization problems, such as function optimization, image processing, and data clustering. Harnessing the collective intelligence of the swarm, PSO presents an efficient and effective approach for resolving intricate optimization challenges across various domains (Raghav & Gulia, 2023).

Artificial Bee Colony (ABC) Algorithm

ABC algorithm seeks to find optimal solutions for the given optimization problem. Initially, a collection of potential solutions, referred to as food sources, is generated randomly. The employed bees explore and exploit these food sources, assessing their quality using an objective function. Onlooker bees probabilistically select food sources based on their quality and exchange information with the employed bees. Scout bees, on the other hand, explore new food sources by abandoning unproductive ones. Through iterative iterations, the swarm gradually converges towards optimal or near-optimal solutions. ABC has demonstrated its effectiveness in various optimization domains, such as function optimization, data clustering, and neural network training. Its successful application to these problems showcases the algorithm's versatility and capability to tackle diverse optimization challenges.

Genetic Algorithm (GA)

This approach to optimization draws inspiration from the principles of natural selection and evolution. It operates using a population-based strategy, with chromosomes serving as representations of potential solutions. Across successive generations, genetic operators, including selection, crossover, and mutation, are employed to generate new solutions. Selection prioritizes individuals with higher fitness, crossover combines genetic information, and mutation introduces variability. These mechanisms collectively steer the algorithm toward optimal solutions. The effectiveness of the Genetic Algorithm has been evidenced across diverse optimization domains, including function optimization, scheduling, and parameter tuning, among others.

Firefly Algorithm (FA)

The Firefly Algorithm takes inspiration from the flashing behavior of fireflies and their attraction to one another. Its objective is to address optimization problems by simulating the movement and interaction observed in fireflies. Each firefly represents a potential solution within the problem space, and its brightness is associated with its objective value. Fireflies move towards brighter individuals, with their movement influenced by factors like attractiveness, distance, and randomization. Brighter fireflies emit stronger attraction signals, while distance affects the level of attractiveness between fireflies. Through iterations, fireflies gradually converge towards brighter regions within the problem space, representing optimal solutions (Kumar et al., 2023).

Harmony Search (HS) Algorithm

The process takes inspiration from the creation and improvisation of music, emulating the method of generating harmony by continuously refining a set of solutions to optimize a particular problem. The primary goal is to tackle optimization issues by producing fresh solution vectors based on a repository of harmonies, which retains the best solutions identified up to that point. This algorithm utilizes a stochastic exploration approach where each element in a solution vector corresponds to a musical note. In the Harmony Search Algorithm, novel harmonies are created and assessed. If these harmonies outperform the least effective harmony in the memory, they take its place. This iterative procedure enables the algorithm to effectively explore and exploit the search spaceThese swarm intelligence algorithms, ACO, PSO, and ABC, Genetic Algorithm, Firefly Algorithm, and Harmony Search Algorithm demonstrate the power of collective behavior and distributed decision making to solving optimization problems, leveraging principles from biology, natural phenomena, and music composition They have been widely applied to a range of real-world problems, showing their effectiveness in finding high-quality solutions in complex search spaces (Bhargavi & Babu, 2019).

SUSTAINABLE LOAD BALANCING USING SWARM INTELLIGENCE

Swarm intelligence algorithms can be applied to achieve sustainable load balancing in cloud environments by leveraging their ability to optimize resource allocation, reduce energy consumption, and improve overall system efficiency. Here are some ways swarm intelligence algorithms can be utilized:

Ant Colony Optimization (ACO)

ACO can be employed to efficiently allocate tasks or virtual machines to physical servers within a cloud environment. The algorithm emulates the behavior of ants that leave pheromone trails to identify the shortest path towards a food source. In the context of load balancing, the ants symbolize tasks or virtual machines, while the servers represent the food sources. By utilizing ACO, tasks can be intelligently assigned to servers, considering factors such as server utilization, network latency, and energy consumption. The pheromone trails serve as a representation of a server's attractiveness or desirability, thereby guiding the allocation decisions. ACO facilitates load balancing by adaptively responding to changing workloads, optimizing resource utilization, reducing energy consumption, and enhancing the sustainability of the cloud environment (Ghumman, 2015; Nishant et al., 2012; Qawqzeh et al., 2021; Surjeet et al., 2021; Ullah, 2019).

Particle Swarm Optimization (PSO)

PSO can be utilized to optimize the resource allocation in a cloud environment, encompassing virtual machines, containers, or workloads. The algorithm emulates the movement and interaction of particles within a multidimensional search space. Each particle denotes a potential solution or resource allocation, with its position indicating the quality of that particular solution. Particles adjust their positions based on their own best-known solution and the global best-known solution among all particles. By employing PSO, resources can be dynamically assigned, taking into account factors such as server load, network bandwidth, and energy consumption. PSO facilitates load balancing by continuously exploring for superior resource allocations, thereby optimizing performance and reducing energy usage (Mishra & Jaiswal, 2012).

Artificial Bee Colony (ABC) Algorithm

The ABC algorithm offers a viable approach for load balancing in cloud environments, as it optimizes the allocation of tasks or workloads to servers. The algorithm draws inspiration from the foraging behavior of honeybees in their quest for food sources. In this analogy, the worker bees represent the tasks or workloads, while the food sources correspond to the servers within the cloud. Just as bees search for improved food sources based on nectar quantity and information exchange, the ABC algorithm optimizes task allocation by considering factors such as server capacity, load, and energy efficiency. By dynamically adjusting the allocation of tasks to servers, ABC promotes load balancing and minimizes energy consumption in the cloud environment (Al-Turjman, 2021).

Genetic Algorithm (GA)

When applied to load balancing in cloud environments, GA addresses the task of allocating tasks or virtual machines to servers as an optimization problem. The algorithm commences with an initial population of candidate solutions, representing different allocation configurations. Fitness criteria, such as server utilization, response time, energy consumption, and cost, are employed to evaluate the solutions. Through the iterative process of selection, crossover, and mutation, the algorithm evolves the population, generating new and potentially superior solutions. The objective is to identify an allocation configuration that achieves load balancing, minimizes energy consumption, and optimizes other performance metrics. By utilizing GA, cloud environments can adapt dynamically to varying workloads, optimize resource allocation, and reduce energy usage, thereby facilitating sustainable load balancing (Mishra & Majhi, 2021).

Firefly Algorithm (FA)

The Firefly Algorithm (FA) constitutes an optimization technique inspired by the light emission patterns of fireflies. When applied to load balancing in cloud environments, FA addresses the challenge of optimizing the allocation of tasks or workloads to servers. Each firefly represents a potential solution or allocation arrangement, with its luminosity indicating the quality of the solution By employing FA, cloud environments can efficiently optimize the allocation of tasks to servers, considering parameters like server load, response time, and energy usage. Brighter fireflies, representing superior allocation configurations, attract other fireflies, thereby promoting load balancing and reducing energy consumption within the cloud ecosystem (Qureshi et al., 2021).

Harmony Search (HS) Algorithm

It is an optimization algorithm that takes inspiration from musicians improvising to create harmonious melodies. When applied to load balancing in cloud environments, HS Algorithm addresses the optimization problem of allocating tasks or workloads to servers. The algorithm maintains a population of solutions known as harmonies, each representing a different allocation configuration. Fitness criteria, such as server load, response time, and energy consumption, are utilized to evaluate the harmonies. The objective is to discover a harmony that achieves load balancing, minimizes energy consumption, and optimizes other performance metrics. By utilizing the HS Algorithm, cloud environments can dynamically adjust task allocation to servers, optimize resource utilization, and foster sustainable load balancing (Bhargavi et al., 2020; Raghav & Vyas, 2019).

By leveraging swarm intelligence algorithms like ACO, PSO, and ABC, Genetic Algorithm, Firefly Algorithm, and Harmony Search Algorithm in cloud environments can achieve sustainable load balancing by optimizing resource allocation, reducing energy consumption, and improving overall system performance. These algorithms adapt to changing workloads, dynamically allocate resources, and optimize the distribution of tasks or workloads based on various factors, leading to a more efficient and environmentally friendly cloud infrastructure and balances the load across servers while minimizing energy usage and other performance metrics.

Application of Swarm Intelligence Algorithms in Load Balancing

Application of Swarm intelligence algorithms can be applied to achieve sustainable load balancing in cloud environments, offering benefits such as improved resource utilization, reduced energy consumption, and enhanced system performance. When designing and implementing these algorithms, several considerations need to be taken into account, including the selection of appropriate algorithm parameters and integration with cloud management systems.

To apply swarm intelligence algorithms for load balancing in cloud environments, the following steps can be followed:

Problem Formulation: Define the load balancing problem, including the objectives and constraints. Identify the resources to be balanced, such as virtual machines (VMs) or tasks, and the metrics to optimize, such as response time, energy consumption, or server utilization.

Algorithm Selection: Choose a suitable swarm intelligence algorithm based on the characteristics of the problem and available resources.

Parameter Configuration: Configure the algorithm parameters to control its behavior. These parameters may include the number of agents (ants, particles, bees, etc.), the exploration-exploitation balance, communication and interaction mechanisms, and convergence criteria. The parameter settings should be adjusted through experimentation and fine-tuning to achieve optimal results (Elmagzoub et al., 2021; Ionescu, 2019).

Problem Representation: Map the load balancing problem to the algorithm's representation format. For example, in VM allocation scenarios, each VM can be represented as a decision variable, and the allocation state can be encoded as a binary or integer vector.

Fitness Evaluation: Define a fitness function that quantifies the quality of a candidate solution based on the load balancing objectives and constraints. The fitness function can incorporate metrics like server load, response time, energy consumption, or other relevant performance indicators.

Swarm Initialization: Initialize the swarm with an initial set of solutions. This can be done randomly or by using heuristics to generate diverse and potentially promising solutions.

Iterative Optimization: Iteratively update the swarm's solutions by applying the algorithm's search mechanisms. These mechanisms may include local search, global search, pheromone communication, velocity updates, or solution exchanges (Li et al., 2020; Qawqzeh et al., 2021).

Convergence and Termination: Define termination conditions to stop the optimization process. These conditions can be based on reaching a maximum number of iterations, achieving a satisfactory solution quality, or satisfying specific performance thresholds.

Integration with Cloud Management Systems: Integrate the load balancing algorithm with the cloud management system to enable real-time monitoring of resource utilization, dynamic adjustment of VM allocations, and efficient resource provisioning. This integration allows the load balancing algorithm to adapt to changing workloads and optimize resource usage (Mishra & Majhi, 2021; Singh, 2018).

By applying swarm intelligence algorithms to load balancing in cloud environments, the allocation of resources can be optimized dynamically, resulting in sustainable load balancing. These algorithms enable efficient utilization of cloud resources, reduction in energy consumption, and improved system performance, ultimately leading to cost savings and environmental benefits.

CASE STUDIES

Swarm intelligence offers several advantages over traditional algorithms when it comes to load balancing in cloud computing. The following case studies and evidence support this claim:

A research paper (Bhargavi et al., 2020) investigated the performance of various "swarm intelligence based load balancing techniques" in cloud environments. The study compared techniques such as whale optimization, spider, dragonfly, and raven roosting. The findings revealed that raven roosting, a swarm intelligence approach, demonstrated superior performance compared to the other techniques. This highlights the effectiveness of swarm intelligence-based load balancing methods in distributing workload within cloud environments, resulting in enhanced overall performance.

A survey paper (Elmagzoub et al., 2021) investigated swarm intelligence-based load balancing techniques, analyzing their objectives, application areas, and targeted challenges. The analysis evaluated the performance of these algorithms based on metrics such as average response time and data center processing time, along with other quality parameters. The findings revealed that swarm intelligence-based load balancing algorithms have been extensively researched and demonstrate potential in achieving efficient load balancing. The survey provides valuable insights into the capabilities and strengths of these algorithms, aiding researchers and practitioners in selecting the most suitable technique for specific load balancing requirements.

In their systematic literature review (SLR), authors (Birje et al., 2017) analyzed 77 selected papers published between 2000 and 2015, offering a comprehensive overview of cloud computing. The review encompasses the historical development, fundamental concepts, technologies, tools, and challenges associated with cloud computing. It emphasizes the growing adoption of cloud computing by major providers while acknowledging the persisting challenges that require attention. This extensive review serves as a valuable reference for researchers seeking insights into the field of cloud computing, providing a consolidated understanding of its evolution, key components, and unresolved issues.

An article (Tapale et al., 2020) introduces a utility-based load balancing approach in cloud computing, utilizing the firefly algorithm. It explores the integration of the firefly algorithm with load balancing techniques and discusses its application in cloud environments. These studies and articles serve as evidence, showcasing the effectiveness of swarm intelligence-based algorithms in achieving efficient load balancing and enhancing various performance metrics in cloud computing. Such approaches highlight the potential of utilizing swarm intelligence techniques to optimize resource allocation and improve overall system performance in cloud-based environments.

Metrics for Evaluating Load Balancing Algorithms

When evaluating swarm intelligence load balancing algorithms, several metrics can be used to assess their performance. Here are some commonly used metrics:

Response time: This metric measures the time taken by the load balancing algorithm to respond to requests and distribute them among the nodes in the system. Lower response time indicates better efficiency and faster task allocation.

Throughput: Throughput refers to the number of requests or tasks that the load balancing algorithm can handle within a given time frame. Higher throughput indicates better scalability and resource utilization.

Resource utilization: This metric assesses how effectively the load balancing algorithm distributes the workload among the available resources. It measures the degree to which system resources, such as CPU, memory, and network bandwidth, are utilized. Higher resource utilization indicates better load balancing .

Load distribution: Load distribution evaluates the balance of tasks or workload across the nodes in the system. It measures the fairness in distributing the load, ensuring that no node is overloaded while others remain underutilized. A well-balanced load distribution results in optimal performance and avoids bottlenecks (Akila et al., 2021; Bhargavi et al., 2020; Junaid et al., 2020; Ramezani et al., 2014).

Scalability: Scalability assesses the load balancing algorithm's ability to handle increasing workload and system size. It measures how well the algorithm performs as the number of nodes or tasks increases. A scalable load balancing algorithm can adapt to changing demands without significant degradation in performance.

Quality of Service (QoS): QoS metrics evaluate the level of service provided to the users or applications in terms of response time, reliability, and other parameters. Load balancing algorithms should maintain acceptable QoS levels for the applications running on the system (Aqeel et al., 2023; Elmagzoub et al., 2021; Pan et al., 2020).

These metrics can be used individually or collectively to evaluate and compare the performance of swarm intelligence load balancing algorithms. By analyzing these metrics, researchers and practitioners can gain insights into the effectiveness and suitability of different algorithms for specific cloud computing scenarios.

Challenges and Limitations Associated With Swarm Intelligence

These swarm algorithms display potential in addressing load balancing complexities and contribute significantly to achieving sustainable load distribution in cloud environments. Nevertheless, it is important to acknowledge the challenges and limitations associated with swarm intelligence-based load balancing techniques in cloud computing. Some of these challenges include:

Scalability: Ensuring that swarm algorithms can handle large-scale cloud environments with a multitude of resources and tasks.

Dynamic Environments: Adapting to real-time workload variations and changes in resource availability as cloud environments are subject to continuous fluctuations.

Heterogeneity: Effectively managing resource heterogeneity in terms of capabilities and task requirements to optimize resource allocation.

Overhead: Minimizing the computational overhead introduced by swarm algorithms to prevent excessive resource consumption.

Convergence Speed: Enhancing the speed at which swarm algorithms converge to rapidly adapt to changing conditions and optimize load balancing (Bhattacharya, et al., 2020; Kiruthiga & Vennila, 2020; Mesbahi & Rahmani, 2016).

Further research and development are required to optimize these algorithms, enhance their performance, and ensure their practicality in real-world cloud scenarios.

Future Directions for Research and Development

The future trajectory of research and development in hybrid algorithms, adaptive techniques, and integration with emerging technologies like edge computing involves several key areas. These areas aim to optimize system performance, efficiency, and autonomy by harnessing the power of AI/ML, cloud computing, fog computing, edge computing, and quantum computing. By exploring these directions, advancements can be made in creating intelligent systems that leverage the strengths of multiple technologies to meet the evolving demands of various industries and applications. Hybrid Algorithms: Researchers are exploring the development of hybrid algorithms that combine multiple optimization or machine learning techniques to improve problem-solving capabilities. Hybridization can involve combining evolutionary algorithms with other metaheuristics, machine learning algorithms with rule-based systems, or combining different optimization algorithms. The objective is to leverage the strengths of each approach and achieve better results in terms of accuracy, convergence speed, and robustness (Kumar et al., 2022; Mishra & Majhi, 2021).

Adaptive Techniques: Adaptive techniques focus on developing algorithms and systems that can dynamically adjust their behavior and parameters based on changing conditions or user requirements. This adaptability can be achieved through the integration of machine learning, reinforcement learning, or control theory approaches. Adaptive techniques enable systems to self-optimize, self-configure, and self-heal, leading to improved performance, fault tolerance, and resource utilization (Bhargavi et al., 2020; Chhabra et al., 2022).

Integration with Edge Computing: Edge computing encompasses the practice of processing data in proximity to its source or end-users, resulting in reduced latency and improved real-time processing capabilities. By bringing computation closer to the edge of the network, this approach enhances responsiveness and efficiency in handling data-intensive tasks. The integration of hybrid algorithms and adaptive techniques with edge computing enables intelligent decision-making at the network edge. It involves developing algorithms that are resource-efficient, can handle dynamic and heterogeneous environments, and support distributed computation and collaboration among edge devices (Birje et al., 2017; Goyal et al., 2021).

Optimization for Edge Computing: As edge computing environments typically have resource-constrained devices and limited computing capabilities, there is a need for optimization techniques tailored to these constraints. Research focuses on developing algorithms that can optimize task placement, resource allocation, and workload management in edge computing architectures. These techniques aim to improve energy efficiency, response time, and overall system performance while considering the unique characteristics of edge devices (Devaraj et al., 2020; Singh et al., 2022).

AI/ML for Autonomic Computing: Autonomic computing aims to design self-managing systems that can autonomously adapt, optimize, and recover from failures. Integrating AI and ML techniques into autonomic computing systems can enable self-learning, prediction, and decision-making capabilities. This involves developing AI/ML models for resource management, anomaly detection, fault prediction, and self-healing mechanisms. The research strives to improve system autonomy, performance, and fault tolerance in various computing paradigms, including cloud, fog, edge, server less, and quantum computing (Gill et al., 2019; Tapale et al., 2020). By focusing on these areas, the study aims to enhance the functionality and reliability of systems in diverse computing environments. The outcomes will drive advancements in the computing field, facilitating the development of more efficient and resilient systems capable of adapting to evolving demands and managing complex workloads. This research holds significant implications for industries and applications that rely on robust and high-performing computing systems.

Overall, the future research and development directions in this field aim to enhance the intelligence, adaptability, and efficiency of computing systems through the integration of hybrid algorithms, adaptive techniques, and emerging technologies like edge computing. These advancements are crucial for addressing the increasing complexity and scale of modern computing environments and enabling the deployment of intelligent and autonomous systems.

CONCLUSION

In conclusion, load balancing in cloud environments is critical for achieving efficient resource allocation and addressing performance bottlenecks. The integration of swarm intelligence algorithms provides a promising approach to enhance load balancing capabilities while promoting sustainability. By leveraging principles such as self-organization, decentralized decision-making, and collective behavior, swarm intelligence algorithms offer improved resource utilization, reduced energy consumption, and enhanced system performance. The efficacy of swarm intelligence-based load balancing in attaining sustainable outcomes has been substantiated through performance evaluation techniques and real-world case studies.

Nonetheless, several challenges, including algorithm scalability, convergence speed, and adaptability to dynamic workload patterns, must be overcome to advance the field. Future research endeavors should concentrate on developing hybrid algorithms, adaptive techniques, and integrating swarm intelligence with emerging technologies such as edge computing. By addressing these challenges and exploring innovative approaches, the optimization of load balancing in cloud environments can be achieved, fostering sustainable development in the field.

REFERENCES

Akila, D., Bhaumik, A., Duraisamy, B., Suseendran, G., & Pal, S. (2021). Improved nature-inspired algorithms in cloud computing for load balancing. *Intelligent Computing and Innovation on Data Science Proceedings of ICTIDS, 2021*, 547–558.

Al-Turjman, F. M. (2021). AI-powered cloud for COVID-19 and other infectious disease diagnosis. *Personal and Ubiquitous Computing*, 27(3), 661–664. doi:10.1007/s00779-021-01625-1 PMID:34413717

Aqeel, I., Khormi, I. M., Khan, S. B., Shuaib, M., Almusharraf, A., Alam, S., & Alkhaldi, N. A. (2023). Load Balancing Using Artificial Intelligence for Cloud-Enabled Internet of Everything in Healthcare Domain. *Sensors (Basel)*, 23(11), 5349. doi:10.3390/s23115349 PMID:37300076

Bhargavi, K., & Babu, B. S. (2019, December). Load balancing scheme for the public cloud using reinforcement learning with raven roosting optimization policy (RROP). In *2019 4th International Conference on Computational Systems and Information Technology for Sustainable Solution (CSITSS)* (Vol. 4, pp. 1-6). IEEE.

Bhargavi, K., Sathish Babu, B., & Pitt, J. (2020). Performance modeling of load balancing techniques in cloud: Some of the recent competitive swarm artificial intelligence-based. *Journal of Intelligent Systems*, 30(1), 40–58. doi:10.1515/jisys-2019-0084

Bhattacharya, SMaddikunta, P. K. RSomayaji, S. R. KLakshmanna, KKaluri, RGadekallu, T. R. (2020). Load balancing of energy cloud using wind driven and firefly algorithms in internet of everything. *Journal of Parallel and Distributed Computing*, 142, 16–26. doi:10.1016/j.jpdc.2020.02.010

Birje, M. N., Challagidad, P., Goudar, R. H., & Tapale, M. (2017). Cloud computing review: Concepts, technology, challenges and security. *International Journal of Cloud Computing (IJCC), Inderscience*, 6(1), 32–57.

Chhabra, A., Huang, K. C., Bacanin, N., & Rashid, T. A. (2022). Optimizing bag-of-tasks scheduling on cloud data centers using hybrid swarm-intelligence meta-heuristic. *The Journal of Supercomputing*, 78(7), 1–63. doi:10.1007/s11227-021-04199-0

Devaraj, A. F. S., Elhoseny, M., Dhanasekaran, S., Lydia, E. L., & Shankar, K. (2020). Hybridization of firefly and improved multi-objective particle swarm optimization algorithm for energy efficient load balancing in cloud computing environments. *Journal of Parallel and Distributed Computing*, 142, 36–45. doi:10.1016/j.jpdc.2020.03.022

Dewan, M., Mudgal, A., Pandey, P., Raghav, Y. Y., & Gupta, T. (2023). Predicting Pregnancy Complications Using Machine Learning. In D. Kumar & P. Maniiarasan (Eds.), *Technological Tools for Predicting Pregnancy Complications* (pp. 141–160). IGI Global. doi:10.4018/979-8-3693-1718-1.ch008

Elmagzoub, M. A., Syed, D., Shaikh, A., Islam, N., Alghamdi, A., & Rizwan, S. (2021). A survey of swarm intelligence based load balancing techniques in cloud computing environment. *Electronics (Basel)*, *10*(21), 2718. doi:10.3390/electronics10212718

Geeks for Geeks. (n.d.). *Load Balancing in Cloud Computing.* GfG, https://www.geeksforgeeks.org/load-balancing-in-cloud-computing/

Ghumman, N. (2015). Dynamic combination of improved max-min and ant colony algorithm for load balancing in cloud system. In *Conference on Computing, Communication and Networking Technologies (ICCCNT)*. IEEE.

Gill, S. S., Tuli, S., Xu, M., Singh, I., Singh, K. V., Lindsay, D., Tuli, S., Smirnova, D., Singh, M., Jain, U., Pervaiz, H., Sehgal, B., Kaila, S. S., Misra, S., Aslanpour, M. S., Mehta, H., Stankovski, V., & Garraghan, P. (2019). Transformative effects of IoT, Blockchain and Artificial Intelligence on cloud computing: Evolution, vision, trends and open challenges. *Internet of Things : Engineering Cyber Physical Human Systems*, *8*, 100118. doi:10.1016/j.iot.2019.100118

Goyal, S., Bhushan, S., Kumar, Y., Rana, A. U. H. S., Bhutta, M. R., Ijaz, M. F., & Son, Y. (2021). An optimized framework for energy-resource allocation in a cloud environment based on the whale optimization algorithm. *Sensors (Basel)*, *21*(5), 1583. doi:10.3390/s21051583 PMID:33668282

Ionescu, L. (2019). Big data, blockchain, and artificial intelligence in cloud-based accounting information systems. *Analysis and Metaphysics*, (18), 44–49.

Junaid, M., Sohail, A., Rais, R. N. B., Ahmed, A., Khalid, O., Khan, I. A., Hussain, S. S., & Ejaz, N. (2020). Modeling an optimized approach for load balancing in cloud. *IEEE Access : Practical Innovations, Open Solutions*, *8*, 173208–173226. doi:10.1109/ACCESS.2020.3024113

Kiruthiga, G., & Vennila, S. M. (2020). Energy efficient load balancing aware task scheduling in cloud computing using multi-objective chaotic darwinian chicken swarm optimization. *Int J Comput Netw Appl*, *7*, 82–92.

Kumar, M. S., Shadrach, F. D., Polamuri, S. R., Poonkodi, R., & Pudi, V. N. (2022, July). A binary Bird Swarm Optimization technique for cloud computing task scheduling and load balancing. In *2022 International Conference on Innovative Computing, Intelligent Communication and Smart Electrical Systems (ICSES)* (pp. 1-6). IEEE.

Li, M., Sun, Z., Jiang, Z., Tan, Z., & Chen, J. (2020). A virtual reality platform for safety training in coal mines with AI and cloud computing. *Discrete Dynamics in Nature and Society*, *2020*, 1–7. doi:10.1155/2020/8889903

Mesbahi, M., & Rahmani, A. M. (2016). Load balancing in cloud computing: A state of the art survey. *Int. J. Mod. Educ. Comput. Sci*, *8*(3), 64–78. doi:10.5815/ijmecs.2016.03.08

Mishra, K., & Majhi, S. K. (2021). A binary Bird Swarm Optimization based load balancing algorithm for cloud computing environment. *Open Computer Science*, *11*(1), 146–160. doi:10.1515/comp-2020-0215

Mishra, R., & Jaiswal, A. (2012). Ant colony optimization: A solution of load balancing in cloud. *International Journal of Web & Semantic Technology*, *3*(2), 33–50. doi:10.5121/ijwest.2012.3203

Nasir, M. A. U., Horii, H., Serafini, M., Kourtellis, N., Raymond, R., Girdzijauskas, S., & Osogami, T. (2017). *Load balancing for skewed streams on heterogeneous cluster*. arXiv preprint arXiv:1705.09073.

Nishant, K., Sharma, P., Krishna, V., Gupta, C., Singh, K. P., & Rastogi, R. (2012, March). Load balancing of nodes in cloud using ant colony optimization. In *2012 UKSim 14th international conference on computer modelling and simulation* (pp. 3-8). IEEE. 10.1109/UKSim.2012.11

Pan, I., Abd Elaziz, M., & Bhattacharyya, S. (Eds.). (2020). *Swarm intelligence for cloud computing*. CRC Press. doi:10.1201/9780429020582

Qawqzeh, Y., Alharbi, M. T., Jaradat, A., & Sattar, K. N. A. (2021). A review of swarm intelligence algorithms deployment for scheduling and optimization in cloud computing environments. *PeerJ. Computer Science*, *7*, e696. doi:10.7717/peerj-cs.696 PMID:34541313

Qureshi, K. N., Jeon, G., & Piccialli, F. (2021). Anomaly detection and trust authority in artificial intelligence and cloud computing. *Computer Networks*, *184*, 107647. doi:10.1016/j.comnet.2020.107647

Raghav, Y. Y., & Gulia, S. (2023). The Rise of Artificial Intelligence and Its Implications on Spirituality. In *Investigating the Impact of AI on Ethics and Spirituality* (pp. 165–178). IGI Global. doi:10.4018/978-1-6684-9196-6.ch011

Raghav, Y. Y., & Vyas, V. (2019, October). A comparative analysis of different load balancing algorithms on different parameters in cloud computing. In *2019 3rd International Conference on Recent Developments in Control, Automation & Power Engineering (RDCAPE)* (pp. 628-634). IEEE. 10.1109/RDCAPE47089.2019.8979122

Raghav, Y. Y., & Vyas, V. (2023). ACBSO: A hybrid solution for load balancing using ant colony and bird swarm optimization algorithms. *International Journal of Information Technology : an Official Journal of Bharati Vidyapeeth's Institute of Computer Applications and Management*, *15*(5), 1–11. doi:10.1007/s41870-023-01340-5

Raghav, Y. Y., Vyas, V., & Rani, H. (2022). Load balancing using dynamic algorithms for cloud environment: A survey. *Materials Today: Proceedings*, *69*, 349–353. doi:10.1016/j.matpr.2022.09.048

Rajeshwari, B. S., Dakshayini, M., & Guruprasad, H. S. (2022). Workload Balancing in a Multi-Cloud Environment: Challenges and Research Directions. *Operationalizing Multi-Cloud Environments: Technologies, Tools and Use Cases*.

Ramezani, F., Lu, J., & Hussain, F. K. (2014). Task-based system load balancing in cloud computing using particle swarm optimization. *International Journal of Parallel Programming*, *42*(5), 739–754. doi:10.1007/s10766-013-0275-4

Singh, K. K. (2018, November). An artificial intelligence and cloud based collaborative platform for plant disease identification, tracking and forecasting for farmers. In 2018 IEEE international conference on cloud computing in emerging markets (CCEM) (pp. 49-56). IEEE. doi:10.1109/CCEM.2018.00016

Singh, S., Nikolovski, S., & Chakrabarti, P. (2022). GWLBC: Gray Wolf Optimization Based Load Balanced Clustering for Sustainable WSNs in Smart City Environment. *Sensors (Basel)*, 22(19), 7113. doi:10.3390/s22197113 PMID:36236208

Surjeet, K., Sabyasachi, P., & Ranjan, A. (2021). *Turkish Journal of Computer and Mathematics Education, 12*(11), 3885-3898.

Tapale, M. T., Goudar, R. H., Birje, M. N., & Patil, R. S. (2020). Utility based load balancing using firefly algorithm in cloud. Journal of Data. *Information & Management, 2*, 215–224.

Ullah, A. (2019). Artificial bee colony algorithm used for load balancing in cloud computing. *IAES International Journal of Artificial Intelligence*, 8(2), 156. doi:10.11591/ijai.v8.i2.pp156-167

Chapter 11
A Comparative Analytics for Dynamic Load Balancing Mechanisms Intended to Improve Task Scheduling in Cloud Computing With Security Challenges

Kiritkumar Patel

ⓘ https://orcid.org/0000-0002-8967-4233

Ganpat University, India

Ajaykumar Patel

Ganpat University, India

Bhavesh Patel

Ganpat University, India

ABSTRACT

Cloud computing refers to a network of computing resources (servers, networks, applications, hardware, and software) interconnected globally. A good usage technique for resource utilization is load balancing. The practice of reassigning the total load to the individual nodes in a particular network is known as task distribution in the cloud. Since there is now no specific research carried out to perform comparative analytics in terms of different parameters of scheduling of task-based algorithms, it is crucial to develop a consistent comparison mechanism among them. FCFS, SJF, OLB, and GPA are the scheduling algorithms that are explored. Distribution of tasks is the main concern of crucial elements that boosts performance and optimizes resource usage. This study surveys the various scheduling methods employed by cloud service providers. There are so many scheduling approaches available to optimize performance and minimize execution time. It also discusses the security challenges in the cloud according to infrastructure and services.

DOI: 10.4018/979-8-3693-0338-2.ch011

INTRODUCTION

Cloud computing nowadays is a major topic of attention in the scientific community. Compared to its competitors, cloud computing offers a more flexible environment. By using cloud computing, you can manage your data from anywhere (Srinivas et al., 2012). Because cloud computing offers resources in enormous quantities and allows users and organizations to use those resources at will, corporations are moving toward it.

Cloud users can easily access resources on demand thanks to the cloud computing model (Soni & Barwar, 2018). On-demand, the cloud offers a wide range of services to its users, including quick elasticity and dynamic network connectivity. The performance, resource management, and efficient job scheduling of the cloud are key factors in its appeal.

The primary emphasis of this essay is various work scheduling strategies. It is possible to describe task scheduling as selecting the most suitable resources for the job's execution. The task can alternatively be described as user queries that are sent to several servers and successfully completed within the given time frame (Kumar & Sharma, 2017). The distribution of tasks among the available resources is the basis for task scheduling.

In a decentralized setting, the major goal of scheduling algorithms is to balance the workload by extending various tasks among servers, which maximizes processor usage and cuts down on user task execution time. Scheduling available resources is always according to the time occupied for their effective execution is the main goal. The work could involve inputting a query, processing that query, and gaining access to the necessary memory and software (Srinivas et al., 2012). The data center then categorizes user requests based on the requests made for the requested services and the services agreement.

Researchers have conducted a survey on many strategies of distributed computing task scheduling in cloud computing. In the current state of growth in technology, it is required for a system to have the capacity to multitask by executing multiple tasks effectively. These kinds of problems are defined in task scheduling algorithms. In task scheduling the networks are established to use various strategies to manage tasks and execute them over various resources as per user expectations to reach the desired milestone. These algorithms are designed to increase throughput and minimize the execution time.

There are many approaches available for the distribution of tasks in cloud computing such as Round Robin, Min Min, FCFS, and Max-Min for handling multiple processes simultaneously over the resources. This paper discussed the merits and demerits of different algorithms in terms of efficiency, throughput, and complexity.

However, there are extra security risks associated with the services offered by third-party cloud service providers. Transferring user assets (data, apps, etc.) from under administrative control into a shared environment where many users are gathered in one place raises security issues. This survey describes the security concerns that arise because of cloud computing's inherent characteristics. The survey also includes the most recent solutions to security problems that have been discussed in the literature. A quick overview of security flaws in mobile cloud computing is also presented. The discussion of unresolved difficulties and potential future study topics is also offered in the conclusion.

LITERATURE REVIEW

The main aim of the paper is that according to the existing research work review was carried out to perform a comparable analysis of the load balancing approach of cloud computing. The following table shows the summarized review of existing models of task scheduling.

Table 1. Literature survey

A Task Scheduling Approach for Cloud Resource Management, By Shi, Y., Suo, K., Kemp, S., & Hodge, J. (2020, July). In *2020 Fourth World Conference on Smart Trends in Systems, Security and Sustainability (WorldS4)* (pp. 131-136). IEEE.	
Research Focus	This research describes a vital usage of cloud resources is task scheduling for assigning tasks to computing resources. Min Min algorithm executes the task with lowest time and BMin is designed to augment the performance for algorithm Min- min.
Outcome	BMin is improved turnaround time and load balancing
Observation	The future scope of the work concentrate towards trying to use other parameters to improve performance

Table 2. Literature survey

Comparison of Task Scheduling Algorithms in Cloud Environment, scopus, Babur Hayat Malik, Mehwashma Amir, Bilal Mazhar, Shehzad Ali, Rabiya Jalil	
Research Focus	The author has discussed how resource utilization approaches are used in the cloud with several parameter settings, like execution time, load balance, Quality of service, performance, response time, and Makespan.
Outcome	Some algorithms consider only load balance while some of them consider response time.
Observation	By extensive study of many approaches most algorithms work with each or two parameters, due to that optimized results can't be achieved effectively. Better milestones can be achieved by tuning more scheduling metrics to generate an efficient algorithm.

Table 3. Literature survey

Evaluating Cloud Computing Scheduling Algorithms Under Different Environment And Scenarios,IEEE, Yash Vijay, Bogdan V Ghita	
Research Focus	The author has developed a set of configurations and usage for the cloud to differentiate the functioning of the scheduling algorithms. Perform the experiment under the different configurations with utilization and were analyzed based on parameters such as Cost and Makespan.
Outcome	FCFS, Generalized Priority,Shortest Job First and Opportunistic Load Balancing, widely used scheduling algorithms in the cloud and were implemented in different environments to be Compared. Author found that there is no such scheduling algorithm that can be used in all circumstances and configurations.
Observation	More parameter specific algorithms can be experimented to address factors like power, throughput etc.

Table 4. Literature survey

A Dynamic Task Scheduling Algorithm Improved by Load Balancing in Cloud Computing, (ICWR,IEEE), Fatemeh Ebadifard *Department of Computer,University of Kashan,Iran*	
Research Focus	The author has proposed an algorithm and it is surveyed with the Round Robin approach which is the method of load balancing of honeybee behavior. Simulation results indicate that in comparison to the honey bee method.
Outcome	The proposed algorithm improves the average make span by 21.25% when increasing the number of tasks. Moreover, the proposed method also reduces the waiting time.
Observation	Author has mentioned the exploration of study by applying other factors like cost reduction or Energy consumption for the service provider

Table 5. Literature survey

Performance Analysis of Load Balancing Architectures in Cloud Computing, Ektemal Al-Rayis Computer Science Department Imam Muhammad Ibn Saud Islamic University	
Research Focus	Author has discussed three different categories: centralized, decentralized or hierarchical. Author has given a basic explanation of this architecture. The author defines one set up in the network simulator Opnet Modeler with all used on figuration. After creating this framework in opnet simulator show all the received result in term of server load and response time and in last conclusion author received final output like hierarchical gave better performance in term of centralized and decentralized architecture
Outcome	Use in network simulator opnet modeler and create framework for public model and SAAS services
Observation	Author has compiled three architecture and its performative effect on the cloud. Author had developed a simulation model for public cloud to measure different scale and performative measures of cloud on three different architectures after competitive analysis author concluded that hierarchical architecture gives dominant performance and also able to split load and and maintain the nature of centralized management of cloud.

The security concerns of cloud computing are covered in a number of papers in the literature. The writers of (Getov, 2013; Rao & Thilagam, 2015) provided reviews of the cloud computing security concerns. The aforementioned studies, however, do not address security solutions; they merely discuss security vulnerabilities. Reference (Chandramouli et al., 2013) examined the security concerns with cloud computing at many levels. The security fixes are also discussed in (Chandramouli et al., 2013). But there hasn't been a thorough consideration of the future, and there's no review of cloud computing. The authors of (Srinivas et al., 2012) provided a thorough analysis of cloud privacy protection with a specific focus on e-health clouds. Additionally, the scope of the study in (Srinivas et al., 2012) is restricted to just privacy. (Yan et al., 2014) examined the security.

In (Yan et al., 2014), the security and privacy issues related to cloud computing were evaluated, and it also covered how to defend against the current flaws. But nothing was said about the technologies as the discussion of the security challenges in (Yan et al., 2014) was based on confidentiality, integrity, availability, accountability, and privacy-preservability creating the vulnerability's root cause. The authors of (Na & Huh, 2015) elaborated on the cloud's security challenges as well as possible defenses against vulnerabilities. However, the poll does not discuss potential future research trajectories. Similar to (Na & Huh, 2015), which provided a thorough analysis of the security concerns related to cloud computing along with a brief review of the most recent and up-to-date security solutions.

The research in (Ali, Dhamotharan, Khan et al, 2015) examined some of the well-liked cloud computing security approaches, including the cube model, the multi-tenancy model, and the risk assessment model. The authors of (Ali, Dhamotharan, Khan et al, 2015) also covered the security concerns with cloud computing. The hazards are, however, explored from the viewpoints of many stakeholder groups, including customers, the government, and service providers.

Similar to this, the article (Rong et al., 2013) discusses cloud computing security challenges and related security solutions. However, the privacy aspect of cloud security is the main topic of discussion. Furthermore, there is little mention of potential future study avenues. Our poll is substantially more detailed and comprehensive than the aforementioned surveys, in which cloud computing security challenges are discussed, with a focus on the most recent security solutions that have been published in the literature. We also offer tabular comparisons of the strategies that are being discussed. Additionally, we quickly go through the security concerns related to mobile cloud computing as well as general approaches that could result in fixes.

ARCHITECTURAL VIEW OF CLOUD COMPUTING

To offer services to end users, cloud computing incorporates a number of computing technologies. It's crucial to briefly explain the elements that make up cloud computing in order to comprehend the security concerns related to it. The definition of cloud computing provided by the National Institute of Standards and Technology (NIST) (Balduzzi et al., 2012) is commonly used (Ficco & Rak, 2014). Listed below are some NIST definitions.

★ **Architectural Characteristics**
- **Ad-hoc self-service:** Without interacting with the CSP directly, customers can order and administer cloud services. When necessary, the accompanying resources and service provision are carried out. Web services and administrative interfaces are typically used for this (Ficco & Rak, 2014).
- **Extensive network access:** Customers must be able to access the services, customer applications, and customer data stored in the cloud via established techniques and protocols. The feature further stipulates that service accessibility should have a diverse environment, either thin or thick (for example, mobile phones, laptops, workstations, tablets). In the literature, ubiquitous network access is sometimes referred to as broad network access (Ficco & Rak, 2014).
- **Pooling of resources:** In a multi-tenant system, the resources of the cloud are pooled and distributed among numerous clients. The clients are open about where the resources are located. A mapping of physical and virtual resources is made available to the customers.
- **Quickly elasticity:** According to consumer demand, the resources can be quickly and elastically scaled. The consumer sees an endless supply of resources that may be paid for on a pay-as-you-go basis as needed.
- **Proportional service:** Dynamically adjusted resource scaling is carried out, and the customer and CSP are informed of service utilization statistics. While the customers are being charged in a certain way, the metering also aids in the automatic optimization of resource utilization in a pay-as-you-go fashion.

- ○ **Multi-tenancy:** The five properties of cloud computing described above are defined by the NIST. Multi-tenancy, however, is now recognised by the Cloud Security Alliance (CSA) as a crucial aspect of cloud computing (although not an essential characteristic) The ability for numerous clients, who may or may not be related, to use a same resource is known as multi-tenancy belonging to the same group. With multi-tenancy, resources are used to their fullest potential and various clients are logically separated.

★ **Service based Modeling**

The NIST defines cloud computing services into three categories: infrastructure as a service (IaaS), platform as a service (PaaS), and software as a service (SaaS) (IaaS). SPI is a term used to describe the cloud service concept (software, platform, and infrastructure)

- ○ **SaaS:** Cloud-based apps from CSP can be accessed by customers online thanks to the SaaS model. Applications like web browsers can be accessed through the thin client interface. The SaaS does not give users the option to make a programme or application. Software as a service (SaaS) is exclusively offered online, making it a model for online software distribution. Customers only pay to use the product; they do not own it (Schwarzkopf et al., 2012).

- ○ **PaaS:** Customer-owned apps require a framework where they may be managed and performed. This includes platform layer resources (the run-time engine that runs the programmes), operating systems, and integrated development environments (IDEs). PaaS is the delivery model for the aforementioned services. Only the apps that are transported to the cloud are under the control of the PaaS, not the underlying cloud infrastructure.

- ○ **IaaS:** The CSP's hardware infrastructure, which includes the network, storage, memory, CPU, and several other computer resources, is referred to as IaaS. The resources are offered as virtualized systems that can be accessed via the Internet. The underlying resources are at the control of the CSP (Na & Huh, 2015).

★ **Modeling based on Deployment Ability**

- ○ **Personal cloud:** The private cloud is a cloud that is operated and managed exclusively for a single enterprise. The physical infrastructure of the organization may or may not be owned by it, and it may be run by another party or by the organization itself. Likewise, private clouds may or may not be situated at the physical location of the company. Whatever the case may be, a private cloud is intended for use by a single enterprise, and no other customers are allowed to access the resources.

- ○ **General purpose cloud:** The CSP is the owner of the physical infrastructure for the cloud, which is accessible to both individuals and businesses. All of the customers share the resources. Customers make payments to the owner of the cloud based on the resources and services they utilize. The CSP manages the physical infrastructure, which is situated away from the clients' sites.

- ○ **Localized cloud:** Many businesses and/or customers share the community cloud, creating a community. The objective, security needs, policy, and compliance issues are often shared interests among the community. Any organization in the community, or a third party, may manage the community cloud. Similar to that, it could be on- or off-premise.

- ○ **Blended cloud:** Two or more clouds are combined to create a hybrid cloud (public, private, or community). Although they all share standardized or proprietary technologies, each participating cloud maintains its position as a separate business.

Figure 1. Load balancing workflow

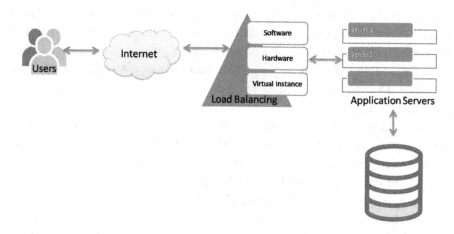

LOAD BALANCING APPROACHES

In this technological growth, there are so many advances to come up with in every aspect. Nowadays load balancer acts as front end and utilized with a single IP address to manage network traffic of targeted workload. It eventually distributes traffic to each avail instance or specific percentage of traffic to each instance.

Many Load balancing algorithms utilize common load balancers for both in local data centers and in public cloud services to distribute traffic to the various workload nodes. The following algorithms are explored in this paper.

- **Round Robin:** Round robin is a load balancing method in which all requests are distributed equally across all the instances/resources. The parameters used for RR are weight and cycle. Round robin works best when all nodes have similar computing capacity. RR doesn't distribute processes among the instances on the priority basis.
- **Weighted RR:** Weighted RR distributes all the processes according to instance capacity. It will divert the traffic to different instances by its measured capacity. The more capable instance receives a high amount of process. WRR works best when all the process size is equal or well known in advance size of packets than the main use of the correct amount of resource bandwidth utilization fulfilled.
- **FCFS:** In FCFS process is forwarding to cloud instances as per their arrival in the ready queue. The process that comes first will have major priority. Drawback of this method is that the process will run till it finishes. Due to this mechanism short processes which are last in queue need to wait until a long process is about to finish. Throughput is not efficient in this algorithm.
- **Min-Min Algorithm:** This algorithm's working strategy is based on an execution time for tasks execution is small that is selected from all tasks for allocation. The efficiency of the Min-Min scheduling technique reduces the overall task completion time. The major drawbacks of the Min-Min scheduling algorithm is that it doesn't count the total load of each instance. Due to this some instances are always overloaded, whereas some are not getting enough work.

- **Max-Min Algorithm:** Max-min algorithm allocates load distribution according to size of task. A large task gets first priority and assigned it to the respective resource rather than smaller tasks and short tasks also executed concurrently. It maintains the task status maintenance table to estimate the real time and load of the server and expected time of completion of task. The drawback of this approach is to finish tasks in minimal time.

COMPARATIVE ANALYTICS

In this paper, resource utilization approaches are comparative studies that have been carried out to optimize the task scheduling in cloud computing. To perform the comparative analytics the below mentioned performance parameters are considered for the all selected load balancing algorithms.

- **Resource Utilization:** It is used to determine resource usage. It is necessary for an effective load balance algorithm which must utilize/maximize resource usage.
- **Performance:** This metric is utilized to map the system's effectiveness.
- **Throughput:** This metric shows the number of task/process execution is completed. high throughput is necessary for better performance.
- **Response time:** It is the span of time taken to complete a submitted request over the system.
- **Scalability:** It is the capacity of an algorithm to balance the load among all the nodes over the cloud.
- **Makespan:** It is the total amount of time needed to complete all tasks by the resources.
- **Migration time:** It is the total amount of time required to move a task from a busy instance to another instance which is less busy or under loaded.
- **Fault tolerance:** This parameter is used to check the algorithm's ability to perform load balancing if certain nodes fail.

SECURITY CHALLENGES

Customers can take advantage of enhanced, optimized, and affordable services thanks to the cloud computing characteristics and models described in the previous section. The models stated above that exhibit the qualities are implemented utilizing a variety of technologies, including virtualization and multi-tenancy. In addition to hazards shared with the traditional IT infrastructure, the technologies together with cloud service and deployment patterns also introduce security risks and vulnerabilities unique to the cloud (Wu et al., 2010). The nature or degree of the security concerns in the cloud may be different from those in traditional IT infrastructure. Nevertheless, the technologies provide quick adaptability and good control but they also pose a few hazards to the system. Data visibility to other users and operation tracing are dangers brought on by multi-tenancy.

Customers are given the option of on-demand self-service through Web-based management interfaces, which increases the risk of illegal access to the management interface compared to traditional systems (Ficco & Rak, 2014). Similar to physical environments, virtualized environments have their own set of hazards and weaknesses, such as hostile virtual machine (VM) cooperation and VM escape. Similarly, from the perspective of the cloud service model, the service models are dependent on one another. The PaaS, which is reliant on the underlying IaaS, is used to build and deploy SaaS applications.

Table 6. Comparative analytics

Load Balancing Algorithms / Performance Metrics	Round Robin	Weighted Round Robin	FCFS	Min-Min	Max-Min
Static/ Dynamic	**Static**	**Static**	**Dynamic**	**Static**	**Static**
Resource Utilization	Resource utilization with variable loads	Better than RR	Manage tasks with FIFO	Effective resource utilization	Optimized resource utilization
Performance	Similar to FCFS but when when data are more variable its perform better	Better than RR because no sorted queues are required	Less performance when data are variable	Good	Effective and scalable
Throughput	Depends on the job load	Utilized in WRR than RR	Increased throughput by cutting down completion time	Better when the limited space and effective execution time	Degradation in throughput for throughput for the Abilene network And less compete in congestion
Response Time	a round robin is better adjusted to average waiting time. It takes low response time	Improved Response time in user faced app	fcfs is better for small brust time. It takes a response time.	Major focus on minimize response time	Mitigate delay in task execution with minimum completion task
Scalability	Efficient scalable but depends on chosen of quantum	Scalable for multiprocessors as well	FCFS is better when guaranteed completion order needed	Scalable when space and time shared mode	Scalable in time shared mode
Makespan	N	N	Arrival time is better and Makespan better only in short burst time	Better then FCFS	Minimal makespan
Migration Time	N	N	N	N	N
Fault Tolerance	N	N	N	N	N
Merits	each task has equal chance and has an equal execution time due to this load is balanced among every instances	simple to identify the assigned server	waiting time of job can be decreased as task assigned to instance on the basis of arrival	task will be executed on the basis of shortest possible times for completion	task with greater requirements are execute first which avoid starvation in the queue
Demerits	Resource utilization is not done effectively as every resource gets an equal amount of tasks. The selection of quantum size is one big issue of RR.	not suitable when size of task is different	underutilization of the VM capacity or vice versa	an uneven and inefficient distribution of resources	imbalanced workloads among instances which reduces the system efficiency.

The service models' operational reliance on one another also introduces a security reliance. SaaS compromise can result from a compromised PaaS. In a nutshell, each service model that has been compromised allows access to additional service model layers. The private cloud deployment paradigm carries over the same set of weaknesses that the traditional IT infrastructure does. Because a single organization is only intended to use the private cloud, Due to the existence of users from various backgrounds and the administrative oversight of a third party, the public, community, and hybrid clouds have more cloud-specific vulnerabilities and dangers (Ibrahim et al., 2016). Multiple tenants using virtualized resources that may be identical to the same actual resources raises a number of security issues.

★ Communicational Level Challenges

Customers often have access to cloud services via the Internet (Younis & Kifayat, 2013). Customers and the cloud communicate using industry-standard Internet protocols and methods (Yu et al., 2012). Between the consumer and the cloud, the communication process results in the transmission of either data/information or applications. Additionally, there is inter-VM communication within the cloud. This chapter categorizes cloud communication into two groups: (a) external cloud communication (with clients); and (b) internal cloud communication (inside the cloud) taking place within the cloud infrastructure).The external communication of the cloud is comparable to any other Internet communication. Therefore, the difficulties that the cloud faces as a result of Internet characteristics are the same difficulties that traditional IT communication faces (Hashizume et al., 2013). These difficulties include man-in-the-middle attacks, eavesdropping, floods caused by IP spoofing, and masquerading (Zhang & Chen, 2013; Zhang et al., 2013). The solutions to these problems are also the same as those that are currently used in conventional settings, such as Secure Socket Layer (SSL), Internet Security Protocol (IPSec), cryptographic algorithms, intrusion detection and prevention systems, traffic cleaning, and digital certificates (Ren et al., 2012; Varadharajan & Tupakula, 2014). We did not detail these issues in this analysis because they are inherent to traditional IT infrastructure. This work concentrates on internal cloud communication since cloud characteristics and technologies create issues peculiar to clouds.

- **Centralized communication system**: Resource pooling permits the sharing of network infrastructure components in addition to the sharing of computing and storage resources (Ficco & Rak, 2014). Sharing network components gives attackers access to cross-tenant data assault (Na & Huh, 2015). The IaaS service model of the cloud is vulnerable because of the resource pooling feature of cloud computing. Such scans are typically not permitted by the service providers because it is difficult to distinguish between a legitimate network vulnerability scan and attacker activity. In a similar vein, IP-based network segmentation is not used because network resources are dynamically allocated and released and cannot be connected with a specific group of users.
- **Virtual network:** In cloud computing systems, virtualized networks are just as crucial to communication as actual networks when it comes to network usage. A logical network constructed over a physical network is known as a virtual network (Wei et al., 2014). the online Networks are in charge of inter-VM communication. The networking of VMs over the same host is supported by software-based network components like bridges, routers, and software-based network configurations. The following security issues can arise due to virtualized networks in a cloud setting. The traffic over a virtualized network cannot be monitored by security and protection measures over a physical network. This turns into a significant difficulty

since malicious VM activity escapes the notice of security tools. Mechanisms for intrusion detection and prevention often use traffic patterns and activity to evaluate abnormalities and identify the possibility of an attack. The aim of such preventive procedures is hampered by virtualized networks (Salah et al., 2012). Multiple VMs share the virtualized network, which makes it vulnerable to attacks like denial of service (DoS), spoofing, and sniffing of the virtual network. It is possible to track the traffic volumes for nefarious ends. In the event of malicious sniffing and spoofing of virtual networks, the cryptographic keys become exposed to leakage (Jansen, 2011).

- **Misconfigurations of security**: In order to offer secure cloud services to the customer, security configurations of the cloud network architecture are crucial (Che et al., 2011). Misconfigurations have the potential to seriously jeopardize user, application, and system security (Eghtesadi et al., 2014). Customers trust that their assets are secure in the cloud, where they outsource their applications and data to the cloud setting. A minor setup error could compromise the system's security. The configurations must be properly in place not only throughout the development, deployment, and operation of the cloud infrastructure, but also during any later changes to the cloud network to maintain the configuration's compliance with the security policies (Che et al., 2011). One of the most frequent configuration errors happens when administrators use a configuration tool that they are accustomed to but may not always meet all security criteria (Che et al., 2011). A variety of security rules may be required as a result of the migration of virtual machines, data, and applications across many physical nodes, changes in traffic patterns, and changes in topology (Singh et al., 2017). To maintain cloud security in such a case, the configuration of the cloud should be managed dynamically. Similar to this, any flaw in protocol setups and session configurations can be used to hijack sessions and obtain sensitive user data (Liu, Bi, & Vasilakos, 2014).

★ Architectural Level Challenges

- **Troubles with virtualization:** One of the strategic elements of the cloud is virtualization. Multiple consumers can share the same physical resources thanks to virtualization. Each user's own virtual machine (VM) is created, thereby giving them a full operating system user. In a multi-tenant environment, multiple VMs can be mapped to the same physical resources, enabling resource pooling. The component that controls virtual machines (VMs) and enables several operating systems to run simultaneously on the same physical system is known as a hypervisor or VM monitor (VMM) (Zhang et al., 2013). However, cloud infrastructure and user security are also hampered by virtualization. Below, we go over the security concerns with virtualization.

  - **Sharing of VM images:** VMs are created by using a VM image. A user has the option of creating their own virtual machine image or using one from the shared image repository (Na & Huh, 2015).

  - **VM separation:** The same physical hardware must be segregated from other virtual machines (VMs) running on it. Even though there is logical isolation between various VMS, access to the same physical resources can result in data breaches and cross-VM assaults. Fine-grained isolation of VMs is required on memory and compute hardware in addition to storage devices (Ali, Khan, & Vasilakos, 2015; Jansen, 2011).

  - **VM elude:** When a hostile user or VM escapes from the control of the VMM or hypervisor, this is known as a VM escape (Salah et al., 2012). A VMM is a piece of software that controls how each VM interacts with the hardware. The possibility of a VM escape can provide an attacker access to other VMs or bring down the VMM (Salah et al., 2012). An effective VM escape attack may grant access.to the hardware for processing and storage. The IaaS service model is impacted, which may have repercussions for other service models (Ren et al., 2012).

- **Moving VMs:** The technique of moving a virtual computer to another physical machine without shutting it down is known as VM migration (Bhadauria et al., 2013). There are many reasons to migrate VMs, including load balancing, fault tolerance, and maintenance (Bhadauria et al., 2013; Na & Huh, 2015). The contents of the VM are exposed to the network during the migration phase, which could result in data exposure worries about integrity and privacy. During migration, attackers can also access the VM's code in addition to its data (Na & Huh, 2015; Salah et al., 2012). To move the VM to a compromised server or under the management of a hacked VMM, an attacker may compromise the migration module. A important step that must be completed securely is the VM migration (Na & Huh, 2015).

- **Rollback of VM:** When necessary, virtualization enables a VM to be rolled back to a previous state. The rollback option gives the user freedom. Rollback, though, also brings up security issues (Song, 2014). For instance, the rewind function can restore the previously disabled security credentials (Na & Huh, 2015). Additionally, the reversion may expose the virtual machine to a vulnerability that has already been fixed (Yu et al., 2013). Additionally, the rollback can return the virtual machine to earlier security policies and errors in configuration (Na & Huh, 2015).

- **Hypervisor problems:** The hypervisor or VMM is the essential component of virtualization. The VMM is in charge of managing and isolating the VMs. Another task carried out by the VMM is creating and managing virtual resources. The operation of VMs running on the host system may be impacted by a VMM (Eghtesadi et al., 2014). All of the virtual machines (VMs) that are controlled by the attacker and managed by the victim's VMM (Eghtesadi et al., 2014). If an attacker seizes control of a VMM, the attacker may also have access to the VMs' metadata (Wei et al., 2014; Zhang et al., 2013).

- **VMware sprawl:** In a situation known as "VM sprawl," the number of virtual machines on the host system keeps growing while the majority of those that have already been created are sitting idle (Hashizume et al., 2013). The host machine's resources are massively squandered as a result of VM sprawl (Younis & Kifayat, 2013).

- **Storage and data concerns:** Users do not have complete control over their data while using the cloud computing model. As opposed to the traditional computer approach, cloud computing gives service providers the ability to decide how servers and data are managed. Users appreciate specific only on the VMs level of control (Rong et al., 2013). Greater data security risks than those associated with the traditional computer approach emerge from the absence of control over the data. Furthermore, unlike the traditional computer model, the properties of cloud computing, such as multi-tenancy and virtualization, also raise the possibility of assaults. The security issues that affect data in a cloud computing environment are summarized in this chapter.

  - **Data integrity and privacy:** Even though cloud computing guarantees cost efficiency and frees users from infrastructure administration tasks, it also has security risks.

In comparison to the traditional computer model, the data in the cloud is significantly more susceptible to hazards in terms of confidentiality, integrity, and availability (Varadharajan & Tupakula, 2014). The best Security threats increase as there are more users and applications. The security strength of the cloud in a shared environment is equal to the security strength of its weakest entity (Ali, Khan, & Vasilakos, 2015). Additionally not standardized (Salah et al., 2012) is the production and maintenance of cryptographic keys for the cloud computing paradigm. Standard cryptographic procedures cannot scale effectively to the cloud computing model due to the lack of secure and standardized key management techniques (Salah et al., 2012). As a result, the field of cryptography also increases the potential hazards to data.

- **Data recovery weakness**: The cloud provides customers with dynamic and on-demand resource provisioning because of its resource pooling and elasticity features. At a later period, the resource allotted to one user may be transferred to another user. A malevolent user can utilize data recovery techniques to access the data of prior users if memory and storage resources are limited (Danna et al., 2012; Ficco & Rak, 2014). The authors in (Danna et al., 2012) were successful in recovering 98% of the Amazon machine pictures files times. The sensitive user data may be seriously threatened by the data recovery vulnerability (Agrawal, 2011).

- **Inappropriately sanitized media:** Physical storage media can be destroyed for a variety of reasons, such as (a) when a disc has to be replaced, (b) when data is no longer required, and (c) when a service is terminated (Salah et al., 2012). The data may be at risk if the CSP does not properly clean the devices (Mell & Grance, 2011). Multi-tenancy can occasionally increase the danger of device sanitization. It might not be possible to destroy a gadget at the conclusion of its life cycle, as with the use of tenants.

- **Data archiving:** Another crucial issue that requires cautious handling is data backup. To guarantee the availability and recovery of data in the event of intentional and unintentional disasters, a frequent data backup is required on the CSP side. Additionally, the backup storage must be secured against tampering and unauthorized access (Ali, Khan, & Vasilakos, 2015).

○ **Security for application programming interfaces (APIs) and web applications:** The Internet is used to deliver services and applications to cloud users, as was covered in Section 1 (Singh et al., 2017). In fact, using and managing a cloud application through the Web is one of the fundamental needs (Zhang & Chen, 2013). The submission given by the CSP is always stored in the cloud, and users can access it anywhere. The fact that cloud apps are not bound to particular users is one of its key features (Yu et al., 2012). It becomes a much bigger problem due to the co-location of numerous users, their data, and other resources. The following were listed as the top 10 web application risks by the Open Web Application Security Project in 2013 ().

- The injection (SQL, OS, and LDAP)
- Broken session management and authentication
- Site-to-Site Scripting (XSS)
- Direct object references that aren't secure
- security configuration error
- Exposed Sensitive Data

- Function Level Access Control is Missing
- Using Known Vulnerable Components to Perform Cross-Site Request Forgery (CSRF)
- Invalidated Forwards and Redirects

To protect online applications and user resources, the risks listed above must be taken into account during web application development, maintenance, and use. The APIs act as a link between the user and cloud services. The security and availability of cloud services are significantly influenced by the security of APIs (Chandramouli et al., 2013). The safe and malicious-free use of cloud services is ensured by the secure APIs (Chen & Zhao, 2012). An API can be compared to a user manual that provides information about CSPs cloud characteristics and architecture. Using the APIs, users create or expand the services (Eghtesadi et al., 2014).

- **Identity administration and access management:** In a cloud context, identity management and access control are also connected to the confidentiality and integrity of data and services. Controlling unwanted access to and monitoring the user's identification are extremely crucial details (Yu et al., 2012). Due to the fact that the owner and resources are in various administrative domains and organization's authentication and authorization may not be exported to the cloud in the existing form, the problem of identity management and access control becomes more complicated in a cloud environment (Salah et al., 2012). Additionally, unlike the typical IT structure, the cloud may deal with users from several organizations with various frameworks for authentication and permission, at the same time and with similar resources.

LEGAL AND CONTRACTUAL LEVEL CHALLENGES

When an enterprise adopts cloud computing, its data and applications are transferred to CSP's administrative authority. This raises a number of concerns, including performance evaluation, adherence to legal requirements, jurisdictional issues, contract enforcement oversight, etc. These issues are associated with the service level agreement (SLA), legal issues and data locations physically.

- **Customer service agreements:** The terms and conditions between the user and CSP are laid out in the SLA. The SLA also specifies (a) the minimum performance standard that CSP must meet, (b) the corrective measures, and (c) the repercussions in the event that the agreement between the user and CSP is broken (Geetha & Robin, 2017). The users must clearly understand the security needs for all of their assets. The SLA should have a detailed agreement on the demand. It is more difficult to claim the loss at a CSP when there are ambiguities. For instance, it becomes challenging to make a claim against a CSP if any service is subcontracted to a third party. A subcontractor's accountability is frequently insufficient (Malik et al., 2018). In a similar vein, contract enforcement monitoring becomes problematic because users cannot entirely rely on CSP statistics. Evaluation of statistics and assigning blame also become a problem in this situation of disagreement between the CSP and user statistics (Jansen, 2011).
- **Legal problems:** The presence of CSP resources in geographically dispersed and occasionally conflicting legal jurisdictions creates legal difficulties related to cloud computing in addition to the technological ones discussed in the previous section (Yu et al., 2013). If the it becomes dif-

ficult for the user to adjust the security rules to comply with the new legal jurisdictions when the user's data is moved to a region with different laws. Data may occasionally exist in many places with various laws governing digital security. Furthermore, the question of jurisdiction—as to which laws would be applicable in the event of a dispute—arises (Chen & Zhao, 2012; Jansen, 2011; Malik et al., 2018).

OPEN CONCERNS AND CONVERSATION FOR CLOUD SECURITY

The explanation of security risks in the sections above explains that, in addition to the traditional security concerns, the cloud also has novel issues brought on by the usage of new technologies and activities. The Web services and application challenges, communication and network issues, data privacy issues, etc. are common issues that existed in the relevant technologies even before the cloud computing paradigm emerged. Virtualization, multi-tenancy, and shared resource pools all present new problems. Furthermore, when handled in the cloud environment, some conventional difficulties become considerably more delicate and important. For instance, the lack of administrative control by the data owner makes data security more important and challenging to manage. The severity is increased by the collocation of the data and applications of diverse organizations. Despite the research community's extensive efforts, there are still unresolved problems that must be solved in order to provide a secure cloud environment. The first and most important requirement is to create a thorough and integrated security solution that covers the majority of the key security needs in the cloud environment. The majority of research activities concentrate on a single problem and attempt to find a solution for it, or in the most promising case, a few problems closely related to it. The specific problem scenario prompts the creation of numerous solutions that address diverse security requirements. In practice, it is neither prudent nor practical to install as many security technologies as there are security requirements. Large-scale deployment and configuration. A more comprehensive security tool will be simple to manage as a result of the solution. There is at least a requirement to synchronize various security measures solutions to achieve the appropriate level of security.

CONCLUSION AND FUTURE SCOPE

In this paper, several algorithms of load balancing have been studied and analyzed. Load balancing is one of the major issues in the field of cloud computing. The main goal of this is to properly distribute the load among all the instances on cloud is necessary for utilizing the resources efficiently. Many algorithms have been discussed with their speciality indications and limitations on the basis of several performative measures like Resources Utilization, Performance, Throughput, Response Time, Scalability, Makespan etc. The article specially focused the comparative analytical study on the basis of all these metrics and concluded usage indications in the context of listed algorithms. The Round Robin performs well when every task gets a fair allocation of CPU. In Weighted RR tasks will be distributed among all the instances based on defined values. FCFS can minimize the waiting time of a task. MinMin increases throughput and minimizes response time. MaxMin minimal makespan by mitigating delay in execution time. For further enhancement of this study, this study further carried out to propose an enhanced and hybrid approach based load balancing algorithm that can give better performance in aspects of all the defined metrics to achieve effective performance.

As per security concerns, although cloud computing has many benefits, it also raises security issues that slow down the adoption of the technology. The security risks present in the cloud should be widely known to all users, whether they are individuals or businesses. Understanding security threats and preventative measures will assist companies in carrying out. They will be urged to switch to the cloud when we carry the cost-benefit study out. Because the cloud uses so many established and cutting-edge technologies, it has both common and uncommon security problems. Multiple users (potentially from different origins) can use the same physical resource thanks to virtualization and multi-tenancy. The aforementioned technologies produce security risks that are unique to clouds, which must be recognised and addressed while taking into account new cloud characteristics. Similar to how traditional physical networks confront security issues, virtual networks too face some particular issues. Because perfect isolation between virtual computers is not possible, it is necessary to design particular approaches that can delineate boundaries that are functionally equal to physical isolation. Cloud computing's geographic reach raises a number of legal questions about users' assets and the laws that govern them. Due to the lack of administrative control of the owner organization, identity management and access control over the business's digital resources also take unique shapes in the cloud.

REFERENCES

Agrawal, R. (2011, June). Legal issues in cloud computing. *IndicThreads*.

Ali, M., Dhamotharan, R., Khan, E., Khan, S. U., Vasilakos, A. V., Li, K., & Zomaya, A. Y. (2015). SeDaSC: Secure data sharing in clouds. *IEEE Systems Journal*, *11*(2), 395–404. doi:10.1109/JSYST.2014.2379646

Ali, M., Khan, S. U., & Vasilakos, A. V. (2015). Security in cloud computing: Opportunities and challenges. *Information Sciences*, *305*, 357–383. doi:10.1016/j.ins.2015.01.025

Ali, M., Khan, S. U., & Vasilakos, A. V. (2015). Security in cloud computing: Opportunities and challenges. *Information Sciences*, *305*, 357–383. doi:10.1016/j.ins.2015.01.025

Ali, S. A., & Alam, M. (2016, December). A relative study of task scheduling algorithms in cloud computing environment. In *2016 2nd International Conference on Contemporary Computing and Informatics (IC3I)* (pp. 105-111). IEEE. 10.1109/IC3I.2016.7917943

Balduzzi, M., Zaddach, J., Balzarotti, D., Kirda, E., & Loureiro, S. (2012, March). A security analysis of amazon's elastic compute cloud service. In *Proceedings of the 27th annual ACM symposium on applied computing* (pp. 1427-1434). ACM. 10.1145/2245276.2232005

Bhadauria, R., Borgohain, R., Biswas, A., & Sanyal, S. (2013). Secure authentication of Cloud data mining API. *arXiv preprint arXiv:1308.0824*.

Chaisiri, S., Lee, B. S., & Niyato, D. (2011). Optimization of resource provisioning cost in cloud computing. *IEEE Transactions on Services Computing*, *5*(2), 164–177. doi:10.1109/TSC.2011.7

Chandramouli, R., Iorga, M., & Chokhani, S. (2013). Cryptographic key management issues and challenges in cloud services. *Secure Cloud Computing*, 1-30.

Che, J., Duan, Y., Zhang, T., & Fan, J. (2011). Study on the security models and strategies of cloud computing. *Procedia Engineering, 23*, 586-593.

Chen, D., & Zhao, H. (2012, March). *Data security and privacy protection issues in cloud computing. In 2012 international conference on computer science and electronics engineering* (Vol. 1). IEEE.

Danna, E., Mandal, S., & Singh, A. (2012, March). *A practical algorithm for balancing the max-min fairness and throughput objectives in traffic engineering. In 2012 Proceedings IEEE INFOCOM.* IEEE.

Dinh, H. T., Lee, C., Niyato, D., & Wang, P. (2013). A survey of mobile cloud computing: Architecture, applications, and approaches. *Wireless Communications and Mobile Computing, 13*(18), 1587–1611. doi:10.1002/wcm.1203

Eghtesadi, A., Jarraya, Y., Debbabi, M., & Pourzandi, M. (2014, March). Preservation of security configurations in the cloud. In *2014 IEEE International Conference on Cloud Engineering* (pp. 17-26). IEEE. 10.1109/IC2E.2014.14

Fang, Y., Wang, F., & Ge, J. (2010, OKaur, B., & Singh, R. (2016). A comparison and analysis of load balancing algorithms in cloud computing. *Adv Comput Sci Technol, 9*(1).

Fernandes, D. A., Soares, L. F., Gomes, J. V., Freire, M. M., & Inácio, P. R. (2014). Security issues in cloud environments: A survey. *International Journal of Information Security, 13*(2), 113–170. doi:10.1007/s10207-013-0208-7

Ficco, M., & Rak, M. (2014). Stealthy denial of service strategy in cloud computing. *IEEE Transactions on Cloud Computing, 3*(1), 80–94. doi:10.1109/TCC.2014.2325045

Geetha, P., & Robin, C. R. (2017, August). A comparative-study of load-cloud balancing algorithms in cloud environments. In *2017 International Conference on Energy, Communication, Data Analytics and Soft Computing (ICECDS)* (pp. 806-810). IEEE. 10.1109/ICECDS.2017.8389549

Getov, V. (2013). Cloud adoption issues: Interoperability and security. *Clouds Big Data Data-intensive Comput., 23*, 53–65.

Gonzalez, N., Miers, C., Redigolo, F., Simplicio, M., Carvalho, T., Näslund, M., & Pourzandi, M. (2012). A quantitative analysis of current security concerns and solutions for cloud computing. *Journal of Cloud Computing: Advances. Systems and Applications, 1*, 1–18.

Hashizume, K., Rosado, D. G., Fernández-Medina, E., & Fernandez, E. B. (2013). An analysis of security issues for cloud computing. *Journal of Internet Services and Applications, 4*(1), 1–13. doi:10.1186/1869-0238-4-5

Hay, B., Nance, K., & Bishop, M. (2011, January). Storm clouds rising: security challenges for IaaS cloud computing. In *2011 44th Hawaii International Conference on System Sciences* (pp. 1-7). IEEE. 10.1109/HICSS.2011.386

Huth, A., & Cebula, J. (2011). The basics of cloud computing. *United States Computer*, 1-4.

Ibrahim, E., El-Bahnasawy, N. A., & Omara, F. A. (2016, March). Task scheduling algorithm in cloud computing environment based on cloud pricing models. In *2016 World Symposium on Computer Applications & Research (WSCAR)* (pp. 65-71). IEEE. 10.1109/WSCAR.2016.20

Jansen, W. A. (2011, January). Cloud hooks: Security and privacy issues in cloud computing. In *2011 44th Hawaii International Conference on System Sciences* (pp. 1-10). IEEE.

Kumar, M., & Sharma, S. C. (2017). Dynamic load balancing algorithm for balancing the workload among virtual machine in cloud computing. *Procedia Computer Science, 115*, 322–329. doi:10.1016/j.procs.2017.09.141

Liu, B., Bi, J., & Vasilakos, A. V. (2014). Toward incentivizing anti-spoofing deployment. *IEEE Transactions on Information Forensics and Security, 9*(3), 436–450. doi:10.1109/TIFS.2013.2296437

Liu, B., Chen, Y., Hadiks, A., Blasch, E., Aved, A., Shen, D., & Chen, G. (2014). Information fusion in a cloud computing era: A systems-level perspective. *IEEE Aerospace and Electronic Systems Magazine, 29*(10), 16–24. doi:10.1109/MAES.2014.130115

Lloyd, W., Pallickara, S., David, O., Lyon, J., Arabi, M., & Rojas, K. (2013). Performance implications of multi-tier application deployments on Infrastructure-as-a-Service clouds: Towards performance modeling. *Future Generation Computer Systems, 29*(5), 1254–1264. doi:10.1016/j.future.2012.12.007

Malik, B. H., Amir, M., Mazhar, B., Ali, S., Jalil, R., & Khalid, J. (2018). Comparison of task scheduling algorithms in cloud environment. *International Journal of Advanced Computer Science and Applications, 9*(5). Advance online publication. doi:10.14569/IJACSA.2018.090550

Mell, P., & Grance, T. (2011). *The NIST definition of cloud computing.* NIST.

Modi, C., Patel, D., Borisaniya, B., Patel, A., & Rajarajan, M. (2013). A survey on security issues and solutions at different layers of Cloud computing. *The Journal of Supercomputing, 63*(2), 561–592. doi:10.1007/s11227-012-0831-5

Na, S. H., & Huh, E. N. (2015). A broker-based cooperative security-SLA evaluation methodology for personal cloud computing. *Security and Communication Networks, 8*(7), 1318–1331. doi:10.1002/sec.1086

Panwar, R., & Mallick, B. (2015). A comparative study of load balancing algorithms in cloud computing. *International Journal of Computer Applications, 117*(24), 33–37. doi:10.5120/20890-3669

Rao, K. S., & Thilagam, P. S. (2015). Heuristics based server consolidation with residual resource defragmentation in cloud data centers. *Future Generation Computer Systems, 50*, 87–98. doi:10.1016/j.future.2014.09.009

Ren, K., Wang, C., & Wang, Q. (2012). Security challenges for the public cloud. *IEEE Internet Computing, 16*(1), 69–73. doi:10.1109/MIC.2012.14

Rodrigues, E. R., Navaux, P. O., Panetta, J., Fazenda, A., Mendes, C. L., & Kale, L. V. (2010, October). A comparative analysis of load balancing algorithms applied to a weather forecast model. In *2010 22nd International Symposium on Computer Architecture and High Performance Computing* (pp. 71-78). IEEE. 10.1109/SBAC-PAD.2010.18

Rong, C., Nguyen, S. T., & Jaatun, M. G. (2013). Beyond lightning: A survey on security challenges in cloud computing. *Computers & Electrical Engineering, 39*(1), 47–54. doi:10.1016/j.compeleceng.2012.04.015

Ryan, M. D. (2013). Cloud computing security: The scientific challenge, and a survey of solutions. *Journal of Systems and Software, 86*(9), 2263–2268. doi:10.1016/j.jss.2012.12.025

Salah, K., Calero, J. M. A., Zeadally, S., Al-Mulla, S., & Alzaabi, M. (2012). Using cloud computing to implement a security overlay network. *IEEE Security and Privacy, 11*(1), 44–53. doi:10.1109/MSP.2012.88

Sankar, K., Kannan, S., & Jennifer, P. (2014). On-demand security architecture for cloud computing. *Middle East Journal of Scientific Research, 20*(2), 241–246.

Schwarzkopf, R., Schmidt, M., Strack, C., Martin, S., & Freisleben, B. (2012). Increasing virtual machine security in cloud environments. *Journal of Cloud Computing: Advances. Systems and Applications, 1*(1), 1–12.

Siahaan, A. P. U. (2016). Comparison analysis of CPU scheduling: FCFS, SJF and Round Robin. *International Journal of Engineering Development and Research, 4*(3), 124–132.

Singh, M., Nandal, P., & Bura, D. (2017, October). Comparative analysis of different load balancing algorithm using cloud analyst. In *International Conference on Recent Developments in Science, Engineering and Technology* (pp. 321-329). Singapore: Springer Singapore.

Soares, L. F., Fernandes, D. A., Gomes, J. V., Freire, M. M., & Inácio, P. R. (2014). Cloud security: state of the art. *Security, Privacy and Trust in Cloud Systems*, 3-44.

Song, M. H. (2014). Analysis of risks for virtualization technology. *Applied Mechanics and Materials, 539*, 374–377. doi:10.4028/www.scientific.net/AMM.539.374

Soni, V., & Barwar, D. N. (2018). Performance Analysis of Enhanced Max-Min and Min-Min Task Scheduling Algorithms in Cloud Computing Environment. In *International Conference on Emerging Trends in Science, Engineering and Management* (pp. 250-255). IEEE.

Srinivas, J., Reddy, K. V. S., & Qyser, A. M. (2012). Cloud computing basics. *International Journal of Advanced Research in Computer and Communication Engineering, 1*(5), 343–347.

Subashini, S., & Kavitha, V. (2011). A survey on security issues in service delivery models of cloud computing. *Journal of Network and Computer Applications, 34*(1), 1–11. doi:10.1016/j.jnca.2010.07.006

Szefer, J., Keller, E., Lee, R. B., & Rexford, J. (2011, October). Eliminating the hypervisor attack surface for a more secure cloud. In *Proceedings of the 18th ACM conference on Computer and communications security* (pp. 401-412). ACM. 10.1145/2046707.2046754

Tari, Z. (2014). Security and privacy in cloud computing. *IEEE Cloud Computing, 1*(01), 54–57. doi:10.1109/MCC.2014.20

Varadharajan, V., & Tupakula, U. (2014). Counteracting security attacks in virtual machines in the cloud using property based attestation. *Journal of Network and Computer Applications, 40*, 31–45. doi:10.1016/j.jnca.2013.08.002

Vijay, Y., & Ghita, B. V. (2017, July). Evaluating cloud computing scheduling algorithms under different environment and scenarios. In *2017 8th International Conference on Computing, Communication and Networking Technologies (ICCCNT)* (pp. 1-5). IEEE. 10.1109/ICCCNT.2017.8204070

Wei, L., Zhu, H., Cao, Z., Dong, X., Jia, W., Chen, Y., & Vasilakos, A. V. (2014). Security and privacy for storage and computation in cloud computing. *Information Sciences, 258*, 371–386. doi:10.1016/j. ins.2013.04.028

Wu, H., Ding, Y., Winer, C., & Yao, L. (2010, November). Network security for virtual machine in cloud computing. In *5th International conference on computer sciences and convergence information technology* (pp. 18-21). IEEE.

Xiao, Z., & Xiao, Y. (2012). Security and privacy in cloud computing. *IEEE Communications Surveys and Tutorials, 15*(2), 843–859. doi:10.1109/SURV.2012.060912.00182

Yan, Z., Zhang, P., & Vasilakos, A. V. (2014). A survey on trust management for Internet of Things. *Journal of Network and Computer Applications, 42*, 120–134. doi:10.1016/j.jnca.2014.01.014

Younis, Y. A., & Kifayat, K. (2013). *Secure cloud computing for critical infrastructure: A survey. Liverpool John Moores University*. Tech. Rep.

Yu, H., Powell, N., Stembridge, D., & Yuan, X. (2012, March). Cloud computing and security challenges. In *Proceedings of the 50th Annual Southeast Regional Conference* (pp. 298-302). ACM. 10.1145/2184512.2184581

Yu, N. H., Hao, Z., Xu, J. J., Zhang, W. M., & Zhang, C. (2013). Review of cloud computing security. *Acta Electonica Sinica, 41*(2), 371.

Zhang, F., & Chen, H. (2013). Security-preserving live migration of virtual machines in the cloud. *Journal of Network and Systems Management, 21*(4), 562–587. doi:10.1007/s10922-012-9253-1

Zhang, F., Chen, J., Chen, H., & Zang, B. (2011, October). Cloudvisor: retrofitting protection of virtual machines in multi-tenant cloud with nested virtualization. In *Proceedings of the twenty-third acm symposium on operating systems principles* (pp. 203-216). ACM. 10.1145/2043556.2043576

Zhang, F., Wang, J., Sun, K., & Stavrou, A. (2013). Hypercheck: A hardware-assistedintegrity monitor. *IEEE Transactions on Dependable and Secure Computing, 11*(4), 332–344. doi:10.1109/TDSC.2013.53

Chapter 12
Cloud Security Based on Data Fragmentation and Improved Encryption for Optimal Performance

Anuj Kumar Gupta

https://orcid.org/0000-0002-7636-0817

CGC College of Engineering, India

ABSTRACT

In the adoption of cloud computing technology, the data security of customer data is prime research these days. The user gets access of the cloud resources that are hosted over the internet that can be hijacked by the attacker. In one example, the access of the virtual machine (VM) as a dedicated resource is given to the end user by the CSP; and when the end user is accessing these resources through an internet-connected PC, there is a possibility of security violation by the attacker, who can take full control of the data. Most of the intrusion detection and prevention system implemented over the cloud infrastructures is rule-based and therefore are only capable to detect the known threats. This research work addressed the security problem by a) selection of optimal data security algorithm, and b) data fragmentation and distribution of data blocks over the multiple cloud nodes that make it difficult to guess about the actual data and its location.

INTRODUCTION

Cloud Computing (CC) is a developing technology that has a connection with other technologies such as Grid Computing (GC) and other domains such as Distributed Computing (Boldrin et al., 2010), Cluster Computing, etc. (Foster, 2008; Gupta, 2015). The major aim of both GC and CC is primarily to achieve full virtualization. Both technologies are synonymous but there are technological differences among them. The Grid Computing major objective is to achieve optimized computing capacity (Dumitru, 2016; Talwar & Gupta, 2016) whereas in the case of Cloud Computing, the aim is to provide a way to

DOI: 10.4018/979-8-3693-0338-2.ch012

handle the needs of an organization by enabling the dynamic and scalable infrastructure to work with (Wu, 2010). Cloud Computing introduced a new paradigm of technology that helps its users to develop applications and store their data somewhere on the internet and they can access their resources from anywhere and anytime by just using the internet connectivity (Vaquero et al., 2008). Based on the need and requirements of the customer, Cloud Computing enable easy and modifiable services to access their work with cloud applications. The services in the form of platforms and infrastructures are provided to the customer for designing applications, storing their data and building their own applications by using the cloud infrastructure to fulfil their route task. These resources are hosted by the CSP over the dedicated resources as a service model. A user can buy these resources on a pay-basis model and merely have internet connectivity and a PC (Hwang et al., 2010; Hwang & Li, 2010).

Now the research question is by hosting and accessing these resources over the public internet what security measurements are installed to protect the user's data (Chavan, 2015; Hashizume & David, 2013). If improper security measures are placed at the side of CSP it may cause the complete loss of the user's data or we can say there are higher risks involved when the customer records are stored in the internet instead of the user's local repository (Yu, 2010). An intruder gains complete access to the user's data transmitted over the connection between the end user and the remote location by just performing the man-in-middle attacks (Ramesh Shahabadkar, 2017). The intruder may also take complete access to the user's data and their sensitive information hosted on cloud infrastructure (Yu, 2010). The users of cloud services are diversified and may include experts and users who don't have any knowledge of technology, thereby putting their data at huge risk in such infrastructures (Hwang et al., 2009; Nick, 2010).

From the above discussions, it is summarized that security is a prime concern with the growing use of Cloud Computing Technology and that should be addressed to provide the data protection of the end users (Hwang & Li, 2010). In this research work, existing security mechanism placed in cloud computing is presented and a solution to protect the customer data fragmentation and its distribution by combining the optimal encryption technique is presented (Ali et al., 2018).

DATA SECURITY IN CLOUD COMPUTING

Data security in cloud computing is a critical concern because it involves storing and processing data on remote servers managed by third-party cloud service providers. While cloud computing offers many benefits, such as scalability, cost-effectiveness, and accessibility, it also introduces unique security challenges. Here are some key considerations and best practices for ensuring data security in cloud computing:

Data Encryption: Data at Rest: Data stored in the cloud should be encrypted using strong encryption algorithms to protect it from unauthorized access. Most cloud providers offer data encryption services.

Data in Transit: Data transferred to and from the cloud should also be encrypted using secure protocols like HTTPS or TLS.

Access Control: Implement strict access controls and permissions. Assign permissions based on the principle of least privilege, ensuring that users and applications only have access to the data and resources they require.

Identity and Authentication: Use multi-factor authentication (MFA) to enhance user identity verification. Implement robust authentication mechanisms to verify the identity of users and devices accessing cloud resources.

Figure 1. Attacker can intrude the cloud network

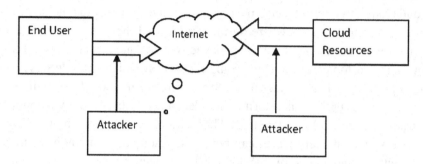

Data Classification: Classify data based on its sensitivity and importance. This allows you to apply appropriate security controls to different types of data.

Data Backups: Regularly back up your data and ensure that these backups are secure. Cloud providers often offer backup services, but it's important to have a backup strategy that aligns with your data retention and recovery requirements.

Data Loss Prevention (DLP): Deploy DLP tools to monitor and control the movement of sensitive data within and outside the cloud environment. These tools can help prevent data leaks.

Security Monitoring and Logging: Set up robust logging and monitoring systems to detect and respond to security incidents. Many cloud providers offer logging and monitoring services that can be integrated with SIEM (Security Information and Event Management) systems.

The growth and scalable model of Cloud Computing comes with lots of security challenges to protect the customer's data. Even though the technology is new and provide a platform to access the applications hosted over the internet easily, still there are challenges and issues to adopt the technology by the end user. One of such challenges that are on top priority by service provider is the security pertaining to the infrastructure and protects the user's data hosted on such infrastructure (Kaur & Singh, 2017). Even though a company use to have top class security installed over it and does update their security policies from time to time, there are still the issues to be addressed to protect the customer data (Goundar et al., 2020). In this regard, through this detailed study we propose security challenges and their solutions pertain to cloud infrastructures.

When the end user access the applications and data hosted over the Cloud Network with public internet connectivity, the intruder can intrude the connection and can take the control of the user's resources that are hosted over the internet connected infrastructures. The major security risks involved in such infrastructures are data loss and leakage (Harika et al., 2014; Oyeyinka & Omotosho, 2015; Sirohi & Shrivastava, 2015; Talib, 2015).

THE PROPOSED SYSTEM

The following diagram depicts the system design of the developed framework during this research implementation. The registered user submits the file as data inputs and then file segmentation module divides the main file into multiple pieces in per similar way to Google File System (GFS) (Revathi et al., 2019). The segmented files are encrypted using the optimal symmetric key encryption algorithm (Chen

Figure 2. System design flow

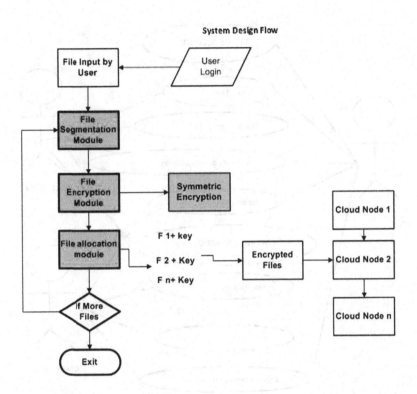

et al., 2004). Here the RSA (Thakur & Kumar, 2011) encryption algorithm is used and performances are measured by changing the key size to get the best optimal results. The in-built cryptography algorithm of Microsoft .NET framework (Gowry, 2012) is implemented and applied to the fragmented data. The main benefit of this research work is to confuse the attacker about the actual data where it is located and not able to get the actual data because it is located over the different cloud nodes and another layer of security is fragment data is encrypted (Revathi et al., 2019).

Workflow of the Implemented Software Code

Figure 2 depict the work flow of the implementation of the software code. The developed application is user driven application in which a user can submit a file to the cloud node resources created in a software program. If the user is registered, he will get the user credentials to upload the files on the cloud nodes. The registered user is authorized to split the main files into multiple chunks and distribute them over the cloud nodes. The pieces of the main files are encrypted with encryption algorithms and distribute them over the cloud nodes. The metadata server is inbuilt in software program to maintain the indexing of the files and storage server is a database repository of SQL server to maintain the user's logs.

Figure 2 describe the software modules in the software program developed in Microsoft .NET framework. There are four major modules:

Figure 3. Workflow diagram of implemented code

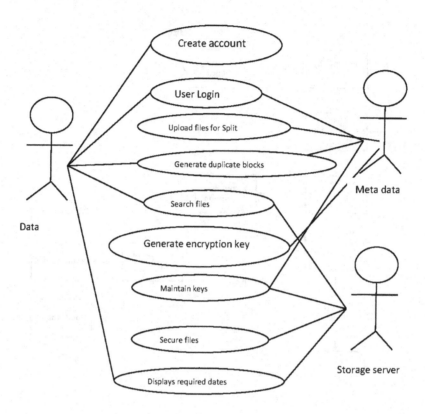

- User registration module
- Upload files modules
- File splitting/data fragmentation module
- Data encryption and decryption module

The user registration module is developed to give the provision to the user to get registered and get the access of the cloud resources as nodes. As mentioned above, the registered user is able to access the cloud nodes and can submit the files into cloud nodes. The submitted main is then divided into multiple data fragments to distribute over the multiple cloud nodes by file splitting program. It is a program which takes the main files and divides them into multiple pieces of same size equal to 7.

Here the numbers of file segments are fixed in a software program that can be changed by the user. Next module is data encryption module that encrypts the segmented files.

EXPERIMENTAL RESULTS

Here the experimental results in the form of system time taken by applying a encryption algorithms with different key size applied on file segments is presented. After the file segmentation process, the multiple chunks of files are encrypted with optimal data encryption algorithm and distributed over the

Figure 4. Software modules in the code

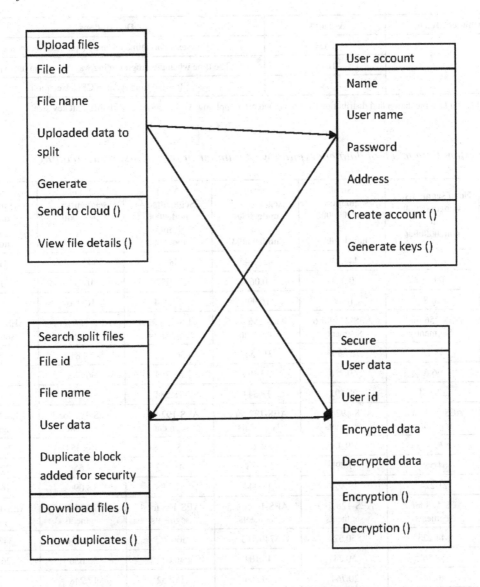

cloud nodes. As discussed above, the main advantage of fragmentation and distribution is to hide the originality of the data so that the attacker will not be able to guess about the actual data and the location of cloud node where it is located. Then by applying another layer of security in the form of data encryption algorithm with strong key size make the guess more difficult to protect the data over the cloud node. For simulation purposes, we have used the Microsoft .NET Framework using Visual Studio 2008 and its in-built cryptography library. The results measurement readings have been taken thoroughly by applying the data encryption algorithm of different key size.

Table 2 describe the readings of system time taken of AES algorithm with different key cipher block corresponding to each fragments. For example, Treal time taken by AES-256 algorithm in seven number of file segments is 467.799 seconds, in a similar for two file segmentation AES-256 algorithm time

Table 1. System time taken as performance matrix

Performance Metrics	Attribute	Descriptions
	Treal	Total execution time taken by a process to execute
	Tuser	The time when the programming was running in user space
	Tsys	It is the time spent in CPU execution

Use Case 1: Data Fragmentation and distribution over the cloud after applying AES encryption with different key size.

Table 2. System time taken of data encryption w.r.t number of fragments, result readings

System Time Taken	No of segments=7 node0000000 to node0000006	No of segments=6 node000000 to node000005	No of segments=5 node00000 to node00004	No of Segments=4 node0000 to node0003	No of segments=3 node000 to node002	No of segments=2 node00 to node01
Treal	467.799	444.343	421.745	453.304	445.902	414.16
Tuser	0.032	0.068	0.064	0.052	0.032	0.052
Tsys	16.8	16.96	16.996	16.984	16.996	17.08
	AES-256 for 7 Segments	AES-256 for 6 Segments	AES-256 for 5 segments	AES-256 for 4 segments	AES-256 for 3 segments	AES-256 for 2 segments
Treal	733.287	757.798	714.544	568.445	454.813	320.761
Tuser	66.6	60.736	53.496	43.284	36.688	28.876
Tsys	22.604	20.192	19.344	18.584	17.812	16.9
	AES-192 for 7 segments	AES-192 for 6 segments	AES-192 for 5 segments	AES-192 for 4 segments	AES-192 for 3 segments	AES-192 for 2 segments
Treal	896.628	939.465	756.698	587.498	468.354	287.962
Tuser	64.552	57.496	49.24	41.972	34.656	27.584
Tsys	21.224	19.864	18.944	18.688	18.096	16.556
	AES-128 for 7 segments	AES-128 for 6 segments	AES-128 for 5 segments	AES-128 for 4 segments	AES-128 for 3 segments	AES-128 for 2 segments
Treal	644.223	850.524	740.413	506.765	452.951	343.739
Tuser	58.56	50.74	46.104	40.044	33.656	26.548
Tsys	20.74	20.764	20.204	18.552	17.248	16.588

taken is 414.16 seconds. Then each fragmented files are encrypted with AES with different key size. This table clearly indicate that more the number of segments, more will be the system time taken, but in the following results it is clearly indicated that in AES-128-bit algorithm is performing better in overall system time taken whereas AES-192 is performing better in system user space. It can be concluded as system time taken by the data encryption algorithm also depends upon the variant of application and its CPU clock requirements.

Result Stats 1: System Time Taken of AES-256 w.r.t. Each Fragmentation

Figure 5. AES-256 performance with data fragments

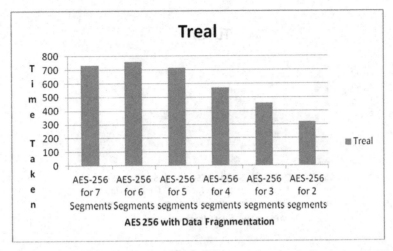

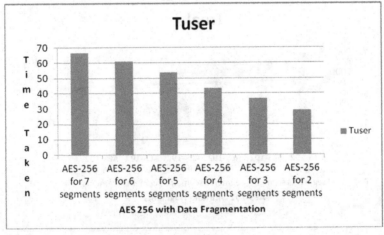

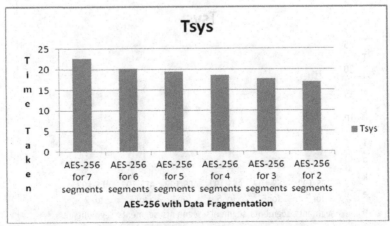

Result Stats 2: System Time Taken of AES-192 w.r.t. Each Fragmentation

Figure 6. AES-192 performance with data fragments

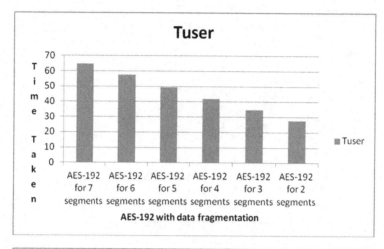

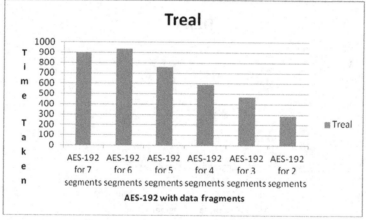

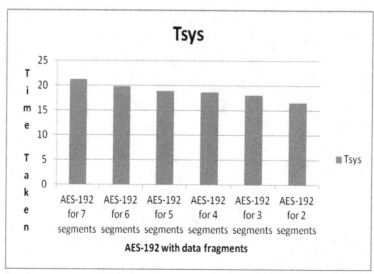

Result Stats 3: System Time Taken of AES-128 w.r.t. Each Fragmentation

Figure 7. AES-128 performance with data fragments

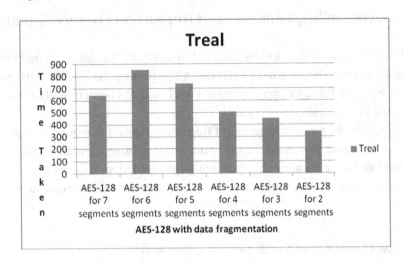

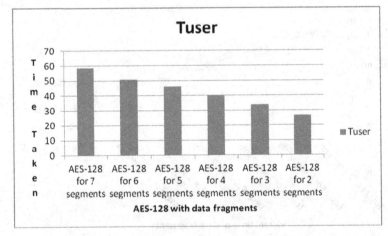

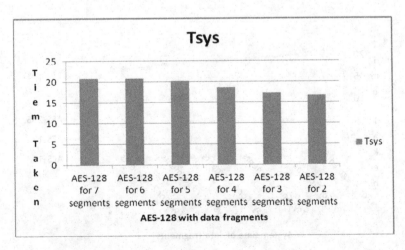

Use Case 2: Comparative Analysis of AES With Different Key Size w.r.t. Each Segmented File

Use Case 3: Data Loss in Segmentation and Replication Over the Cloud Nodes

In this use case, the percentage of data loss is depicted by applying the data fragmentation and its replication over the cloud nodes. The stats have been taken by splitting the big file into smaller pieces of
equal size and then applying the data encryption over it. The data encryption algorithm is adding the
data padding along with the actual size of data.

As depicted in Figure 9, the more the number of fragmented data, the more distribution of data loss.
However, the comparative data loss is smaller in more number of segmentation compared to a small
number of segmentation. By performing this research implementation, it is advised to set the count of
data segmentation which is hard (data segmentation=7) coded in our software code to get more efficient
results.

Figure 8. Comparison of different AES with number of fragments

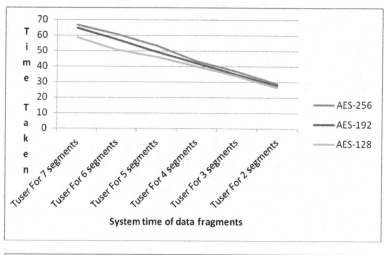

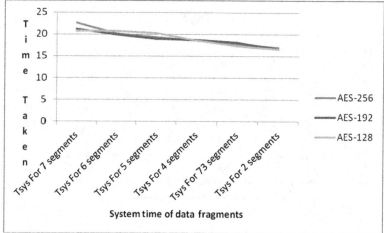

Table 3. Effect of data fragmentation on actual data size

No of Segments	Segmented and encrypted data size (in Mbytes)	Combined Data Size (In Mbytes)	Data Loss	%Data Loss
7	6033	5700	333	5.519
6	5266	5000	300	5.051
5	4419	4200	300	4.956
4	3428	3275	200	4.463
3	2805	2700	105	3.743
2	1998	1930	68	3.403

Table 4. Percentage of data loss

Segments	% of data loss
No of Segments=7	5.519
No of Segments=6	5.051
No of Segments=5	4.956
No of Segments=4	4.463
No of Segments=3	3.743
No of Segments=2	3.403

Figure 9. Percentage distribution of data loss w.r.t each fragmentation

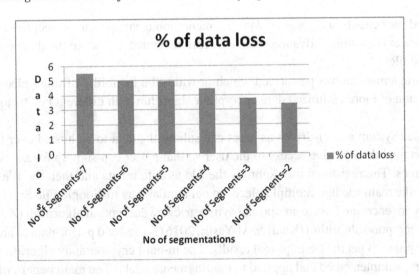

CONCLUSION AND FUTURE WORK

Cloud computing technology has grown exponentially and is very well adopted by the end users that make the technical and cultural shift from localization to globalization with the inclusion of internet-connected resources. A customer can access their data hosted anywhere in the global world by merely having internet connectivity. Cloud resources are maintained and controlled by the third party as Cloud Service Providers (CSP) and these pay less attention to secure the user's data. The cloud service provider can take care of infrastructure security and protect the network those are under their control but the end user who is not so technical guy has a belief that data hosted over the cloud network is fool proof and secured. Normally the data hosted on cloud resources are more vulnerable to attacks than the data hosted on a PC locally because data flow is always through a public internet which is always an insecure infrastructure and always prone to attacks. Moreover, the volume of users of cloud computing is increasing in an exponential manner which definitely puts the internet-based environment under the reach of the end user but it also leads to threats pertaining to these resources.

In research, many authors have proposed multiple approaches to ensure the data security and protection of end users. Researchers also depicted that only applying traditional cryptographic algorithms may not be useful in the context of cloud computing because it increases overhead to the cloud infrastructures, moreover, the security is wholly dependent upon the type of encryption algorithm and key used in that. To avoid such algorithms, the researchers explored another phenomenon of data security of the user hosted on CSP. It includes data fragmentation and its dispersal over multiple cloud nodes.

In this research thesis, the need and requirements for the protection of user's data are presented by addressing the security problems in cloud infrastructures. Then solution is presented to solve this research problem by incorporating novel data fragmentation techniques and distribution of data files over the cloud nodes along with advanced and optimal data encryption algorithm. For the protection of end-user data, we propose a schematic algorithmic novel combined approach for data security which will involve lightweight encryption with data fragmentation and replication techniques to ensure data protection.

The core benefits of the proposed approach are:

- It explored the benefits and usage of data fragmentation techniques to protect the user's data
- It incorporates the optimal advanced data encryption algorithm prior to the disbursal of the user's segmented files.
- Scalable implementation is performed which provides the flexibility of more pieces of files, and incorporation of more optimized data encryption algorithm with different key factors.

The developed system is user-driven as users can submit the data to be hosted over the cloud. The user registration module is to give access to the user so that a user can sign up for access to the cloud nodes as resources. The registered user submits the file as data inputs and then the file segmentation module divides the main file into multiple pieces in per similar way to Google File System (GFS). The segmented files are encrypted using an optimal symmetric key encryption algorithm (Zaz et al., 2012). Here the RSA encryption algorithm (Khan & Al-Yasiri, 2016) is used and performances are measured by changing the key size to get the best optimal results. The in-built cryptography algorithm of Microsoft .NET framework is implemented and applied to the fragmented data. The main benefit of this research work is to confuse the attacker about the actual data where it is located and not able to get the actual data because it is located over the different cloud nodes and another layer of security is fragment data encrypted. The performance benchmarking is listed and presented through system time taken in the form of Treal, Tsys and Tuser after enabling the data fragmentation and data encryption processes on a system.

The developed system is tested on the limited simulated environment using the Microsoft .NET framework and its in-build cryptography algorithm. The testing of the AES data encryption algorithm is performed with different key sizes and data segmentations. The exploration and testing of more symmetric key encryption algorithms such as DES, Blowfish and more Asymmetric cryptography algorithms is left for future work.

REFERENCES

Ali, M., Bilal, K,. Khan, S., Veeravalli, B., Li, K., & Zomaya, A. (2018). DROPS: Division and Replication of Data in the Cloud for Optimal Performance and Security. *IEEE Transactions on Cloud Computing*. doi:10.1109/TCC.2015.2400460

Boldrin, F., Taddia, C., & Mazzini, G. (2010). Web Distributed Computing Systems Implementation and Modeling. *International Journal of Adaptive, Resilient and Autonomic Systems*, *1*(1), 75–91. doi:10.4018/jaras.2010071705

Chavan, R. (2015, November). A Review on Secure Methodology Fragmentation and Replication of data in Cloud for Data Secrecy and Ideal Performance. *International Journal of Advanced Research in Computer Engineering and Technology*, *4*(11).

Chen, G., Mao, Y., & Charles, K. (2004). Chui, A symmetric image encryption scheme based on 3D chaotic cat maps. *Chaos, Solitons, and Fractals*, *21*(3), 749–761. doi:10.1016/j.chaos.2003.12.022

Dumitru, I. (2016). Grid Computing: Enabled Resource Management Models. In I. Management Association (Ed.), Project Management: Concepts, Methodologies, Tools, and Applications (pp. 2290-2303). IGI Global. doi:10.4018/978-1-5225-0196-1.ch114

Foster, I. (2008). Cloud computing and grid computing 360 degrees compared. In *Grid Computing Environments Workshop*. IEEE.

Gowry, S. (2012). *Paramasivam, Cryptography in Microsoft.NET*. C-Sharp Corner. https://www.c-sharpcorner.com/article/cryptography-in-microsoft-net-part-i-encryption

Gupta, A. K. (2015). Cloud Computing: Concepts and Challenges. *Asian Journal of Computer Science and Technology*, *4*(2), 27-30.

Harika, A. V., Haleema, P. K., Subalakshmi, R. J., & Iyengar, N. Ch. S. N. (2014). Quality-based solution for adaptable and scalable access control in cloud computing. *International Journal of Grid and Distributed Computing*, *7*(6), 137–148. doi:10.14257/ijgdc.2014.7.6.11

Hashizume, K., & David, G. (2013). Rosado, Eduardo FernndezMedina, Eduardo B Fernandez, An analysis of security issues for cloud computing. *Journal of Internet Services and Applications*, *4*(1), 5. doi:10.1186/1869-0238-4-5

Hwang, K., Fox, G., & Dongarra, J. (2010). *Distributed Systems and Cloud Computing: Clusters, Grids/P2P, and Internet Clouds*. Morgan Kaufmann.

Hwang, K., Kulkarni, S., & Hu, Y. (2009). Cloud Security with Virtualized Defence and Reputation-Based Trust Management. *IEEE Int'l Conf. Dependable, Autonomic, and Secure Computing (DASC 09)*. IEEE CS Press.

Hwang, K., & Li, D. (2010, September-October). Trusted Cloud Computing with Secure Resources and Data Colouring. *IEEE Internet Computing, 14*(5), 14–22. doi:10.1109/MIC.2010.86

Kaur, S., & Singh, A. (2017). security issues in cloud computing. *International Education and Research Journal.*

Khan, N., & Al-Yasiri, A. (2016). Cloud Security Threats and Techniques to Strengthen Cloud Computing Adoption Framework. *International Journal of Information Technology and Web Engineering, 11*(3), 50–64. doi:10.4018/IJITWE.2016070104

]Mollah, M. (2012). Next generation of computing through cloud computing technology. In *2012 25th IEEE CCECE.* IEEE.

Nick, J. (2010). *Journey to the Private Cloud: Security and Compliance.* Tech. Presentation, EMC, Tsinghua Univ.

Oyeyinka, F. I., & Omotosho, O. J. (2015). A modified things role-based access control model for securing utilities in cloud computing. *Int. J. Innov. Res. Inf. Security, 5*(2), 21–25.

Ramesh Shahabadkar, S. (2017). *Secure Framework of Authentication Mechanism over Cloud Environment, CSOC.* Software Engineering Trends and Techniques in Intelligent Systems.

Revathi, T., Muneeswaran, K., & Blessa Binolin Pepsi, M. (2019). *Hadoop History and Architecture.* IGI Global. doi:10.4018/978-1-5225-3790-8.ch003

Sanjay, G. H. G. S.-T. L. (n.d.). The Google File System, *Proceedings of the 19th ACM Symposium on Operating Systems Principles.* ACM.

Sirohi, A., & Shrivastava, V. (2015). Implementing data storage in cloud computing with HMAC encryption algorithm to improve data security. *International Journal of Advanced Research in Computer Science and Software Engineering, 5*(8), 678–684.

Talib, A. M. (2015). Ensuring security, confidentiality and fine-grained data access control of cloud data storage implementation environment. *J. Inf. Security, 6*(2), 118–130. doi:10.4236/jis.2015.62013

Talwar, B., & Gupta, A. K. (2016). A Survey on Cloud Computing Model Configuration Security Issues with Proposed Solutions. *International Journal of Exploration in Science and Technology, 1*(2), 43-49.

Thakare, V. R., & Singh, K. J. (2020). Cloud Security Architecture Based on Fully Homomorphic Encryption. In S. Goundar, S. Bhushan, & P. Rayani (Eds.), *Architecture and Security Issues in Fog Computing Applications* (pp. 83–89). IGI Global. doi:10.4018/978-1-7998-0194-8.ch005

Thakur, J., & Kumar, N. (2011). DES, AES and Blowfish: Symmetric Key Cryptography Algorithms Simulation Based Performance Analysis. *International Journal of Emerging Technology and Advanced Engineering.* www.ijetae.com

Vaquero, L., Rodero-Merino, L., Caceres, J., & Lindner, M. (2008). *ACM Computer Communication Review.* ACM.

Wu, R. (2010). Information flow control in cloud computing. In *Collaborative Computing: Networking, Applications and Work sharing (Collaborate Com), 6th International Conference.* IEEE.

Yu, S. (2010). Achieving secure, scalable, and fine-grained data access control in cloud computing. In IN- *FOCOM, 2010 Proceedings IEEE*, (pp. 1-9). IEEE.

Zaz, Y., El Fadil, L., & El Kayyali, M. (2012). Securing EPR Data Using Cryptography and Image Watermarking. *International Journal of Mobile Computing and Multimedia Communications*, 4(2), 76–87. doi:10.4018/jmcmc.2012040106

Chapter 13
An AI-Integrated Green Power Monitoring System:
Empowering Small and Medium Enterprises

Varuna Kumara

iD https://orcid.org/0000-0002-9671-0546

Department of Electronics and Communication Engineering, Moodlakatte Institute of Technology, Kundapura, India

Durgesh M Sharma

iD https://orcid.org/0000-0002-9378-3061

Shri Ramdeobaba College of Engineering and Management, Nagpur, India

J. Samson Isaac

Department of Biomedical Engineering, Karunya Institute of Technology and Sciences, Coimbatore, India

S. Saravanan

iD https://orcid.org/0000-0001-8255-2623

Department of Electrical and Electronics Engineering, B.V. Raju Institute of Technology, Narsapur, India

D. Suganthi

iD https://orcid.org/0000-0003-2089-9108

Department of Computer Science, Saveetha College of Liberal Arts and Sciences, SIMATS, Thandalam, India

Sampath Boopathi

iD https://orcid.org/0000-0002-2065-6539

Mechanical Engineering, Muthayammal Engineering College, Namakkal, India

ABSTRACT

The book explores the use of artificial intelligence (AI) in power monitoring systems for SMEs to enhance energy efficiency, reduce operational costs, and ensure sustainability. It discusses current energy challenges faced by SMEs, emphasizes real-time monitoring, and highlights the benefits of AI integration. The chapter details the components of an AI-integrated power monitoring system, including data acquisition, analysis, and control strategies. It examines AI techniques like machine learning, deep learning, and predictive analytics for identifying energy usage patterns. The chapter also discusses successful cases of SMEs using AI-based systems, highlighting their optimization of energy consumption and reduced costs.

DOI: 10.4018/979-8-3693-0338-2.ch013

INTRODUCTION

SMEs are crucial for global economic growth, employment, and innovation. However, they face challenges in managing energy consumption due to rising costs, environmental concerns, and operational sustainability. This book chapter explores the integration of Artificial Intelligence (AI) into power monitoring systems, a promising technological solution that could revolutionize SMEs' energy resource management. By minimizing operational costs and reducing environmental footprint, AI can help SMEs reduce their environmental footprint and improve their energy management strategies(Lu et al., 2022).

SMEs face unique energy challenges due to limited resources, requiring efficient resource allocation. Traditional power monitoring systems may not provide real-time insights for optimizing energy usage, reducing downtime, and cutting operational costs. This chapter explores the importance of real-time power monitoring and the role of AI in making it more accessible and effective for SMEs(Brandalero et al., 2020).

AI integration in power monitoring systems can improve energy efficiency, reduce operational costs, and ensure long-term sustainability for SMEs. Technologies like machine learning, deep learning, and predictive analytics enable the identification of energy usage patterns, enabling data-informed decisions. This chapter examines how AI integration in SME power monitoring can enhance energy efficiency, reduce operational costs, and ensure the sustainability of SMEs(Jung et al., 2021).

This chapter discusses the energy challenges faced by SMEs and the importance of effective power monitoring. It highlights the potential benefits of AI integration in power monitoring, emphasizing the value of real-time data in energy management. The chapter then delves into the core components of an AI-integrated power monitoring system, focusing on AI techniques for energy usage analysis(Žigienė et al., 2019). It presents case studies and success stories of SMEs that have improved through AI integration. It also discusses regulatory and ethical considerations surrounding AI in power monitoring. The chapter concludes by anticipating future trends and challenges in AI's role in SMEs' energy management(Nascimento et al., 2021).

SMEs, known for their agility and innovation, face significant energy challenges that hinder their competitiveness and sustainability. With rising global energy demands and environmental concerns, efficient energy use is crucial. Due to limited budgets and resources, SMEs often struggle to do more with less, leading to increased operational costs and hindered market competitiveness(Crockett et al., 2021). AI-driven solutions for power monitoring can create a level playing field for SMEs, allowing them to harness advanced energy management systems previously accessible only to large corporations. Real-time monitoring of energy consumption is vital for SMEs to adapt and respond to changes in usage patterns, mitigating potential issues before they become critical. AI integration brings predictive analytics and anomaly detection to the forefront, enabling SMEs to anticipate equipment failures, optimize energy usage during peak and non-peak hours, and make informed decisions to cut costs and reduce their carbon footprint(Bauer et al., 2020).

AI plays a crucial role in power monitoring, enabling cost savings, efficiency improvements, and environmental sustainability. It can identify energy waste areas and suggest corrective actions, reducing greenhouse gas emissions and promoting a greener business approach. AI-enhanced power monitoring aligns SMEs with evolving energy regulations, ensuring compliance and competitiveness in a world that values sustainability(Grashof & Kopka, 2023). This book chapter explores AI-integrated power monitoring for SMEs, exploring technologies, applications, and benefits. It provides insights into real-world success stories, regulatory and ethical considerations, and future trends. The goal is to provide a comprehensive perspective on how AI can empower SMEs to manage energy resources efficiently, reduce operational costs, and secure a sustainable future.

SMEs are crucial for global economic growth, innovation, and job creation. However, they face unique energy management challenges like high costs, unpredictable demand, and resource limitations. The integration of Artificial Intelligence in power monitoring systems can help SMEs manage their energy consumption effectively, enhancing their competitiveness and sustainability(Baabdullah et al., 2021). SMEs, with diverse sectors and limited energy management resources, face significant operational costs due to inefficient energy use. The volatility of energy prices exacerbates the financial impact of inefficient energy use. AI-integrated power monitoring offers SMEs insights into energy consumption patterns, optimizing resource allocation, and mitigating financial volatility, thereby enhancing their competitiveness and efficiency.

AI-integrated power monitoring involves data acquisition from sensor networks and IoT devices, which are then analyzed using machine learning algorithms like linear regression, decision trees, and support vector machines. These algorithms help SMEs understand energy usage factors, predict future demand, and optimize resource allocation. Deep learning models like Recurrent Neural Networks and Convolutional Neural Networks are particularly useful for handling time-series data and image analysis, making them ideal for SMEs dealing with complex energy consumption data(Mohammadian & Rezaie, 2020).

The power monitoring system is improved by incorporating AI-driven predictive analytics and anomaly detection. Predictive analytics forecasts future energy consumption patterns, enabling SMEs to optimize usage and reduce costs. Anomaly detection identifies irregularities in energy consumption, potentially indicating equipment malfunctions or security breaches, reducing downtime and maintenance costs.

AI integration in SMEs can optimize energy consumption, reduce downtime, and enhance sustainability. Case studies show that a manufacturing company reduced energy consumption by 15% and operational costs by 10%, a food processing plant reduced downtime by 30% and maintenance costs by 20%, and a retail business enhanced sustainability by 12% and reduced energy costs by 12%(Han & Trimi, 2022). However, SMEs must adhere to regulatory and ethical standards, such as data privacy and security, to fully utilize AI. Balancing innovation and responsibility can help SMEs navigate emerging technologies, tackle challenges, and drive energy management innovation.

BACKGROUND AND MOTIVATION

SMEs are vital for economic growth and job creation, demonstrating their ability to innovate and adapt to market changes. However, they often face unique challenges, including efficient power management, which is a significant challenge they face in various industries. The energy landscape has shifted towards sustainability, efficiency, and carbon reduction, making SMEs crucial for environmental sustainability. However, fluctuating energy prices, supply disruptions, and operational costs necessitate effective energy management. To address these challenges, SMEs need reliable, cost-effective solutions to monitor, analyze, and optimize their energy usage.

Traditional power monitoring systems provide historical energy consumption insights but lack real-time data and advanced analytics for proactive energy management. The integration of Artificial Intelligence (AI) has emerged as a transformative solution. AI-integrated power monitoring systems are being explored for SMEs to optimize energy consumption, forecast demand, and detect anomalies. This technology offers real-time insights into energy patterns, reducing operational costs and enhancing profitability, a crucial advantage in competitive markets. This approach is crucial for SMEs to stay competitive(Alaskari et al., 2021; Onu & Mbohwa, 2021).

Secondly, environmental concerns have driven an increased focus on sustainability. AI-driven power monitoring enables SMEs to track and reduce their carbon footprint by identifying areas of energy waste and implementing energy-saving measures. This not only aligns with global environmental goals but also enhances the reputation and marketability of SMEs committed to sustainability. This chapter explores the potential of AI to improve energy management for SMEs, highlighting its potential to level the playing field and make advanced solutions more accessible and cost-effective(Crockett et al., 2021; Žigienė et al., 2019). The chapter focuses on the growing energy challenges faced by SMEs, the transformative potential of AI in addressing these challenges, and the goals of enhancing energy efficiency, sustainability, and competitiveness in the SME sector. It delves into the concepts, technologies, applications, and practical implications of AI-integrated power monitoring for SMEs.

OBJECTIVES

- To elucidate the energy challenges specifically encountered by Small and Medium Enterprises (SMEs) and underscore the need for effective power monitoring in their operations.
- To explore the potential benefits of integrating Artificial Intelligence (AI) into power monitoring systems, highlighting its role in enhancing energy efficiency, reducing operational costs, and promoting sustainability in SMEs.
- To examine the core components of an AI-integrated power monitoring system, providing an in-depth understanding of how data acquisition, analysis, and control strategies contribute to efficient energy management.
- To delve into various AI techniques, such as machine learning, deep learning, and predictive analytics, to showcase their effectiveness in identifying energy usage patterns and anomalies, enabling SMEs to make data-informed decisions.
- To present practical case studies and success stories of SMEs that have implemented AI-driven power monitoring systems, offering real-world examples of how AI can optimize energy consumption, reduce downtime, and lower maintenance costs.
- To address the regulatory and ethical considerations related to AI in power monitoring, emphasizing the importance of data privacy, security, and compliance with energy regulations.
- To anticipate future trends and challenges in the field, providing insights into emerging technologies and the potential role of AI in driving innovation in SME energy management.
- To provide a comprehensive perspective on the integration of AI into power monitoring systems for SMEs, demonstrating how it can empower these enterprises to manage their energy resources efficiently, reduce operational costs, and secure their place in a sustainable and competitive future.

The objectives outline the book chapter's exploration of AI-integrated power monitoring in the context of Small and Medium Enterprises.

Figure 1. The challenges for examining energy demand trends

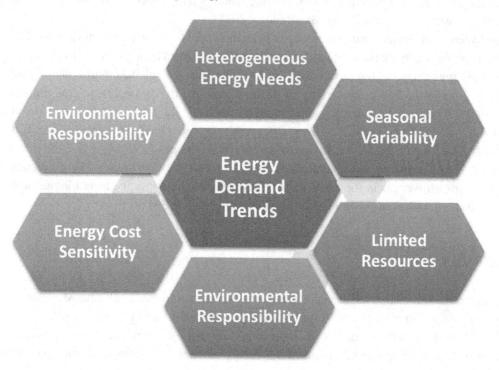

ENERGY CHALLENGES IN SMALL AND MEDIUM ENTERPRISES (SMEs)

Energy Demand Trends

SMEs, a diverse group of businesses, contribute significantly to economic growth but often face unique energy challenges(Pereira et al., 2020; Prashar, 2019; Qamar et al., 2022). Understanding these challenges begins with examining energy demand trends, which are influenced by various factors, highlighting their dynamic nature (Figure 1).

- **Heterogeneous Energy Needs:** SMEs span various industries, each with its unique energy requirements. Retail businesses, for instance, primarily rely on lighting and heating, while manufacturing SMEs may have heavy machinery that demands substantial electricity. These diverse energy needs make it challenging to implement standardized energy management strategies.
- **Seasonal Variability:** Many SMEs experience seasonal fluctuations in their energy demands. For example, a ski resort's energy usage drastically differs between the winter and summer seasons. Managing these fluctuations efficiently is essential to avoid overconsumption and excessive costs.
- **Limited Resources:** Unlike large corporations with dedicated energy departments and sizable budgets, SMEs often have limited resources to invest in energy management. This constraint makes it difficult to implement sophisticated power monitoring and efficiency improvement solutions.
- **Energy Cost Sensitivity:** SMEs are acutely aware of the impact of energy costs on their bottom line. Fluctuations in energy prices can directly affect profitability, making cost control a paramount concern.

- **Environmental Responsibility:** In an era of growing environmental consciousness, SMEs are increasingly expected to reduce their carbon footprint and adopt sustainable energy practices. Balancing the need for energy efficiency with environmental responsibility is a complex challenge.
- **Technology Accessibility:** SMEs may not have the resources or technical expertise to implement advanced energy monitoring and management systems. The lack of access to modern technology can hinder their ability to optimize energy consumption.
- **Aging Infrastructure:** Some SMEs operate in older facilities with outdated equipment and infrastructure. Upgrading these systems to meet modern energy efficiency standards can be cost-prohibitive.

Understanding energy demand trends is crucial for SMEs to manage their resources effectively. Innovative solutions like AI-integrated power monitoring systems are needed to adapt to the evolving energy landscape while remaining competitive and sustainable. This chapter explores how AI technologies can optimize energy consumption for SMEs.

Operational Challenges and the Need for Effective Power Monitoring in SMEs:

SMEs face operational challenges related to energy consumption, necessitating the implementation of effective power monitoring solutions. Real-time power monitoring is crucial to address these key operational challenges and ensure efficient energy usage(Qamar et al., 2022).

- **Unpredictable Energy Costs:** SMEs often struggle with fluctuating energy costs. The unpredictability of energy prices can strain operational budgets, affecting profitability and long-term sustainability. Effective power monitoring is essential for optimizing energy usage and mitigating the financial impact of cost fluctuations.
- **Downtime and Productivity Loss:** Unscheduled downtime due to equipment failures or energy disruptions can be disastrous for SMEs. Manufacturing processes come to a halt, and service-oriented businesses experience service interruptions. Real-time power monitoring can detect anomalies and irregularities, allowing SMEs to perform predictive maintenance and prevent costly downtime.
- **Inefficient Resource Allocation:** SMEs may allocate resources inefficiently without accurate insights into their energy consumption patterns. For instance, they might be overusing energy during non-peak hours or underutilizing equipment during peak times. Effective power monitoring enables SMEs to allocate resources optimally and reduce waste.
- **Environmental Impact:** Many SMEs are increasingly concerned about their environmental footprint. Excessive energy consumption not only affects operational costs but also contributes to greenhouse gas emissions. Sustainable business practices have become a requirement for maintaining a positive reputation and adhering to environmental regulations.
- **Competitive Disadvantage:** SMEs face competition from larger corporations that often have dedicated energy management teams and resources to implement advanced monitoring systems. Without access to similar technology and expertise, SMEs may find it challenging to remain competitive and innovative in their operations.

SMEs need effective power monitoring solutions to address operational challenges and remain agile, efficient, and sustainable in a competitive marketplace. The integration of Artificial Intelligence (AI) into power monitoring systems is crucial for accessibility and effectiveness. AI-driven systems provide real-time data and predictive analytics, enhancing operational efficiency. This chapter explores how AI technologies can transform power monitoring in SMEs, helping them thrive amidst operational obstacles.

AI INTEGRATION IN POWER MONITORING SYSTEMS

Leveraging Artificial Intelligence

This section explores the integration of Artificial Intelligence (AI) in power monitoring systems, highlighting its significant benefits for Small and Medium Enterprises (SMEs) and its impact on various industries (Figure 2).

- **Real-Time Insights:** AI enables power monitoring systems to provide real-time insights into energy consumption patterns. It continuously analyzes data, allowing SMEs to respond promptly to changing energy demands, thereby optimizing their resource allocation.
- **Predictive Analytics:** AI-driven power monitoring systems use predictive analytics to forecast future energy usage based on historical data and current trends. This capability empowers SMEs to proactively adjust their energy consumption, reducing costs and minimizing waste(Agrawal et al., 2024; Kavitha et al., 2023; Srinivas et al., 2023).
- **Anomaly Detection:** AI can detect anomalies or irregularities in energy consumption. Sudden spikes or drops in energy usage, which might be indicative of equipment malfunctions, can be identified in real-time, enabling preventive maintenance and cost savings.
- **Adaptive Control:** AI can control equipment and systems to adapt to changing energy conditions. For instance, it can optimize HVAC systems, lighting, and machinery to minimize energy consumption without compromising productivity.
- **Energy Efficiency Recommendations:** AI can provide recommendations to enhance energy efficiency. SMEs can use these insights to implement energy-saving measures, from adjusting equipment settings to scheduling energy-intensive tasks during non-peak hours(Agrawal et al., 2024; B et al., 2024; Satav, Lamani, et al., 2024).
- **Cost Reduction:** By optimizing energy consumption and reducing operational costs, AI-driven power monitoring systems contribute to significant cost savings. This is especially crucial for SMEs with limited budgets and resources.
- **Sustainability:** AI integration supports SMEs in their sustainability efforts by identifying areas of energy waste and suggesting eco-friendly practices. This aligns with environmental regulations and enhances the company's reputation(Satav, Hasan, et al., 2024; Satav, Lamani, et al., 2024; Venkateswaran, Vidhya, Ayyannan, et al., 2023).
- **Competitive Advantage:** AI allows SMEs to remain competitive by providing them with advanced energy management tools that were once primarily available to larger corporations. This can differentiate them in the market and attract environmentally conscious customers.

Figure 2. Integration of artificial intelligence (AI) in power monitoring systems

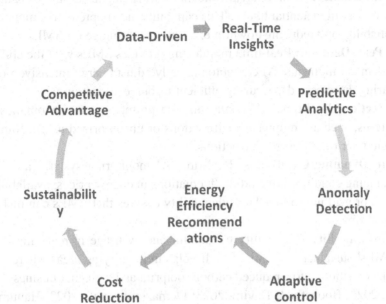

- **Data-Driven Decision-Making:** AI facilitates data-driven decision-making by offering action-able insights. SMEs can make informed choices regarding energy usage, operational processes, and investments, leading to improved long-term strategies.

This chapter explores the use of AI in power monitoring systems, its core components, energy usage analysis techniques, and practical case studies to demonstrate the tangible benefits of AI in SME energy management, thereby enabling sustainable growth and overcoming energy challenges.

Benefits of AI Integration in Power Monitoring Systems: Role of Real-time Monitoring

The integration of Artificial Intelligence (AI) into power monitoring systems offers numerous benefits, including real-time monitoring, which can significantly improve the energy management capabilities of Small and Medium Enterprises (SMEs).

- **Improved Energy Efficiency:** Real-time monitoring, empowered by AI, provides SMEs with instantaneous insights into their energy consumption. This allows for on-the-fly adjustments to optimize energy efficiency, resulting in reduced waste and lower operational costs.
- **Cost Reduction:** Real-time monitoring enables SMEs to track energy usage continuously. This, in turn, helps identify and address cost inefficiencies promptly. For instance, if energy usage spikes unexpectedly, real-time monitoring can trigger an alert, allowing swift action to prevent additional costs(Boopathi et al., 2018; Kavitha et al., 2023; Venkateswaran, Kumar, Diwakar, et al., 2023).

- **Predictive Maintenance:** AI-driven real-time monitoring can detect subtle changes in equipment performance, indicating potential issues. This capability aids in predictive maintenance, ensuring equipment reliability and reducing downtime, a critical advantage for SMEs.
- **Response to Peak Demand:** Real-time monitoring provides SMEs with the ability to respond to peak energy demand moments. AI can automatically adjust energy-intensive processes to minimize costs during these periods, ensuring efficient resource allocation.
- **Anomaly Detection:** Real-time AI monitoring can promptly detect anomalies in energy consumption patterns, such as equipment malfunctions or unauthorized usage. Rapid detection and notification allow for timely corrective actions.
- **Adaptation to Dynamic Conditions:** Real-time AI monitoring systems are adaptive and can respond to changing conditions, including fluctuations in energy prices, availability of renewable energy sources, or grid instability. This adaptability ensures that SMEs can make data-informed decisions in real-time.
- **Enhanced Sustainability:** The ability to monitor energy usage in real-time is instrumental in supporting SMEs' sustainability initiatives. It helps in identifying areas where energy waste can be minimized, contributing to a reduced carbon footprint and a greener business image(Boopathi, Kumar, et al., 2023; Boopathi & Davim, 2023; Domakonda et al., 2022; Hanumanthakari et al., 2023; Hussain & Srimathy, 2023; Samikannu et al., 2022; Venkateswaran, Vidhya, Ayyannan, et al., 2023).
- **Data-Driven Decision-Making:** Real-time monitoring coupled with AI generates a continuous stream of data that can be harnessed for informed decision-making. This data can be used to evaluate the effectiveness of energy-saving initiatives and drive long-term sustainability strategies(Dhanya et al., 2023; Kavitha et al., 2023; Pramila et al., 2023).
- **Competitive Advantage:** SMEs equipped with real-time AI monitoring systems gain a competitive edge by being able to respond swiftly to changing energy conditions, improve operational efficiency, and align with sustainability trends, attracting customers who value responsible energy use.

This chapter explores the use of AI integration in real-time monitoring for SMEs to optimize energy consumption and gain a competitive edge in their markets. It discusses the core components of AI-integrated power monitoring systems, energy usage analysis techniques, and practical case studies showcasing the benefits of real-time AI monitoring in SME energy management.

COMPONENTS OF AN AI-INTEGRATED POWER MONITORING SYSTEM

This section delves into the fundamental components of an AI-integrated power monitoring system (Figure 3), focusing on data acquisition, analysis, and control strategies, which are essential for optimizing energy management for SMEs(Kavitha et al., 2023; Kumar et al., 2023).

Figure 3. The various components of AI-integrated power monitoring system

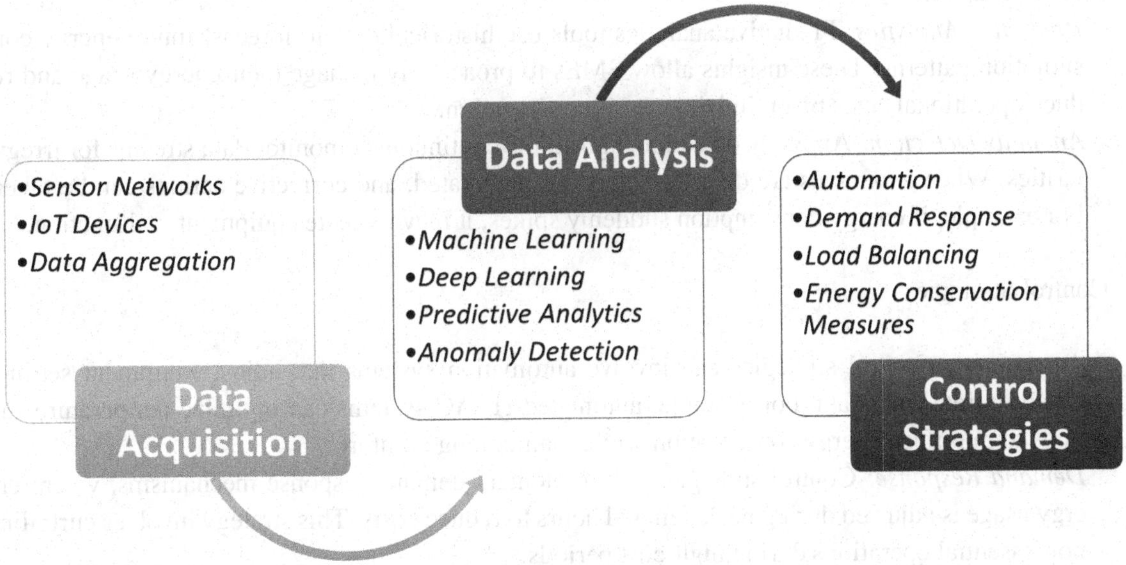

Data Acquisition

- *Sensor Networks:* Sensor networks are the foundation of data acquisition. These sensors collect data from various sources such as energy meters, smart devices, and industrial equipment. They continuously measure parameters like voltage, current, power factor, and energy consumption.
- *IoT Devices:* Internet of Things (IoT) devices are often used for data collection. They provide a bridge between physical devices and the digital world, enabling seamless data transmission and real-time monitoring. For example, smart meters, environmental sensors, and equipment sensors can be connected through IoT devices.
- *Data Aggregation:* Data collected from these sources is aggregated into a centralized database, making it accessible for analysis. This database can be hosted on-site or in the cloud, depending on the SME's infrastructure and data management strategy.

Data Analysis

- *Machine Learning:* AI algorithms, specifically machine learning, are employed to analyze the collected data. These algorithms can recognize patterns, identify anomalies, and make predictions based on historical and real-time data. For instance, machine learning models can identify equipment that needs maintenance or predict peak energy demand times(Boopathi & Kanike, 2023; Maheswari et al., 2023; Ramudu et al., 2023; Syamala et al., 2023).
- *Deep Learning:* Deep learning, a subset of machine learning, is used for more complex and nuanced data analysis tasks. Deep neural networks can uncover hidden insights in large datasets and improve the accuracy of predictions. They are particularly useful for image analysis and time-

series data(Boopathi, 2023a; Hema et al., 2023; Syamala et al., 2023; Venkateswaran, Vidhya, Naik, et al., 2023).

- *Predictive Analytics:* Predictive analytics tools use historical data to forecast future energy consumption patterns. These insights allow SMEs to proactively manage their energy usage and reduce operational costs by optimizing resource allocation.
- *Anomaly Detection:* Anomaly detection algorithms continuously monitor data streams for irregularities. When anomalies are detected, alerts are generated, and corrective actions can be taken. For example, if energy consumption suddenly spikes, it may indicate equipment malfunction.

Control Strategies

- *Automation:* Control strategies can involve automation systems that adjust equipment settings based on real-time data. For example, automated HVAC systems can optimize temperature settings to minimize energy consumption while maintaining comfort.
- *Demand Response:* Control strategies can implement demand response mechanisms, where energy usage is adjusted during peak demand hours to reduce costs. This strategy involves curtailing non-essential operations during high-cost periods.
- *Load Balancing:* Control strategies include load balancing, which evenly distributes energy demand across the grid. This not only prevents overloading but also ensures that energy-intensive processes run efficiently during off-peak hours.
- *Energy Conservation Measures:* Based on data analysis, control strategies can suggest energy conservation measures such as changing equipment usage schedules, adjusting lighting levels, or implementing energy-efficient practices.

This chapter explores the AI-integrated power monitoring system, focusing on data acquisition, analysis, and control strategies. It discusses various AI techniques for energy usage analysis and practical case studies demonstrating the benefits of implementing such systems in SMEs, highlighting the importance of data collection, analysis, and control strategies.

AI TECHNIQUES FOR ENERGY USAGE ANALYSIS

Machine Learning Algorithms

This section explores machine learning algorithms used in AI-integrated power monitoring systems, providing SMEs with powerful tools for analyzing and optimizing energy consumption in SMEs(Chandrika et al., 2023; Domakonda et al., 2022; Gnanaprakasam et al., 2023; Maguluri et al., 2023).

- **Linear Regression:** Linear regression is used to model the relationship between energy consumption and various factors, such as temperature or time of day. It can help SMEs understand how different variables influence their energy usage.
- **Decision Trees:** Decision trees are used for classification and regression tasks. In energy usage analysis, they can help identify patterns and categorize data into different consumption profiles, aiding in anomaly detection and predictive maintenance.

- **Random Forest:** Random forests are an ensemble learning technique that uses multiple decision trees. They are effective for analyzing complex energy consumption patterns and can enhance the accuracy of predictions and anomaly detection.

- **Support Vector Machines (SVM):** SVM is used for classifying data. In energy monitoring, SVM can be used to classify energy consumption patterns into various categories, allowing SMEs to identify irregularities and predict energy demand.

- **k-Means Clustering:** k-Means clustering groups similar energy consumption data points together. This can help SMEs identify clusters of equipment or processes with similar energy usage patterns and optimize their operations accordingly.

- **Neural Networks:** Neural networks, including feedforward and recurrent neural networks, can analyze time-series data from energy meters and predict future energy consumption patterns. Recurrent neural networks are particularly effective for sequence data, such as hourly energy usage.

- **Principal Component Analysis (PCA):** PCA is used for dimensionality reduction. In energy usage analysis, it can help SMEs identify the most important variables that influence energy consumption, enabling focused energy-saving strategies.

- **Long Short-Term Memory (LSTM):** LSTM is a type of recurrent neural network suitable for analyzing sequences, such as energy consumption data over time. It is valuable for predicting energy demand and detecting anomalies in real-time.

- **Gradient Boosting:** Gradient boosting algorithms like XGBoost and LightGBM are used for accurate energy usage predictions. They can capture complex relationships between variables and deliver precise insights.

- **Time-Series Analysis:** Time-series analysis techniques, such as Autoregressive Integrated Moving Average (ARIMA) and Exponential Smoothing, are used for forecasting energy usage based on historical data. These models are valuable for predicting future energy demand and optimizing resource allocation.

Machine learning algorithms can help Small and Medium-sized Enterprises (SMEs) understand their energy usage patterns, predict future demand, and identify inefficiencies. This helps optimize energy management, reduce operational costs, and enhance sustainability. The chapter will explore the role of deep learning and predictive analytics in energy usage analysis and present practical case studies showcasing their benefits.

Deep Learning Models

Deep learning models, a subset of AI, are gaining popularity for energy usage analysis in SMEs (Figure 4) due to their ability to analyze complex, high-dimensional data, offering numerous energy management applications(Anitha et al., 2023; Boopathi et al., 2022; Gunasekaran & Boopathi, 2023; Koshariya, Kalaiyarasi, et al., 2023; Koshariya, Khatoon, et al., 2023; Vanitha et al., 2023; Venkateswaran, Vidhya, Ayyannan, et al., 2023).

- **Recurrent Neural Networks (RNN):** RNNs are particularly suited for analyzing time-series data, which is common in energy usage. They can predict future energy consumption patterns based on historical data, helping SMEs anticipate demand and make data-informed decisions.

Figure 4. Deep learning models for energy usage analysis

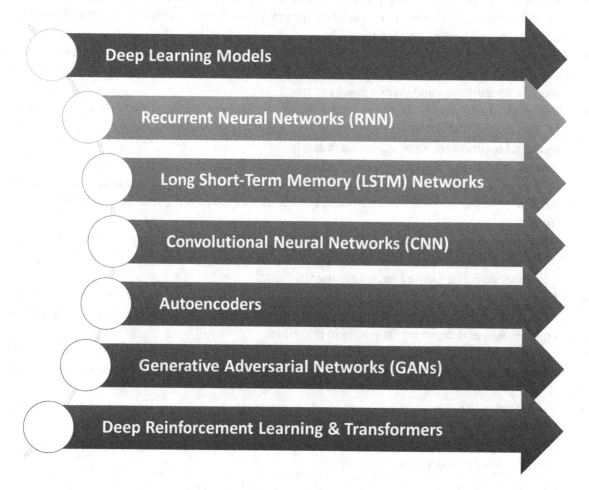

- **Long Short-Term Memory (LSTM) Networks:** LSTMs are a type of RNN specifically designed for sequence data. They excel in capturing dependencies over long time periods. SMEs can use LSTMs to predict energy consumption and detect anomalies, especially in applications where time intervals are irregular.
- **Convolutional Neural Networks (CNN):** CNNs are widely used in image analysis, but they are also valuable for energy monitoring systems that use visual data, such as infrared images to detect hotspots in electrical panels. SMEs can identify inefficient equipment or overheating issues using CNNs.
- **Autoencoders:** Autoencoders are used for dimensionality reduction and feature learning. SMEs can employ autoencoders to create compressed representations of energy data, making it easier to identify patterns and anomalies in a reduced feature space.
- **Generative Adversarial Networks (GANs):** GANs can be used to generate synthetic energy consumption data. This artificial data can help SMEs train models more effectively and create representative datasets for analysis and forecasting.

Figure 5. The predict future energy consumption using predictive analytics

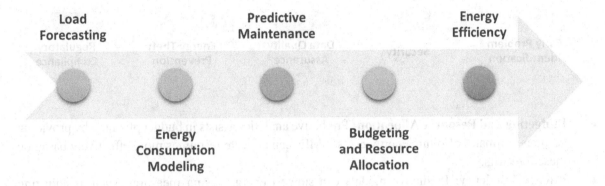

- **Deep Reinforcement Learning:** Deep reinforcement learning can optimize energy consumption in real-time. SMEs can use this approach to create algorithms that control equipment and systems to reduce energy waste while maintaining productivity.
- **Transformers:** Transformers, known for their effectiveness in natural language processing, can be applied to time-series data and are particularly useful for forecasting energy usage and identifying patterns in data collected from various sensors.

Deep learning models are useful for SMEs to analyze complex energy consumption data, enabling accurate predictions, anomaly detection, and real-time control. This helps in making informed decisions about energy consumption, maintenance, and resource allocation. This chapter will explore practical case studies showcasing how deep learning models have improved efficiency and cost reduction in SME energy management.

Predictive Analytics and Anomaly Detection

AI techniques like predictive analytics and anomaly detection are crucial for improving energy usage analysis in SMEs.

Predictive Analytics

Predictive analytics uses historical and real-time data to predict future energy consumption patterns, offering numerous benefits for SMEs and energy management (Figure 5).

- **Load Forecasting:** Predictive analytics aids SMEs in predicting peak energy demand times, optimizing resource allocation for efficient energy use and cost reduction.
- **Energy Consumption Modeling:** Predictive models enable SMEs to create detailed energy consumption profiles for various equipment or processes, enabling effective planning and budgeting for energy-efficient operations.
- **Predictive Maintenance:** By analyzing equipment performance data, predictive analytics can predict when maintenance is needed, reducing downtime and maintenance costs. This is particularly valuable for SMEs reliant on critical machinery.

Figure 6. Anomaly detection process for SMEs

- **Budgeting and Resource Allocation:** Predictive analytics assists in budget planning by providing accurate estimates of future energy costs. SMEs can allocate resources more effectively based on these forecasts.
- **Energy Efficiency:** Predictive models can suggest energy-saving measures, such as adjusting equipment schedules or implementing energy-efficient practices, helping SMEs reduce their environmental impact and operational costs.

Anomaly Detection

Anomaly detection is crucial for SMEs to identify deviations from normal energy consumption behavior, ensuring operational reliability and efficiency (Figure 6).

- **Early Problem Identification:** Anomaly detection can swiftly identify irregularities, such as sudden spikes or drops in energy usage. This can be indicative of equipment malfunction or operational issues, enabling SMEs to take corrective actions promptly.
- **Security:** Anomaly detection can also help SMEs detect unusual energy consumption patterns that may indicate unauthorized access or security breaches. It ensures the integrity of the power supply and protects sensitive data and operations.
- **Data Quality Assurance:** Anomaly detection can reveal data quality issues or sensor malfunctions. By flagging inconsistent data, it maintains the accuracy and reliability of energy usage data, essential for sound decision-making(Agrawal et al., 2023; Dhanya et al., 2023; Rahamathunnisa et al., 2023; Srinivas et al., 2023).
- **Energy Theft Prevention:** For utilities and energy service providers working with SMEs, anomaly detection can help detect energy theft or tampering, ensuring fair billing and preventing losses.
- **Regulatory Compliance:** Anomaly detection systems contribute to regulatory compliance by ensuring that energy consumption aligns with established standards. This is especially important for SMEs in industries with strict energy regulations.

Predictive analytics and anomaly detection are crucial tools for SMEs to optimize energy consumption, reduce operational costs, and improve sustainability. These AI techniques analyze historical and real-time data, identifying deviations from normal behavior, giving them a competitive edge in the dynamic energy landscape. This chapter will explore the role of AI in energy management through practical case studies and success stories.

CASE STUDIES AND SUCCESS STORIES

Three case studies showcase SMEs' successful implementation of AI-integrated power monitoring systems, enhancing energy consumption, reducing downtime and maintenance costs, and boosting profitability and sustainability(Chaudhuri et al., 2022; Gill et al., 2022).

SME: Optimizing Energy Consumption

SME successfully tackled energy inefficiency and fluctuating operational costs by implementing an AI-integrated power monitoring system.

Challenges

- Erratic energy consumption patterns.
- Inefficient equipment utilization.
- High operational costs due to energy waste.
- Limited budget for energy management solutions.

Solution

- Installed a real-time power monitoring system.
- Utilized machine learning algorithms to analyze historical data.
- Integrated predictive analytics to forecast energy demand.
- Automated equipment control for energy optimization.

Results

- Reduced energy consumption by 15%.
- Lowered operational costs by 10%.
- Improved equipment reliability and minimized downtime.
- Enhanced environmental sustainability and reduced carbon footprint.
- Achieved a return on investment (ROI) within 12 months.

SME: Reducing Downtime and Maintenance Costs

SME successfully addressed equipment breakdowns and maintenance costs by implementing AI-integrated power monitoring in their small-scale food processing plant(Brandalero et al., 2020; Velmurugan et al., 2021).

Challenges

- Frequent equipment failures and unexpected downtime.

- Escalating maintenance costs.
- Unpredictable energy consumption patterns.
- Inefficient resource allocation.

Solution

- Implemented real-time power monitoring with predictive maintenance.
- Utilized anomaly detection for early problem identification.
- Automated equipment control strategies.
- Conducted predictive analytics to forecast maintenance needs.

Results

- Reduced downtime by 30%.
- Slashed maintenance costs by 20%.
- Improved equipment reliability and longevity.
- Enhanced operational efficiency.
- Realized a positive impact on overall profitability.

SME: Enhancing Profitability and Sustainability

SME is a small retail business aiming to improve profitability while adhering to sustainable practices. By integrating AI into their energy management, they achieved a balance between profitability and environmental responsibility(Chaudhuri et al., 2022; Pereira et al., 2020; Qamar et al., 2022; Žigienė et al., 2019).

Challenges:
- Fluctuating energy costs.
- Rising environmental concerns.
- Need for cost reduction and sustainability.
- Limited budget for energy management solutions.

Solution:
- Installed AI-driven power monitoring for real-time data analysis.
- Utilized AI recommendations for energy conservation measures.
- Embraced load optimization strategies.
- Implemented automated lighting and HVAC control.

Results:
- Reduced energy costs by 12%.
- Enhanced energy efficiency and sustainability.
- Attracted environmentally conscious customers.

- ○ Improved reputation and marketability.
- ○ Demonstrated a commitment to corporate social responsibility.

These case studies illustrate the transformative power of AI-integrated power monitoring systems in addressing specific challenges faced by SMEs. Whether the goal is optimizing energy consumption, reducing downtime and maintenance costs, or enhancing profitability and sustainability, AI-driven solutions empower SMEs to thrive in a competitive and sustainable future.

REGULATORY AND ETHICAL CONSIDERATIONS

As Small and Medium Enterprises (SMEs) adopt AI-integrated power monitoring systems, it is vital to address regulatory and ethical concerns related to data privacy, security, compliance with energy regulations, and the ethical use of AI in power monitoring(Maguluri et al., 2023; Ugandar et al., 2023).

Data Privacy and Security

Challenge: AI-integrated power monitoring systems require the collection, storage, and analysis of sensitive energy consumption data. Ensuring the privacy and security of this data is crucial.

Solutions:

- ○ **Data Encryption:** Implement robust encryption methods to protect data during transmission and storage.
- ○ **Access Control:** Restrict data access to authorized personnel only and use multi-factor authentication.
- ○ **Regular Audits:** Conduct routine security audits and vulnerability assessments.
- ○ **Data Masking:** Anonymize or pseudonymize sensitive data to prevent personal or sensitive information exposure.

Compliance With Energy Regulations

Challenge: SMEs must adhere to energy regulations and standards, which can be complex and demanding. Compliance is essential to avoid legal issues and maintain a positive reputation.

Solutions:

- ○ **Stay Informed:** Stay updated on the latest energy regulations and ensure that the AI-integrated power monitoring system complies with them.
- ○ **Data Retention Policies:** Implement data retention policies in line with regulatory requirements.
- ○ **Third-Party Verification:** Employ third-party experts to verify and validate the compliance of the monitoring system.
- ○ **Documentation:** Maintain comprehensive records and documentation of compliance efforts.

Ethical Use of AI in Power Monitoring

Challenge: Ensuring the ethical use of AI in power monitoring is vital to maintain trust and prevent AI-related controversies.

Solutions:

- ○ **Transparent Data Handling:** Clearly communicate data collection, analysis, and usage to stakeholders.
- ○ **Consent and Control:** Allow users to opt in or out of data collection and provide control over their data.
- ○ **Bias Mitigation:** Implement mechanisms to reduce algorithmic bias and discrimination in AI models.
- ○ **Algorithm Transparency:** Make AI algorithms used in power monitoring transparent and interpretable.

By addressing data privacy and security, ensuring compliance with energy regulations, and promoting the ethical use of AI in power monitoring, SMEs can foster trust among customers, regulators, and other stakeholders. It is essential to strike a balance between innovation and responsibility as SMEs navigate the integration of AI into their energy management systems.

FUTURE TRENDS AND CHALLENGES

The article delves into the future trends and challenges in power monitoring in SMEs, highlighting the pivotal role of AI in driving innovation and exploring potential solutions(Anitha et al., 2023; Boopathi, 2023b; Boopathi, Pandey, et al., 2023; Gunasekaran & Boopathi, 2023).

Emerging Technologies

1. Edge Computing:
   - ○ *Trend:* Edge computing is gaining traction in power monitoring. AI algorithms are being deployed at the edge, enabling real-time analysis of data at the source.
   - ○ *Benefits:* Reduced latency, improved responsiveness, and enhanced data privacy.
2. Renewable Energy Integration:
   - ○ *Trend:* SMEs are increasingly adopting renewable energy sources. AI is used to manage the integration of intermittent renewables into the energy mix.
   - ○ *Benefits:* Reduced reliance on fossil fuels, lower energy costs, and reduced carbon footprint.
3. Advanced Energy Storage:
   - ○ *Trend:* Advanced energy storage solutions, including batteries and supercapacitors, are becoming more affordable. AI helps optimize energy storage systems for SMEs.
   - ○ *Benefits:* Enhanced energy resilience, reduced peak energy demand costs, and increased sustainability.

4. Decentralized Energy Grids:
   ○ *Trend:* The rise of decentralized energy grids and microgrids, often incorporating renewable energy sources, necessitates AI for efficient energy distribution.
   ○ *Benefits:* Enhanced energy reliability, local control, and reduced transmission losses.

Challenges and Potential Solutions

1. Data Privacy and Security:
   ○ *Challenge:* With increasing data collection and sharing, data privacy and security challenges are amplified(Maguluri et al., 2023; Ugandar et al., 2023; Venkateswaran, Kumar, Diwakar, et al., 2023).
   ○ *Solutions:* Continuously update cybersecurity measures, employ encryption, conduct regular audits, and educate staff on security best practices.
2. Energy Efficiency Awareness:
   ○ *Challenge:* SMEs may not be fully aware of the benefits of AI-integrated power monitoring systems.
   ○ *Solutions:* Raise awareness through education and training, and showcase successful case studies and return on investment (ROI).
3. Scalability and Integration:
   ○ *Challenge:* Integrating AI solutions seamlessly and cost-effectively into existing SME infrastructure.
   ○ *Solutions:* Seek scalable solutions, invest in robust IT infrastructure, and explore cloud-based systems.
4. Skills and Expertise:
   ○ *Challenge:* SMEs may lack the internal expertise to manage AI-integrated systems.
   ○ *Solutions:* Collaborate with experts, provide training to staff, and consider outsourcing management to specialized providers.

The Role of AI in Driving Innovation

AI is poised to play a central role in driving innovation in SME energy management(Boopathi, Kumar, et al., 2023; Domakonda et al., 2022; Hussain & Srimathy, 2023; Ingle et al., 2023; Kumara et al., 2023). It empowers SMEs to:

- **Optimize Energy Consumption:** AI helps SMEs identify patterns, reduce waste, and achieve higher energy efficiency.
- **Predict Future Demand:** AI forecasting models assist in resource allocation and cost reduction.
- **Automate Decision-Making:** AI-driven automation responds to real-time data, ensuring energy optimization.
- **Enhance Sustainability:** AI supports environmentally responsible practices and compliance with regulations.

SMEs that embrace AI in their power monitoring systems can navigate emerging technologies, address challenges, and drive innovation in their energy management practices. This sets the stage for a more sustainable and competitive future.

CONCLUSION

This chapter explores the potential of AI-integrated power monitoring systems for Small and Medium Enterprises (SMEs). It addresses unique energy challenges such as diverse energy needs, seasonal variability, limited resources, and cost sensitivity. It also highlights the growing environmental responsibility and the need for technology accessibility for efficient energy management.

The study explores the components of AI-integrated power monitoring systems, focusing on data acquisition, analysis, and control strategies, which enable SMEs to efficiently collect and optimize energy consumption data.

Machine learning algorithms like linear regression, decision trees, and support vector machines were used for energy usage analysis. Deep learning models like recurrent neural networks, LSTM networks, and CNNs were introduced for managing energy data. Annomaly detection and predictive analytics were explored for SMEs to identify irregularities and predict future energy demand. AI integration improved energy consumption, reduced costs, and enhanced profitability and sustainability in three SMEs.

The paper discusses the ethical and regulatory aspects of AI-integrated power monitoring for SMEs, emphasizing data privacy, security, energy regulation compliance, and ethical AI use. It also explores future trends and challenges, such as edge computing, renewable energy integration, advanced energy storage, and decentralized energy grids. Key challenges include data privacy, energy efficiency awareness, scalability, and skills requirements. AI is seen as a driving force in SME energy management, offering opportunities for optimization, demand prediction, decision-making automation, and sustainability enhancement.

AI-integrated power monitoring systems offer significant benefits for SMEs, enhancing energy efficiency, reducing operational costs, and promoting sustainable practices, positioning them for success in the rapidly changing energy landscape.

REFERENCES

Agrawal, A. V., Magulur, L. P., Priya, S. G., Kaur, A., Singh, G., & Boopathi, S. (2023). Smart Precision Agriculture Using IoT and WSN. In *Handbook of Research on Data Science and Cybersecurity Innovations in Industry 4.0 Technologies* (pp. 524–541). IGI Global. doi:10.4018/978-1-6684-8145-5.ch026

Agrawal, A. V., Shashibhushan, G., Pradeep, S., Padhi, S. N., Sugumar, D., & Boopathi, S. (2024). Synergizing Artificial Intelligence, 5G, and Cloud Computing for Efficient Energy Conversion Using Agricultural Waste. In Practice, Progress, and Proficiency in Sustainability (pp. 475–497). IGI Global. doi:10.4018/979-8-3693-1186-8.ch026

Alaskari, O., Pinedo-Cuenca, R., & Ahmad, M. (2021). Framework for implementation of Enterprise Resource Planning (ERP) systems in small and medium enterprises (SMEs): A case study. *Procedia Manufacturing*, *55*, 424–430. doi:10.1016/j.promfg.2021.10.058

Anitha, C., Komala, C., Vivekanand, C. V., Lalitha, S., & Boopathi, S. (2023). Artificial Intelligence driven security model for Internet of Medical Things (IoMT). *IEEE Explore*, 1–7.

B, M. K., K, K. K., Sasikala, P., Sampath, B., Gopi, B., & Sundaram, S. (2024). Sustainable Green Energy Generation From Waste Water. In *Practice, Progress, and Proficiency in Sustainability* (pp. 440–463). IGI Global. doi:10.4018/979-8-3693-1186-8.ch024

Baabdullah, A. M., Alalwan, A. A., Slade, E. L., Raman, R., & Khatatneh, K. F. (2021). SMEs and artificial intelligence (AI): Antecedents and consequences of AI-based B2B practices. *Industrial Marketing Management*, 98, 255–270. doi:10.1016/j.indmarman.2021.09.003

Bauer, M., van Dinther, C., & Kiefer, D. (2020). *Machine learning in SME: an empirical study on enablers and success factors*. Research Gate.

Boopathi, S. (2023a). Deep Learning Techniques Applied for Automatic Sentence Generation. In *Promoting Diversity, Equity, and Inclusion in Language Learning Environments* (pp. 255–273). IGI Global. doi:10.4018/978-1-6684-3632-5.ch016

Boopathi, S. (2023b). Internet of Things-Integrated Remote Patient Monitoring System: Healthcare Application. In *Dynamics of Swarm Intelligence Health Analysis for the Next Generation* (pp. 137–161). IGI Global. doi:10.4018/978-1-6684-6894-4.ch008

Boopathi, S., & Davim, J. P. (2023). *Sustainable Utilization of Nanoparticles and Nanofluids in Engineering Applications*. IGI Global. doi:10.4018/978-1-6684-9135-5

Boopathi, S., & Kanike, U. K. (2023). Applications of Artificial Intelligent and Machine Learning Techniques in Image Processing. In *Handbook of Research on Thrust Technologies' Effect on Image Processing* (pp. 151–173). IGI Global. doi:10.4018/978-1-6684-8618-4.ch010

Boopathi, S., Kumar, P. K. S., Meena, R. S., Sudhakar, M., & Associates. (2023). Sustainable Developments of Modern Soil-Less Agro-Cultivation Systems: Aquaponic Culture. In Human Agro-Energy Optimization for Business and Industry (pp. 69–87). IGI Global.

Boopathi, S., Pandey, B. K., & Pandey, D. (2023). Advances in Artificial Intelligence for Image Processing: Techniques, Applications, and Optimization. In Handbook of Research on Thrust Technologies' Effect on Image Processing (pp. 73–95). IGI Global.

Boopathi, S., Saranya, A., Raghuraman, S., & Revanth, R. (2018). Design and Fabrication of Low Cost Electric Bicycle. *International Research Journal of Engineering and Technology*, 5(3), 146–147.

Boopathi, S., Sureshkumar, M., & Sathiskumar, S. (2022). Parametric Optimization of LPG Refrigeration System Using Artificial Bee Colony Algorithm. *International Conference on Recent Advances in Mechanical Engineering Research and Development*, (pp. 97–105). IEEE.

Brandalero, M., Ali, M., Le Jeune, L., Hernandez, H. G. M., Veleski, M., Da Silva, B., Lemeire, J., Van Beeck, K., Touhafi, A., Goedemé, T., & ... (2020). Aitia: Embedded ai techniques for embedded industrial applications. *2020 International Conference on Omni-Layer Intelligent Systems (COINS)*, (pp. 1–7). IEEE. 10.1109/COINS49042.2020.9191672

Chandrika, V., Sivakumar, A., Krishnan, T. S., Pradeep, J., Manikandan, S., & Boopathi, S. (2023). Theoretical Study on Power Distribution Systems for Electric Vehicles. In *Intelligent Engineering Applications and Applied Sciences for Sustainability* (pp. 1–19). IGI Global. doi:10.4018/979-8-3693-0044-2.ch001

Chaudhuri, R., Chatterjee, S., Vrontis, D., & Chaudhuri, S. (2022). Innovation in SMEs, AI dynamism, and sustainability: The current situation and way forward. *Sustainability (Basel)*, *14*(19), 12760. doi:10.3390/su141912760

Crockett, K. A., Gerber, L., Latham, A., & Colyer, E. (2021). Building trustworthy AI solutions: A case for practical solutions for small businesses. *IEEE Transactions on Artificial Intelligence*.

Dhanya, D., Kumar, S. S., Thilagavathy, A., Prasad, D., & Boopathi, S. (2023). Data Analytics and Artificial Intelligence in the Circular Economy: Case Studies. In Intelligent Engineering Applications and Applied Sciences for Sustainability (pp. 40–58). IGI Global.

Domakonda, V. K., Farooq, S., Chinthamreddy, S., Puviarasi, R., Sudhakar, M., & Boopathi, S. (2022). Sustainable Developments of Hybrid Floating Solar Power Plants: Photovoltaic System. In Human Agro-Energy Optimization for Business and Industry (pp. 148–167). IGI Global.

Gill, S. S., Xu, M., Ottaviani, C., Patros, P., Bahsoon, R., Shaghaghi, A., Golec, M., Stankovski, V., Wu, H., Abraham, A., Singh, M., Mehta, H., Ghosh, S. K., Baker, T., Parlikad, A. K., Lutfiyya, H., Kanhere, S. S., Sakellariou, R., Dustdar, S., & Uhlig, S. (2022). AI for next generation computing: Emerging trends and future directions. *Internet of Things : Engineering Cyber Physical Human Systems*, *19*, 100514. doi:10.1016/j.iot.2022.100514

Gnanaprakasam, C., Vankara, J., Sastry, A. S., Prajval, V., Gireesh, N., & Boopathi, S. (2023). Long-Range and Low-Power Automated Soil Irrigation System Using Internet of Things: An Experimental Study. In Contemporary Developments in Agricultural Cyber-Physical Systems (pp. 87–104). IGI Global.

Grashof, N., & Kopka, A. (2023). Artificial intelligence and radical innovation: An opportunity for all companies? *Small Business Economics*, *61*(2), 771–797. doi:10.1007/s11187-022-00698-3

Gunasekaran, K., & Boopathi, S. (2023). Artificial Intelligence in Water Treatments and Water Resource Assessments. In *Artificial Intelligence Applications in Water Treatment and Water Resource Management* (pp. 71–98). IGI Global. doi:10.4018/978-1-6684-6791-6.ch004

Han, H., & Trimi, S. (2022). Towards a data science platform for improving SME collaboration through Industry 4.0 technologies. *Technological Forecasting and Social Change*, *174*, 121242. doi:10.1016/j.techfore.2021.121242

Hanumanthakari, S., Gift, M. M., Kanimozhi, K., Bhavani, M. D., Bamane, K. D., & Boopathi, S. (2023). Biomining Method to Extract Metal Components Using Computer-Printed Circuit Board E-Waste. In *Handbook of Research on Safe Disposal Methods of Municipal Solid Wastes for a Sustainable Environment* (pp. 123–141). IGI Global. doi:10.4018/978-1-6684-8117-2.ch010

Hema, N., Krishnamoorthy, N., Chavan, S. M., Kumar, N., Sabarimuthu, M., & Boopathi, S. (2023). A Study on an Internet of Things (IoT)-Enabled Smart Solar Grid System. In *Handbook of Research on Deep Learning Techniques for Cloud-Based Industrial IoT* (pp. 290–308). IGI Global. doi:10.4018/978-1-6684-8098-4.ch017

Hussain, Z., & Srimathy, G. (2023). *IoT and AI Integration for Enhanced Efficiency and Sustainability.* Research Gate.

Ingle, R. B., Senthil, T. S., Swathi, S., Muralidharan, N., Mahendran, G., & Boopathi, S. (2023). Sustainability and Optimization of Green and Lean Manufacturing Processes Using Machine Learning Techniques. IGI Global. doi:10.4018/978-1-6684-8238-4.ch012

Jung, W.-K., Kim, D.-R., Lee, H., Lee, T.-H., Yang, I., Youn, B. D., Zontar, D., Brockmann, M., Brecher, C., & Ahn, S.-H. (2021). Appropriate smart factory for SMEs: Concept, application and perspective. *International Journal of Precision Engineering and Manufacturing, 22*(1), 201–215. doi:10.1007/s12541-020-00445-2

Kavitha, C. R., Varalatchoumy, M., Mithuna, H. R., Bharathi, K., Geethalakshmi, N. M., & Boopathi, S. (2023). Energy Monitoring and Control in the Smart Grid: Integrated Intelligent IoT and ANFIS. In M. Arshad (Ed.), (pp. 290–316). Advances in Bioinformatics and Biomedical Engineering. IGI Global. doi:10.4018/978-1-6684-6577-6.ch014

Koshariya, A. K., Kalaiyarasi, D., Jovith, A. A., Sivakami, T., Hasan, D. S., & Boopathi, S. (2023). AI-Enabled IoT and WSN-Integrated Smart Agriculture System. In *Artificial Intelligence Tools and Technologies for Smart Farming and Agriculture Practices* (pp. 200–218). IGI Global. doi:10.4018/978-1-6684-8516-3.ch011

Koshariya, A. K., Khatoon, S., Marathe, A. M., Suba, G. M., Baral, D., & Boopathi, S. (2023). Agricultural Waste Management Systems Using Artificial Intelligence Techniques. In *AI-Enabled Social Robotics in Human Care Services* (pp. 236–258). IGI Global. doi:10.4018/978-1-6684-8171-4.ch009

Kumar, P. R., Meenakshi, S., Shalini, S., Devi, S. R., & Boopathi, S. (2023). Soil Quality Prediction in Context Learning Approaches Using Deep Learning and Blockchain for Smart Agriculture. In R. Kumar, A. B. Abdul Hamid, & N. I. Binti Ya'akub (Eds.), (pp. 1–26). Advances in Computational Intelligence and Robotics. IGI Global. doi:10.4018/978-1-6684-9151-5.ch001

Kumara, V., Mohanaprakash, T., Fairooz, S., Jamal, K., Babu, T., & Sampath, B. (2023). Experimental Study on a Reliable Smart Hydroponics System. In *Human Agro-Energy Optimization for Business and Industry* (pp. 27–45). IGI Global. doi:10.4018/978-1-6684-4118-3.ch002

Lu, Y., Yang, L., Shi, B., Li, J., & Abedin, M. Z. (2022). A novel framework of credit risk feature selection for SMEs during industry 4.0. *Annals of Operations Research*, 1–28. doi:10.1007/s10479-022-04849-3 PMID:35910041

Maguluri, L. P., Arularasan, A. N., & Boopathi, S. (2023). Assessing Security Concerns for AI-Based Drones in Smart Cities. In R. Kumar, A. B. Abdul Hamid, & N. I. Binti Ya'akub (Eds.), (pp. 27–47). Advances in Computational Intelligence and Robotics. IGI Global. doi:10.4018/978-1-6684-9151-5.ch002

Maheswari, B. U., Imambi, S. S., Hasan, D., Meenakshi, S., Pratheep, V., & Boopathi, S. (2023). Internet of Things and Machine Learning-Integrated Smart Robotics. In Global Perspectives on Robotics and Autonomous Systems: Development and Applications (pp. 240–258). IGI Global. doi:10.4018/978-1-6684-7791-5.ch010

Mohammadian, H. D., & Rezaie, F. (2020). The role of IoE-Education in the 5 th wave theory readiness & its effect on SME 4.0 HR competencies. *2020 IEEE Global Engineering Education Conference (EDUCON)*, (pp. 1604–1613). IEEE. 10.1109/EDUCON45650.2020.9125249

Nascimento, A. M., de Melo, V. V., Queiroz, A. C. M., Brashear-Alejandro, T., & de Souza Meirelles, F. (2021). Artificial intelligence applied to small businesses: The use of automatic feature engineering and machine learning for more accurate planning. *Revista de Contabilidade e Organizações*, *15*, 1–15.

Onu, P., & Mbohwa, C. (2021). Industry 4.0 opportunities in manufacturing SMEs: Sustainability outlook. *Materials Today: Proceedings*, *44*, 1925–1930. doi:10.1016/j.matpr.2020.12.095

Pereira, I. P., Ferreira, F. A., Pereira, L. F., Govindan, K., Meidutė-Kavaliauskienė, I., & Correia, R. J. (2020). A fuzzy cognitive mapping-system dynamics approach to energy-change impacts on the sustainability of small and medium-sized enterprises. *Journal of Cleaner Production*, *256*, 120154. doi:10.1016/j.jclepro.2020.120154

Pramila, P., Amudha, S., Saravanan, T., Sankar, S. R., Poongothai, E., & Boopathi, S. (2023). Design and Development of Robots for Medical Assistance: An Architectural Approach. In Contemporary Applications of Data Fusion for Advanced Healthcare Informatics (pp. 260–282). IGI Global.

Prashar, A. (2019). Towards sustainable development in industrial small and Medium-sized Enterprises: An energy sustainability approach. *Journal of Cleaner Production*, *235*, 977–996. doi:10.1016/j.jclepro.2019.07.045

Qamar, S., Ahmad, M., Oryani, B., & Zhang, Q. (2022). Solar energy technology adoption and diffusion by micro, small, and medium enterprises: Sustainable energy for climate change mitigation. *Environmental Science and Pollution Research International*, *29*(32), 49385–49403. doi:10.1007/s11356-022-19406-5 PMID:35218487

Rahamathunnisa, U., Subhashini, P., Aancy, H. M., Meenakshi, S., Boopathi, S., & ... (2023). Solutions for Software Requirement Risks Using Artificial Intelligence Techniques. In *Handbook of Research on Data Science and Cybersecurity Innovations in Industry 4.0 Technologies* (pp. 45–64). IGI Global.

Ramudu, K., Mohan, V. M., Jyothirmai, D., Prasad, D., Agrawal, R., & Boopathi, S. (2023). Machine Learning and Artificial Intelligence in Disease Prediction: Applications, Challenges, Limitations, Case Studies, and Future Directions. In Contemporary Applications of Data Fusion for Advanced Healthcare Informatics (pp. 297–318). IGI Global.

Samikannu, R., Koshariya, A. K., Poornima, E., Ramesh, S., Kumar, A., & Boopathi, S. (2022). Sustainable Development in Modern Aquaponics Cultivation Systems Using IoT Technologies. In *Human Agro-Energy Optimization for Business and Industry* (pp. 105–127). IGI Global.

Satav, S. D., Hasan, D. S., Pitchai, R., Mohanaprakash, T. A., Sultanuddin, S. J., & Boopathi, S. (2024). Next Generation of Internet of Things (NGIoT) in Healthcare Systems. In Practice, Progress, and Proficiency in Sustainability (pp. 307–330). IGI Global. doi:10.4018/979-8-3693-1186-8.ch017

Satav, S. D., & Lamani, D. G, H. K., Kumar, N. M. G., Manikandan, S., & Sampath, B. (2024). Energy and Battery Management in the Era of Cloud Computing. In Practice, Progress, and Proficiency in Sustainability (pp. 141–166). IGI Global. doi:10.4018/979-8-3693-1186-8.ch009

Srinivas, B., Maguluri, L. P., Naidu, K. V., Reddy, L. C. S., Deivakani, M., & Boopathi, S. (2023). Architecture and Framework for Interfacing Cloud-Enabled Robots. In *Handbook of Research on Data Science and Cybersecurity Innovations in Industry 4.0 Technologies* (pp. 542–560). IGI Global. doi:10.4018/978-1-6684-8145-5.ch027

Syamala, M., Komala, C., Pramila, P., Dash, S., Meenakshi, S., & Boopathi, S. (2023). Machine Learning-Integrated IoT-Based Smart Home Energy Management System. In *Handbook of Research on Deep Learning Techniques for Cloud-Based Industrial IoT* (pp. 219–235). IGI Global. doi:10.4018/978-1-6684-8098-4.ch013

Ugandar, R. E., Rahamathunnisa, U., Sajithra, S., Christiana, M. B. V., Palai, B. K., & Boopathi, S. (2023). Hospital Waste Management Using Internet of Things and Deep Learning: Enhanced Efficiency and Sustainability. In M. Arshad (Ed.), (pp. 317–343). Advances in Bioinformatics and Biomedical Engineering. IGI Global. doi:10.4018/978-1-6684-6577-6.ch015

Vanitha, S., Radhika, K., & Boopathi, S. (2023). Artificial Intelligence Techniques in Water Purification and Utilization. In *Human Agro-Energy Optimization for Business and Industry* (pp. 202–218). IGI Global. doi:10.4018/978-1-6684-4118-3.ch010

Velmurugan, K., Venkumar, P., & Sudhakara, P. R. (2021). SME 4.0: Machine learning framework for real-time machine health monitoring system. *Journal of Physics: Conference Series*, *1911*(1), 012026. doi:10.1088/1742-6596/1911/1/012026

Venkateswaran, N., Kumar, S. S., Diwakar, G., Gnanasangeetha, D., & Boopathi, S. (2023). Synthetic Biology for Waste Water to Energy Conversion: IoT and AI Approaches. In M. Arshad (Ed.), (pp. 360–384). Advances in Bioinformatics and Biomedical Engineering. IGI Global. doi:10.4018/978-1-6684-6577-6.ch017

Venkateswaran, N., Vidhya, K., Ayyannan, M., Chavan, S. M., Sekar, K., & Boopathi, S. (2023). A Study on Smart Energy Management Framework Using Cloud Computing. In 5G, Artificial Intelligence, and Next Generation Internet of Things: Digital Innovation for Green and Sustainable Economies (pp. 189–212). IGI Global. doi:10.4018/978-1-6684-8634-4.ch009

Venkateswaran, N., Vidhya, R., Naik, D. A., Raj, T. M., Munjal, N., & Boopathi, S. (2023). Study on Sentence and Question Formation Using Deep Learning Techniques. In *Digital Natives as a Disruptive Force in Asian Businesses and Societies* (pp. 252–273). IGI Global. doi:10.4018/978-1-6684-6782-4.ch015

Žigienė, G., Rybakovas, E., & Alzbutas, R. (2019). Artificial intelligence based commercial risk management framework for SMEs. *Sustainability (Basel)*, *11*(16), 4501. doi:10.3390/su11164501

ABBREVIATIONS

AI: Artificial Intelligence
ARIMA: Autoregressive Integrated Moving Average
CNN: Convolutional Neural Networks
GANs: Generative Adversarial Networks

HVAC: Heating, Ventilation, and Air Conditioning
IoT: Internet of Things
LSTM: Long Short-Term Memory
RNN: Recurrent Neural Networks
ROI: Return on Investment
SMEs: Small and Medium Enterprises

Chapter 14
Water Resource Managements in Soil and Soilless Irrigation Systems Using AI Techniques

R. Jeya

ⓘ https://orcid.org/0000-0002-8650-3244

Department of Computing Technologies, School of Computing, SRM Institute of Science and Technology, Kattankulathur, India

M. Rajalakshmi

ⓘ https://orcid.org/0000-0002-2393-7811

Department of Computing Technologies, School of Computing, SRM Institute of Science and Technology, Kattankulathur, India

G. R. Venkatakrishnan

ⓘ https://orcid.org/0000-0001-6538-930X

Department of Electrical and Electronics Engineering, Sri Sivasubramaniya Nadar College of Engineering, Kalavakkam, India

K. Pradeep Mohan Kumar

Department of Computing Technologies, School of Computing, SRM Institute of Science and Technolog, Kattankulathur, India

R. Rengaraj

Department of Electrical and Electronics Engineering, Sri Sivasubramaniya Nadar College of Engineering, Kalavakkam, India

Sampath Boopathi

ⓘ https://orcid.org/0000-0002-2065-6539

Mechanical Engineering, Muthayammal Engineering College, Namakkal, India

ABSTRACT

This chapter explores the integration of AI techniques in water resource management for soil-based and soilless irrigation systems in agriculture. It emphasizes the importance of AI in optimizing water use and data-driven decision-making. AI-powered techniques like machine learning and predictive analytics enable precise water optimization. Soilless systems like hydroponics, aquaponics, and aeroponics also contribute to water efficiency. AI is crucial in weather forecasting, climate adaptation, crop water estimation, and water use optimization in water-stressed environments. The chapter discusses successful AI implementations, cost-benefit analysis, ethical, social, environmental considerations, equity, access, and sustainability. Future prospects, advancements, and challenges in AI techniques for water management are explored, emphasizing the need for AI adoption in water-efficient farming practices.

DOI: 10.4018/979-8-3693-0338-2.ch014

INTRODUCTION

Water resource management is crucial for sustainable agriculture, especially in the face of water scarcity and global population demands. Efficient water use is essential for long-term viability and environmental conservation. AI advancements have revolutionized water management strategies in agriculture, integrating AI techniques in soil-based and soilless irrigation systems. This integration leads to informed decisions, improved water efficiency, higher crop yields, and reduced environmental impact. The text discusses water resource management in agriculture, emphasizing its importance for food security and sustainable development. It highlights challenges faced by conventional irrigation methods, such as inefficiencies, over-irrigation, and water wastage. AI techniques are crucial for optimizing water use, as they process vast amounts of data, recognize patterns, and make accurate predictions. Integrating AI in soil and soilless irrigation systems could revolutionize traditional farming practices and create a water-smart agriculture era(Vanitha et al., 2023).

This chapter explores AI applications like machine learning, data analytics, predictive modeling, and real-time monitoring for monitoring soil moisture levels, crop water requirements, and adapting irrigation strategies. It also discusses the use of AI in soilless systems like hydroponics, aquaponics, and aeroponics for improved crop growth. However, it also addresses challenges and limitations, including ethical considerations, equitable access to AI-driven irrigation technologies, and environmental sustainability. This chapter explores AI techniques in water resource management for soil and soilless irrigation systems, aiming to inspire agricultural stakeholders to adopt water-efficient and sustainable farming practices. AI integration can contribute to global food security, address challenges like water scarcity, climate change, and population growth(Srivastava et al., 2022).

This review explores the use of AI techniques like machine learning and data analytics in precision irrigation. It emphasizes the optimization of irrigation scheduling, monitoring soil moisture, and predicting crop water requirements, resulting in improved water use efficiency. This review explores the use of AI techniques like machine learning and data analytics in precision irrigation. It emphasizes the optimization of irrigation scheduling, monitoring soil moisture, and predicting crop water requirements, resulting in improved water use efficiency. The research paper explores AI implementation in agricultural water management, focusing on challenges and opportunities. It discusses climate adaptation strategies, smart irrigation controllers, and data analytics for addressing water scarcity and enhancing reuse practices(Malik et al., 2021).

This systematic literature review explores the applications of AI in agriculture, including water resource management. It highlights AI techniques in irrigation systems, including soil moisture sensing, data-driven decision-making, and adaptive irrigation approaches. This review paper discusses machine learning techniques for smart water management in precision agriculture, focusing on AI's potential to optimize irrigation schedules, predict crop water needs, and improve water recycling and reuse practices(Afzaal et al., 2023).

This review explores AI's role in sustainable agriculture, focusing on water resource management. It examines applications in hydroponics, aquaponics, and aeroponics, focusing on optimizing water and nutrient delivery. AI-driven decision-making and real-time soil moisture sensing result in water-efficient irrigation practices and improved crop yields. This research paper presents an AI-based optimization approach for optimal water allocation in agricultural river basins. It uses genetic algorithms and other techniques to achieve optimal distribution for irrigation, considering constraints and stakeholders' needs(Kalyani & Collier, 2021).

This review article discusses the use of Artificial Intelligence (AI) in improving water management in agriculture, focusing on decision support systems, precision irrigation, and crop water requirements estimation. It highlights the potential benefits of AI-driven water resource management in agriculture. The study presents an AI-based decision support system for real-time irrigation scheduling, analyzing weather data, soil moisture levels, and crop characteristics to optimize irrigation schedules and minimize water use in agriculture. The paper presents an AI-based smart irrigation system for precision agriculture, integrating AI algorithms with IoT devices and sensors. This system automates irrigation practices, resulting in water-saving and improved crop yield(Garc\'\ia et al., 2021).

This survey explores the use of deep learning in agriculture, specifically water resource management, for accurate crop water demand forecasting and irrigation optimization. The study, published in Sensors in 2021, explores the potential applications of deep learning in agriculture. The research paper presents an AI-based smart irrigation system for water-saving and sustainable agriculture. It combines AI techniques with soil moisture sensors and weather data to optimize irrigation strategies, conserving water and improving crop quality. This systematic review explores AI applications in precision water management in agriculture, focusing on irrigation systems, sensor-based data analysis, and machine learning models. The study aims to optimize water use for various crops and farming scenarios(Xiang et al., 2021).

The research paper explores AI-driven precision irrigation for sustainable water management in agriculture, using algorithms to predict crop water needs, monitor soil moisture, and optimize irrigation scheduling for water-efficient farming practices. This survey paper explores AI techniques for efficient water management in agriculture, focusing on reducing water consumption, improving crop yield, and minimizing environmental impact(Dharmaraj & Vijayanand, 2018). AI-driven approaches promote sustainable agricultural practices, reducing water consumption and promoting crop yield. This study explores AI-driven approaches in precision water management for intelligent agriculture, focusing on soil moisture sensing, weather forecasting, and data analytics. The goal is to optimize irrigation strategies for water conservation and improved crop productivity. This paper explores AI techniques for smart water management in agriculture, focusing on challenges such as data integration, scalability, and stakeholder engagement. It provides insights into ongoing efforts to fully realize the benefits of AI in water resource management. This review paper explores innovative AI practices and case studies in water sustainability in agriculture, focusing on real-world applications and success stories. It highlights lessons learned from implementing AI-driven water management strategies.

WATER DYNAMICS IN AGRICULTURE

Water efficiency is crucial for sustainable agriculture due to its finite nature and essential role in crop growth and productivity. Conventional irrigation methods face challenges, but AI-driven water management techniques offer advantages in addressing these issues. This section highlights the importance of water efficiency in sustainable agriculture, addressing water requirements and challenges, and integrating AI-driven techniques for improved practices(Parihar et al., 2019).

Figure 1. Water efficiency in sustainable agriculture

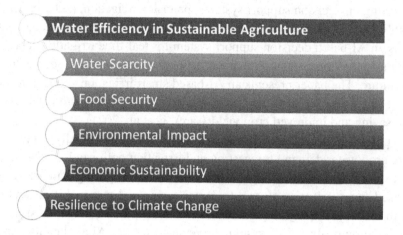

Water Efficiency in Sustainable Agriculture

Water efficiency in agriculture is crucial for maximizing crop yield, minimizing water wastage, and preserving resources for future generations. It is a cornerstone of sustainable agriculture, ensuring long-term viability and preserving water resources for future generations(Parihar et al., 2019). The various factors for water Efficiency in Sustainable Agriculture is depicted in Figure 1.

- Water Scarcity: Water scarcity is a global concern, with many regions facing limited water availability due to factors such as climate change, over-extraction, and competing demands. Inefficient water use can exacerbate water scarcity issues, leading to negative consequences for agriculture and food security.
- Food Security: Agriculture is the primary source of food production. Efficient water management ensures a stable and secure food supply, even in water-stressed regions, helping to meet the nutritional needs of the growing global population.
- Environmental Impact: Over-irrigation and water wastage can lead to environmental degradation, such as soil salinization, depletion of aquifers, and water pollution. Water-efficient practices help minimize these adverse effects on ecosystems.
- Economic Sustainability: Water is a significant input cost for agriculture. By optimizing water use, farmers can reduce expenses, increase profitability, and achieve economic sustainability in their operations.
- Resilience to Climate Change: As climate patterns become more unpredictable, water-efficient practices enhance agricultural resilience to droughts and extreme weather events, ensuring continued crop production.

Water Requirements and Challenges in Conventional Irrigation Methods

Traditional irrigation methods like surface, sprinkler, and flood irrigation face challenges in water requirements and management, affecting crop growth and productivity(Raza et al., 2012).

- Inefficient Water Distribution: Conventional irrigation methods may result in uneven water distribution, leading to over-irrigation in some areas and under-irrigation in others. This inefficiency can negatively impact crop growth and yield.
- High Water Losses: Surface and flood irrigation methods are prone to significant water losses due to evaporation, runoff, and deep percolation. These losses reduce the overall water use efficiency in agriculture.
- Lack of Precision: Conventional methods often lack precision in delivering water to crops based on their actual needs. As a result, crops may receive more or less water than required, affecting their health and productivity.
- Climate Sensitivity: Conventional irrigation practices are less adaptable to changing climate conditions, making them vulnerable to water scarcity and other climate-related challenges.
- Environmental Impact: Over-irrigation and poor water management can lead to environmental problems, such as soil erosion, waterlogging, and nutrient leaching, contributing to ecological imbalances.

Advantages of AI-Driven Water Management in Agriculture

AI-driven water management techniques, including machine learning, data analytics, and predictive modeling, can revolutionize agriculture's water resource management by overcoming challenges from conventional irrigation methods and improving water efficiency(Malik et al., 2021).

- Precision Irrigation Scheduling: AI-powered systems can analyze vast amounts of data, including weather forecasts, soil moisture levels, and crop characteristics, to determine precise irrigation schedules tailored to crop water requirements. This results in optimal water use, reducing water wastage and improving crop yields.
- Real-Time Monitoring: AI-enabled sensors and IoT devices can provide real-time data on soil moisture, weather conditions, and crop health. This allows farmers to make data-driven decisions and respond promptly to changes in water needs, optimizing irrigation practices.
- Data-Driven Decision-Making: AI algorithms can analyze historical and real-time data to identify patterns and trends related to water use and crop performance. Such insights enable farmers to make informed decisions, enhancing the overall efficiency and productivity of agricultural operations.
- Adaptive Irrigation: AI-driven systems can adapt irrigation schedules based on changing environmental conditions, crop growth stages, and water availability. This adaptability ensures that crops receive the right amount of water at the right time, irrespective of weather fluctuations.
- Water Recycling and Reuse: AI techniques can optimize water recycling and reuse in agriculture by analyzing water quality and treatment needs. This promotes sustainable water practices and reduces the demand for freshwater resources.
- Climate Adaptation: AI models can predict climate patterns and extreme weather events, allowing farmers to prepare for and mitigate the impacts of droughts, floods, and other climate-related challenges on water resources.
- Enhanced Crop Selection: AI can assist in selecting crop varieties that are more resilient to water stress and better suited to specific environmental conditions, maximizing water use efficiency.

- Cost Savings: By optimizing water use, AI-driven water management can lead to cost savings for farmers, making agriculture more economically viable and sustainable.
- Environmental Sustainability: Efficient water management through AI techniques contributes to environmental sustainability by conserving water resources and reducing the ecological impact of agricultural activities.
- Scalability: AI-driven water management solutions can be scaled up or down to fit various agricultural settings, making them adaptable to different farm sizes and types of crops.

Water efficiency is crucial for sustainable agriculture, as water scarcity and global food demands demand innovative solutions. AI-driven water management techniques offer advantages like precision irrigation scheduling, real-time monitoring, data-driven decision-making, and climate adaptation. These technologies enhance water use, increase crop productivity, and ensure long-term viability for a food-secure and environmentally sustainable future.

AI TECHNIQUES FOR WATER MANAGEMENT

AI techniques, especially machine learning, have the potential to revolutionize water management in agriculture by analyzing complex interactions between environmental factors, crop characteristics, and water needs. This section explores machine learning applications, data-driven decision-making in irrigation scheduling, and predictive analytics for optimizing water use in farming practices (Fig. 2).

Machine Learning Applications in Agriculture

Machine learning, a subset of AI, improves systems' performance over time without explicit programming. Its applications in agriculture include efficient water management, enhancing data-driven decision-making(P. Prema et al., 2022).

- Crop Yield Prediction: Machine learning models can analyze historical crop yield data alongside environmental factors like temperature, precipitation, and soil moisture to predict future crop yields accurately. These predictions aid farmers in better planning and resource allocation, including water usage.
- Crop Water Requirements: Machine learning algorithms can be trained using data on crop types, growth stages, and weather conditions to estimate crop-specific water requirements. This information is vital for optimizing irrigation schedules and ensuring crops receive the right amount of water at each stage.
- Soil Moisture Monitoring: Machine learning-based sensors and IoT devices can monitor soil moisture levels across farmland. The data collected allows farmers to gauge soil water content accurately, enabling precise irrigation practices and preventing over-irrigation.
- Disease and Pest Detection: Machine learning algorithms can identify patterns associated with disease or pest outbreaks in crops based on visual data (e.g., images of leaves or fruits). Early detection helps farmers take timely measures, avoiding unnecessary application of water and chemicals.

Figure 2. AI Techniques for water management

- Automated Irrigation Control: Machine learning-driven smart irrigation systems can autonomously adjust water delivery based on real-time data, such as weather forecasts and soil moisture levels. This automation ensures water is applied when and where it is needed most.
- Weed Detection and Management: Machine learning models can differentiate between crops and weeds, enabling targeted weed management strategies. By minimizing the competition for water, crops benefit from optimized water use.

Data-Driven Decision-Making in Irrigation Scheduling

Data-driven irrigation scheduling uses real-time and historical data to determine the optimal timing, frequency, and quantity of water for crops, considering factors like growth stage, weather, soil moisture, and environmental variables(Malik et al., 2021).

- Real-Time Data Integration: Data from sensors, weather stations, satellite imagery, and other sources are integrated to provide a comprehensive view of the field's conditions. This data informs decision-making, helping farmers respond promptly to changes in water requirements.
- Precision Irrigation: Data-driven decision-making enables precision irrigation, where water is applied in optimal quantities, avoiding under- or over-irrigation. Precision irrigation maximizes water use efficiency, leading to improved crop yields.
- Decision Support Systems (DSS): AI-driven DSS provide farmers with valuable insights and recommendations based on analyzed data. These systems help farmers make informed decisions about irrigation practices, ensuring water is utilized effectively.

- Dynamic Scheduling: Data-driven irrigation scheduling is dynamic and flexible, adjusting irrigation plans based on real-time weather updates and crop water needs. This adaptability allows farmers to respond to changing environmental conditions.
- Reduced Water Waste: Data-driven irrigation scheduling minimizes water waste by delivering water only when necessary. By avoiding unnecessary irrigation, water resources are

Predictive Analytics for Optimizing Water Use

Predictive analytics uses historical data to identify patterns, trends, and predict future events, crucial in agriculture for optimizing water use(Vanitha et al., 2023).

- Water Demand Forecasting: By analyzing historical water use data and considering factors such as crop type, growth stage, and weather patterns, predictive analytics can forecast future water demands. This information assists farmers in planning and managing water resources efficiently.
- Water Allocation: Predictive analytics helps in allocating water resources effectively among different crops or regions based on their water requirements and expected yields. This allocation ensures equitable and optimized water distribution.
- Risk Assessment: Predictive analytics can assess the risks associated with water scarcity or extreme weather events, enabling farmers to implement mitigation measures in advance.
- Decision Optimization: By integrating predictive analytics with other variables like energy costs, crop prices, and water availability, farmers can optimize decisions related to irrigation, such as when to irrigate, which crops to prioritize, and when to utilize water-saving techniques.
- Irrigation Cost Optimization: Predictive analytics can identify cost-efficient irrigation practices by analyzing data on water usage, energy consumption, and crop performance. This optimization leads to reduced operational costs for farmers.

AI techniques, especially machine learning, have proven invaluable in agriculture for water resource management. They aid farmers in crop yield prediction and weed detection, enabling informed decisions about irrigation practices and water usage. Data-driven decision-making in irrigation scheduling reduces water waste and enhances crop yields. Predictive analytics optimize water use by forecasting water demand, assessing risks, and identifying cost-efficient irrigation strategies. Integrating AI techniques in agriculture ensures global food security and preserves precious water resources for future generations.

SOIL MOISTURE SENSING AND MANAGEMENT

AI-powered soil moisture sensors play a crucial role in agricultural water management, ensuring accurate measurement and monitoring of soil moisture. These sensors enable farmers to optimize irrigation practices, ensuring crops receive the right amount of water at the right time. Adaptive irrigation based on real-time moisture data is another important aspect of these sensors, while automated irrigation systems with AI-controlled water delivery are also explored(Shock et al., 1998). The soil moisture sensing and management is shown in Fig. 3.

Figure 3. Soil moisture sensing and management

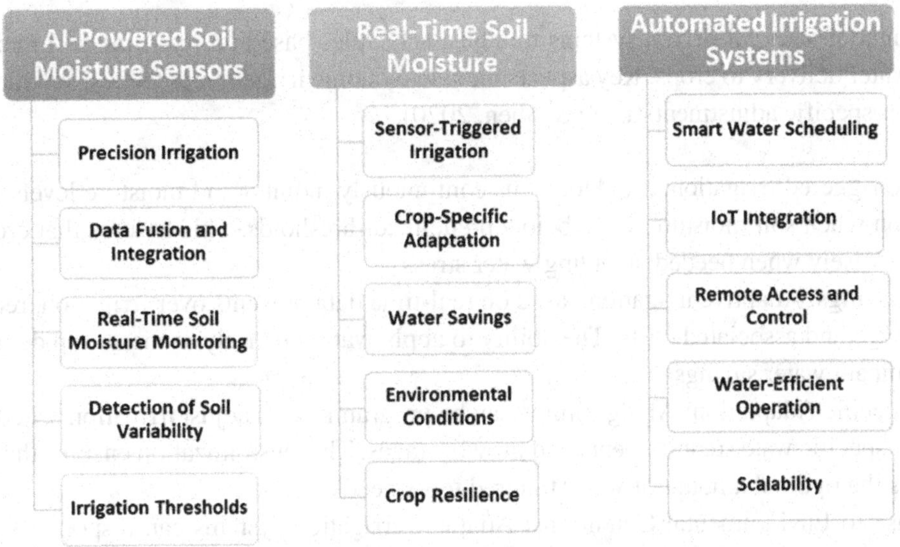

AI-Powered Soil Moisture Sensors and Their Applications

Traditional soil moisture sensors are limited by manual operation and lack of real-time data feedback. AI-powered sensors use machine learning algorithms to interpret data, providing accurate, actionable information to farmers. Key applications include agriculture(Fang & Shen, 2020).

- Real-Time Soil Moisture Monitoring: AI-powered sensors continuously measure soil moisture levels, providing real-time data on the water content in the soil. This enables farmers to make timely decisions about irrigation scheduling based on actual soil moisture conditions.
- Data Fusion and Integration: AI algorithms can integrate soil moisture data with other environmental factors such as weather forecasts, crop water requirements, and historical data. This data fusion allows for a comprehensive understanding of soil-water dynamics, leading to more informed irrigation decisions.
- Precision Irrigation: By precisely measuring soil moisture levels at various depths, AI-powered sensors enable precision irrigation, delivering water to the root zone where crops can efficiently uptake it. This reduces water wastage and optimizes water use.
- Detection of Soil Variability: AI techniques can identify spatial and temporal variability in soil moisture across the field. This knowledge helps farmers tailor irrigation practices to specific areas, accommodating variations in soil types and crop needs.
- Irrigation Thresholds: AI-powered sensors can define irrigation thresholds based on crop water requirements, growth stage, and soil characteristics. When soil moisture falls below a certain threshold, irrigation is triggered, ensuring timely water supply to sustain healthy plant growth.

Adaptive Irrigation Based on Real-Time Soil Moisture Data

Adaptive irrigation uses AI-driven systems to adjust schedules based on real-time soil moisture data, optimizing water delivery to crops. Key aspects include dynamic irrigation practices, soil moisture sensors, and crop-specific adjustments(Fang & Shen, 2020).

- Sensor-Triggered Irrigation: AI algorithms continuously monitor soil moisture levels and trigger irrigation when soil moisture drops below predefined thresholds. This ensures that crops receive water precisely when needed, avoiding water stress.
- Water Savings: Adaptive irrigation based on real-time data prevents over-irrigation, reducing water wastage and associated costs. The ability to apply water precisely to meet crop demands leads to significant water savings.
- Crop-Specific Adaptation: AI algorithms can be programmed to adjust irrigation schedules based on crop-specific water requirements and growth stages. This customization ensures that each crop receives the optimal amount of water tailored to its needs.
- Response to Environmental Conditions: Adaptive irrigation systems can respond to changes in weather conditions, adjusting irrigation schedules to account for rainfall events or unexpected temperature fluctuations.
- Increased Crop Resilience: By responding to variations in soil moisture, adaptive irrigation promotes crop resilience to water stress, enhancing their ability to withstand drought conditions.

Automated Irrigation Systems and AI-Controlled Water Delivery

Automated irrigation systems use AI algorithms to control water delivery, enhancing efficiency, precision, and ease of operation. These systems can be fully or partially automated, utilizing real-time data for real-time water distribution(Hellegers & Perry, 2006; Shock et al., 1998).

- Smart Water Scheduling: AI algorithms analyze data from soil moisture sensors, weather forecasts, and other sources to create optimized irrigation schedules. This ensures that water is applied efficiently and only when necessary.
- IoT Integration: Automated irrigation systems often employ IoT devices and sensors, allowing seamless communication between components for efficient water delivery and remote monitoring.
- Remote Access and Control: AI-driven automated systems can be controlled remotely through mobile applications or web interfaces, providing farmers with convenient access to irrigation management even when away from the farm.
- Water-Efficient Operation: By continuously analyzing data, AI-controlled automated systems can adjust irrigation duration and frequency to minimize water wastage while maintaining crop health.
- Scalability: AI-powered automated irrigation systems can be scaled to fit various farm sizes and types, making them adaptable to different agricultural settings.

AI-powered soil moisture sensors, adaptive irrigation based on real-time data, and automated irrigation systems with AI-controlled water delivery improve water management in agriculture. These technologies offer precise, data-driven approaches, optimizing water use and enhancing crop productivity.

Figure 4. AI applications in soilless systems

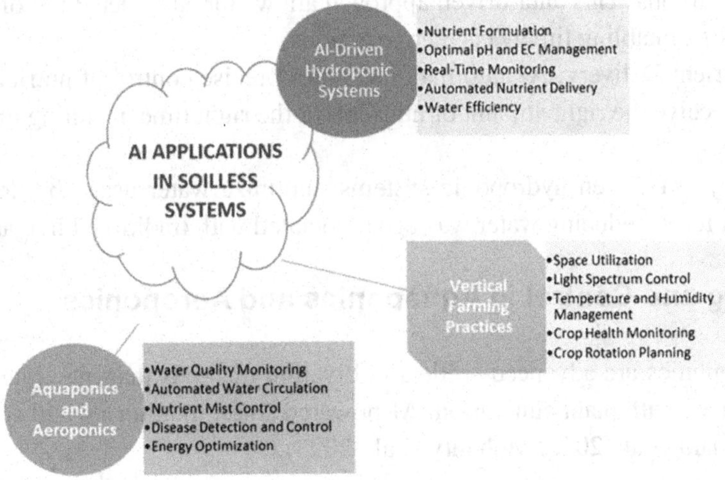

Farmers can make informed decisions about irrigation practices, resulting in sustainable and efficient water resource management.

AI APPLICATIONS IN SOILLESS SYSTEMS

Soilless cultivation systems, including hydroponics, aquaponics, and aeroponics, offer innovative approaches to agriculture by enabling crop cultivation without traditional soil mediums. These systems provide controlled environments for precise nutrient and water delivery, resulting in efficient resource utilization and increased crop yields (Fig. 4). AI technologies play a vital role in advancing soilless systems, optimizing processes and maximizing their potential. This section explores AI-driven applications in soilless systems, focusing on precise nutrient and water delivery, smart monitoring and control, and AI-based optimization of vertical farming practices(Boopathi et al., 2023).

AI-Driven Hydroponic Systems for Precise Nutrient and Water Delivery

Hydroponics is a soilless cultivation method using nutrient-rich water solutions to deliver nutrients to plant roots. AI-driven systems use advanced algorithms for precise nutrient and water management, offering numerous benefits(Koshariya, Kalaiyarasi, et al., 2023a; Koshariya, Khatoon, et al., 2023).

- Nutrient Formulation: AI algorithms analyze plant requirements, growth stages, and environmental data to develop customized nutrient solutions tailored to the specific needs of each crop.
- Optimal pH and EC Management: AI-controlled hydroponic systems continuously monitor and adjust the pH and electrical conductivity (EC) levels of the nutrient solution, ensuring optimal nutrient uptake by plants.

- Real-Time Monitoring: AI sensors provide real-time data on plant health, nutrient levels, and environmental conditions. This data-driven approach allows for early detection of nutrient deficiencies or imbalances, enabling timely corrective actions.
- Automated Nutrient Delivery: AI automation enables precise control of nutrient delivery, ensuring that plants receive the right amount of nutrients at the right time, resulting in improved growth and productivity.
- Water Efficiency: AI-driven hydroponic systems minimize water usage by delivering nutrients directly to plant roots, reducing water wastage associated with traditional irrigation methods.

Smart Monitoring and Control in Aquaponics and Aeroponics

Aquaponics and aeroponics are advanced soilless cultivation methods that integrate fish farming and misted nutrient solutions with plant cultivation. AI-powered smart monitoring and control systems improve efficiency(Kumara et al., 2023; Mohanty et al., 2023).

- Water Quality Monitoring: AI sensors continuously monitor water quality parameters, such as pH, dissolved oxygen, ammonia, and nitrate levels in aquaponic systems. This real-time data ensures a balanced and healthy environment for both fish and plants.
- Automated Water Circulation: AI algorithms control water circulation in aquaponic systems, optimizing nutrient distribution from fish waste to plant roots and maintaining water oxygenation.
- Nutrient Mist Control: In aeroponics, AI-controlled misting systems deliver nutrients in a fine mist to plant roots. AI algorithms adjust misting cycles based on plant requirements and growth stages, promoting efficient nutrient absorption.
- Disease Detection and Control: AI-driven cameras and image analysis can detect signs of disease or stress in both fish and plants. Early detection allows for timely intervention and disease control.
- Energy Optimization: AI can optimize energy usage in aquaponic and aeroponic systems by adjusting lighting and environmental controls based on plant growth requirements and weather conditions.

AI-Based Optimization of Vertical Farming Practices

Vertical farming is a soilless method utilizing vertical layers for efficient use of space and resources, with AI-based optimization offering numerous benefits(Kumara et al., 2023; Samikannu et al., 2023).

- Space Utilization: AI algorithms optimize crop placement within vertical farming structures, maximizing sunlight exposure and minimizing shading to improve overall crop productivity.
- Light Spectrum Control: AI-controlled LED lighting systems can adjust light spectra to match specific crop requirements at different growth stages, enhancing photosynthesis and crop quality.
- Temperature and Humidity Management: AI-driven environmental controls maintain optimal temperature and humidity levels within vertical farming environments, ensuring optimal growth conditions for crops.
- Crop Health Monitoring: AI sensors monitor plant health indicators, such as leaf color and size, to detect signs of stress or nutrient deficiencies. AI analytics offer insights into potential issues, allowing for timely interventions.

- Crop Rotation Planning: AI can optimize crop rotation schedules in vertical farming setups, preventing soil depletion and minimizing the risk of disease outbreaks.

AI applications in soilless systems, like hydroponics, aquaponics, and aeroponics, revolutionize agricultural practices. Hydroponic systems ensure precise nutrient and water delivery, promoting efficient resource utilization and increased crop yields. Aquaponics and aeroponics optimize water quality and nutrient delivery, while vertical farming practices enhance productivity and sustainability. The integration of AI technologies in soilless systems offers a glimpse into the future of agriculture, achieving efficient resource management and high crop yields through data-driven precision and innovation(Vanitha et al., 2023; Vennila et al., 2023).

INTEGRATING AI WITH SMART IRRIGATION CONTROLLERS

IoT-based Smart Irrigation Systems and AI Integration, Self-Learning Irrigation Controllers for Adaptive Water Management, and Benefits and Challenges of AI-Controlled Smart Irrigation

IoT-Based Smart Irrigation Systems and AI Integration

IoT-based smart irrigation systems leverage the power of connected sensors, actuators, and controllers to optimize water usage in agriculture. The integration of AI with these systems further enhances their efficiency and effectiveness. Key aspects of IoT-based smart irrigation systems with AI integration include(Koshariya, Kalaiyarasi, et al., 2023b; Kumara et al., 2023):

- Real-Time Data Collection: IoT sensors continuously monitor various environmental factors such as soil moisture, weather conditions, temperature, and humidity. The data collected in real-time serves as input for AI algorithms.
- Data Analytics and Decision-Making: AI algorithms analyze the vast amount of data collected from IoT sensors to make data-driven decisions. These decisions include when and how much to irrigate, considering crop water requirements, soil conditions, and weather forecasts.
- Predictive Modeling: AI integration enables predictive modeling, anticipating changes in weather patterns and soil moisture levels. This proactive approach allows for preemptive adjustments to irrigation schedules, preventing water stress or overwatering.
- Dynamic Irrigation Scheduling: AI algorithms dynamically adjust irrigation schedules based on real-time data and historical patterns. This adaptability ensures that irrigation is precisely tailored to meet the changing needs of the crops and the environment.

Self-Learning Irrigation Controllers for Adaptive Water Management

Self-learning irrigation controllers represent a significant advancement in smart irrigation technology. These controllers utilize AI and machine learning capabilities to continuously improve their performance without explicit programming(Koshariya, Kalaiyarasi, et al., 2023b; Rahamathunnisa et al., 2023).

- Machine Learning Capabilities: Self-learning controllers employ machine learning algorithms to analyze historical data and user feedback. Over time, they learn from patterns and optimize irrigation schedules accordingly.
- Personalized Irrigation: These controllers adapt to the specific needs of each crop and the prevailing environmental conditions. They adjust irrigation patterns based on individual plant growth stages, ensuring optimal water delivery.
- Sensor Integration: Self-learning controllers are integrated with various sensors to collect real-time data on soil moisture, temperature, and weather conditions. The combination of data from these sensors allows for precise decision-making.
- Continuous Improvement: By continuously learning from past performance and making adjustments, self-learning irrigation controllers can adapt to changes in the environment and achieve more efficient water management.

Benefits and Challenges of AI-Controlled Smart Irrigation

- Water Conservation: By optimizing irrigation schedules and precisely delivering water based on crop needs, AI-controlled systems reduce water wastage, promoting water conservation.
- Increased Crop Productivity: AI-driven smart irrigation ensures that crops receive the right amount of water at the right time, resulting in improved crop health and higher yields.
- Cost Savings: Efficient water usage and improved crop yields lead to cost savings for farmers, offsetting the initial investment in AI-controlled smart irrigation systems.
- Environmental Sustainability: Reduced water usage and efficient resource management contribute to environmental sustainability and mitigate the impact of agriculture on water resources.

CASE STUDIES OF AI IMPLEMENTATION IN WATER RESOURCE MANAGEMENTS

AI-Driven Precision Irrigation: A Case Study in Water Resource Management

This case study explores AI-driven precision irrigation in large-scale agricultural settings, highlighting its benefits in optimizing water resource management, improving crop yields, and conserving water. By utilizing real-time data and advanced algorithms, the AI system offers valuable insights for decision-making, leading to cost savings and sustainable agricultural practices(Abbasnia et al., 2019; Schaible & Aillery, 2012; Shock et al., 1998).

Water scarcity and food production demands challenge modern agriculture, leading to precision irrigation techniques. AI technologies are applied to improve efficiency, crop productivity, and economic benefits in precision irrigation.

- AI-Driven Precision Irrigation System: The case study introduces an AI-driven precision irrigation system deployed in a large agricultural farm. The system comprises a network of soil moisture sensors, weather stations, and IoT devices that collect real-time data on soil moisture, weather conditions, and crop health.

- Data-Driven Decision-Making: The AI system employs machine learning algorithms to analyze the collected data and make data-driven decisions regarding irrigation scheduling and water delivery. The algorithms take into account crop-specific water requirements, growth stages, and environmental conditions to optimize irrigation practices.
- Results and Benefits: The case study demonstrates significant improvements in water resource management and crop productivity. The AI-driven precision irrigation system achieved:
  a. Water Savings: The precision irrigation system reduced water consumption by up to 30% compared to conventional irrigation methods. This resulted in substantial water savings, mitigating water scarcity challenges.
  b. Increased Crop Yields: The precise delivery of water and nutrients improved crop health and yield. Crop yields increased by an average of 15-20%, enhancing farm profitability.
  c. Cost Savings: The reduction in water usage and increased crop yields led to substantial cost savings for the farmers. The AI implementation paid for itself within the first year of operation.
  d. Sustainable Practices: By optimizing water use and reducing water wastage, the AI-driven precision irrigation system contributed to more sustainable agricultural practices.
- Cost-Benefit Analysis of AI Adoption in Different Agricultural Settings: The case study also includes a cost-benefit analysis comparing AI-driven precision irrigation with conventional irrigation methods in different agricultural settings. The analysis considers factors such as initial investment, operational costs, water savings, crop yield improvements, and economic returns.
  a. Large-Scale Farms: For large-scale farms with extensive irrigation needs, the cost-benefit analysis reveals that AI-driven precision irrigation offers significant long-term economic benefits, outweighing the initial investment costs.
  b. Small and Medium-Scale Farms: Even for smaller farms, the cost savings achieved through water conservation and increased crop yields make AI adoption financially viable over time.
- Lessons Learned and Best Practices: The case study concludes with key lessons learned and best practices for successful AI implementation in water resource management:
  a. Data Quality: Accurate and reliable data collection is essential for AI algorithms to make informed decisions. Regular maintenance and calibration of sensors are crucial to ensure data accuracy.
  b. Integration and Scalability: Integrating AI technologies seamlessly with existing irrigation systems and scaling the technology to different farm sizes are essential considerations for successful adoption.
  c. Continuous Monitoring: Continuous monitoring of system performance and periodic adjustments to algorithms based on real-world feedback are necessary to optimize results continually.
  d. Stakeholder Engagement: Involving farmers and stakeholders in the development and deployment of AI-driven systems fosters acceptance and adoption, leading to successful implementation.

The case study highlights the positive impact of AI-driven precision irrigation on water resource management in agriculture, enabling farmers to achieve water efficiency, increased crop productivity, and economic benefits. This success serves as a blueprint for other agricultural settings to implement AI solutions for sustainable water resource management and improved practices.

AI-Enhanced Water Recycling and Reuse: A Case Study in Sustainable Agriculture

The case study showcases AI-enhanced water recycling and reuse in agriculture, optimizing treatment and purification processes, increasing recycling efficiency, and promoting responsible reuse practices. It highlights the economic and environmental benefits of AI-driven water recycling and offers valuable insights into sustainable water management strategies(Mehta et al., 2020; Raza et al., 2012).

Water scarcity and environmental concerns highlight the importance of recycling and reuse in agriculture. AI technologies are integrated to maximize reuse, reduce demand, and minimize environmental impact in water recycling systems.

- AI-Driven Water Treatment and Purification: The case study introduces an AI-driven water treatment and purification system installed on a large agricultural estate. The system employs advanced AI algorithms to monitor water quality parameters, predict treatment requirements, and optimize purification processes.
- Real-Time Data Analysis: AI technologies continuously analyze real-time data from water quality sensors, flow meters, and treatment units. Machine learning algorithms identify contaminants and adjust treatment processes based on water quality variations.
- Results and Benefits: The case study demonstrates the effectiveness of AI-enhanced water recycling and reuse, yielding several key benefits:
  a. Enhanced Water Quality: AI-driven water treatment ensures consistent water quality, meeting irrigation and agricultural use standards. This leads to healthier crops and increased productivity.
  b. Increased Water Recycling Efficiency: The AI system optimizes water recycling processes, resulting in a higher percentage of water being successfully recycled and reused in agricultural operations.
  c. Reduced Freshwater Demand: By recycling and reusing water, the agricultural estate reduces its reliance on freshwater sources, mitigating the strain on local water supplies.
  d. Cost Savings: The AI-enhanced water recycling system reduces the need for purchasing and transporting freshwater, leading to significant cost savings in the long run.
  e. Environmental Impact: The reduction in freshwater demand and improved water treatment processes contribute to environmental sustainability, conserving natural water resources and reducing pollution.
- AI-Driven Decision-Making for Water Reuse: The case study delves into the AI-driven decision-making process for water reuse. AI algorithms analyze water quality data and crop water requirements to determine the most suitable water sources for different agricultural activities, optimizing water allocation.
- Lessons Learned and Best Practices: The case study identifies valuable lessons learned and best practices for successful AI implementation in water recycling and reuse:
  a. Customization: Tailoring AI algorithms to the specific water quality requirements of different crops and irrigation systems ensures optimized water reuse.
  b. Continuous Monitoring and Maintenance: Regular monitoring and maintenance of water recycling systems are crucial for ensuring consistent water quality and treatment efficiency.

c. Data Security and Privacy: Protecting water quality data and maintaining data privacy are paramount to gaining trust from stakeholders and ensuring system integrity.

d. Awareness and Education: Raising awareness among farmers and the community about the benefits of AI-enhanced water recycling fosters support and acceptance of these technologies.

The case study highlights the positive impact of AI-enhanced water recycling and reuse in agriculture, optimizing treatment, increasing efficiency, and promoting responsible practices. This approach leads to economic savings, environmental sustainability, and increased resilience to water scarcity challenges. The case study serves as a blueprint for other agricultural settings to implement AI-driven solutions for sustainable agricultural practices.

AI-OPTIMIZED NUTRIENT DELIVERY IN HYDROPONICS: A CASE STUDY IN SOILLESS IRRIGATION SYSTEM

This case study showcases the successful implementation of AI-optimized nutrient delivery in hydroponic farming, utilizing AI technologies to manage nutrient levels, promoting efficient plant uptake and maximizing crop yields. It highlights the economic and environmental benefits of AI-driven nutrient delivery and offers valuable insights into the future of soilless agriculture. Hydroponics is an efficient soilless irrigation system that delivers controlled nutrients to plant roots. AI technologies revolutionize nutrient management, enabling precise crop-specific optimization and improved efficiency(Kumara et al., 2023; Rahamathunnisa et al., 2023; S. et al., 2022).

- AI-Driven Nutrient Management System: The case study introduces an AI-driven nutrient management system deployed in a commercial hydroponic greenhouse. The system utilizes advanced AI algorithms to analyze real-time data from nutrient sensors and adjust nutrient solutions accordingly.
- Data-Driven Nutrient Formulation: AI algorithms process data on crop types, growth stages, environmental conditions, and nutrient levels in the solution. The AI system formulates custom nutrient solutions tailored to each crop's specific needs, maximizing nutrient uptake and growth.
- Results and Benefits: The case study showcases the positive outcomes of AI-optimized nutrient delivery in hydroponics:
  a. Precision Nutrient Delivery: The AI system ensures that crops receive precise nutrient concentrations based on their individual requirements at different growth stages. This leads to healthier plants and increased crop yields.
  b. Enhanced Crop Productivity: By providing crops with the ideal nutrient balance, the hydroponic greenhouse achieved a significant increase in crop productivity compared to traditional soil-based methods.
  c. Resource Efficiency: AI-driven nutrient delivery minimizes nutrient wastage, resulting in reduced nutrient consumption and more sustainable agricultural practices.
  d. Reduced Environmental Impact: The AI system prevents nutrient imbalances, minimizing the risk of nutrient leaching and pollution in the surrounding environment.
- AI-Enabled Crop-Specific Optimization: The case study delves into AI-enabled crop-specific optimization, where machine learning algorithms continuously adapt nutrient formulations based on

plant health data and historical performance. This dynamic adjustment ensures the best possible outcomes for each crop.

- Lessons Learned and Best Practices: The case study identifies essential lessons learned and best practices for successful AI implementation in nutrient management for hydroponics:
  a. Data Accuracy: Ensuring accurate and reliable data collection from nutrient sensors is critical to providing precise nutrient solutions.
  b. Algorithm Validation: Regular validation and fine-tuning of AI algorithms based on real-world performance data are essential to optimize nutrient delivery.
  c. Scalability: The AI-driven nutrient management system can be scaled for different crop varieties and greenhouse sizes, making it adaptable to various agricultural settings.
  d. d. Integration with Automation: Integrating the AI system with automated nutrient delivery mechanisms allows for seamless and efficient nutrient management.

The case study showcases AI-optimized nutrient delivery in hydroponics, revolutionizing soilless irrigation systems. By utilizing AI technologies, hydroponic farmers can achieve precision nutrient delivery, increased crop productivity, resource efficiency, and reduced environmental impact. This case study serves as a model for sustainable, data-driven agricultural practices in future soilless irrigation systems.

ETHICAL AND SOCIAL CONSIDERATIONS IN AI-DRIVEN WATER MANAGEMENT IN AGRICULTURE

Implications of AI in Water Management on Rural Communities

AI-driven water management technologies impact rural communities positively and negatively in agriculture(Boopathi, 2023; Koshariya, Kalaiyarasi, et al., 2023b).

- Positive Impact: AI technologies can improve productivity, economic growth, and knowledge transfer in rural areas. By enhancing water efficiency, crop yields, and promoting economic growth, these practices benefit rural farmers, job creators, and communities. Additionally, AI adoption can facilitate skill development and modern agricultural practices, empowering rural communities.
- Negative Impact: AI technologies may create a digital divide, leaving farmers and communities behind due to lack of access or knowledge. This could lead to job displacement for rural workers and inequitable access to AI-driven irrigation technologies, affecting rural communities' ability to access and afford these technologies.

Addressing Equity and Access to AI-Driven Irrigation Technologies

- Education and Training: Providing training and support to rural farmers on the use and maintenance of AI technologies can empower them to harness the benefits of these systems effectively(Afzaal et al., 2023; Srivastava et al., 2022).

- Affordable Financing: Offering financial assistance, subsidies, or affordable financing options can make AI-driven irrigation technologies more accessible to small-scale and resource-constrained farmers.
- Public-Private Partnerships: Collaborations between governments, private companies, and non-profit organizations can facilitate technology dissemination and ensure broader access to AI-driven solutions.
- Customization for Local Needs: Tailoring AI technologies to suit the specific requirements of local crops and environmental conditions can enhance the relevance and effectiveness of these systems.
- Community Involvement: Involving local communities in the design and implementation of AI projects fosters ownership and acceptance of the technology, promoting sustainable adoption.

Environmental Sustainability and Responsible AI Use in Agriculture

- Energy Consumption: AI-powered systems may consume significant energy for data processing and operation. Adopting renewable energy sources can mitigate the environmental impact.
- Data Privacy and Security: AI-driven systems rely on data collection, raising concerns about data privacy and potential misuse. Implementing robust data security measures and adhering to data protection regulations are crucial.
- Responsible Resource Management: AI technologies should prioritize water conservation and efficient resource utilization to align with sustainable agricultural practices.
- Monitoring and Regulation: Regular monitoring and regulation of AI systems in agriculture are necessary to prevent overuse of resources and ensure adherence to ethical guidelines.
- Long-Term Impact Assessment: Conducting thorough impact assessments on AI-driven water management projects can identify potential environmental risks and inform adaptive strategies.

CONCLUSION

- AI technologies in water resource management in agriculture offer a transformative approach to tackle challenges. Integrating AI in soil and soilless irrigation systems enables precision water management, resource optimization, and increased crop productivity, while promoting sustainability and environmental responsibility.
- AI-driven water resource management has proven successful in agricultural settings, such as precision irrigation, water recycling, and reuse systems. Data-driven decisions lead to water savings, increased crop yields, and reduced environmental impact. AI-enhanced systems also offer economic savings and reduced freshwater demand.
- AI technology adoption in water management raises ethical and social concerns. Supporting rural communities in adopting AI-driven solutions is crucial. Ensuring equity, education, and financial assistance can bridge the digital divide and promote inclusive technology adoption.
- Environmental sustainability and responsible AI use are crucial in agriculture, balancing resource efficiency and technological advancement. Long-term impact assessments, data privacy measures, and ethical guidelines are essential for responsible AI integration in water management practices.

- The integration of AI techniques and water resource management in agriculture can create a more efficient, productive, and sustainable future. By addressing ethical, social, and environmental concerns, AI-driven innovations can create a transformative, resilient agricultural sector that meets current challenges and ensures food security for future generations.

REFERENCES

Abbasnia, A., Yousefi, N., Mahvi, A. H., Nabizadeh, R., Radfard, M., Yousefi, M., & Alimohammadi, M. (2019). Evaluation of groundwater quality using water quality index and its suitability for assessing water for drinking and irrigation purposes: Case study of Sistan and Baluchistan province (Iran). *Human and Ecological Risk Assessment*, 25(4), 988–1005. doi:10.1080/10807039.2018.1458596

Afzaal, H., Farooque, A. A., Esau, T. J., Schumann, A. W., Zaman, Q. U., Abbas, F., & Bos, M. (2023). Artificial neural modeling for precision agricultural water management practices. In *Precision Agriculture* (pp. 169–186). Elsevier. doi:10.1016/B978-0-443-18953-1.00005-2

Boopathi, S. (2023). *Deep Learning Techniques Applied for Automatic Sentence Generation.* doi:10.4018/978-1-6684-3632-5.ch016

Boopathi, S., Kumar, P. K. S., Meena, R. S., Sudhakar, M., & Associates. (2023). Sustainable Developments of Modern Soil-Less Agro-Cultivation Systems: Aquaponic Culture. In Human Agro-Energy Optimization for Business and Industry (pp. 69–87). IGI Global.

Dharmaraj, V., & Vijayanand, C. (2018). Artificial intelligence (AI) in agriculture. *International Journal of Current Microbiology and Applied Sciences*, 7(12), 2122–2128. doi:10.20546/ijcmas.2018.712.241

Fang, K., & Shen, C. (2020). Near-real-time forecast of satellite-based soil moisture using long short-term memory with an adaptive data integration kernel. *Journal of Hydrometeorology*, 21(3), 399–413. doi:10.1175/JHM-D-19-0169.1

Hellegers, P. J. G. J., & Perry, C. J. (2006). Can irrigation water use be guided by market forces? Theory and practice. *Water: Research and Development*, 22(1), 79–86.

Kalyani, Y., & Collier, R. (2021). A systematic survey on the role of cloud, fog, and edge computing combination in smart agriculture. *Sensors (Basel)*, 21(17), 5922. doi:10.3390/s21175922 PMID:34502813

Koshariya, A. K., Kalaiyarasi, D., Jovith, A. A., Sivakami, T., Hasan, D. S., & Boopathi, S. (2023a). AI-Enabled IoT and WSN-Integrated Smart Agriculture System. In *Artificial Intelligence Tools and Technologies for Smart Farming and Agriculture Practices* (pp. 200–218). IGI Global. doi:10.4018/978-1-6684-8516-3.ch011

Koshariya, A. K., Kalaiyarasi, D., Jovith, A. A., Sivakami, T., Hasan, D. S., & Boopathi, S. (2023b). AI-Enabled IoT and WSN-Integrated Smart. *Practice, Progress, and Proficiency in Sustainability*, 200–218. doi:10.4018/978-1-6684-8516-3.ch011

Koshariya, A. K., Khatoon, S., Marathe, A. M., Suba, G. M., Baral, D., & Boopathi, S. (2023). Agricultural Waste Management Systems Using Artificial Intelligence Techniques. In *AI-Enabled Social Robotics in Human Care Services* (pp. 236–258). IGI Global. doi:10.4018/978-1-6684-8171-4.ch009

Kumara, V., Mohanaprakash, T. A., Fairooz, S., Jamal, K., Babu, T., & B., S. (2023). Experimental Study on a Reliable Smart Hydroponics System. In *Human Agro-Energy Optimization for Business and Industry* (pp. 27–45). IGI Global. doi:10.4018/978-1-6684-4118-3.ch002

Malik, H., Fatema, N., & Alzubi, J. A. (2021). AI and Machine Learning Paradigms for Health Monitoring System: Intelligent Data Analytics. In Springer- Studies in Big Data 86 (Vol. 86). Springer Nature.

Mehta, C. R., Chandel, N. S., & Rajwade, Y. A. (2020). Smart farm mechanization for sustainable indian agriculture. *AMA, Agricultural Mechanization in Asia, Africa and Latin America, 51*(4), 99-105+95.

Mohanty, A., Venkateswaran, N., Ranjit, P. S., Tripathi, M. A., & Boopathi, S. (2023). Innovative strategy for profitable automobile industries: Working capital management. In *Handbook of Research on Designing Sustainable Supply Chains to Achieve a Circular Economy* (pp. 412–428). IGI Global. doi:10.4018/978-1-6684-7664-2.ch020

Parihar, C. M., Nayak, H. S., Rai, V. K., Jat, S. L., Parihar, N., Aggarwal, P., & Mishra, A. K. (2019). Soil water dynamics, water productivity and radiation use efficiency of maize under multi-year conservation agriculture during contrasting rainfall events. *Field Crops Research, 241*, 107570. doi:10.1016/j.fcr.2019.107570

Prema, P., Veeramani, A., & Sivakumar, T. (2022). Machine Learning Applications in Agriculture. *Journal of Agriculture Research and Technology. Special*, (01), 126–129. doi:10.56228/JART.2022.SP120

Rahamathunnisa, U., Sudhakar, K., Murugan, T. K., Thivaharan, S., Rajkumar, M., & Boopathi, S. (2023). *Cloud Computing Principles for Optimizing Robot Task Offloading Processes.*, doi:10.4018/978-1-6684-8171-4.ch007

Raza, A., Friedel, J. K., & Bodner, G. (2012). Improving water use efficiency for sustainable agriculture. *Agroecology and Strategies for Climate Change*, 167–211.

S., P. K., Sampath, B., R., S. K., Babu, B. H., & N., A. (2022). Hydroponics, Aeroponics, and Aquaponics Technologies in Modern Agricultural Cultivation. In *Trends, Paradigms, and Advances in Mechatronics Engineering* (pp. 223–241). IGI Global. doi:10.4018/978-1-6684-5887-7.ch012

Samikannu, R., Koshariya, A. K., Poornima, E., Ramesh, S., Kumar, A., & Boopathi, S. (2023). Sustainable Development in Modern Aquaponics Cultivation Systems Using IoT Technologies. In *Human Agro-Energy Optimization for Business and Industry* (pp. 105–127). IGI Global. doi:10.4018/978-1-6684-4118-3.ch006

Schaible, G., & Aillery, M. (2012). Water conservation in irrigated agriculture: Trends and challenges in the face of emerging demands. *USDA-ERS Economic Information Bulletin, 99*.

Shock, C. C., Barnum, J. M., & Seddigh, M. (1998). Calibration of Watermark Soil Moisture Sensors for Irrigation Management. *Proceedings of the International Irrigation Show, September*, 139–146. https://www.researchgate.net/publication/228762944

Srivastava, A., Jain, S., Maity, R., & Desai, V. R. (2022). Demystifying artificial intelligence amidst sustainable agricultural water management. *Current Directions in Water Scarcity Research*, 7, 17–35. doi:10.1016/B978-0-323-91910-4.00002-9

Vanitha, S. K. R., & Boopathi, S. (2023). Artificial Intelligence Techniques in Water Purification and Utilization. In *Human Agro-Energy Optimization for Business and Industry* (pp. 202–218). IGI Global., doi:10.4018/978-1-6684-4118-3.ch010

Vennila, T., Karuna, M. S., Srivastava, B. K., Venugopal, J., Surakasi, R., & B., S. (2023). New Strategies in Treatment and Enzymatic Processes. In *Human Agro-Energy Optimization for Business and Industry* (pp. 219–240). IGI Global. doi:10.4018/978-1-6684-4118-3.ch011

Xiang, X., Li, Q., Khan, S., & Khalaf, O. I. (2021). Urban water resource management for sustainable environment planning using artificial intelligence techniques. *Environmental Impact Assessment Review*, *86*, 106515. doi:10.1016/j.eiar.2020.106515

Chapter 15
Integrating Artificial Intelligence and Machine Learning in the Design and Manufacturing of Green and Flexible Electronics

Manish Kumar Singh

(iD) https://orcid.org/0000-0001-8801-536X

School of Electronics Engineering (SENSE), VIT-AP University, India

Anamika Lata

School of Electronics Engineering (SENSE), VIT-AP University, India

ABSTRACT

This chapter explores the integration of AI and ML techniques in the design and manufacturing of green and flexible electronics. It emphasizes the significance of these technologies for sustainable development and discusses the challenges and opportunities they present. The chapter provides an overview of AI and ML algorithms applicable to the field, including materials selection, intelligent manufacturing, energy efficiency prediction, and design optimization. Case studies highlight successful applications of AI and ML in green and flexible electronics. Overall, this chapter demonstrates how AI and ML contribute to the sustainability, efficiency, and performance of electronic devices, including AI-assisted materials selection, intelligent manufacturing processes, predictive modeling for energy efficiency, and optimization of flexible electronic designs using machine learning. It demonstrates the effectiveness of AI and ML in achieving sustainable development in the field of green and flexible electronics.

INTRODUCTION

The chapter begins with an introduction to the significance of green and flexible electronics in sustainable development, highlighting the unique challenges and opportunities in this field. Subsequently, it provides

DOI: 10.4018/979-8-3693-0338-2.ch015

a detailed overview of relevant AI and ML algorithms, encompassing supervised and unsupervised learning methods that can be applied in the design and manufacturing processes of these electronic devices.

One critical aspect addressed in the chapter is AI-assisted materials selection for green electronics. It explores the utilization of machine learning approaches to identify and predict sustainable materials with desirable properties for electronic devices. By accurately forecasting material properties, researchers and engineers can make informed decisions, optimizing performance while minimizing environmental impact.

Furthermore, the chapter delves into intelligent manufacturing processes for sustainable electronics. It showcases AI-driven approaches that facilitate eco-friendly and efficient manufacturing of green and flexible electronics. Through the optimization of manufacturing parameters and implementation of quality control measures using ML techniques, the chapter demonstrates the simultaneous achievement of sustainability and productivity. Energy efficiency is a pivotal consideration in electronic device design. In this regard, the chapter illustrates how predictive modeling with ML can be employed to estimate power requirements, optimize energy consumption, and develop energy-saving strategies for flexible electronic devices. Additionally, it discusses the application of ML techniques in optimizing the design of flexible electronic components through simulation, modeling, and analysis. To exemplify the practical applications of AI and ML in green and flexible electronics, the chapter provides case studies highlighting successful projects. These case studies showcase the sustainable and efficient outcomes achieved by integrating AI and ML techniques in the design, manufacturing, and optimization of green and flexible electronic devices.

Throughout the chapter, the challenges and limitations associated with the integration of AI and ML in green and flexible electronics are addressed. Moreover, emerging trends and future prospects in sustainable electronic design and manufacturing are explored, offering opportunities for further research and collaboration.

Chapter Overview: This chapter focuses on the integration of artificial intelligence (AI) and machine learning (ML) techniques in the design and manufacturing processes of green and flexible electronics. It explores how AI and ML can contribute to the sustainability, efficiency, and performance of electronic devices in the context of green and flexible electronics. The chapter covers various aspects, including AI-assisted materials selection, intelligent manufacturing processes, predictive modeling for energy efficiency, and optimization of flexible electronic designs using machine learning. Additionally, it highlights case studies and examples that demonstrate the effectiveness of AI and ML in achieving sustainable development in the field of green and flexible electronics.

Chapter Outline/ Table of Contents:

GREEN AND FLEXIBLE ELECTRONICS

Green and flexible electronics focus on developing electronic devices and systems that prioritize sustainability and environmental friendliness. These advancements aim to minimize energy consumption, reduce material waste, and enhance the recyclability of electronic products. The integration of artificial intelligence (AI) and machine learning (ML) techniques in green and flexible electronics has the potential to revolutionize the field. By leveraging AI and ML, designers can optimize various aspects of electronic design and manufacturing, resulting in energy-efficient and environmentally-conscious electronic devices. These advancements contribute to a more sustainable future by addressing the ecological impact of electronics and promoting the use of renewable resources.

Overview of the Importance of Green and Flexible Electronics in Sustainable Development

Green and flexible electronics have gained significant attention and importance in the pursuit of sustainable development goals. These fields aim to address the environmental challenges associated with conventional electronics and offer enhanced functionality, energy efficiency, and versatility. Green electronics focus on minimizing the ecological footprint of electronic devices throughout their lifecycle, from material sourcing to end-of-life disposal. This involves the use of environmentally friendly materials, energy-efficient designs, and strategies for recycling and waste reduction (Irimia-Vladu, 2014). On the other hand, flexible electronics emphasize the development of electronic components and systems that can conform to various shapes and surfaces, enabling applications such as wearable devices, flexible displays, and conformable sensors (Someya et al., 2016).

Green and flexible electronics hold promise for various sectors, including healthcare, energy, transportation, and consumer electronics. In the healthcare sector, flexible and wearable electronic devices can revolutionize medical monitoring, diagnostics, and drug delivery systems, offering personalized and non-invasive solutions (Nasiri & Khosravani, 2020). In the energy sector, green electronics contribute to the development of energy-efficient devices, renewable energy systems, and smart grids, promoting energy conservation and reducing greenhouse gas emissions (Zhu et al., 2016). Flexible electronics find applications in transportation through the development of lightweight and energy-efficient sensors, displays, and energy storage devices for electric vehicles, improving overall efficiency and sustainability (Lipomi & Bao, 2011). Additionally, green and flexible electronics offer novel opportunities in consumer electronics, enabling the design of thinner, lighter, and more energy-efficient devices with enhanced functionalities (Chhowalla et al., 2013).

Challenges and Opportunities in the Field

Despite the immense potential of green and flexible electronics, several challenges need to be addressed to fully realize their benefits and widespread adoption. One of the primary challenges lies in the development of sustainable and environmentally friendly materials suitable for electronic devices. This involves identifying materials with low toxicity, high recyclability, and reduced reliance on rare or hazardous elements. Researchers and manufacturers are actively exploring alternatives to conventional materials, such as lead-free solder, organic semiconductors, and biodegradable substrates, to reduce the environmental impact of electronic devices (Klauk, 2010).

Achieving high-performance and reliable functionality in flexible electronics presents engineering and manufacturing challenges. Flexible substrates and interconnects require materials and fabrication processes that can withstand mechanical stress and maintain electrical performance over extended use. Ensuring robustness and durability in flexible electronic systems is essential for their successful integration into various applications (Pang et al., 2012).

Energy efficiency is a critical consideration in green and flexible electronics. With the increasing demand for portable and wearable devices, optimizing energy consumption is vital. The development of power-efficient components, low-power circuit designs, and intelligent power management techniques is crucial to extend battery life and minimize environmental impact. Furthermore, exploring energy harvesting technologies, such as solar cells or kinetic energy harvesters, can contribute to the sustainability of electronic devices by reducing reliance on traditional power sources (Shi et al., 2019).

The integration of green and flexible electronics into existing infrastructure and manufacturing processes poses logistical and economic challenges. Adapting conventional manufacturing techniques to accommodate flexible substrates, developing reliable and cost-effective fabrication processes, and establishing supply chains for sustainable materials are critical steps. However, these challenges also present opportunities for technological advancements, job creation, and the development of new markets focused on sustainable and flexible electronic solutions (Wang et al., 2020).

In summary, green and flexible electronics have emerged as key drivers of sustainable development, offering the potential to address environmental concerns and revolutionize various sectors. The development of sustainable materials, advancements in flexible device engineering, and the optimization of energy efficiency are ongoing research areas. Overcoming these challenges and capitalizing on the opportunities presented by green and flexible electronics can lead to significant advancements in technology, environmental stewardship, and the realization of a sustainable future.

ARTIFICIAL INTELLIGENCE AND MACHINE LEARNING TECHNIQUES FOR GREEN AND FLEXIBLE ELECTRONICS

Artificial Intelligence and Machine Learning Techniques: Artificial intelligence (AI) and machine learning (ML) techniques are computational approaches that enable systems to learn, reason, and make informed decisions without explicit programming. In the context of green and flexible electronics, AI and ML techniques play a crucial role in analyzing large datasets, identifying patterns, and optimizing electronic design and manufacturing processes. These techniques offer valuable insights into areas such as design optimization, materials selection, manufacturing process optimization, energy efficiency prediction, and quality control. By leveraging AI and ML, designers can make data-driven decisions, reduce energy consumption, minimize waste, and improve the overall sustainability of electronic devices.

Introduction to AI and ML Algorithms Relevant to Green and Flexible Electronics

Artificial intelligence (AI) and machine learning (ML) algorithms have emerged as transformative technologies with significant applications in the field of green and flexible electronics. These algorithms enable intelligent decision-making, pattern recognition, and data analysis, leading to improved energy efficiency, optimization of material usage, and enhanced performance in electronic devices.

In the context of green and flexible electronics, AI and ML algorithms offer promising solutions for addressing key challenges and leveraging opportunities. One of the primary areas where these algorithms find application is in material selection. ML algorithms can analyze vast datasets of material properties, including mechanical flexibility, thermal conductivity, environmental impact, and cost, to identify the most suitable materials for flexible electronic applications (Brishty, Urner, & Grau, 2022). By considering multiple parameters simultaneously and applying advanced algorithms such as neural networks and decision trees, these techniques can efficiently assess the properties of various materials, aiding in the design and development of sustainable and flexible electronic devices.

Another critical aspect of green and flexible electronics is energy management. AI-based algorithms provide opportunities for optimizing the energy consumption of electronic systems. Through techniques like reinforcement learning and predictive modeling, these algorithms can learn from historical data and real-time inputs to make intelligent decisions regarding power usage, optimizing the balance between performance and energy efficiency (Entezari et al., 2023). By dynamically adjusting power consumption based on usage patterns, environmental conditions, and user requirements, these algorithms can significantly contribute to achieving sustainability goals in the field.

Furthermore, AI and ML algorithms have shown potential in fault diagnosis and performance optimization in green and flexible electronics. These algorithms can analyze sensor data, detect anomalies, and identify potential failures in electronic devices, enabling proactive maintenance and reducing electronic waste (Ali et al., 2023). Moreover, ML techniques can optimize the performance of flexible electronics by modeling and predicting device behavior, allowing for intelligent control and adaptation to environmental changes (Liu et al., 2020).

In summary, AI and ML algorithms are revolutionizing the field of green and flexible electronics by providing intelligent solutions for material selection, energy management, fault diagnosis, and performance optimization. Leveraging these algorithms can drive sustainable development, enhance energy efficiency, and promote the adoption of flexible and eco-friendly electronic technologies.

Supervised and Unsupervised Learning Methods Applicable to the Field

Supervised and unsupervised learning methods are fundamental branches of machine learning (ML) that find wide-ranging applications in the field of green and flexible electronics, enabling advanced data analysis and decision-making processes.

Supervised Learning Techniques

Supervised learning techniques involve training ML models using labeled data, where the desired output is known. In the context of green and flexible electronics, supervised learning algorithms play a vital role in various tasks, facilitating intelligent decision-making and enhancing sustainability.

One application of supervised learning in the field is electronic waste classification. By analyzing image or sensor data, supervised learning algorithms can identify and sort different materials, contributing to efficient recycling processes and reducing the environmental impact of electronic waste (Jana et al., 2021). These algorithms can learn from labeled datasets, recognizing patterns and characteristics that indicate specific materials, enabling effective sorting and recycling practices.

Another significant application of supervised learning is energy consumption prediction. By training models on historical data that includes energy consumption records and relevant input parameters, such as usage patterns, environmental conditions, and device characteristics, supervised learning algorithms can accurately predict the energy consumption of electronic devices (Liu et al., 2015). This prediction capability aids in the development of energy-efficient designs and power management strategies, enabling the optimization of energy usage and reducing the carbon footprint associated with electronic devices.

Unsupervised Learning Techniques

In contrast, unsupervised learning techniques are employed when the data is unlabelled or when the objective is to discover hidden patterns or structures within the data. Unsupervised learning plays a crucial role in exploring and uncovering insights in the field of green and flexible electronics.

Clustering algorithms, a popular unsupervised learning technique, group together similar devices or materials based on their properties (Wen & Aris, 2022). By identifying common characteristics, clustering algorithms enable the identification of clusters or groups of devices with similar performance or properties. This information can be leveraged to drive targeted improvements, such as optimizing material usage, enhancing device performance, and streamlining manufacturing processes, leading to increased sustainability and resource efficiency.

Dimensionality reduction techniques, such as principal component analysis (PCA), are another important tool in unsupervised learning. These techniques extract essential features from large datasets by reducing the dimensionality of the data, enabling more efficient data representation and analysis (Wu et al., 2021). In the context of green and flexible electronics, dimensionality reduction techniques can be applied to tasks such as fault diagnosis and performance optimization. By capturing the most critical factors and reducing data complexity, these techniques facilitate effective fault detection and diagnosis, enabling timely maintenance and reducing electronic waste.

Supervised and unsupervised learning methods, with their respective strengths and applications, contribute significantly to the advancement of green and flexible electronics. These ML techniques offer valuable insights, enable efficient data analysis, and facilitate informed decision-making, ultimately driving the development of sustainable and environmentally friendly electronic technologies.

AI-ASSISTED MATERIALS SELECTION FOR GREEN ELECTRONICS

AI-assisted materials selection in green electronics involves utilizing AI and ML techniques to identify and optimize the use of sustainable materials in electronic devices. With the vast amount of data available on material properties, availability, cost, and environmental impact, ML models can guide designers in selecting materials that align with sustainability principles. These models analyze and prioritize factors such as recyclability, non-toxicity, and energy efficiency to enhance the sustainability of electronic devices. By integrating AI and ML into materials selection processes, designers can make informed decisions that minimize the ecological footprint and promote the circular economy principles within the electronic industry

Machine Learning Approaches for Sustainable Materials Selection in Electronic Devices

Machine learning techniques play a vital role in sustainable materials selection for electronic devices. These approaches leverage large datasets and advanced algorithms to identify materials with desirable properties, considering factors such as mechanical flexibility, thermal conductivity, environmental impact, and cost.

One prominent machine learning approach used in materials selection is the use of neural networks. Neural networks can learn complex relationships between material properties and device performance, enabling the identification of optimal materials for specific applications. By training on extensive datasets that include material properties and device performance metrics, neural networks can predict the performance of new materials and provide valuable insights into their suitability for green electronics (Brishty, Urner, & Grau, 2022). For instance, researchers have successfully employed neural networks to predict the mechanical flexibility of materials for flexible electronic devices. By training the network on a dataset of material properties and experimental bending tests, the model can predict the flexibility of new materials, aiding in the selection of materials with optimal mechanical characteristics (Liu et al., 2021).

Decision trees and random forests are other ML techniques utilized in materials selection. These algorithms employ a hierarchical structure to model decision-making processes based on input features and target outputs. By constructing decision rules based on material properties and their impact on device performance, decision tree-based models can assist in selecting materials that meet specific criteria, such as eco-friendliness, energy efficiency, and durability. Random forests, which combine multiple decision trees, can provide enhanced accuracy and robustness in materials selection (Altun et al., 2010). These techniques have been applied in the design of sustainable electronic devices, helping identify materials with low environmental impact, high thermal conductivity, and excellent electrical properties (Liu et al., 2018).

Prediction of Material Properties and Their Impact on Device Performance and Sustainability

Another area where AI and ML techniques contribute to green electronics is in the prediction of material properties and their impact on device performance and sustainability. These techniques enable accurate modeling and prediction of material behavior, aiding in the selection of materials that align with sustainable development goals.

Support vector machines (SVM) have been widely used for predicting material properties in green electronics. SVM algorithms can effectively handle complex and high-dimensional data, making them suitable for predicting material properties based on various input parameters. By training on historical data that includes material properties and relevant input features, SVM models can forecast the behavior of new materials, helping researchers and designers select materials with desired properties for sustainable electronic devices. For example, SVM models have been employed to predict the bandgap energy of organic semiconductors, a crucial material property for efficient solar cells and light-emitting devices (Wang et al., 2022). These predictions enable the identification of materials with optimal bandgap energy, enhancing device performance and sustainability.

Additionally, regression analysis techniques, such as linear regression and support vector regression (SVR), are utilized for predicting material properties and their impact on device performance. These techniques establish mathematical relationships between material characteristics and device performance metrics, enabling the estimation of how changes in material properties will affect device behavior. By quantifying the impact of material properties on performance and sustainability, regression models support informed decision-making in materials selection. For instance, SVR models have been employed to predict the thermal conductivity of materials used in heat dissipation applications, enabling the selection of materials with optimal thermal management properties for energy-efficient devices (Boobalan & Kannaiyan, 2022).

In summary, AI and ML approaches have transformed materials selection for green electronics by enabling sustainable materials choices and predicting the impact of material properties on device performance. Neural networks, decision trees, random forests, SVM, and regression analysis techniques empower researchers and designers to make informed decisions, optimizing the performance, energy efficiency, and sustainability of electronic devices.

INTELLIGENT MANUFACTURING PROCESSES FOR SUSTAINABLE ELECTRONICS

Intelligent manufacturing processes refer to the application of AI and ML techniques in the manufacturing of sustainable electronics. These techniques enable eco-friendly and efficient production through methods such as computer vision, anomaly detection, optimization of manufacturing parameters, and quality control. AI-driven approaches optimize resource utilization, reduce waste, and improve product quality, leading to more sustainable and efficient manufacturing processes for electronic devices. By automating and streamlining production operations, AI and ML contribute to increased efficiency, reduced energy consumption, and minimized environmental impact. These advancements also facilitate improved quality control and defect detection, ensuring the production of high-quality and reliable green electronic devices.

AI-Driven Approaches for Eco-Friendly and Efficient Manufacturing of Green and Flexible Electronics

AI-driven approaches have emerged as powerful tools in achieving eco-friendly and efficient manufacturing of green and flexible electronics. These approaches leverage AI techniques, such as computer vision, natural language processing, and expert systems, to analyze data and make informed decisions, contributing to sustainable manufacturing practices.

Computer vision techniques enable the recognition and analysis of visual data, aiding in the inspection of electronic components and the identification of potential defects or quality issues. By training ML models on large datasets of images, computer vision algorithms can detect anomalies and classify components, ensuring the production of high-quality and reliable electronic devices (Fang et al., 2020). Additionally, computer vision can assist in the identification and sorting of recyclable materials, enabling effective waste management practices in the electronics industry.

Natural language processing techniques facilitate the analysis and understanding of textual data, such as product specifications, manufacturing instructions, and quality control reports. By extracting information and identifying patterns from textual data, ML algorithms can optimize manufacturing processes, identify areas for improvement, and support decision-making for sustainable manufacturing (Elgendy & Elragal, 2014). For instance, ML models can analyze manufacturing instructions to identify energy-efficient practices or suggest eco-friendly alternatives in the production of electronic devices.

Expert systems, which incorporate knowledge and expertise from domain specialists, provide intelligent decision support in manufacturing processes. By encoding rules and heuristics, expert systems can guide decision-making, ensuring compliance with sustainability standards and optimizing manufacturing operations (Shortliffe, 1986). These systems enable the implementation of best practices for sustainable manufacturing, such as energy-efficient process design, waste reduction strategies, and the use of environmentally friendly materials.

Optimization of Manufacturing Parameters Using ML Techniques

ML techniques offer valuable insights and optimization capabilities for manufacturing processes in the production of sustainable electronics. By leveraging historical data, ML algorithms can identify optimal manufacturing parameters, leading to improved product quality, reduced energy consumption, and minimized environmental impact.

One common ML technique used for optimization is regression analysis. Regression models can establish mathematical relationships between manufacturing parameters and desired outcomes, such as energy efficiency, material utilization, or production yield. By analyzing the data and identifying key factors, regression models can guide decision-making and help manufacturers optimize their processes accordingly (Ascher et al., 2022). For example, regression models can identify the optimal curing time and temperature for flexible electronic devices, ensuring efficient production while maintaining desired performance characteristics.

Furthermore, reinforcement learning techniques enable the optimization of manufacturing processes through trial and error. Reinforcement learning algorithms learn from experience and feedback, adjusting manufacturing parameters to maximize desired outcomes, such as energy efficiency or waste reduction. By interacting with the manufacturing environment and receiving rewards or penalties, these algorithms can autonomously optimize process parameters and make real-time adjustments, leading to sustainable and efficient manufacturing (Huang et al., 2019).

Quality Control and Defect Detection With AI in Manufacturing Processes

Ensuring product quality and detecting defects are critical aspects of sustainable manufacturing in the electronics industry. AI techniques, such as image processing, anomaly detection, and predictive analytics, play a crucial role in effective quality control and defect detection.

Image processing algorithms enable the inspection of electronic components, circuit boards, and final products to detect visual defects or anomalies. By analyzing images or video streams, these algorithms can identify deviations from expected standards, such as incorrect component placement, soldering defects, or surface irregularities. ML models trained on large datasets of labeled images can classify and detect such defects with high accuracy, enabling timely interventions and reducing waste (Czimmermann et al., 2020).

An additional technique employed in quality control is anomaly detection. Anomaly detection algorithms analyze sensor data or process parameters to identify deviations from normal behavior. By establishing baseline patterns, ML models can detect anomalies in real time, alerting manufacturers to potential quality issues or process abnormalities. This proactive approach enables timely corrective actions, reducing waste and improving overall product quality (Zipfel et al., 2023).

Predictive analytics techniques utilize ML algorithms to analyze historical data and predict potential defects or quality issues before they occur. By identifying patterns and correlations between process parameters and quality outcomes, predictive models can provide early warnings and insights into factors that may lead to suboptimal quality or performance. This information allows manufacturers to make data-driven decisions and implement preventive measures, ensuring sustainable and defect-free production (Ferrero Bermejo et al., 2019).

In summary, the integration of AI and ML techniques in manufacturing processes has transformed the production of sustainable electronics. AI-driven approaches enable eco-friendly and efficient manufacturing through computer vision, natural language processing, and expert systems. ML techniques optimize manufacturing parameters through regression analysis and reinforcement learning, while AI techniques such as image processing, anomaly detection, and predictive analytics support quality control and defect detection. By leveraging these intelligent manufacturing processes, the electronics industry can achieve higher product quality, improved energy efficiency, and reduced environmental impact.

PREDICTIVE MODELING FOR ENERGY EFFICIENCY IN FLEXIBLE ELECTRONICS

Predictive modeling utilizes ML algorithms to analyze historical data and predict energy consumption in flexible electronic devices. By considering device parameters, operational conditions, and usage patterns, predictive models estimate power requirements, optimize energy allocation, and develop energy-saving strategies. These models enable designers to make data-driven decisions, optimize energy efficiency, and reduce the environmental impact of flexible electronic devices. By accurately predicting and managing energy consumption, flexible electronics can contribute to sustainable energy consumption practices.

These advancements in energy efficiency also extend the battery life of portable devices and reduce the overall carbon footprint associated with electronic devices.

Use of ML Models for Predicting and Optimizing Energy Consumption in Flexible Electronic Devices

ML models have shown significant promise in predicting and optimizing energy consumption in flexible electronic devices. By leveraging historical data and complex algorithms, ML models can identify patterns and relationships between device parameters, operational conditions, and energy consumption.

One common approach is the use of regression analysis to develop ML models that predict the energy consumption of flexible electronic devices. These models establish mathematical relationships between device characteristics, such as circuit design, materials used, operational parameters, and the corresponding energy consumption. By analyzing these relationships, ML models can accurately estimate the energy requirements of new devices and assist in the design process to optimize energy efficiency (Benedetti et al., 2019).

Furthermore, ML techniques such as artificial neural networks (ANNs) have been employed to predict energy consumption in flexible electronic devices. ANNs can learn complex patterns and non-linear relationships between input features (e.g., device configuration, operating conditions) and energy consumption. By training on a dataset that includes various device configurations and corresponding energy consumption measurements, ANNs can predict the energy consumption of new devices with high accuracy (Di Franco & Santurro, 2021). These predictions enable designers to identify energy-intensive components or design choices, facilitating the development of energy-saving strategies.

Techniques for Estimating Power Requirements and Energy-Saving Strategies

Estimating power requirements accurately is crucial for optimizing energy efficiency in flexible electronics. ML techniques can assist in estimating power requirements and developing energy-saving strategies through the analysis of device characteristics and operational parameters.

One approach is the use of decision tree-based models to estimate power requirements. Decision trees analyze device parameters such as power supply voltage, clock frequency, and active components to predict power consumption. By considering the impact of different design choices on power consumption, decision tree models can guide designers in making informed decisions that promote energy efficiency (Dayarathna et al., 2015).

Additionally, reinforcement learning techniques can be employed to optimize energy-saving strategies in flexible electronics. Reinforcement learning algorithms can learn from experience and feedback, interacting with the device environment to make decisions that maximize energy efficiency. By adjusting operational parameters, such as clock frequency, power supply voltage, or component activation, reinforcement learning algorithms can autonomously optimize energy consumption while meeting performance requirements (Yang et al., 2020).

Furthermore, predictive modeling can be utilized to develop energy-saving strategies in flexible electronics. By analyzing historical data on device usage patterns, ML models can predict energy demand at different times or under specific conditions. These predictions enable the development of energy management strategies, such as dynamic power allocation, load balancing, or intelligent scheduling of tasks, to optimize energy efficiency in flexible electronic systems (Xin et al., 2018).

In summary, predictive modeling combined with ML techniques offers valuable insights into energy efficiency in flexible electronics. ML models can accurately predict and optimize energy consumption in devices, enabling designers to make informed decisions for energy-efficient designs. Techniques such as regression analysis, artificial neural networks, decision trees, and reinforcement learning empower designers to estimate power requirements and develop energy-saving strategies. By leveraging these techniques, the field of flexible electronics can advance sustainable development goals by improving energy efficiency and reducing environmental impact.

MACHINE LEARNING FOR OPTIMIZATION OF FLEXIBLE ELECTRONIC DESIGNS

Machine learning plays a crucial role in optimizing the design of flexible electronic components. ML-based approaches, such as genetic algorithms and artificial neural networks, analyze design parameters, performance metrics, and constraints to identify optimal design configurations. These techniques enable designers to explore a vast design space, improve performance, enhance reliability, and promote resource efficiency in flexible electronic devices. By leveraging ML algorithms, designers can identify design choices that minimize material usage, reduce energy consumption, and enhance overall device performance. These advancements contribute to the development of sustainable and efficient flexible electronic designs, supporting the transition towards more eco-friendly electronic systems.

ML-based Approaches for Optimizing the Design of Flexible Electronic Components

ML-based approaches play a crucial role in optimizing the design of flexible electronic components. These approaches leverage ML algorithms to analyze large datasets, identify patterns, and make informed decisions for improved design outcomes.

One notable ML technique used in design optimization is genetic algorithms. Genetic algorithms employ a population-based search approach inspired by the principles of natural evolution. By generating and evolving a population of potential design solutions, genetic algorithms can iteratively improve flexible electronic component designs based on predefined fitness criteria. Through repeated generations, these algorithms converge toward optimal design configurations, considering multiple factors such as performance, reliability, and manufacturability (Javaid et al., 2022). Genetic algorithms have been successfully applied to optimize the layout of flexible electronic circuits, leading to improved electrical performance and reliability (Zebulum et al., 2018).

Another ML technique is the use of artificial neural networks (ANNs) for design optimization. ANNs can learn complex relationships between design parameters, performance metrics, and constraints. By training on datasets that include various design configurations and corresponding performance data, ANNs can predict the performance of new designs and guide optimization efforts. For instance, ANNs have been employed to optimize the mechanical properties of flexible substrates, enabling the selection of materials and dimensions that enhance the reliability and flexibility of flexible electronic components (Patra et al., 2017).

Simulation, Modeling, and Analysis Using Machine Learning Techniques

Simulation, modeling, and analysis are integral parts of the design optimization process for flexible electronic components. ML techniques can be employed to enhance these processes, enabling accurate predictions, faster simulations, and comprehensive analysis.

ML-based surrogate modeling is a powerful technique used to create efficient approximations of computationally expensive simulations. Surrogate models, such as Gaussian processes or support vector regression, learn from a limited set of simulation results and can provide accurate predictions for a wide range of design parameters. By utilizing surrogate models, designers can rapidly explore different design configurations, assess their performance, and accelerate the optimization process (Thrampoulidis et al., 2021).

Additionally, ML techniques can be utilized for feature extraction and dimensionality reduction in simulation and analysis. High-dimensional data generated from simulations can be challenging to interpret and analyze. ML algorithms, such as principal component analysis or t-SNE, can identify key features and reduce the dimensionality of the data, facilitating visualization, interpretation, and efficient analysis of simulation results (Khalid et al., 2014).

Furthermore, ML-based anomaly detection methods can identify unusual or unexpected behavior in simulation results, providing insights into design weaknesses, potential failure modes, or areas for improvement. By analyzing the simulation data and identifying anomalies, designers can refine and optimize their designs to enhance performance, reliability, and efficiency (Şengönül et al., 2023).

In summary, ML techniques are invaluable in the optimization of flexible electronic designs. Genetic algorithms and artificial neural networks enable efficient design optimization of flexible electronic components, considering various performance criteria. ML-based surrogate modeling enhances simulation and analysis processes, enabling faster evaluations and comprehensive design exploration. Feature extraction, dimensionality reduction, and anomaly detection techniques empower designers to interpret simulation results and identify areas for improvement. By leveraging these ML-based approaches, designers can achieve optimized designs with enhanced performance, reliability, and manufacturability.

CASE STUDIES: AI AND ML APPLICATIONS IN GREEN AND FLEXIBLE ELECTRONICS

The successful application of artificial intelligence (AI) and machine learning (ML) techniques in the design, manufacturing, and optimization of green and flexible electronic devices has resulted in remarkable sustainability and efficiency improvements. Real-world projects exemplify how AI and ML have played a pivotal role in advancing the field of green and flexible electronics.

Examples of Successful Applications of AI and ML in Green and Flexible Electronics

One notable example of AI and ML applications is in the design optimization of flexible solar cells. Researchers have utilized ML algorithms to analyze large datasets of material properties, device configurations, and performance metrics to identify the most efficient combinations of materials for improved solar energy conversion. By training ML models on this data, researchers have successfully predicted and optimized solar cell efficiency, leading to significant advancements in the development of flexible and sustainable energy sources (Abadi et al., 2022).

Another successful application is in the manufacturing process of green electronic devices. AI and ML techniques, such as computer vision and anomaly detection, have been employed for quality control and defect detection. By analyzing images or sensor data, ML models can identify defects, irregularities, or inconsistencies in the manufacturing process, ensuring the production of high-quality and reliable green electronic devices (Qin et al., 2022). These AI-driven quality control techniques have led to reduced waste, improved product quality, and increased overall manufacturing efficiency.

Furthermore, AI and ML have played a crucial role in energy management for flexible electronic devices. ML models have been utilized to develop predictive models for energy consumption, allowing for the optimization of power allocation and energy-saving strategies. By analyzing usage patterns and operational parameters, ML models can predict energy demand, identify peak usage periods, and optimize power allocation in real-time, resulting in enhanced energy efficiency and reduced environmental impact (Ahmad et al., 2022).

Real-World Projects Demonstrating Sustainability and Efficiency Achieved Through AI and ML Techniques

A real-world project demonstrating the sustainability and efficiency achieved through AI and ML techniques is the optimization of power management in wearable electronics. Researchers have implemented ML algorithms to analyze user behavior and sensor data to develop intelligent power management systems for wearables. These systems can dynamically adjust power allocation, activate power-saving modes, and optimize resource utilization based on user activities, resulting in extended battery life, reduced energy consumption, and improved user experience (Seng et al., 2023).

Another project focuses on the development of AI-assisted recycling systems for electronic waste. ML algorithms have been utilized to analyze and classify electronic waste components, facilitating efficient sorting and recycling processes. By automatically identifying recyclable materials, these systems contribute to reducing landfill waste and promoting sustainable recycling practices (Nowakowski & Pamuła, 2020).

Additionally, AI and ML techniques have been applied to optimize material usage and manufacturing processes in the production of flexible electronic components. By analyzing data on material properties, manufacturing parameters, and performance requirements, ML models can guide the selection of optimal materials and optimize manufacturing processes to reduce material waste, improve yield rates, and enhance overall manufacturing efficiency (Cioffi et al., 2020).

These case studies demonstrate the tangible benefits of AI and ML in the green and flexible electronics industry, showcasing the sustainable development and improved efficiency achieved through the application of these techniques.

CHALLENGES AND FUTURE DIRECTIONS

While the integration of AI and ML in green and flexible electronics brings numerous benefits, several challenges and future directions must be considered. Challenges include data availability and quality, the interpretability of ML models, and the transferability of ML models to different contexts and conditions. Overcoming these challenges requires standardized data collection procedures, explainable AI techniques, and the development of robust and adaptable ML models. Future directions include emerging trends such as generative design, optimized material selection, digital twins, IoT-enabled systems, and predictive maintenance. These trends have the potential to further enhance sustainability and efficiency in green and flexible electronics. Collaboration among researchers, industry stakeholders, and policy-makers is essential to address challenges, drive advancements, and ensure the responsible and ethical implementation of AI and ML techniques in the field.

Limitations and Challenges in Integrating AI and ML in Green and Flexible Electronics

While the integration of artificial intelligence (AI) and machine learning (ML) in green and flexible electronics has shown tremendous promise, several limitations and challenges need to be addressed for further advancements in the field.

One key challenge is the availability and quality of data. ML algorithms heavily rely on large datasets for training and validation. However, in the domain of green and flexible electronics, acquiring comprehensive and well-annotated datasets can be challenging. Data collection, especially for emerging materials and technologies, may be limited, leading to potential biases or insufficient representation of the design space. Additionally, the reliability and accuracy of data are crucial, as inaccurate or incomplete data can impact the performance and reliability of ML models (LeCun et al., 2015). Addressing these data challenges requires collaboration among researchers, industry stakeholders, and regulatory bodies to establish standardized data collection procedures and promote data-sharing initiatives.

Another challenge lies in the interpretability and explainability of ML models. Complex ML algorithms, such as deep learning neural networks, often operate as black boxes, making it difficult to understand the decision-making process. Interpreting and explaining the results and decisions of ML models is essential for designers, engineers, and regulators to gain confidence and trust in the use of AI and ML techniques. Efforts are being made to develop explainable AI techniques, enabling the transparency and interpretability of ML models, thus facilitating the adoption of AI-driven solutions in green and flexible electronics (Van Erp et al., 2021).

Furthermore, the transferability and generalizability of ML models across different contexts and conditions present challenges. ML models trained on specific datasets and conditions may not perform optimally when applied to different scenarios or variations in materials, designs, or operational environments. Developing robust ML models that can adapt and generalize to different situations is critical for achieving widespread adoption and scalability of AI and ML techniques in the field (Jayal et al., 2010).

Emerging Trends and Future Prospects in Sustainable Electronic Design and Manufacturing

Despite the challenges, emerging trends and future prospects in sustainable electronic design and manufacturing hold significant promise for the integration of AI and ML techniques.

One emerging trend is the use of generative design, where AI and ML algorithms collaborate with designers to explore a vast design space and identify novel, efficient, and sustainable solutions. Generative design algorithms can optimize designs based on predefined performance criteria and constraints, enabling the discovery of innovative designs that are resource-efficient, lightweight, and environmentally friendly (Mi et al., 2020). Integrating AI and ML techniques into the generative design process can enhance exploration and optimization capabilities, leading to the development of more sustainable and efficient electronic devices.

Another future prospect lies in the optimization of material selection and supply chain management. AI and ML algorithms can analyze vast amounts of data related to material properties, availability, cost, and environmental impact to support sustainable material selection decisions. By considering factors such as recyclability, toxicity, and energy consumption in material production, ML models can assist in identifying materials with improved sustainability profiles (Mishra et al., 2020). Additionally, ML techniques can optimize supply chain operations by analyzing historical data, predicting demand, and optimizing inventory management, thereby minimizing waste and reducing the environmental impact of the entire product lifecycle.

Furthermore, the advancement of digital twins and simulation-based design approaches holds great potential for sustainable electronic design and manufacturing. Digital twins, virtual replicas of physical devices or systems, combined with AI and ML techniques, allow for rapid prototyping, optimization, and performance prediction. By simulating and analyzing various design configurations and operational conditions, designers can optimize energy consumption, reliability, and overall performance before physical production, reducing material waste, and streamlining the design iteration process (Chin & Harlow, 1982).

The integration of AI and ML techniques with Internet of Things (IoT) technologies and edge computing further enhances the sustainability and efficiency of flexible electronic systems. AI-driven IoT devices and edge computing enable real-time data analysis, decision-making, and optimization at the edge of the network, reducing the need for extensive data transmission and central processing. This distributed intelligence approach not only improves system responsiveness but also reduces energy consumption and overall environmental impact (Chandola et al., 2009).

In addition to design and manufacturing, AI and ML techniques can contribute to the implementation of sustainable practices in the operation and maintenance of electronic devices. Predictive maintenance models, powered by ML algorithms, can analyze sensor data and historical maintenance records to predict equipment failures, optimize maintenance schedules, and reduce downtime. By detecting and addressing issues proactively, the lifespan of electronic devices can be extended, minimizing electronic waste and improving resource efficiency (Zheng et al., 2018).

Looking ahead, collaboration among researchers, industry stakeholders, and policymakers is crucial for addressing the challenges and realizing the full potential of AI and ML in green and flexible electronics. Investments in research and development, infrastructure, and regulatory frameworks that support sustainability goals are essential. Moreover, interdisciplinary collaborations between experts in AI, ML, materials science, electronics engineering, and sustainability will foster innovation and drive the adoption of sustainable practices in the industry. A schematic representation has been shown in Fig.1 for the highly automated, self-evolving futuristic AI control system (Tai et al., 2020).

In gist, while challenges exist, the integration of AI and ML techniques in green and flexible electronics holds tremendous promise for sustainable electronic design and manufacturing. Overcoming data limitations, ensuring the interpretability of ML models, and addressing transferability challenges are key areas of focus. The emerging trends of generative design, optimized material selection, digital twins, IoT-enabled systems, and predictive maintenance demonstrate the potential for AI and ML to contribute to sustainability and efficiency. By embracing these trends and fostering collaborative efforts, the field of green and flexible electronics can pave the way for a more sustainable and environmentally friendly future.

Figure 1. Self-evolving and closed loop automated process: Futuristic approach (Tai et al., 2020)

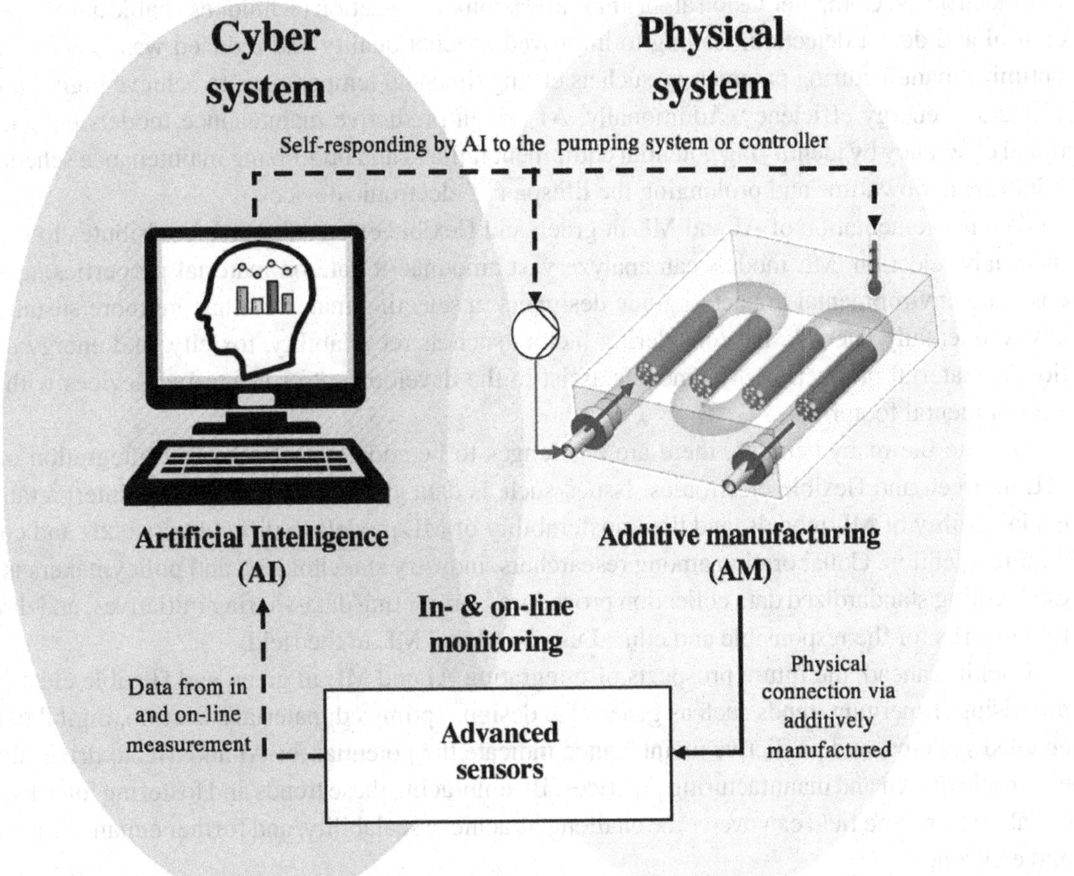

CONCLUSION

The integration of artificial intelligence (AI) and machine learning (ML) techniques in the design and manufacturing of green and flexible electronics has brought about transformative advancements in the pursuit of sustainable development. This convergence of AI and ML with green and flexible electronics has yielded significant improvements in energy efficiency, material utilization, manufacturing processes, and overall environmental impact. As a result, the field of green and flexible electronics is poised to contribute to a more sustainable and environmentally friendly future.

One of the key benefits of integrating AI and ML in green and flexible electronics is the ability to optimize design processes. ML algorithms have the capability to analyze large volumes of data and identify patterns and correlations that can inform the design of more efficient and sustainable electronic components. Through techniques such as generative design, ML models can explore vast design spaces and identify innovative solutions that are resource-efficient, lightweight, and environmentally friendly. This optimization of design processes has the potential to greatly enhance the energy efficiency and overall performance of green and flexible electronic devices.

Moreover, AI and ML techniques have revolutionized the manufacturing processes of green and flexible electronics. Computer vision algorithms and anomaly detection techniques enable automated quality control and defect detection, leading to improved product quality and reduced waste. ML models can optimize manufacturing parameters, such as curing time and temperature, to achieve higher production yields and energy efficiency. Additionally, AI-driven predictive maintenance models enhance operational efficiency by identifying potential equipment failures and optimizing maintenance schedules, thus minimizing downtime and prolonging the lifespan of electronic devices.

The implementation of AI and ML in green and flexible electronics also contributes to sustainable materials selection. ML models can analyze vast amounts of data on material properties, availability, cost, and environmental impact to guide designers in selecting materials that are more sustainable and environmentally friendly. By considering factors such as recyclability, toxicity, and energy consumption in material production, ML models assist in the development of electronic devices with reduced environmental footprints.

Despite the many benefits, there are challenges to be addressed for the full integration of AI and ML in green and flexible electronics. Issues such as data availability and quality, interpretability and explainability of ML models, and the transferability of ML models to different contexts and conditions require attention. Collaboration among researchers, industry stakeholders, and policymakers is vital for establishing standardized data collection procedures, promoting data-sharing initiatives, and developing frameworks for the responsible and ethical use of AI and ML in the field.

Looking ahead, the future prospects of integrating AI and ML in green and flexible electronics are promising. Emerging trends such as generative design, optimized material selection, digital twins, IoT-enabled systems, and predictive maintenance indicate the potential for AI and ML to drive sustainable electronic design and manufacturing practices. By embracing these trends and fostering interdisciplinary collaborations, the field can overcome challenges, achieve scalability, and further enhance sustainability and efficiency.

As a whole, the integration of artificial intelligence and machine learning in the design and manufacturing of green and flexible electronics has ushered in a new era of sustainable development. With their optimization capabilities, AI and ML techniques have revolutionized design processes, manufacturing operations, and materials selection. By addressing challenges and capitalizing on emerging trends, the field of green and flexible electronics is poised to play a pivotal role in creating a more sustainable and environmentally conscious future.

REFERENCES

Abadi, E. A. J., Sahu, H., Javadpour, S. M., & Goharimanesh, M. (2022). Interpretable machine learning for developing high-performance organic solar cells. *Materials Today. Energy*, *25*, 100969. doi:10.1016/j.mtener.2022.100969

Ahmad, T., Zhu, H., Zhang, D., Tariq, R., Bassam, A., Ullah, F., AlGhamdi, A. S., & Alshamrani, S. S. (2022). Energetics Systems and artificial intelligence: Applications of industry 4.0. *Energy Reports*, *8*, 334–361. doi:10.1016/j.egyr.2021.11.256

Ali, L., Sivaramakrishnan, K., Kuttiyathil, M. S., Chandrasekaran, V., Ahmed, O. H., Al-Harahsheh, M., & Altarawneh, M. (2023). Prediction of Thermogravimetric Data in Bromine Captured from Brominated Flame Retardants (BFRs) in e-Waste Treatment Using Machine Learning Approaches. *Journal of Chemical Information and Modeling, 63*(8), 2305–2320. doi:10.1021/acs.jcim.3c00183 PMID:37036888

Altun, K., Barshan, B., & Tunçel, O. (2010). Comparative study on classifying human activities with miniature inertial and magnetic sensors. *Pattern Recognition, 43*(10), 3605–3620. doi:10.1016/j.patcog.2010.04.019

Ascher, S., Watson, I., & You, S. (2022). Machine learning methods for modelling the gasification and pyrolysis of biomass and waste. *Renewable & Sustainable Energy Reviews, 155*, 111902. doi:10.1016/j.rser.2021.111902

Benedetti, M., Lloyd, E., Sack, S., & Fiorentini, M. (2019). Parameterized quantum circuits as machine learning models. *Quantum Science and Technology, 4*(4), 043001. doi:10.1088/2058-9565/ab4eb5

Boobalan, C., & Kannaiyan, S. K. (2022). A correlation to predict the thermal conductivity of MXene-silicone oil based nano-fluids and data driven modeling using artificial neural networks. *International Journal of Energy Research, 46*(15), 21538–21547. doi:10.1002/er.7786

Brishty, F. P., Urner, R., & Grau, G. (2022). Machine learning based data-driven inkjet printed electronics: Jetting prediction for novel inks. *Flexible and Printed Electronics, 7*(1), 015009. doi:10.1088/2058-8585/ac5a39

Brishty, F. P., Urner, R., & Grau, G. (2022). Machine learning based data driven inkjet printed electronics: Jetting prediction for novel inks. *Flexible and Printed Electronics, 7*(1), 015009. doi:10.1088/2058-8585/ac5a39

Chandola, V., Banerjee, A., & Kumar, V. (2009). Anomaly detection: A survey. *ACM Computing Surveys, 41*(3), 1–58. doi:10.1145/1541880.1541882

Chhowalla, M., Shin, H. S., Eda, G., Li, L. J., Loh, K. P., & Zhang, H. (2013). The chemistry of two-dimensional layered transition metal dichalcogenide nanosheets. *Nature Chemistry, 5*(4), 263–275. doi:10.1038/nchem.1589 PMID:23511414

Chin, R. T., & Harlow, C. A. (1982). Automated visual inspection: A survey. *IEEE Transactions on Pattern Analysis and Machine Intelligence, PAMI-4*(6), 557–573. doi:10.1109/TPAMI.1982.4767309 PMID:22499630

Cioffi, R., Travaglioni, M., Piscitelli, G., Petrillo, A., & De Felice, F. (2020). Artificial intelligence and machine learning applications in smart production: Progress, trends, and directions. *Sustainability (Basel), 12*(2), 492. doi:10.3390/su12020492

Czimmermann, T., Ciuti, G., Milazzo, M., Chiurazzi, M., Roccella, S., Oddo, C. M., & Dario, P. (2020). Visual-based defect detection and classification approaches for industrial applications—A survey. *Sensors (Basel), 20*(5), 1459. doi:10.3390/s20051459 PMID:32155900

Dayarathna, M., Wen, Y., & Fan, R. (2015). Data center energy consumption modeling: A survey. *IEEE Communications Surveys and Tutorials, 18*(1), 732–794. doi:10.1109/COMST.2015.2481183

Di Franco, G., & Santurro, M. (2021). Machine learning, artificial neural networks and social research. *Quality & Quantity, 55*(3), 1007–1025. doi:10.1007/s11135-020-01037-y

Elgendy, N., & Elragal, A. (2014). Big data analytics: a literature review paper. In *Advances in Data Mining. Applications and Theoretical Aspects: 14th Industrial Conference.* Springer International Publishing.

Entezari, A., Aslani, A., Zahedi, R., & Noorollahi, Y. (2023). Artificial intelligence and machine learning in energy systems: A bibliographic perspective. *Energy Strategy Reviews, 45*, 101017. doi:10.1016/j.esr.2022.101017

Fang, W., Love, P. E., Luo, H., & Ding, L. (2020). Computer vision for behaviour-based safety in construction: A review and future directions. *Advanced Engineering Informatics, 43*, 100980. doi:10.1016/j.aei.2019.100980

Ferrero Bermejo, J., Gómez Fernández, J. F., Olivencia Polo, F., & Crespo Márquez, A. (2019). A review of the use of artificial neural network models for energy and reliability prediction. A study of the solar PV, hydraulic and wind energy sources. *Applied Sciences (Basel, Switzerland), 9*(9), 1844. doi:10.3390/app9091844

Huang, X., Hong, S. H., Yu, M., Ding, Y., & Jiang, J. (2019). Demand response management for industrial facilities: A deep reinforcement learning approach. *IEEE Access : Practical Innovations, Open Solutions, 7*, 82194–82205. doi:10.1109/ACCESS.2019.2924030

Irimia-Vladu, M. (2014). "Green" electronics: Biodegradable and biocompatible materials and devices for a sustainable future. *Chemical Society Reviews, 43*(2), 588–610. doi:10.1039/C3CS60235D PMID:24121237

Jana, R. K., Ghosh, I., Das, D., & Dutta, A. (2021). Determinants of electronic waste generation in Bitcoin network: Evidence from the machine learning approach. *Technological Forecasting and Social Change, 173*, 121101. doi:10.1016/j.techfore.2021.121101

Javaid, M., Haleem, A., Singh, R. P., Suman, R., & Rab, S. (2022). Significance of machine learning in healthcare: Features, pillars and applications. *International Journal of Intelligent Networks, 3*, 58–73. doi:10.1016/j.ijin.2022.05.002

Jayal, A. D., Badurdeen, F., Dillon, O. W. Jr, & Jawahir, I. S. (2010). Sustainable manufacturing: Modeling and optimization challenges at the product, process and system levels. *CIRP Journal of Manufacturing Science and Technology, 2*(3), 144–152. doi:10.1016/j.cirpj.2010.03.006

Khalid, S., Khalil, T., & Nasreen, S. (2014, August). *A survey of feature selection and feature extraction techniques in machine learning. In 2014 science and information conference.* IEEE.

Klauk, H. (2010). Organic thin-film transistors. *Chemical Society Reviews, 39*(7), 2643–2666. doi:10.1039/b909902f PMID:20396828

LeCun, Y., Bengio, Y., & Hinton, G. (2015). Deep learning. *Nature, 521*(7553), 436-444.

Lipomi, D. J., & Bao, Z. (2011). Stretchable, elastic materials and devices for solar energy conversion. *Energy & Environmental Science, 4*(9), 3314–3328. doi:10.1039/c1ee01881g

Liu, D., Chen, Q., & Mori, K. (2015, August). *Time series forecasting method of building energy consumption using support vector regression. In 2015 IEEE international conference on Information and automation.* IEEE.

Liu, Y., Cao, G., Zhao, N., Mulligan, K., & Ye, X. (2018). Improve ground-level PM2. 5 concentration mapping using a random forests-based geostatistical approach. *Environmental Pollution, 235,* 272–282. doi:10.1016/j.envpol.2017.12.070 PMID:29291527

Liu, Y., Chen, H., Zhang, L., Wu, X., & Wang, X. J. (2020). Energy consumption prediction and diagnosis of public buildings based on support vector machine learning: A case study in China. *Journal of Cleaner Production, 272,* 122542. doi:10.1016/j.jclepro.2020.122542

Liu, Z., Zhang, T., Yang, M., Gao, W., Wu, S., Wang, K., Dong, F., Dang, J., Zhou, D., & Zhang, J. (2021). Hydrogel pressure distribution sensors based on an imaging strategy and machine learning. *ACS Applied Electronic Materials, 3*(8), 3599–3609. doi:10.1021/acsaelm.1c00488

Mi, S., Feng, Y., Zheng, H., Li, Z., Gao, Y., & Tan, J. (2020). Integrated intelligent green scheduling of predictive maintenance for complex equipment based on information services. *IEEE Access : Practical Innovations, Open Solutions, 8,* 45797–45812. doi:10.1109/ACCESS.2020.2977667

Mishra, M., Nayak, J., Naik, B., & Abraham, A. (2020). Deep learning in electrical utility industry: A comprehensive review of a decade of research. *Engineering Applications of Artificial Intelligence, 96,* 104000. doi:10.1016/j.engappai.2020.104000

Nasiri, S., & Khosravani, M. R. (2020). Progress and challenges in the fabrication of wearable sensors for health monitoring. *Sensors and Actuators. A, Physical, 312,* 112105. doi:10.1016/j.sna.2020.112105

Nowakowski, P., & Pamuła, T. (2020). Application of deep learning object classifier to improve e-waste collection planning. *Waste Management (New York, N.Y.), 109,* 1–9. doi:10.1016/j.wasman.2020.04.041 PMID:32361385

Pang, C., Lee, G. Y., Kim, T. I., Kim, S. M., Kim, H. N., Ahn, S. H., & Suh, K. Y. (2012). A flexible and highly sensitive strain-gauge sensor using reversible interlocking of nanofibres. *Nature Materials, 11*(9), 795–801. doi:10.1038/nmat3380 PMID:22842511

Patra, T. K., Meenakshisundaram, V., Hung, J. H., & Simmons, D. S. (2017). Neural-network-biased genetic algorithms for materials design: Evolutionary algorithms that learn. *ACS Combinatorial Science, 19*(2), 96–107. doi:10.1021/acscombsci.6b00136 PMID:27997791

Qin, J., Hu, F., Liu, Y., Witherell, P., Wang, C. C., Rosen, D. W., Simpson, T. W., Lu, Y., & Tang, Q. (2022). Research and application of machine learning for additive manufacturing. *Additive Manufacturing, 52,* 102691. doi:10.1016/j.addma.2022.102691

Seng, K. P., Ang, L. M., Peter, E., & Mmonyi, A. (2023). Machine Learning and AI Technologies for Smart Wearables. *Electronics (Basel), 12*(7), 1509. doi:10.3390/electronics12071509

Şengönül, E., Samet, R., Abu Al-Haija, Q., Alqahtani, A., Alturki, B., & Alsulami, A. A. (2023). An Analysis of Artificial Intelligence Techniques in Surveillance Video Anomaly Detection: A Comprehensive Survey. *Applied Sciences (Basel, Switzerland), 13*(8), 4956. doi:10.3390/app13084956

Shi, Q., He, T., & Lee, C. (2019). More than energy harvesting–Combining triboelectric nanogenerator and flexible electronics technology for enabling novel micro-/nano-systems. *Nano Energy*, *57*, 851–871. doi:10.1016/j.nanoen.2019.01.002

Shortliffe, E. H. (1986). Medical expert systems—Knowledge tools for physicians. *The Western Journal of Medicine*, *145*(6), 830. PMID:3811349

Someya, T., Bao, Z., & Malliaras, G. G. (2016). The rise of plastic bioelectronics. *Nature*, *540*(7633), 379–385. doi:10.1038/nature21004 PMID:27974769

Tai, X. Y., Zhang, H., Niu, Z., Christie, S. D., & Xuan, J. (2020). The future of sustainable chemistry and process: Convergence of artificial intelligence, data and hardware. *Energy and AI*, *2*, 100036. doi:10.1016/j.egyai.2020.100036

Thrampoulidis, E., Mavromatidis, G., Lucchi, A., & Orehounig, K. (2021). A machine learning-based surrogate model to approximate optimal building retrofit solutions. *Applied Energy*, *281*, 116024. doi:10.1016/j.apenergy.2020.116024

Van Erp, M., Reynolds, C., Maynard, D., Starke, A., Ibáñez Martín, R., Andres, F., Leite, M. C. A., Alvarez de Toledo, D., Schmidt Rivera, X., Trattner, C., Brewer, S., Adriano Martins, C., Kluczkovski, A., Frankowska, A., Bridle, S., Levy, R. B., Rauber, F., Tereza da Silva, J., & Bosma, U. (2021). Using natural language processing and artificial intelligence to explore the nutrition and sustainability of recipes and food. *Frontiers in Artificial Intelligence*, *3*, 621577. doi:10.3389/frai.2020.621577 PMID:33733227

Wang, P., Hu, M., Wang, H., Chen, Z., Feng, Y., Wang, J., Ling, W., & Huang, Y. (2020). The evolution of flexible electronics: From nature, beyond nature, and to nature. *Advancement of Science*, *7*(20), 2001116. doi:10.1002/advs.202001116 PMID:33101851

Wang, T., Zhang, K., Thé, J., & Yu, H. (2022). Accurate prediction of band gap of materials using stacking machine learning model. *Computational Materials Science*, *201*, 110899. doi:10.1016/j.commatsci.2021.110899

Wen, T. Y., & Aris, S. A. M. (2022). Hybrid approach of eeg stress level classification using k-means clustering and support vector machine. *IEEE Access : Practical Innovations, Open Solutions*, *10*, 18370–18379. doi:10.1109/ACCESS.2022.3148380

Wu, Y., Sun, X., Zhang, Y., Zhong, X., & Cheng, L. (2021). A power transformer fault diagnosis method-based hybrid improved seagull optimization algorithm and support vector machine. *IEEE Access : Practical Innovations, Open Solutions*, *10*, 17268–17286. doi:10.1109/ACCESS.2021.3127164

Xin, Y., Kong, L., Liu, Z., Chen, Y., Li, Y., Zhu, H., Gao, M., Hou, H., & Wang, C. (2018). Machine learning and deep learning methods for cybersecurity. *IEEE Access : Practical Innovations, Open Solutions*, *6*, 35365–35381. doi:10.1109/ACCESS.2018.2836950

Yang, T., Zhao, L., Li, W., & Zomaya, A. Y. (2020). Reinforcement learning in sustainable energy and electric systems: A survey. *Annual Reviews in Control*, *49*, 145–163. doi:10.1016/j.arcontrol.2020.03.001

Zebulum, R. S., Pacheco, M. A., & Vellasco, M. M. B. (2018). *Evolutionary electronics: automatic design of electronic circuits and systems by genetic algorithms*. CRC press. doi:10.1201/9781420041590

Zheng, P., Wang, H., Sang, Z., Zhong, R. Y., Liu, Y., Liu, C., Mubarok, K., Yu, S., & Xu, X. (2018). Smart manufacturing systems for Industry 4.0: Conceptual framework, scenarios, and future perspectives. *Frontiers of Mechanical Engineering, 13*(2), 137–150. doi:10.1007/s11465-018-0499-5

Zhu, H., Luo, W., Ciesielski, P. N., Fang, Z., Zhu, J. Y., Henriksson, G., Himmel, M. E., & Hu, L. (2016). Wood-derived materials for green electronics, biological devices, and energy applications. *Chemical Reviews, 116*(16), 9305–9374. doi:10.1021/acs.chemrev.6b00225 PMID:27459699

Zipfel, J., Verworner, F., Fischer, M., Wieland, U., Kraus, M., & Zschech, P. (2023). Anomaly detection for industrial quality assurance: A comparative evaluation of unsupervised deep learning models. *Computers & Industrial Engineering, 177*, 109045. doi:10.1016/j.cie.2023.109045

Compilation of References

Abadi, E. A. J., Sahu, H., Javadpour, S. M., & Goharimanesh, M. (2022). Interpretable machine learning for developing high-performance organic solar cells. *Materials Today. Energy, 25*, 100969. doi:10.1016/j.mtener.2022.100969

Abbasi, A., & Kamal, M. M. (2020). Adopting Industry 4.0 technologies in citizens' electronic-engagement considering sustainability development. In *European, Mediterranean, and Middle Eastern Conference on Information Systems* (pp. 304-313). Springer, Cham.

Abbasnia, A., Yousefi, N., Mahvi, A. H., Nabizadeh, R., Radfard, M., Yousefi, M., & Alimohammadi, M. (2019). Evaluation of groundwater quality using water quality index and its suitability for assessing water for drinking and irrigation purposes: Case study of Sistan and Baluchistan province (Iran). *Human and Ecological Risk Assessment, 25*(4), 988–1005. doi:10.1080/10807039.2018.1458596

Abuzreda, A., Hamad, T., Elayatt, A., & Ahmad, I. (2023). A Review of Different Renewable Energy Resource s and Their Energy Efficiency Technologies. *Adn Envi Wa s Mana Rec, 6*(1), 384–389.

Acioli, C., Scavarda, A., & Reis, A. (2021). Applying Industry 4.0 technologies in the COVID–19 sustainable chains. *International Journal of Productivity and Performance Management, 70*(5), 988–1016. doi:10.1108/IJPPM-03-2020-0137

Adel, A. (2022). Future of industry 5.0 in society: Human-centric solutions, challenges and prospective research areas. *Journal of Cloud Computing (Heidelberg, Germany), 11*(1), 1–15. doi:10.1186/s13677-022-00314-5 PMID:36101900

Aderibigbe, J. K. (2022). Accentuating Society 5.0 New Normal: The Strategic Role of Industry 4.0 Collaborative Partnership and Emotional Resilience. In Agile Management and VUCA-RR: Opportunities and Threats in Industry 4.0 towards Society 5.0 (pp. 39-55). Emerald Publishing Limited.

Afzaal, H., Farooque, A. A., Esau, T. J., Schumann, A. W., Zaman, Q. U., Abbas, F., & Bos, M. (2023). Artificial neural modeling for precision agricultural water management practices. In *Precision Agriculture* (pp. 169–186). Elsevier. doi:10.1016/B978-0-443-18953-1.00005-2

Agrawal, A. V., Pitchai, R., Senthamaraikannan, C., Balaji, N. A., Sajithra, S., & Boopathi, S. (2023). Digital Education System During the COVID-19 Pandemic. In Using Assistive Technology for Inclusive Learning in K-12 Classrooms (pp. 104–126). IGI Global. doi:10.4018/978-1-6684-6424-3.ch005

Agrawal, A. V., Shashibhushan, G., Pradeep, S., Padhi, S. N., Sugumar, D., & Boopathi, S. (2024). Synergizing Artificial Intelligence, 5G, and Cloud Computing for Efficient Energy Conversion Using Agricultural Waste. In Practice, Progress, and Proficiency in Sustainability (pp. 475–497). IGI Global. doi:10.4018/979-8-3693-1186-8.ch026

Agrawal, R. (2011, June). Legal issues in cloud computing. *IndicThreads.*

Agrawal, A. V., Magulur, L. P., Priya, S. G., Kaur, A., Singh, G., & Boopathi, S. (2023). Smart Precision Agriculture Using IoT and WSN. In *Handbook of Research on Data Science and Cybersecurity Innovations in Industry 4.0 Technologies* (pp. 524–541). IGI Global. doi:10.4018/978-1-6684-8145-5.ch026

Agrawal, M., & Rajapatel, M. S. (2020). Global perspective on electric vehicle 2020. *International Journal of Engineering Research & Technology (Ahmedabad)*, *9*(1), 8–11.

Ahmad, T., Zhu, H., Zhang, D., Tariq, R., Bassam, A., Ullah, F., AlGhamdi, A. S., & Alshamrani, S. S. (2022). Energetics Systems and artificial intelligence: Applications of industry 4.0. *Energy Reports*, *8*, 334–361. doi:10.1016/j.egyr.2021.11.256

Ahmed, J., Mrugalska, B., & Akkaya, B. (2022). Agile management and VUCA 2.0 (VUCA-RR) during Industry 4.0. In Agile Management and VUCA-RR: Opportunities and Threats in Industry 4.0 towards Society 5.0 (pp. 13-26). Emerald Publishing Limited.

Akhtar, M. N., Shaikh, A. J., Khan, A., Awais, H., Bakar, E. A., & Othman, A. R. (2021). Smart Sensing with Edge Computing in Precision Agriculture for Soil Assessment and Heavy Metal Monitoring. *Agriculture*, *11*(6), 475. doi:10.3390/agriculture11060475

Akila, D., Bhaumik, A., Duraisamy, B., Suseendran, G., & Pal, S. (2021). Improved nature-inspired algorithms in cloud computing for load balancing. *Intelligent Computing and Innovation on Data Science Proceedings of ICTIDS*, *2021*, 547–558.

Akkaya, B., & Ahmed, J. (2022). VUCA-RR Toward Industry 5.0. In Agile Management and VUCA-RR: Opportunities and Threats in Industry 4.0 towards Society 5.0 (pp. 1-11). Emerald Publishing Limited.

Akkaya, B., Guah, M. W., Jermsittiparsert, K., Bulinska-Stangrecka, H., & Koçyiğit, Y. K. (Eds.). (2022). *Agile Management and VUCA-RR: Opportunities and Threats in Industry 4.0 towards Society 5.0*. Emerald Group Publishing.

Alankrita, S. (2020). *Application of AI in Renewable Energy*. IEEE. https://ieeexplore.ieee.org/document/9200065

Alaskari, O., Pinedo-Cuenca, R., & Ahmad, M. (2021). Framework for implementation of Enterprise Resource Planning (ERP) systems in small and medium enterprises (SMEs): A case study. *Procedia Manufacturing*, *55*, 424–430. doi:10.1016/j.promfg.2021.10.058

Al-Fuqaha, A., Guizani, M., Mohammadi, M., Aledhari, M., & Ayyash, M. (2015). Internet of things: A survey on enabling technologies, protocols, and applications. *IEEE Communications Surveys and Tutorials*, *17*(4), 2347–2376. doi:10.1109/COMST.2015.2444095

Ali, M., Bilal, K,. Khan, S., Veeravalli, B., Li, K., & Zomaya, A. (2018). DROPS: Division and Replication of Data in the Cloud for Optimal Performance and Security. *IEEE Transactions on Cloud Computing*. doi:10.1109/TCC.2015.2400460

Ali, S. A., & Alam, M. (2016, December). A relative study of task scheduling algorithms in cloud computing environment. In *2016 2nd International Conference on Contemporary Computing and Informatics (IC3I)* (pp. 105-111). IEEE. 10.1109/IC3I.2016.7917943

Ali, L., Sivaramakrishnan, K., Kuttiyathil, M. S., Chandrasekaran, V., Ahmed, O. H., Al-Harahsheh, M., & Altarawneh, M. (2023). Prediction of Thermogravimetric Data in Bromine Captured from Brominated Flame Retardants (BFRs) in e-Waste Treatment Using Machine Learning Approaches. *Journal of Chemical Information and Modeling*, *63*(8), 2305–2320. doi:10.1021/acs.jcim.3c00183 PMID:37036888

Ali, M. (2021). Vocational students' perception and readiness in facing globalization, industry revolution 4.0 and society 5.0. []. IOP Publishing.]. *Journal of Physics: Conference Series*, *1833*(1), 012050. doi:10.1088/1742-6596/1833/1/012050

Ali, M., Dhamotharan, R., Khan, E., Khan, S. U., Vasilakos, A. V., Li, K., & Zomaya, A. Y. (2015). SeDaSC: Secure data sharing in clouds. *IEEE Systems Journal*, *11*(2), 395–404. doi:10.1109/JSYST.2014.2379646

Ali, M., Khan, S. U., & Vasilakos, A. V. (2015). Security in cloud computing: Opportunities and challenges. *Information Sciences*, *305*, 357–383. doi:10.1016/j.ins.2015.01.025

Alimuzzaman, M. D. (2015). Agricultural drone. *Journal of Food Security*, *3*(5), 12–27.

Alshahrani, A., Omer, S., Su, Y., Mohamed, E., & Alotaibi, S. (2021). *The technical challenges facing the integration of small-scale and large-scale PV systems into the grid*. Science Direct. https://www.sciencedirect.com/science/article/abs/pii/S0038092X21004825

Alsharif, M. H., Jahid, A., Kelechi, A. H., & Kannadasan, R. (2023). Green IoT: A review and future research directions. *Symmetry*, *15*(3), 757. doi:10.3390/sym15030757

Altıntaş, H., & Kassouri, Y. (2020). The impact of energy technology innovations on cleaner energy supply and carbon footprints in Europe: A linear versus nonlinear approach. *Journal of Cleaner Production*, *276*, 124140. doi:10.1016/j.jclepro.2020.124140

Altun, K., Barshan, B., & Tunçel, O. (2010). Comparative study on classifying human activities with miniature inertial and magnetic sensors. *Pattern Recognition*, *43*(10), 3605–3620. doi:10.1016/j.patcog.2010.04.019

Al-Turjman, F. M. (2021). AI-powered cloud for COVID-19 and other infectious disease diagnosis. *Personal and Ubiquitous Computing*, *27*(3), 661–664. doi:10.1007/s00779-021-01625-1 PMID:34413717

Anand, A. (2002, January). ICTs: Empowering Women, Assisting Development. *Gender, Technology and Development*, *6*(1), 121–127. doi:10.1080/09718524.2002.11910017

Andeobu, L., Wibowo, S., & Grandhi, S. (2022, August). Artificial intelligence applications for sustainable solid waste management practices in Australia: A systematic review. *The Science of the Total Environment*, *834*, 155389. doi:10.1016/j.scitotenv.2022.155389 PMID:35460765

Andronie, M., Lăzăroiu, G., Iatagan, M., Hurloiu, I., & Dijmărescu, I. (2021). Sustainable cyber-physical production systems in big data-driven smart urban economy: A systematic literature review. *Sustainability (Basel)*, *13*(2), 751. doi:10.3390/su13020751

Anitha, C., Komala, C., Vivekanand, C. V., Lalitha, S., & Boopathi, S. (2023). Artificial Intelligence driven security model for Internet of Medical Things (IoMT). *IEEE Explore*, 1–7.

Anpalagan, A., Ejaz, W., Sharma, S. K., Da Costa, D. B., Jo, M., & Kim, J. (2021). Guest Editorial Special Issue on "Green Communication and Computing Technologies for 6G Networks" in IEEE. Transactions of the on Green Communications and Networking. *IEEE Transactions on Green Communications and Networking*, *5*(4), 1653–1656. doi:10.1109/TGCN.2021.3125233

Aqeel, I., Khormi, I. M., Khan, S. B., Shuaib, M., Almusharraf, A., Alam, S., & Alkhaldi, N. A. (2023). Load Balancing Using Artificial Intelligence for Cloud-Enabled Internet of Everything in Healthcare Domain. *Sensors (Basel)*, *23*(11), 5349. doi:10.3390/s23115349 PMID:37300076

Aquilani, B., Piccarozzi, M., Abbate, T., & Codini, A. (2020). The role of open innovation and value co-creation in the challenging transition from industry 4.0 to society 5.0: Toward a theoretical framework. *Sustainability (Basel)*, *12*(21), 8943. doi:10.3390/su12218943

Ascher, S., Watson, I., & You, S. (2022). Machine learning methods for modelling the gasification and pyrolysis of biomass and waste. *Renewable & Sustainable Energy Reviews*, *155*, 111902. doi:10.1016/j.rser.2021.111902

Atina, V. Z., Mahmudi, A. Y., & Abdillah, H. (2021). Industry Preparation In Ceper Klaten On Society 5.0. *International Journal of Economics, Business and Accounting Research (IJEBAR), 5*(2).

Atrey, A., Jain, N., & Iyengar, N. (2013). A study on green cloud computing. *International Journal of Grid and Distributed Computing, 6*(6), 93–102. doi:10.14257/ijgdc.2013.6.6.08

Atzori, L., Iera, A., & Morabito, G. (2017). Understanding the internet of things: Definition, potentials, and societal role of a fast evolving paradigm. *Ad Hoc Networks, 56*, 122–140. doi:10.1016/j.adhoc.2016.12.004

B, M. K., K, K. K., Sasikala, P., Sampath, B., Gopi, B., & Sundaram, S. (2024). Sustainable Green Energy Generation From Waste Water. In *Practice, Progress, and Proficiency in Sustainability* (pp. 440–463). IGI Global. doi:10.4018/979-8-3693-1186-8.ch024

Baabdullah, A. M., Alalwan, A. A., Slade, E. L., Raman, R., & Khatatneh, K. F. (2021). SMEs and artificial intelligence (AI): Antecedents and consequences of AI-based B2B practices. *Industrial Marketing Management, 98*, 255–270. doi:10.1016/j.indmarman.2021.09.003

Bachmann, N., Tripathi, S., Brunner, M., & Jodlbauer, H. (2022, February 22). The Contribution of Data-Driven Technologies in Achieving the Sustainable Development Goals. *Sustainability (Basel), 14*(5), 2497. doi:10.3390/su14052497

Bakıcı, T., Almirall, E., & Wareham, J. (2013). A smart city initiative: The case of Barcelona. *Journal of the Knowledge Economy, 4*(2), 135–148. doi:10.1007/s13132-012-0084-9

Balduzzi, M., Zaddach, J., Balzarotti, D., Kirda, E., & Loureiro, S. (2012, March). A security analysis of amazon's elastic compute cloud service. In *Proceedings of the 27th annual ACM symposium on applied computing* (pp. 1427-1434). ACM. 10.1145/2245276.2232005

Bartoloni, S., Calò, E., Marinelli, L., Pascucci, F., Dezi, L., Carayannis, E., Revel, G. M., & Gregori, G. L. (2022). Towards designing society 5.0 solutions: The new Quintuple Helix-Design Thinking approach to technology. *Technovation, 113*, 102413. doi:10.1016/j.technovation.2021.102413

Bauer, M., van Dinther, C., & Kiefer, D. (2020). *Machine learning in SME: an empirical study on enablers and success factors*. Research Gate.

Benedetti, M., Lloyd, E., Sack, S., & Fiorentini, M. (2019). Parameterized quantum circuits as machine learning models. *Quantum Science and Technology, 4*(4), 043001. doi:10.1088/2058-9565/ab4eb5

Bhadauria, R., Borgohain, R., Biswas, A., & Sanyal, S. (2013). Secure authentication of Cloud data mining API. *arXiv preprint arXiv:1308.0824.*

Bhargavi, K., & Babu, B. S. (2019, December). Load balancing scheme for the public cloud using reinforcement learning with raven roosting optimization policy (RROP). In *2019 4th International Conference on Computational Systems and Information Technology for Sustainable Solution (CSITSS)* (Vol. 4, pp. 1-6). IEEE.

Bhargavi, K., Sathish Babu, B., & Pitt, J. (2020). Performance modeling of load balancing techniques in cloud: Some of the recent competitive swarm artificial intelligence-based. *Journal of Intelligent Systems, 30*(1), 40–58. doi:10.1515/jisys-2019-0084

Bhat, J. R., & Alqahtani, S. A. (2021). 6G ecosystem: Current status and future perspective. *IEEE Access : Practical Innovations, Open Solutions, 9*, 43134–43167. doi:10.1109/ACCESS.2021.3054833

Bhattacharya, SMaddikunta, P. K. RSomayaji, S. R. KLakshmanna, KKaluri, RGadekallu, T. R. (2020). Load balancing of energy cloud using wind driven and firefly algorithms in internet of everything. *Journal of Parallel and Distributed Computing, 142*, 16–26. doi:10.1016/j.jpdc.2020.02.010

Bindhu, V., & Joe, M. (2019). Green cloud computing solution for operational cost efficiency and environmental impact reduction. *Journal of ISMAC*, *1*(02), 120–128.

Birje, M. N., Challagidad, P., Goudar, R. H., & Tapale, M. (2017). Cloud computing review: Concepts, technology, challenges and security. *International Journal of Cloud Computing (IJCC), Inderscience*, *6*(1), 32–57.

Boldrin, F., Taddia, C., & Mazzini, G. (2010). Web Distributed Computing Systems Implementation and Modeling. *International Journal of Adaptive, Resilient and Autonomic Systems*, *1*(1), 75–91. doi:10.4018/jaras.2010071705

Boobalan, C., & Kannaiyan, S. K. (2022). A correlation to predict the thermal conductivity of MXene-silicone oil based nano-fluids and data driven modeling using artificial neural networks. *International Journal of Energy Research*, *46*(15), 21538–21547. doi:10.1002/er.7786

Boopathi, S. (2021). Improving of Green Sand-Mould Quality using Taguchi Technique. *Journal of Engineering Research*.

Boopathi, S. (2023a). Deep Learning Techniques Applied for Automatic Sentence Generation. In Promoting Diversity, Equity, and Inclusion in Language Learning Environments (pp. 255–273). IGI Global. doi:10.4018/978-1-6684-3632-5.ch016

Boopathi, S., Kumar, P. K. S., Meena, R. S., Sudhakar, M., & Associates. (2023). Sustainable Developments of Modern Soil-Less Agro-Cultivation Systems: Aquaponic Culture. In Human Agro-Energy Optimization for Business and Industry (pp. 69–87). IGI Global.

Boopathi, S., Pandey, B. K., & Pandey, D. (2023). Advances in Artificial Intelligence for Image Processing: Techniques, Applications, and Optimization. In Handbook of Research on Thrust Technologies' Effect on Image Processing (pp. 73–95). IGI Global.

Boopathi, S. (2022). An investigation on gas emission concentration and relative emission rate of the near-dry wire-cut electrical discharge machining process. *Environmental Science and Pollution Research International*, *29*(57), 86237–86246. doi:10.1007/s11356-021-17658-1 PMID:34837614

Boopathi, S. (2023). Internet of Things-Integrated Remote Patient Monitoring System: Healthcare Application. In *Dynamics of Swarm Intelligence Health Analysis for the Next Generation* (pp. 137–161). IGI Global. doi:10.4018/978-1-6684-6894-4.ch008

Boopathi, S., & Davim, J. P. (2023). *Sustainable Utilization of Nanoparticles and Nanofluids in Engineering Applications*. IGI Global. doi:10.4018/978-1-6684-9135-5

Boopathi, S., & Kanike, U. K. (2023). Applications of Artificial Intelligent and Machine Learning Techniques in Image Processing. In *Handbook of Research on Thrust Technologies' Effect on Image Processing* (pp. 151–173). IGI Global. doi:10.4018/978-1-6684-8618-4.ch010

Boopathi, S., Saranya, A., Raghuraman, S., & Revanth, R. (2018). Design and Fabrication of Low Cost Electric Bicycle. *International Research Journal of Engineering and Technology*, *5*(3), 146–147.

Boopathi, S., Sureshkumar, M., & Sathiskumar, S. (2022). Parametric Optimization of LPG Refrigeration System Using Artificial Bee Colony Algorithm. *International Conference on Recent Advances in Mechanical Engineering Research and Development*, (pp. 97–105). IEEE.

Bourechak, A., Zedadra, O., Kouahla, M. N., Guerrieri, A., Seridi, H., & Fortino, G. (2023). At the Confluence of Artificial Intelligence and Edge Computing in IoT-Based Applications: A Review and New Perspectives. *Sensors (Basel)*, *23*(3), 1639. doi:10.3390/s23031639 PMID:36772680

Brandalero, M., Ali, M., Le Jeune, L., Hernandez, H. G. M., Veleski, M., Da Silva, B., Lemeire, J., Van Beeck, K., Touhafi, A., Goedemé, T., & ... (2020). Aitia: Embedded ai techniques for embedded industrial applications. *2020 International Conference on Omni-Layer Intelligent Systems (COINS)*, (pp. 1–7). IEEE. 10.1109/COINS49042.2020.9191672

Breque, M., De Nul, L., & Petridis, A. (2021). *Industry 5.0: towards a sustainable, human-centric and resilient European industry.*

Brishty, F. P., Urner, R., & Grau, G. (2022). Machine learning based data-driven inkjet printed electronics: Jetting prediction for novel inks. *Flexible and Printed Electronics*, *7*(1), 015009. doi:10.1088/2058-8585/ac5a39

Brown, N., & Sandholm, T. (2018, January 26). Superhuman AI for heads-up no-limit poker: Libratus beats top professionals. *Science*, *359*(6374), 418–424. doi:10.1126/science.aao1733 PMID:29249696

Caiado, R., Nascimento, D., Quelhas, O., Tortorella, G., & Rangel, L. (2018). Towards sustainability through green, lean and six sigma integration at service industry: Review and framework. *Technological and Economic Development of Economy*, *24*(4), 1659–1678. doi:10.3846/tede.2018.3119

Calp, M. H., & Bütüner, R. (2022). Society 5.0: Effective technology for a smart society. In Artificial Intelligence and Industry 4.0 (pp. 175-194). Academic Press.

Carayannis, E. G., Dezi, L., Gregori, G., & Calo, E. (2022b). Smart environments and techno-centric and human-centric innovations for Industry and Society 5.0: A quintuple helix innovation system view towards smart, sustainable, and inclusive solutions. *Journal of the Knowledge Economy*, *13*(2), 926–955. doi:10.1007/s13132-021-00763-4

Carayannis, E. G., Draper, J., & Bhaneja, B. (2021). Towards fusion energy in the Industry 5.0 and Society 5.0 context: Call for a global commission for urgent action on fusion energy. *Journal of the Knowledge Economy*, *12*(4), 1891–1904. doi:10.1007/s13132-020-00695-5

Carayannis, E. G., & Morawska-Jancelewicz, J. (2022a). The futures of Europe: Society 5.0 and Industry 5.0 as driving forces of future universities. *Journal of the Knowledge Economy*, *13*(4), 1–27. doi:10.1007/s13132-021-00854-2

Caro Anzola, E. W., & Mendoza Moreno, M. Á. (2021). Enhanced Living Environments (ELE): A Paradigm Based on Integration of Industry 4.0 and Society 5.0 Contexts with Ambient Assisted Living (AAL). In *International Workshop on Gerontechnology* (pp. 121-132). Springer, Cham. 10.1007/978-3-030-72567-9_12

Červený, L., Sloup, R., Červená, T., Riedl, M., & Palátová, P. (2022). Industry 4.0 as an Opportunity and Challenge for the Furniture Industry-A Case Study. *Sustainability (Basel)*, *14*(20), 13325. doi:10.3390/su142013325

Chaisiri, S., Lee, B. S., & Niyato, D. (2011). Optimization of resource provisioning cost in cloud computing. *IEEE Transactions on Services Computing*, *5*(2), 164–177. doi:10.1109/TSC.2011.7

Chan, C. C. (1993). An overview of electric vehicle technology. *Proceedings of the IEEE*, *81*(9), 1202–1213. doi:10.1109/5.237530

Chandola, V., Banerjee, A., & Kumar, V. (2009). Anomaly detection: A survey. *ACM Computing Surveys*, *41*(3), 1–58. doi:10.1145/1541880.1541882

Chandramouli, R., Iorga, M., & Chokhani, S. (2013). Cryptographic key management issues and challenges in cloud services. *Secure Cloud Computing*, 1-30.

Chandrika, V., Sivakumar, A., Krishnan, T. S., Pradeep, J., Manikandan, S., & Boopathi, S. (2023). Theoretical Study on Power Distribution Systems for Electric Vehicles. In *Intelligent Engineering Applications and Applied Sciences for Sustainability* (pp. 1–19). IGI Global. doi:10.4018/979-8-3693-0044-2.ch001

Chapman, D. (2021). Environmentally sustainable urban development and internet of things connected sensors in cognitive smart cities. *Geopolitics, History, and International Relations, 13*(2), 51–64. doi:10.22381/GHIR13220214

Chaudhuri, R., Chatterjee, S., Vrontis, D., & Chaudhuri, S. (2022). Innovation in SMEs, AI dynamism, and sustainability: The current situation and way forward. *Sustainability (Basel), 14*(19), 12760. doi:10.3390/su141912760

Chavan, R. (2015, November). A Review on Secure Methodology Fragmentation and Replication of data in Cloud for Data Secrecy and Ideal Performance. *International Journal of Advanced Research in Computer Engineering and Technology, 4*(11).

Chavhan, S., Gupta, D., Gochhayat, S., & Khanna, A. (2022). Edge Computing AI-IoT Integrated Energy-efficient Intelligent Transportation System for Smart Cities. *ACM Transactions on Internet Technology, 22*(4), 1–18. doi:10.1145/3507906

Che, J., Duan, Y., Zhang, T., & Fan, J. (2011). Study on the security models and strategies of cloud computing. *Procedia Engineering, 23*, 586-593.

Chen Liu, A. C., Law, O. M. K., Liao, J., & Chen, J. Y. C. (2021). *Traffic Safety System Edge AI Computing. 2021 IEEE/ACM Symposium on Edge Computing (SEC)*, San Jose, CA, USA. doi:10.1145/3453142.3491410

Chen, D., & Zhao, H. (2012, March). *Data security and privacy protection issues in cloud computing. In 2012 international conference on computer science and electronics engineering* (Vol. 1). IEEE.

Chen, G., Mao, Y., & Charles, K. (2004). Chui, A symmetric image encryption scheme based on 3D chaotic cat maps. *Chaos, Solitons, and Fractals, 21*(3), 749–761. doi:10.1016/j.chaos.2003.12.022

Chhabra, A., Huang, K. C., Bacanin, N., & Rashid, T. A. (2022). Optimizing bag-of-tasks scheduling on cloud data centers using hybrid swarm-intelligence meta-heuristic. *The Journal of Supercomputing, 78*(7), 1–63. doi:10.1007/s11227-021-04199-0

Chhowalla, M., Shin, H. S., Eda, G., Li, L. J., Loh, K. P., & Zhang, H. (2013). The chemistry of two-dimensional layered transition metal dichalcogenide nanosheets. *Nature Chemistry, 5*(4), 263–275. doi:10.1038/nchem.1589 PMID:23511414

Chin, R. T., & Harlow, C. A. (1982). Automated visual inspection: A survey. *IEEE Transactions on Pattern Analysis and Machine Intelligence, PAMI-4*(6), 557–573. doi:10.1109/TPAMI.1982.4767309 PMID:22499630

Chong, C. T., Van Fan, Y., Lee, C. T., & Klemeš, J. J. (2022). Post COVID-19 ENERGY sustainability and carbon emissions neutrality. *Energy, 241*, 122801. doi:10.1016/j.energy.2021.122801 PMID:36570560

Cioffi, R., Travaglioni, M., Piscitelli, G., Petrillo, A., & De Felice, F. (2020). Artificial intelligence and machine learning applications in smart production: Progress, trends, and directions. *Sustainability (Basel), 12*(2), 492. doi:10.3390/su12020492

Cohn, P., Green, A., Langstaff, M., & Roller, M. (2017). *Commercial drones are here: The future of unmanned aerial systems*. McKinsey & Company.

Cotta, J., Breque, M., De Nul, L., & Petridis, A. (2021). *Industry 5.0: towards a sustainable, human-centric and resilient European industry. European Commission Research and Innovation (R&I)*. Series Policy Brief.

Coumans, F. (2018). Smart Factories Need Space and Time Anchors. *GIM International – the worldwide magazine for geoinformatics*.

Cowan, R., & Hultén, S. (1996). Escaping lock-in: The case of the electric vehicle. *Technological Forecasting and Social Change, 53*(1), 61–79. doi:10.1016/0040-1625(96)00059-5

Crockett, K. A., Gerber, L., Latham, A., & Colyer, E. (2021). Building trustworthy AI solutions: A case for practical solutions for small businesses. *IEEE Transactions on Artificial Intelligence*.

Csiszer, A. (2022). Towards Society 5.0 in Perspective of Agile Society. In Agile Management and VUCA-RR: Opportunities and Threats in Industry 4.0 towards Society 5.0 (pp. 169-190). Emerald Publishing Limited.

Czimmermann, T., Ciuti, G., Milazzo, M., Chiurazzi, M., Roccella, S., Oddo, C. M., & Dario, P. (2020). Visual-based defect detection and classification approaches for industrial applications—A survey. *Sensors (Basel)*, 20(5), 1459. doi:10.3390/s20051459 PMID:32155900

Daly, A., Hagendorff, T., Li, H., Mann, M., Marda, V., Wagner, B., Wang, W., & Witteborn, S. (2019). Artificial Intelligence, Governance and Ethics: Global Perspectives. SSRN *Electronic Journal*. doi:10.2139/ssrn.3414805

Danna, E., Mandal, S., & Singh, A. (2012, March). *A practical algorithm for balancing the max-min fairness and throughput objectives in traffic engineering. In 2012 Proceedings IEEE INFOCOM*. IEEE.

Danowitz, A. (2010). *Solar Thermal vs. Photovoltaic*. Stanford Press. http://large.stanford.edu/courses/2010/ph240/danowitz2/ https://www.nrel.gov/grid/solar-resource/renewable-resource-data.html?utm_medium=print&utm_source=grid&utm_campaign=rredc

Darsana, I. M., & Sudjana, I. M. (2022). A Literature Study of Indonesian Tourism Human Resources Development in the Era of Society 5.0. *Al-Ishlah: Jurnal Pendidikan*, 14(3), 2691–2700. doi:10.35445/alishlah.v14i3.2014

Dassisti, M., Siragusa, N., & Semeraro, C. (2018). Exergetic model as a guideline for implementing the smart-factory paradigm in small medium enterprises: The brovedani case. *Procedia CIRP*, 67, 534–539. doi:10.1016/j.procir.2017.12.256

Dautaj, M., & Rossi, M. (2021). Towards a New Society: Solving the Dilemma Between Society 5.0 and Industry 5.0. In *IFIP International Conference on Product Lifecycle Management* (pp. 523-536). Springer, Cham.

Dayarathna, M., Wen, Y., & Fan, R. (2015). Data center energy consumption modeling: A survey. *IEEE Communications Surveys and Tutorials*, 18(1), 732–794. doi:10.1109/COMST.2015.2481183

Debauche, O., Saïd, M., Mahmoudi, S., Manneback, P., Bindelle, J., & Lebeau, F. (2020). Edge Computing and Artificial Intelligence for Real-time Poultry Monitoring. *Procedia Computer Science*, 175, 534–541. doi:10.1016/j.procs.2020.07.076

Dellosa, J. (2021). *AI in Renewable Energy Systems*. IEEE. https://ieeexplore.ieee.org/document/9584587

Deng, S., Zhao, H., Fang, W., Yin, J., Dustdar, S., & Zomaya, A. (2019). *Edge Intelligence: The Confluence of Edge Computing and Artificial Intelligence*.

Deng, Z., Wang, X., Jiang, Z., Zhou, N., Ge, H., & Dong, B. (2023). Evaluation of deploying data-driven predictive controls in buildings on a large scale for greenhouse gas emission reduction. *Energy*, 270, 126934. doi:10.1016/j.energy.2023.126934

Devaraj, A. F. S., Elhoseny, M., Dhanasekaran, S., Lydia, E. L., & Shankar, K. (2020). Hybridization of firefly and improved multi-objective particle swarm optimization algorithm for energy efficient load balancing in cloud computing environments. *Journal of Parallel and Distributed Computing*, 142, 36–45. doi:10.1016/j.jpdc.2020.03.022

Dewan, M., Mudgal, A., Pandey, P., Raghav, Y. Y., & Gupta, T. (2023). Predicting Pregnancy Complications Using Machine Learning. In D. Kumar & P. Maniiarasan (Eds.), *Technological Tools for Predicting Pregnancy Complications* (pp. 141–160). IGI Global. doi:10.4018/979-8-3693-1718-1.ch008

Dhanya, D., Kumar, S. S., Thilagavathy, A., Prasad, D., & Boopathi, S. (2023). Data Analytics and Artificial Intelligence in the Circular Economy: Case Studies. In Intelligent Engineering Applications and Applied Sciences for Sustainability (pp. 40–58). IGI Global.

Dharmaraj, V., & Vijayanand, C. (2018). Artificial intelligence (AI) in agriculture. *International Journal of Current Microbiology and Applied Sciences*, 7(12), 2122–2128. doi:10.20546/ijcmas.2018.712.241

Dhar, P. (2020). The carbon impact of artificial intelligence. *Nature Machine Intelligence*, 2(8), 423–425. doi:10.1038/s42256-020-0219-9

Di Franco, G., & Santurro, M. (2021). Machine learning, artificial neural networks and social research. *Quality & Quantity*, 55(3), 1007–1025. doi:10.1007/s11135-020-01037-y

Di Nardo, M., & Yu, H. (2021). Special issue "Industry 5.0: The prelude to the sixth industrial revolution". *Applied System Innovation*, 4(3), 45. doi:10.3390/asi4030045

Dib, R., Zervos, A., Eckhart, M., David, M.E.A., Kirsty, H., & Peter, H. (2021). Governments, R.; Bariloche, F. Renewables 2021 Global Status Report. *REN21 Renewables Now*.

Ding, N., Prasad, K., & Lie, T. T. (2017). The electric vehicle: A review. *International Journal of Electric and Hybrid Vehicles*, 9(1), 49–66. doi:10.1504/IJEHV.2017.082816

Dinh, H. T., Lee, C., Niyato, D., & Wang, P. (2013). A survey of mobile cloud computing: Architecture, applications, and approaches. *Wireless Communications and Mobile Computing*, 13(18), 1587–1611. doi:10.1002/wcm.1203

Domakonda, V. K., Farooq, S., Chinthamreddy, S., Puviarasi, R., Sudhakar, M., & Boopathi, S. (2022). Sustainable Developments of Hybrid Floating Solar Power Plants: Photovoltaic System. In Human Agro-Energy Optimization for Business and Industry (pp. 148–167). IGI Global.

Dumitru, I. (2016). Grid Computing: Enabled Resource Management Models. In I. Management Association (Ed.), Project Management: Concepts, Methodologies, Tools, and Applications (pp. 2290-2303). IGI Global. doi:10.4018/978-1-5225-0196-1.ch114

Durairaj, M., Jayakumar, S., Karpagavalli, V., Maheswari, B. U., Boopathi, S., & ... (2023). Utilization of Digital Tools in the Indian Higher Education System During Health Crises. In *Multidisciplinary Approaches to Organizational Governance During Health Crises* (pp. 1–21). IGI Global. doi:10.4018/978-1-7998-9213-7.ch001

Dwijendra, N. K. A., Sharma, S., Asary, A. R., Majdi, A., Muda, I., Mutlak, D. A., Parra, R. M. R., & Hammid, A. T. (2022). Economic performance of a hybrid renewable energy system with optimal design of resources. *Environmental and Climate Technologies*, 26(1), 441–453. doi:10.2478/rtuect-2022-0034

Eberle, U., & Von Helmolt, R. (2010). Sustainable transportation based on electric vehicle concepts: A brief overview. *Energy & Environmental Science*, 3(6), 689–699. doi:10.1039/c001674h

Eghtesadi, A., Jarraya, Y., Debbabi, M., & Pourzandi, M. (2014, March). Preservation of security configurations in the cloud. In *2014 IEEE International Conference on Cloud Engineering* (pp. 17-26). IEEE. 10.1109/IC2E.2014.14

Ehwanudin, E., Irhamudin, I., & Wijaya, A. (2022). Relevansi Konsep Pendidikan Aswaja Anahdliyah Era Industry 4.0 dan Society 5.0 di Pendidikan Tinggi Islam. *Berkala Ilmiah Pendidikan*, 2(2), 94–104. doi:10.51214/bip.v2i2.420

Elgendy, N., & Elragal, A. (2014). Big data analytics: a literature review paper. In *Advances in Data Mining. Applications and Theoretical Aspects: 14th Industrial Conference*. Springer International Publishing.

Elim, H. I., & Zhai, G. (2020). Control system of multitasking interactions between society 5.0 and industry 5.0: A conceptual introduction & its applications. []. IOP Publishing.]. *Journal of Physics: Conference Series, 1463*(1), 012035. doi:10.1088/1742-6596/1463/1/012035

Ellitan, L. (2020). Competing in the era of industrial revolution 4.0 and society 5.0. *Jurnal Maksipreneur: Manajemen, Koperasi, dan Entrepreneurship, 10*(1), 1-12.

Elmagzoub, M. A., Syed, D., Shaikh, A., Islam, N., Alghamdi, A., & Rizwan, S. (2021). A survey of swarm intelligence based load balancing techniques in cloud computing environment. *Electronics (Basel), 10*(21), 2718. doi:10.3390/electronics10212718

Elsevier. (n.d.). *Forthcoming Special Issues.* Elesvier.https://www.journals.elsevier.com/environmental-challenges/forthcoming-special-issues/artificial-intelligence-applications-for-green-energy-systems

Entezari, A., Aslani, A., Zahedi, R., & Noorollahi, Y. (2023). Artificial intelligence and machine learning in energy systems: A bibliographic perspective. *Energy Strategy Reviews, 45*, 101017. doi:10.1016/j.esr.2022.101017

Eriksson, N. (2018). *Conceptual study of a future drone detection system-Countering a threat posed by a disruptive technology.*

Esmaeilian, B., Wang, B., Lewis, K., Duarte, F., Ratti, C., & Behdad, S. (2018). The future of waste management in smart and sustainable cities: A review and concept paper. *Waste Management, 81*, 177-195.

Etezadi-Amoli, M., Choma, K., & Stefani, J. (2010). Rapid-charge electric-vehicle stations. *IEEE Transactions on Power Delivery, 25*(3), 1883–1887. doi:10.1109/TPWRD.2010.2047874

Fakhar, A., Haidar, A. M. A., Abdullah, M. O., & Das, N. (2023). Smart grid mechanism for green energy management: A comprehensive review. *International Journal of Green Energy, 20*(3), 284–308. doi:10.1080/15435075.2022.2038610

Fanariotis, A., Orphanoudakis, T., Kotrotsios, K., Fotopoulos, V., Keramidas, G., & Karkazis, P. (2023). Power Efficient Machine Learning Models Deployment on Edge IoT Devices. *Sensors (Basel), 23*(3), 1595. doi:10.3390/s23031595 PMID:36772635

Fang, Y., Wang, F., & Ge, J. (2010, OKaur, B., & Singh, R. (2016). A comparison and analysis of load balancing algorithms in cloud computing. *Adv Comput Sci Technol, 9*(1).

Fang, K., & Shen, C. (2020). Near-real-time forecast of satellite-based soil moisture using long short-term memory with an adaptive data integration kernel. *Journal of Hydrometeorology, 21*(3), 399–413. doi:10.1175/JHM-D-19-0169.1

Fang, W., Love, P. E., Luo, H., & Ding, L. (2020). Computer vision for behaviour-based safety in construction: A review and future directions. *Advanced Engineering Informatics, 43*, 100980. doi:10.1016/j.aei.2019.100980

Favaretto, M., De Clercq, E., & Elger, B. S. (2019, February 5). Big Data and discrimination: Perils, promises and solutions. A systematic review. *Journal of Big Data, 6*(1), 12. doi:10.1186/s40537-019-0177-4

Fernandes, D. A., Soares, L. F., Gomes, J. V., Freire, M. M., & Inácio, P. R. (2014). Security issues in cloud environments: A survey. *International Journal of Information Security, 13*(2), 113–170. doi:10.1007/s10207-013-0208-7

Fernando, Y., Jabbour, C. J. C., & Wah, W. X. (2019). Pursuing green growth in technology firms through the connections between environmental innovation and sustainable business performance: Does service capability matter? *Resources, Conservation and Recycling, 141*, 8–20. doi:10.1016/j.resconrec.2018.09.031

Fernando, Y., Saedan, R., Shaharudin, M. S., & Mohamed, A. (2021). Integrity in halal food supply chain towards the society 5.0. *Journal of Governance and Integrity, 4*(2), 103–114. doi:10.15282/jgi.4.2.2021.5948

Ferreira, C. M., & Serpa, S. (2018). Society 5.0 and social development. *Management and Organizational Studies, 5*(4), 26–31. doi:10.5430/mos.v5n4p26

Ferrero Bermejo, J., Gómez Fernández, J. F., Olivencia Polo, F., & Crespo Márquez, A. (2019). A review of the use of artificial neural network models for energy and reliability prediction. A study of the solar PV, hydraulic and wind energy sources. *Applied Sciences (Basel, Switzerland), 9*(9), 1844. doi:10.3390/app9091844

Ficco, M., & Rak, M. (2014). Stealthy denial of service strategy in cloud computing. *IEEE Transactions on Cloud Computing, 3*(1), 80–94. doi:10.1109/TCC.2014.2325045

Foster, I. (2008). Cloud computing and grid computing 360 degrees compared. In *Grid Computing Environments Workshop*. IEEE.

Fowziya, S., Sivaranjani, S., Devi, N. L., Boopathi, S., Thakur, S., & Sailaja, J. M. (2023). Influences of nano-green lubricants in the friction-stir process of TiAlN coated alloys. *Materials Today: Proceedings*. Advance online publication. doi:10.1016/j.matpr.2023.06.446

Fox, S. J. (2019). Policing-the technological revolution: Opportunities & challenges! *Technology in Society, 56*, 69–78. doi:10.1016/j.techsoc.2018.09.006

Fraga-Lamas, P., Lopes, S. I., & Fernández-Caramés, T. M. (2021). Green IoT and edge AI as key technological enablers for a sustainable digital transition towards a smart circular economy: An industry 5.0 use case. *Sensors (Basel), 21*(17), 5745. doi:10.3390/s21175745 PMID:34502637

Frederico, G. F. (2021). From supply chain 4.0 to supply chain 5.0: Findings from a systematic literature review and research directions. *Logistics, 5*(3), 49. doi:10.3390/logistics5030049

Fukuda, K. (2020). Science, technology and innovation ecosystem transformation toward society 5.0. *International Journal of Production Economics, 220*, 107460. doi:10.1016/j.ijpe.2019.07.033

Gea, T., Paradells, J., Lamarca, M., & Roldan, D. (2013, July). Smart cities as an application of internet of things: Experiences and lessons learnt in barcelona. In *2013 Seventh International Conference on Innovative Mobile and Internet Services in Ubiquitous Computing* (pp. 552-557). IEEE. 10.1109/IMIS.2013.158

Geeks for Geeks. (n.d.). *Load Balancing in Cloud Computing*. GfG, https://www.geeksforgeeks.org/load-balancing-in-cloud-computing/

Geetha, P., & Robin, C. R. (2017, August). A comparative-study of load-cloud balancing algorithms in cloud environments. In *2017 International Conference on Energy, Communication, Data Analytics and Soft Computing (ICECDS)* (pp. 806-810). IEEE. 10.1109/ICECDS.2017.8389549

Gera, B., Raghuvanshi, Y. S., Rawlley, O., Gupta, S., Dua, A., & Sharma, P. (2023). Leveraging AI-enabled 6G-driven IoT for sustainable smart cities. *International Journal of Communication Systems, 36*(16), e5588. doi:10.1002/dac.5588

Getov, V. (2013). Cloud adoption issues: Interoperability and security. *Clouds Big Data Data-intensive Comput., 23*, 53–65.

Ghani, I., Niknejad, N., & Jeong, S. R. (2015). Energy saving in green cloud computing data centers: A review. *Journal of Theoretical and Applied Information Technology, 74*(1).

Ghumman, N. (2015). Dynamic combination of improved max-min and ant colony algorithm for load balancing in cloud system. In *Conference on Computing, Communication and Networking Technologies (ICCCNT)*. IEEE.

Gibbs, M. & Kanjo, E. (2023). *Realising the Power of Edge Intelligence: Addressing the Challenges in AI and tiny ML Applications for Edge Computing*.

Gill, S. S., Tuli, S., Xu, M., Singh, I., Singh, K. V., Lindsay, D., Tuli, S., Smirnova, D., Singh, M., Jain, U., Pervaiz, H., Sehgal, B., Kaila, S. S., Misra, S., Aslanpour, M. S., Mehta, H., Stankovski, V., & Garraghan, P. (2019). Transformative effects of IoT, Blockchain and Artificial Intelligence on cloud computing: Evolution, vision, trends and open challenges. *Internet of Things : Engineering Cyber Physical Human Systems, 8*, 100118. doi:10.1016/j.iot.2019.100118

Gill, S. S., Xu, M., Ottaviani, C., Patros, P., Bahsoon, R., Shaghaghi, A., Golec, M., Stankovski, V., Wu, H., Abraham, A., Singh, M., Mehta, H., Ghosh, S. K., Baker, T., Parlikad, A. K., Lutfiyya, H., Kanhere, S. S., Sakellariou, R., Dustdar, S., & Uhlig, S. (2022). AI for next generation computing: Emerging trends and future directions. *Internet of Things : Engineering Cyber Physical Human Systems, 19*, 100514. doi:10.1016/j.iot.2022.100514

Gladden, M. E. (2019). Who will be the members of Society 5.0? Towards an anthropology of technologically posthumanized future societies. *Social Sciences (Basel, Switzerland), 8*(5), 148. doi:10.3390/socsci8050148

Gnanaprakasam, C., Vankara, J., Sastry, A. S., Prajval, V., Gireesh, N., & Boopathi, S. (2023). Long-Range and Low-Power Automated Soil Irrigation System Using Internet of Things: An Experimental Study. In Contemporary Developments in Agricultural Cyber-Physical Systems (pp. 87–104). IGI Global.

Gong, T., Zhu, L., Yu, F. R., & Tang, T. (2023). Edge Intelligence in Intelligent Transportation Systems: A Survey, 2023. IEEE Transactions on Intelligent Transportation Systems. IEEE. doi:10.1109/TITS.2023.3275741

Gong, K., Yang, J., Wang, X., Jiang, C., Xiong, Z., Zhang, M., Guo, M., Lv, R., Wang, S., & Zhang, S. (2022). Comprehensive review of modeling, structure, and integration techniques of smart buildings in the cyber-physical-social system. *Frontiers in Energy, 16*(1), 1–21. doi:10.1007/s11708-021-0792-6

Gonzalez, N., Miers, C., Redigolo, F., Simplicio, M., Carvalho, T., Näslund, M., & Pourzandi, M. (2012). A quantitative analysis of current security concerns and solutions for cloud computing. *Journal of Cloud Computing: Advances. Systems and Applications, 1*, 1–18.

Gowry, S. (2012). *Paramasivam, Cryptography in Microsoft.NET*. C-Sharp Corner. https://www.c-sharpcorner.com/article/cryptography-in-microsoft-net-part-i-encryption

Goyal, S., Bhushan, S., Kumar, Y., Rana, A. U. H. S., Bhutta, M. R., Ijaz, M. F., & Son, Y. (2021). An optimized framework for energy-resource allocation in a cloud environment based on the whale optimization algorithm. *Sensors (Basel), 21*(5), 1583. doi:10.3390/s21051583 PMID:33668282

Goyal, Y., Arya, M. S., & Nagpal, S. (2015, October). Energy efficient hybrid policy in green cloud computing. In *2015 International Conference on Green Computing and Internet of Things (ICGCIoT)* (pp. 1065-1069). IEEE. 10.1109/ICGCIoT.2015.7380621

Grashof, N., & Kopka, A. (2023). Artificial intelligence and radical innovation: An opportunity for all companies? *Small Business Economics, 61*(2), 771–797. doi:10.1007/s11187-022-00698-3

Gubbi, J., Buyya, R., Marusic, S., & Palaniswami, M. (2013). Internet of things (IoT): A vision, architectural elements, and future directions. *Future Generation Computer Systems, 29*(7), 1645–1660. doi:10.1016/j.future.2013.01.010

Gunasekaran, K., & Boopathi, S. (2023). Artificial Intelligence in Water Treatments and Water Resource Assessments. In *Artificial Intelligence Applications in Water Treatment and Water Resource Management* (pp. 71–98). IGI Global. doi:10.4018/978-1-6684-6791-6.ch004

Guo, L., Mu, S., Deng, Y., Shi, C., Yan, B., & Xiao, Z. (2023). Efficient Binary Weight Convolutional Network Accelerator for Speech Recognition. *Sensors (Basel), 23*(3), 1530. doi:10.3390/s23031530 PMID:36772567

Guo, Y., Xia, X., Zhang, S., & Zhang, D. (2018). Environmental regulation, government R&D funding and green technology innovation: Evidence from China provincial data. *Sustainability (Basel)*, *10*(4), 940. doi:10.3390/su10040940

Gupta, A. K. (2015). Cloud Computing: Concepts and Challenges. *Asian Journal of Computer Science and Technology*, *4*(2), 27-30.

Han, H., & Trimi, S. (2022). Towards a data science platform for improving SME collaboration through Industry 4.0 technologies. *Technological Forecasting and Social Change*, *174*, 121242. doi:10.1016/j.techfore.2021.121242

Hannan, E., & Liu, S. (2021, August 9). AI: New source of competitiveness in higher education. *Competitiveness Review*, *33*(2), 265–279. doi:10.1108/CR-03-2021-0045

Hanumanthakari, S., Gift, M. M., Kanimozhi, K., Bhavani, M. D., Bamane, K. D., & Boopathi, S. (2023). Biomining Method to Extract Metal Components Using Computer-Printed Circuit Board E-Waste. In *Handbook of Research on Safe Disposal Methods of Municipal Solid Wastes for a Sustainable Environment* (pp. 123–141). IGI Global. doi:10.4018/978-1-6684-8117-2.ch010

Hao, T., Hwang, K., Zhan, J., Li, Y., & Cao, Y. (2022). Scenario-based AI Benchmark Evaluation of Distributed Cloud/Edge Computing Systems. *IEEE Transactions on Computers*. IEEE. . doi:10.1109/TC.2022.3176803

Hao, T., Zhan, J., Hwang, K., Gao, W., & Wen, X. (2020). *AI-oriented Medical Workload Allocation for Hierarchical Cloud/Edge/Device Computing*.

Harayama, Y., & Fukuyama, M. (2017). *Society 5.0: Aiming for a new human-centered society Japan's science and technology policies for addressing global social challenges*. Hitachi. https://www.hitachi.com/rev/archive/2017/r2017_06/trends/ index.html

Harika, A. V., Haleema, P. K., Subalakshmi, R. J., & Iyengar, N. Ch. S. N. (2014). Quality-based solution for adaptable and scalable access control in cloud computing. *International Journal of Grid and Distributed Computing*, *7*(6), 137–148. doi:10.14257/ijgdc.2014.7.6.11

Hashizume, K., Rosado, D. G., Fernández-Medina, E., & Fernandez, E. B. (2013). An analysis of security issues for cloud computing. *Journal of Internet Services and Applications*, *4*(1), 1–13. doi:10.1186/1869-0238-4-5

Hassan, R., Qamar, F., Hasan, M. K., Aman, A. H. M., & Ahmed, A. S. (2020). Internet of Things and its applications: A comprehensive survey. *Symmetry*, *12*(10), 1674. doi:10.3390/sym12101674

Haupt, S. (2020). *Applications of Artificial Intelligence in Renewable Energy*. Energies. https://www.mdpi.com/journal/energies/special_issues/Artificial_Intelligence_Renewable_Energy

Hay, B., Nance, K., & Bishop, M. (2011, January). Storm clouds rising: security challenges for IaaS cloud computing. In *2011 44th Hawaii International Conference on System Sciences* (pp. 1-7). IEEE. 10.1109/HICSS.2011.386

Hellegers, P. J. G. J., & Perry, C. J. (2006). Can irrigation water use be guided by market forces? Theory and practice. *Water: Research and Development*, *22*(1), 79–86.

Hema, N., Krishnamoorthy, N., Chavan, S. M., Kumar, N., Sabarimuthu, M., & Boopathi, S. (2023). A Study on an Internet of Things (IoT)-Enabled Smart Solar Grid System. In *Handbook of Research on Deep Learning Techniques for Cloud-Based Industrial IoT* (pp. 290–308). IGI Global. doi:10.4018/978-1-6684-8098-4.ch017

Hoque, M., Farhad, S. S. B., Dewanjee, S., Alom, Z., Mokhtar, R. A., Saeed, R. A., Khalifa, O. O., Ali, E. S., & Abdul Azim, M. A. (2022). Green communication in 6G. doi:10.1049/icp.2022.2273

Huang, S., Wang, B., Li, X., Zheng, P., Mourtzis, D., & Wang, L. (2022). Industry 5.0 and Society 5.0—Comparison, complementation and co-evolution. *Journal of Manufacturing Systems, 64*, 424–428. doi:10.1016/j.jmsy.2022.07.010

Huang, X., Hong, S. H., Yu, M., Ding, Y., & Jiang, J. (2019). Demand response management for industrial facilities: A deep reinforcement learning approach. *IEEE Access : Practical Innovations, Open Solutions, 7*, 82194–82205. doi:10.1109/ACCESS.2019.2924030

Hussain, Z., & Srimathy, G. (2023). *IoT and AI Integration for Enhanced Efficiency and Sustainability.*

Hussain, Z., & Srimathy, G. (2023). *IoT and AI Integration for Enhanced Efficiency and Sustainability.* Research Gate.

Huth, A., & Cebula, J. (2011). The basics of cloud computing. *United States Computer*, 1-4.

Hwang, K., Fox, G., & Dongarra, J. (2010). *Distributed Systems and Cloud Computing: Clusters, Grids/P2P, and Internet Clouds.* Morgan Kaufmann.

Hwang, K., Kulkarni, S., & Hu, Y. (2009). Cloud Security with Virtualized Defence and Reputation-Based Trust Management. *IEEE Int'l Conf. Dependable, Autonomic, and Secure Computing (DASC 09).* IEEE CS Press.

Hwang, K., & Li, D. (2010, September-October). Trusted Cloud Computing with Secure Resources and Data Colouring. *IEEE Internet Computing, 14*(5), 14–22. doi:10.1109/MIC.2010.86

Ibrahim, E., El-Bahnasawy, N. A., & Omara, F. A. (2016, March). Task scheduling algorithm in cloud computing environment based on cloud pricing models. In *2016 World Symposium on Computer Applications & Research (WSCAR)* (pp. 65-71). IEEE. 10.1109/WSCAR.2016.20

Ingle, R. B., Senthil, T. S., Swathi, S., Muralidharan, N., Mahendran, G., & Boopathi, S. (2023). Sustainability and Optimization of Green and Lean Manufacturing Processes Using Machine Learning Techniques. In IGI Global. doi:10.4018/978-1-6684-8238-4.ch012

Ionescu, L. (2019). Big data, blockchain, and artificial intelligence in cloud-based accounting information systems. *Analysis and Metaphysics*, (18), 44–49.

Irena International Renewable Energy Agency. (n.d.). *Future of Solar Photovoltaic Deployment, Investment, Technology, Grid Integration and Socio-Economic Aspects.* MDPI. https://www.mdpi.com/2076-3417/12/19/10056 https://solarbuildermag.com/wp-content/uploads/2023/02/robot-AI-solar-panels.jpg

Irimia-Vladu, M. (2014). "Green" electronics: Biodegradable and biocompatible materials and devices for a sustainable future. *Chemical Society Reviews, 43*(2), 588–610. doi:10.1039/C3CS60235D PMID:24121237

Islam, A., Islam, M., Hossain Uzir, M. U., Abd Wahab, S., & Abdul Latiff, A. S. (2020). The panorama between COVID-19 pandemic and Artificial Intelligence (AI): Can it be the catalyst for Society 5.0. *International Journal of Scientific Research and Management, 8*(12), 2011–2025. doi:10.18535/ijsrm/v8i12.em02

Issa, M., Ilinca, A., & Martini, F. (2022). Ship energy efficiency and maritime sector initiatives to reduce carbon emissions. *Energies, 15*(21), 7910. doi:10.3390/en15217910

Jain, A., Mishra, M., Peddoju, S. K., & Jain, N. (2013, April). *Energy efficient computing-green cloud computing. In 2013 international conference on energy efficient technologies for sustainability.* IEEE.

Jana, R. K., Ghosh, I., Das, D., & Dutta, A. (2021). Determinants of electronic waste generation in Bitcoin network: Evidence from the machine learning approach. *Technological Forecasting and Social Change, 173*, 121101. doi:10.1016/j.techfore.2021.121101

Jansen, W. A. (2011, January). Cloud hooks: Security and privacy issues in cloud computing. In *2011 44th Hawaii International Conference on System Sciences* (pp. 1-10). IEEE.

Jatmiko, B., Sembodo, T. B., Langke, A. Y., Sukirdi, S., & Hulu, Y. (2021). Gereja sebagai Hamba yang Melayani: Sebuah Perspektif Eklesiologi Transformatif di Era Society 5.0. *CARAKA: Jurnal Teologi Biblika dan Praktika, 2*(2), 234-253.

Javaid, M., Haleem, A., Singh, R. P., & Suman, R. (2022). Artificial intelligence applications for industry 4.0: A literature-based study. *Journal of Industrial Integration and Management, 7*(01), 83–111. doi:10.1142/S2424862221300040

Javaid, M., Haleem, A., Singh, R. P., Suman, R., & Gonzalez, E. S. (2022). Understanding the adoption of Industry 4.0 technologies in improving environmental sustainability. *Sustainable Operations and Computers, 3*, 203–217. doi:10.1016/j.susoc.2022.01.008

Javaid, M., Haleem, A., Singh, R. P., Suman, R., & Rab, S. (2022). Significance of machine learning in healthcare: Features, pillars and applications. *International Journal of Intelligent Networks, 3*, 58–73. doi:10.1016/j.ijin.2022.05.002

Jayal, A. D., Badurdeen, F., Dillon, O. W. Jr, & Jawahir, I. S. (2010). Sustainable manufacturing: Modeling and optimization challenges at the product, process and system levels. *CIRP Journal of Manufacturing Science and Technology, 2*(3), 144–152. doi:10.1016/j.cirpj.2010.03.006

Joshi, K., Anandaram, H., Khanduja, M., Kumar, R., Saini, V., & Mohialden, Y. (2022). *Recent Challenges on Edge AI with Its Application: A Brief Introduction*. Springer. . doi:10.1007/978-3-031-18292-1_5

Junaid, M., Sohail, A., Rais, R. N. B., Ahmed, A., Khalid, O., Khan, I. A., Hussain, S. S., & Ejaz, N. (2020). Modeling an optimized approach for load balancing in cloud. *IEEE Access : Practical Innovations, Open Solutions, 8*, 173208–173226. doi:10.1109/ACCESS.2020.3024113

Jung, W.-K., Kim, D.-R., Lee, H., Lee, T.-H., Yang, I., Youn, B. D., Zontar, D., Brockmann, M., Brecher, C., & Ahn, S.-H. (2021). Appropriate smart factory for SMEs: Concept, application and perspective. *International Journal of Precision Engineering and Manufacturing, 22*(1), 201–215. doi:10.1007/s12541-020-00445-2

Jungwirth, D., & Haluza, D. (2023). Artificial Intelligence and the Sustainable Development Goals: An Exploratory Study in the Context of the Society Domain. *Journal of Software Engineering and Applications, 16*(04), 91–112. doi:10.4236/jsea.2023.164006

Kadarisman, M., Wijayanto, A. W., & Sakti, A. D. (2022). Government Agencies' Readiness Evaluation towards Industry 4.0 and Society 5.0 in Indonesia. *Social Sciences (Basel, Switzerland), 11*(8), 331. doi:10.3390/socsci11080331

Kalyani, Y., & Collier, R. (2021). A systematic survey on the role of cloud, fog, and edge computing combination in smart agriculture. *Sensors (Basel), 21*(17), 5922. doi:10.3390/s21175922 PMID:34502813

Kanase-Patil, A. (2020). *A review of AI-based optimization techniques for the sizing of integrated renewable energy systems*. Taylor & Francis. https://www.tandfonline.com/doi/abs/10.1080/21622515.2020.1836035

Kang, K. D., Kang, H., Ilankoon, I. M. S. K., & Chong, C. Y. (2020). Electronic waste collection systems using Internet of Things (IoT): Household electronic waste management in Malaysia. *Journal of Cleaner Production, 252*, 119801. doi:10.1016/j.jclepro.2019.119801

Karuppasamy, M., & Balakannan, S. P. (2019). An improving data delivery method using EEDD algorithm for energy conservation in green cloud network. *Soft Computing, 23*(18), 8643–8649. doi:10.1007/s00500-019-04027-x

Kasinathan, P., Pugazhendhi, R., Elavarasan, R. M., Ramachandaramurthy, V. K., Ramanathan, V., Subramanian, S., Kumar, S., Nandhagopal, K., Raghavan, R. R. V., Rangasamy, S., Devendiran, R., & Alsharif, M. H. (2022). Realization of Sustainable Development Goals with Disruptive Technologies by Integrating Industry 5.0, Society 5.0, Smart Cities and Villages. *Sustainability (Basel)*, *14*(22), 15258. doi:10.3390/su142215258

Katiyar, S., & Farhana, A. (2021, October 1). Smart Agriculture: The Future of Agriculture using AI and IoT. *Journal of Computational Science*, *17*(10), 984–999. doi:10.3844/jcssp.2021.984.999

Kaur, S., & Singh, A. (2017). security issues in cloud computing. *International Education and Research Journal*.

Kavitha, C. R., Varalatchoumy, M., Mithuna, H. R., Bharathi, K., Geethalakshmi, N. M., & Boopathi, S. (2023). Energy Monitoring and Control in the Smart Grid: Integrated Intelligent IoT and ANFIS. In M. Arshad (Ed.), (pp. 290–316). Advances in Bioinformatics and Biomedical Engineering. IGI Global. doi:10.4018/978-1-6684-6577-6.ch014

Khalid, S., Khalil, T., & Nasreen, S. (2014, August). *A survey of feature selection and feature extraction techniques in machine learning. In 2014 science and information conference*. IEEE.

Khan, N., Jhariya, M. K., Raj, A., Banerjee, A., & Meena, R. S. (2021). Eco-designing for sustainability. *Ecological intensification of natural resources for sustainable agriculture*, 565-595.

Khan, N., & Al-Yasiri, A. (2016). Cloud Security Threats and Techniques to Strengthen Cloud Computing Adoption Framework. *International Journal of Information Technology and Web Engineering*, *11*(3), 50–64. doi:10.4018/IJITWE.2016070104

Khosravi, A., & Buyya, R. (2018). Energy and carbon footprint-aware management of geo-distributed cloud data centers: A taxonomy, state of the art, and future directions. *Sustainable Development: Concepts, Methodologies, Tools, and Applications*, 1456-1475.

Kiepas, A. (2021). Humanity-Organization-Technology in View of Industry 4.0/Society 5.0. *Polish Pol. Sci. YB*, *50*(3), 21–32. doi:10.15804/ppsy202135

King, A. (2017). Technology: The future of agriculture. *Nature*, *544*(7651), S21–S23. doi:10.1038/544S21a PMID:28445450

Kiruthiga, G., & Vennila, S. M. (2020). Energy efficient load balancing aware task scheduling in cloud computing using multi-objective chaotic darwinian chicken swarm optimization. *Int J Comput Netw Appl*, *7*, 82–92.

Klauk, H. (2010). Organic thin-film transistors. *Chemical Society Reviews*, *39*(7), 2643–2666. doi:10.1039/b909902f PMID:20396828

Konhäuser, W. (2023). From 5G technology to 6G green deals. In Enabling technologies, (pp. 75–93). River Publishers.

Koshariya, A. K., Kalaiyarasi, D., Jovith, A. A., Sivakami, T., Hasan, D. S., & Boopathi, S. (2023). AI-Enabled IoT and WSN-Integrated Smart Agriculture System. In *Artificial Intelligence Tools and Technologies for Smart Farming and Agriculture Practices* (pp. 200–218). IGI Global. doi:10.4018/978-1-6684-8516-3.ch011

Koshariya, A. K., Khatoon, S., Marathe, A. M., Suba, G. M., Baral, D., & Boopathi, S. (2023). Agricultural Waste Management Systems Using Artificial Intelligence Techniques. In *AI-Enabled Social Robotics in Human Care Services* (pp. 236–258). IGI Global. doi:10.4018/978-1-6684-8171-4.ch009

Krishnan, S. R., Nallakaruppan, M. K., Chengoden, R., Koppu, S., Iyapparaja, M., Sadhasivam, J., & Sethuraman, S. (2022). Smart Water Resource Management Using Artificial Intelligence—A Review. *Sustainability (Basel)*, *14*(20), 13384. doi:10.3390/su142013384

Kumar, S., & Buyya, R. (2012). Green cloud computing and environmental sustainability. *Harnessing green IT: principles and practices*, 315-339.

Kumara, V., Mohanaprakash, T., Fairooz, S., Jamal, K., Babu, T., & Sampath, B. (2023). Experimental Study on a Reliable Smart Hydroponics System. In *Human Agro-Energy Optimization for Business and Industry* (pp. 27–45). IGI Global. doi:10.4018/978-1-6684-4118-3.ch002

Kumar, M. S., Shadrach, F. D., Polamuri, S. R., Poonkodi, R., & Pudi, V. N. (2022, July). A binary Bird Swarm Optimization technique for cloud computing task scheduling and load balancing. In *2022 International Conference on Innovative Computing, Intelligent Communication and Smart Electrical Systems (ICSES)* (pp. 1-6). IEEE.

Kumar, M., & Sharma, S. C. (2017). Dynamic load balancing algorithm for balancing the workload among virtual machine in cloud computing. *Procedia Computer Science, 115*, 322–329. doi:10.1016/j.procs.2017.09.141

Kumar, P. R., Meenakshi, S., Shalini, S., Devi, S. R., & Boopathi, S. (2023). Soil Quality Prediction in Context Learning Approaches Using Deep Learning and Blockchain for Smart Agriculture. In R. Kumar, A. B. Abdul Hamid, & N. I. Binti Ya'akub (Eds.), (pp. 1–26). Advances in Computational Intelligence and Robotics. IGI Global. doi:10.4018/978-1-6684-9151-5.ch001

Kumar, R., Gupta, S. K., Wang, H.-C., Kumari, C. S., & Korlam, S. S. V. P. (2023). From efficiency to sustainability: Exploring the potential of 6G for a greener future. *Sustainability (Basel), 15*(23), 16387. doi:10.3390/su152316387

Kurniasih, D., Setyoko, P. I., & Saputra, A. S. (2022). Digital Transformation of Health Quality Services in the Healthcare Industry during Disruption and Society 5.0 Era. *International Journal of Social and Management Studies, 3*(5), 139–143.

Kynčlová, P., Upadhyaya, S., & Nice, T. (2020, May). Composite index as a measure on achieving Sustainable Development Goal 9 (SDG-9) industry-related targets: The SDG-9 index. *Applied Energy, 265*, 114755. doi:10.1016/j.apenergy.2020.114755

LeCun, Y., Bengio, Y., & Hinton, G. (2015). Deep learning. *Nature, 521*(7553), 436-444.

Leng, J., Sha, W., Wang, B., Zheng, P., Zhuang, C., Liu, Q., Wuest, T., Mourtzis, D., & Wang, L. (2022). Industry 5.0: Prospect and retrospect. *Journal of Manufacturing Systems, 65*, 279–295. doi:10.1016/j.jmsy.2022.09.017

Leonardi, N., Manca, M., Paternò, F., & Santoro, C. (2019). Trigger-action programming for personalising humanoid robot behaviour. In *Proceedings of the 2019 CHI Conference on Human Factors in Computing Systems-CHI '19*, Glasgow, UK, 4–9 May 2019; ACM Press: New York, NY, USA, Pp. 1-13. 10.1145/3290605.3300675

Liang, T., Zhang, Y.-J., & Qiang, W. (2022). Does technological innovation benefit energy firms' environmental performance? The moderating effect of government subsidies and media coverage. *Technological Forecasting and Social Change, 180*, 121728. doi:10.1016/j.techfore.2022.121728

Li, M., Sun, Z., Jiang, Z., Tan, Z., & Chen, J. (2020). A virtual reality platform for safety training in coal mines with AI and cloud computing. *Discrete Dynamics in Nature and Society, 2020*, 1–7. doi:10.1155/2020/8889903

Lin, Z., Wang, H., Li, W., & Chen, M. (2023). Impact of green finance on carbon emissions based on a two-stage LMDI decomposition method. *Sustainability (Basel), 15*(17), 12808. doi:10.3390/su151712808

Lipomi, D. J., & Bao, Z. (2011). Stretchable, elastic materials and devices for solar energy conversion. *Energy & Environmental Science, 4*(9), 3314–3328. doi:10.1039/c1ee01881g

Li, S., Xu, L. D., & Zhao, S. (2018). 5G internet of things: A survey. *Journal of Industrial Information Integration, 10*, 1–9. doi:10.1016/j.jii.2018.01.005

Liu, B., Bi, J., & Vasilakos, A. V. (2014). Toward incentivizing anti-spoofing deployment. *IEEE Transactions on Information Forensics and Security*, 9(3), 436–450. doi:10.1109/TIFS.2013.2296437

Liu, B., Chen, Y., Hadiks, A., Blasch, E., Aved, A., Shen, D., & Chen, G. (2014). Information fusion in a cloud computing era: A systems-level perspective. *IEEE Aerospace and Electronic Systems Magazine*, 29(10), 16–24. doi:10.1109/MAES.2014.130115

Liu, D., Chen, Q., & Mori, K. (2015, August). *Time series forecasting method of building energy consumption using support vector regression. In 2015 IEEE international conference on Information and automation.* IEEE.

Liu, Y., Cao, G., Zhao, N., Mulligan, K., & Ye, X. (2018). Improve ground-level PM2. 5 concentration mapping using a random forests-based geostatistical approach. *Environmental Pollution*, 235, 272–282. doi:10.1016/j.envpol.2017.12.070 PMID:29291527

Liu, Y., Chen, H., Zhang, L., Wu, X., & Wang, X. J. (2020). Energy consumption prediction and diagnosis of public buildings based on support vector machine learning: A case study in China. *Journal of Cleaner Production*, 272, 122542. doi:10.1016/j.jclepro.2020.122542

Liu, Z., Zhang, T., Yang, M., Gao, W., Wu, S., Wang, K., Dong, F., Dang, J., Zhou, D., & Zhang, J. (2021). Hydrogel pressure distribution sensors based on an imaging strategy and machine learning. *ACS Applied Electronic Materials*, 3(8), 3599–3609. doi:10.1021/acsaelm.1c00488

Li, Y. (2020, November). Research Direction of Smart Home Real-time Monitoring. In *2020 International Conference on Computer Engineering and Intelligent Control (ICCEIC)* (pp. 220-232). IEEE. 10.1109/ICCEIC51584.2020.00051

Lloyd, W., Pallickara, S., David, O., Lyon, J., Arabi, M., & Rojas, K. (2013). Performance implications of multi-tier application deployments on Infrastructure-as-a-Service clouds: Towards performance modeling. *Future Generation Computer Systems*, 29(5), 1254–1264. doi:10.1016/j.future.2012.12.007

Lu, M., Fu, G., Osman, N. B., & Konbr, U. (2021). Green energy harvesting strategies on edge-based urban computing in sustainable internet of things. *Sustainable Cities and Society*, 75, 103349. doi:10.1016/j.scs.2021.103349

Luo, B., Khan, A. A., Wu, X., & Li, H. (2023). Navigating carbon emissions in G-7 economies: A quantile regression analysis of environmental-economic interplay. *Environmental Science and Pollution Research International*, 30(47), 1–16. doi:10.1007/s11356-023-29722-z PMID:37707736

Lu, Y., Yang, L., Shi, B., Li, J., & Abedin, M. Z. (2022). A novel framework of credit risk feature selection for SMEs during industry 4.0. *Annals of Operations Research*, 1–28. doi:10.1007/s10479-022-04849-3 PMID:35910041

Maddikunta, P. K. R., Pham, Q. V., Prabadevi, B., Deepa, N., Dev, K., Gadekallu, T. R., & Liyanage, M. (2022). Industry 5.0: A survey on enabling technologies and potential applications. *Journal of Industrial Information Integration*, 26, 100257. doi:10.1016/j.jii.2021.100257

Maguluri, L. P., Arularasan, A. N., & Boopathi, S. (2023). Assessing Security Concerns for AI-Based Drones in Smart Cities. In R. Kumar, A. B. Abdul Hamid, & N. I. Binti Ya'akub (Eds.), (pp. 27–47). Advances in Computational Intelligence and Robotics. IGI Global. doi:10.4018/978-1-6684-9151-5.ch002

Maheswari, B. U., Imambi, S. S., Hasan, D., Meenakshi, S., Pratheep, V., & Boopathi, S. (2023). Internet of Things and Machine Learning-Integrated Smart Robotics. In Global Perspectives on Robotics and Autonomous Systems: Development and Applications (pp. 240–258). IGI Global. doi:10.4018/978-1-6684-7791-5.ch010

Maier, M. (2021). 6G as if people mattered: from industry 4.0 toward society 5.0. In *2021 International Conference on Computer Communications and Networks (ICCCN)* (pp. 1-10). IEEE.

Malik, H., Fatema, N., & Alzubi, J. A. (2021). AI and Machine Learning Paradigms for Health Monitoring System: Intelligent Data Analytics. In Springer- Studies in Big Data 86 (Vol. 86). Springer Nature.

Malik, B. H., Amir, M., Mazhar, B., Ali, S., Jalil, R., & Khalid, J. (2018). Comparison of task scheduling algorithms in cloud environment. *International Journal of Advanced Computer Science and Applications*, 9(5). Advance online publication. doi:10.14569/IJACSA.2018.090550

Manshahia, M. (2023). *Advances in Artificial Intelligence for Renewable Energy Systems and Energy Autonomy*. Springer. https://link.springer.com/book/10.1007/978-3-031-26496-2

Marda, V. (2018, October 15). Artificial intelligence policy in India: A framework for engaging the limits of data-driven decision-making. *Philosophical Transactions. Series A, Mathematical, Physical, and Engineering Sciences*, 376(2133), 20180087. doi:10.1098/rsta.2018.0087 PMID:30323001

Masuda, Y., Zimmermann, A., Shepard, D. S., Schmidt, R., & Shirasaka, S. (2021). An adaptive enterprise architecture design for a digital healthcare platform: toward digitized society-industry 4.0, society 5.0. In *2021 IEEE 25th International Enterprise Distributed Object Computing Workshop (EDOCW)* (pp. 138-146). IEEE.

Mavrodieva, A. V., & Shaw, R. (2020). Disaster and climate change issues in Japan's Society 5.0-A discussion. *Sustainability (Basel)*, 12(5), 1893. doi:10.3390/su12051893

Medina-Borja, A. (2017). Smart human-centered service systems of the future. *Future Services & Societal Systems in Society, 5*.

Mehrabi, Z., McDowell, M. J., Ricciardi, V., Levers, C., Martinez, J. D., Mehrabi, N., Wittman, H., Ramankutty, N., & Jarvis, A. (2020, November 2). The global divide in data-driven farming. *Nature Sustainability*, 4(2), 154–160. doi:10.1038/s41893-020-00631-0

Mehta, C. R., Chandel, N. S., & Rajwade, Y. A. (2020). Smart farm mechanization for sustainable indian agriculture. *AMA, Agricultural Mechanization in Asia, Africa and Latin America*, 51(4), 99-105+95.

Mei, B., Khan, A. A., Khan, S. U., Ali, M. A. S., & Luo, J. (2023). Variation of digital economy's effect on carbon emissions: Improving energy efficiency and structure for energy conservation and emission reduction. *Environmental Science and Pollution Research International*, 30(37), 87300–87313. doi:10.1007/s11356-023-28010-0 PMID:37422562

Mell, P., & Grance, T. (2011). *The NIST definition of cloud computing*. NIST.

Menezes, B., Yaqot, M., Hassaan, S., Franzoi, R., AlQashouti, N., & Al-Banna, A. (2022). Digital Transformation in the Era of Industry 4.0 and Society 5.0: A perspective. In *2022 2nd International Conference on Emerging Smart Technologies and Applications (eSmarTA)* (pp. 1-6). IEEE.

Mesbahi, M., & Rahmani, A. M. (2016). Load balancing in cloud computing: A state of the art survey. *Int. J. Mod. Educ. Comput. Sci*, 8(3), 64–78. doi:10.5815/ijmecs.2016.03.08

Midilli, A., Dincer, I., & Ay, M. (2006). Green energy strategies for sustainable development. *Energy Policy*, 34(18), 3623–3633. doi:10.1016/j.enpol.2005.08.003

Mi, S., Feng, Y., Zheng, H., Li, Z., Gao, Y., & Tan, J. (2020). Integrated intelligent green scheduling of predictive maintenance for complex equipment based on information services. *IEEE Access : Practical Innovations, Open Solutions*, 8, 45797–45812. doi:10.1109/ACCESS.2020.2977667

Mishra, A., Gangisetti, G., Khazanchi, D. (2023). *Integrating Edge-AI in Structural Health Monitoring domain*.

Mishra, P., & Singh, G. (2023). 6G-IoT framework for sustainable smart city: Vision and challenges. *IEEE Consumer Electronics Magazine*. Springer International Publishing, (1–8). doi:10.1109/MCE.2023.3307225

Mishra, K., & Majhi, S. K. (2021). A binary Bird Swarm Optimization based load balancing algorithm for cloud computing environment. *Open Computer Science, 11*(1), 146–160. doi:10.1515/comp-2020-0215

Mishra, M., Nayak, J., Naik, B., & Abraham, A. (2020). Deep learning in electrical utility industry: A comprehensive review of a decade of research. *Engineering Applications of Artificial Intelligence, 96*, 104000. doi:10.1016/j.engappai.2020.104000

Mishra, R., & Jaiswal, A. (2012). Ant colony optimization: A solution of load balancing in cloud. *International Journal of Web & Semantic Technology, 3*(2), 33–50. doi:10.5121/ijwest.2012.3203

Modi, C., Patel, D., Borisaniya, B., Patel, A., & Rajarajan, M. (2013). A survey on security issues and solutions at different layers of Cloud computing. *The Journal of Supercomputing, 63*(2), 561–592. doi:10.1007/s11227-012-0831-5

Mohammadian, H. D., & Rezaie, F. (2020). The role of IoE-Education in the 5 th wave theory readiness & its effect on SME 4.0 HR competencies. *2020 IEEE Global Engineering Education Conference (EDUCON)*, (pp. 1604–1613). IEEE. 10.1109/EDUCON45650.2020.9125249

Mohanty, A., Venkateswaran, N., Ranjit, P., Tripathi, M. A., & Boopathi, S. (2023). Innovative Strategy for Profitable Automobile Industries: Working Capital Management. In Handbook of Research on Designing Sustainable Supply Chains to Achieve a Circular Economy (pp. 412–428). IGI Global.

Mohanty, A., Venkateswaran, N., Ranjit, P. S., Tripathi, M. A., & Boopathi, S. (2023). Innovative strategy for profitable automobile industries: Working capital management. In *Handbook of Research on Designing Sustainable Supply Chains to Achieve a Circular Economy* (pp. 412–428). IGI Global. doi:10.4018/978-1-6684-7664-2.ch020

Mortier, T. (2020). *EY Global Digital & Innovation lead for Energy*. EY. https://www.ey.com/en_in/power-utilities/why-artificial-intelligence-is-a-game-changer-for-renewable-energy

Mourtzis, D., Angelopoulos, J., & Panopoulos, N. (2022). A literature review of the challenges and opportunities of the transition from industry 4.0 to society 5.0. *Energies, 15*(17), 6276. doi:10.3390/en15176276

Mruzek, M., Gajdáč, I., Kučera, Ľ., & Barta, D. (2016). Analysis of parameters influencing electric vehicle range. *Procedia Engineering, 134*, 165–174. doi:10.1016/j.proeng.2016.01.056

Mukherjee, A., Panja, A. K., Obaidat, M. S., & De, D. (2022). 6G based green mobile edge computing for Internet of things (IoT). In *Green mobile cloud computing* (pp. 265–282). Springer International Publishing. doi:10.1007/978-3-031-08038-8_13

Mustapha, U. F., Alhassan, A.-W., Jiang, D.-N., & Li, G.-L. (2021). Sustainable aquaculture development: A review on the roles of cloud computing, internet of things and artificial intelligence (CIA). *Reviews in Aquaculture, 13*(4), 2076–2091. doi:10.1111/raq.12559

Myilsamy Sureshkumar, V. R. P., S. Boopathi, M. & Sabareesh. (2018). The improving Wear Resistance Properties of Molybdenum Alloy Under Cryogenic Treatment. *International Journal of Mechanical and Production Engineering Research and Development, 8*(7), 724–728.

Nair, M. M., Tyagi, A. K., & Sreenath, N. (2021). The future with industry 4.0 at the core of society 5.0: open issues, future opportunities and challenges. In *2021 International Conference on Computer Communication and Informatics (ICCCI)* (pp. 1-7). IEEE. 10.1109/ICCCI50826.2021.9402498

Narvaez Rojas, C., Alomia Peñafiel, G. A., Loaiza Buitrago, D. F., & Tavera Romero, C. A. (2021). Society 5.0: A Japanese concept for a superintelligent society. *Sustainability (Basel)*, *13*(12), 6567. doi:10.3390/su13126567

Na, S. H., & Huh, E. N. (2015). A broker-based cooperative security-SLA evaluation methodology for personal cloud computing. *Security and Communication Networks*, *8*(7), 1318–1331. doi:10.1002/sec.1086

Nascimento, A. M., de Melo, V. V., Queiroz, A. C. M., Brashear-Alejandro, T., & de Souza Meirelles, F. (2021). Artificial intelligence applied to small businesses: The use of automatic feature engineering and machine learning for more accurate planning. *Revista de Contabilidade e Organizações*, *15*, 1–15.

Nasir, M. A. U., Horii, H., Serafini, M., Kourtellis, N., Raymond, R., Girdzijauskas, S., & Osogami, T. (2017). *Load balancing for skewed streams on heterogeneous cluster*. arXiv preprint arXiv:1705.09073.

Nasiri, S., & Khosravani, M. R. (2020). Progress and challenges in the fabrication of wearable sensors for health monitoring. *Sensors and Actuators. A, Physical*, *312*, 112105. doi:10.1016/j.sna.2020.112105

Nastiti, F. E., & Ni'mal'Abdu, A. R. (2020). Kesiapan pendidikan Indonesia menghadapi era society 5.0. *Jurnal Kajian Teknologi Pendidikan*, *5*(1), 61–66. doi:10.17977/um039v5i12020p061

Ndiaye, M., Salhi, S., & Madani, B. (2020). When green technology meets optimization modeling: the case of routing drones in logistics, agriculture, and healthcare. *Modeling and Optimization in Green Logistics*, 127-145.

Nick, J. (2010). *Journey to the Private Cloud: Security and Compliance*. Tech. Presentation, EMC, Tsinghua Univ.

Nieuważny, J., Masui, F., Ptaszynski, M., Rzepka, R., & Nowakowski, K. (2020). How religion and morality correlate in age of society 5.0: Statistical analysis of emotional and moral associations with Buddhist religious terms appearing on Japanese blogs. *Cognitive Systems Research*, *59*, 329–344. doi:10.1016/j.cogsys.2019.09.026

Nishant, K., Sharma, P., Krishna, V., Gupta, C., Singh, K. P., & Rastogi, R. (2012, March). Load balancing of nodes in cloud using ant colony optimization. In *2012 UKSim 14th international conference on computer modelling and simulation* (pp. 3-8). IEEE. 10.1109/UKSim.2012.11

Nishanth, J., Deshmukh, M. A., Kushwah, R., Kushwaha, K. K., Balaji, S., & Sampath, B. (2023). Particle Swarm Optimization of Hybrid Renewable Energy Systems. In *Intelligent Engineering Applications and Applied Sciences for Sustainability* (pp. 291–308). IGI Global. doi:10.4018/979-8-3693-0044-2.ch016

Nonami, K. (2016). Drone technology, cutting-edge drone business, and future prospects. *Journal of robotics and mechatronics*, *28*(3), 262-272.

Nowakowski, P., & Pamuła, T. (2020). Application of deep learning object classifier to improve e-waste collection planning. *Waste Management (New York, N.Y.)*, *109*, 1–9. doi:10.1016/j.wasman.2020.04.041 PMID:32361385

Obschonka, M., & Audretsch, D. B. (2019). Artificial intelligence and big data in entrepreneurship: A new era has begun. *Small Business Economics*, *55*(3), 529–539. doi:10.1007/s11187-019-00202-4

Ofori, E. K., Li, J., Gyamfi, B. A., Opoku-Mensah, E., & Zhang, J. (2023). Green industrial transition: Leveraging environmental innovation and environmental tax to achieve carbon neutrality. Expanding on STRIPAT model. *Journal of Environmental Management*, *343*, 118121. doi:10.1016/j.jenvman.2023.118121 PMID:37224684

Onday, O. (2019). Japan's society 5.0: Going beyond industry 4.0. *Business and Economics Journal*, *10*(2), 1–6.

Onu, P., & Mbohwa, C. (2021). Industry 4.0 opportunities in manufacturing SMEs: Sustainability outlook. *Materials Today: Proceedings*, *44*, 1925–1930. doi:10.1016/j.matpr.2020.12.095

Østbø, N. P., Berg, J. P., Kukharuk, A., & Skorobogatova, N. (2022). Industry 4.0 and society 5.0: visions of a sustainable future. *МІЖНАРОДНЕ НАУКОВО-ТЕХНІЧНЕ СПІВРОБІТНИЦТВО: ПРИНЦИПИ*, 84.

Owe, A., & Baum, S. D. (2021, June 6). Moral consideration of nonhumans in the ethics of artificial intelligence. *AI and Ethics*, *1*(4), 517–528. doi:10.1007/s43681-021-00065-0

Oyeyinka, F. I., & Omotosho, O. J. (2015). A modified things role-based access control model for securing utilities in cloud computing. *Int. J. Innov. Res. Inf. Security*, *5*(2), 21–25.

Pandey, V., Sircar, A., Bist, N., Solanki, K., & Yadav, K. (2023). Accelerating the renewable energy sector through Industry 4.0: Optimization opportunities in the digital revolution. *International Journal of Innovation Studies*, *7*(2), 171–188. doi:10.1016/j.ijis.2023.03.003

Pang, C., Lee, G. Y., Kim, T. I., Kim, S. M., Kim, H. N., Ahn, S. H., & Suh, K. Y. (2012). A flexible and highly sensitive strain-gauge sensor using reversible interlocking of nanofibres. *Nature Materials*, *11*(9), 795–801. doi:10.1038/nmat3380 PMID:22842511

Pan, I., Abd Elaziz, M., & Bhattacharyya, S. (Eds.). (2020). *Swarm intelligence for cloud computing*. CRC Press. doi:10.1201/9780429020582

Panwar, R., & Mallick, B. (2015). A comparative study of load balancing algorithms in cloud computing. *International Journal of Computer Applications*, *117*(24), 33–37. doi:10.5120/20890-3669

Parihar, C. M., Nayak, H. S., Rai, V. K., Jat, S. L., Parihar, N., Aggarwal, P., & Mishra, A. K. (2019). Soil water dynamics, water productivity and radiation use efficiency of maize under multi-year conservation agriculture during contrasting rainfall events. *Field Crops Research*, *241*, 107570. doi:10.1016/j.fcr.2019.107570

Paschek, D., Luminosu, C. T., & Ocakci, E. (2022). Industry 5.0 challenges and perspectives for manufacturing systems in the society 5.0. *Sustainability and Innovation in Manufacturing Enterprises*, 17-63.

Paternò, F., Manca, M., & Santoro, C. (2019). *End user personalization of social humanoid robots. 2019*. https://www.google.com.hk/url?sa=t&rct=j&q=&esrc=s&source=web&cd=&cad=rja&uact=8&ved=2ahUKEwilvaGXnbT7

Patil, A., & Patil, D. (2019, February). An *analysis report on green cloud computing current trends and future research challenges*. In *International Conference on Sustainable Computing in Science, Technology and Management (SUSCOM)*. Amity University Rajasthan. 10.2139/ssrn.3355151

Patra, T. K., Meenakshisundaram, V., Hung, J. H., & Simmons, D. S. (2017). Neural-network-biased genetic algorithms for materials design: Evolutionary algorithms that learn. *ACS Combinatorial Science*, *19*(2), 96–107. doi:10.1021/acscombsci.6b00136 PMID:27997791

Peng, H., Zhang, X., Li, H., Xu, L., & Wang, X. (2023). An AI-Enhanced Strategy of Service Offloading for IoV in Mobile Edge Computing. *Electronics (Basel)*, *12*(12), 2719. doi:10.3390/electronics12122719

Pereira, A. G., Lima, T. M., & Santos, F. C. (2020). Industry 4.0 and Society 5.0: Opportunities and threats. *International Journal of Recent Technology and Engineering*, *8*(5), 3305–3308. doi:10.35940/ijrte.D8764.018520

Pereira, I. P., Ferreira, F. A., Pereira, L. F., Govindan, K., Meidutė-Kavaliauskienė, I., & Correia, R. J. (2020). A fuzzy cognitive mapping-system dynamics approach to energy-change impacts on the sustainability of small and medium-sized enterprises. *Journal of Cleaner Production*, *256*, 120154. doi:10.1016/j.jclepro.2020.120154

Petrolo, R., Loscri, V., & Mitton, N. (2017). Towards a smart city based on cloud of things, a survey on the smart city vision and paradigms. *Transactions on Emerging Telecommunications Technologies*, *28*(1), e2931. doi:10.1002/ett.2931

Peyman, M., Copado, P. J., Tordecilla, R. D., Martins, L. D. C., Xhafa, F., & Juan, A. A. (2021). Edge computing and iot analytics for agile optimization in intelligent transportation systems. *Energies*, *14*(19), 6309. doi:10.3390/en14196309

Polat, L., & Erkollar, A. (2020). Industry 4.0 vs. Society 5.0. In *The International Symposium for Production Research* (pp. 333-345). Springer, Cham.

Pomšár, L., Brecko, A., & Zolotová, I. (2022). *Brief overview of Edge AI accelerators for energy-constrained edge.* 2022 IEEE 20th Jubilee World Symposium on Applied Machine Intelligence and Informatics (SAMI), Poprad, Slovakia. 10.1109/SAMI54271.2022.9780669

Popkova, E. G., & Sergi, B. S. (2018). Will industry 4.0 and other innovations impact Russia's development. *Exploring the future of Russia's economy and markets: Towards sustainable economic development*, (pp. 51-68). Research Gate.

Potočan, V., Mulej, M., & Nedelko, Z. (2020). Society 5.0: Balancing of Industry 4.0, economic advancement and social problems. *Kybernetes*.

Pradhan, D., & Priyanka, K. C. (2021). Green-Cloud Computing (G-CC) data center and its architecture toward efficient usage of energy. In Future trends in 5G and 6G (pp. 163–182). CRC Press.

Pramila, P., Amudha, S., Saravanan, T., Sankar, S. R., Poongothai, E., & Boopathi, S. (2023). Design and Development of Robots for Medical Assistance: An Architectural Approach. In Contemporary Applications of Data Fusion for Advanced Healthcare Informatics (pp. 260–282). IGI Global.

Prasad, R., & Ruggieri, M. (2021). Editorial: Special issue on "sustainable green environment (SGE)". *Wireless Personal Communications*, *121*(2), 1117–1122. doi:10.1007/s11277-021-09195-4 PMID:34703081

Prashar, A. (2019). Towards sustainable development in industrial small and Medium-sized Enterprises: An energy sustainability approach. *Journal of Cleaner Production*, *235*, 977–996. doi:10.1016/j.jclepro.2019.07.045

Prema, P., Veeramani, A., & Sivakumar, T. (2022). Machine Learning Applications in Agriculture. *Journal of Agriculture Research and Technology*. *Special*, (01), 126–129. doi:10.56228/JART.2022.SP120

Qamar, S., Ahmad, M., Oryani, B., & Zhang, Q. (2022). Solar energy technology adoption and diffusion by micro, small, and medium enterprises: Sustainable energy for climate change mitigation. *Environmental Science and Pollution Research International*, *29*(32), 49385–49403. doi:10.1007/s11356-022-19406-5 PMID:35218487

Qawqzeh, Y., Alharbi, M. T., Jaradat, A., & Sattar, K. N. A. (2021). A review of swarm intelligence algorithms deployment for scheduling and optimization in cloud computing environments. *PeerJ. Computer Science*, *7*, e696. doi:10.7717/peerj-cs.696 PMID:34541313

Qin, J., Hu, F., Liu, Y., Witherell, P., Wang, C. C., Rosen, D. W., Simpson, T. W., Lu, Y., & Tang, Q. (2022). Research and application of machine learning for additive manufacturing. *Additive Manufacturing*, *52*, 102691. doi:10.1016/j.addma.2022.102691

Qureshi, K. N., Jeon, G., & Piccialli, F. (2021). Anomaly detection and trust authority in artificial intelligence and cloud computing. *Computer Networks*, *184*, 107647. doi:10.1016/j.comnet.2020.107647

Radu, L. D. (2017). Green cloud computing: A literature survey. *Symmetry*, *9*(12), 295. doi:10.3390/sym9120295

Raghav, Y. Y., & Vyas, V. (2019, October). A comparative analysis of different load balancing algorithms on different parameters in cloud computing. In *2019 3rd International Conference on Recent Developments in Control, Automation & Power Engineering (RDCAPE)* (pp. 628-634). IEEE. 10.1109/RDCAPE47089.2019.8979122

Raghav, Y. Y., & Gulia, S. (2023). The Rise of Artificial Intelligence and Its Implications on Spirituality. In *Investigating the Impact of AI on Ethics and Spirituality* (pp. 165–178). IGI Global. doi:10.4018/978-1-6684-9196-6.ch011

Raghav, Y. Y., & Vyas, V. (2023). ACBSO: A hybrid solution for load balancing using ant colony and bird swarm optimization algorithms. *International Journal of Information Technology : an Official Journal of Bharati Vidyapeeth's Institute of Computer Applications and Management, 15*(5), 1–11. doi:10.1007/s41870-023-01340-5

Raghav, Y. Y., Vyas, V., & Rani, H. (2022). Load balancing using dynamic algorithms for cloud environment: A survey. *Materials Today: Proceedings, 69*, 349–353. doi:10.1016/j.matpr.2022.09.048

Raha, A. (2021). *Design Considerations for Edge Neural Network Accelerators: An Industry Perspective.* 2021 34th International Conference on VLSI Design and 2021 20th International Conference on Embedded Systems (VLSID), Guwahati, India. 10.1109/VLSID51830.2021.00061

Rahamathunnisa, U., Subhashini, P., Aancy, H. M., Meenakshi, S., Boopathi, S., & ... (2023). Solutions for Software Requirement Risks Using Artificial Intelligence Techniques. In *Handbook of Research on Data Science and Cybersecurity Innovations in Industry 4.0 Technologies* (pp. 45–64). IGI Global.

Rahamathunnisa, U., Sudhakar, K., Murugan, T. K., Thivaharan, S., Rajkumar, M., & Boopathi, S. (2023). Cloud Computing Principles for Optimizing Robot Task Offloading Processes. In *AI-Enabled Social Robotics in Human Care Services* (pp. 188–211). IGI Global. doi:10.4018/978-1-6684-8171-4.ch007

Rahman, A., Pasaribu, E., Nugraha, Y., Khair, F., Soebandrija, K. E. N., & Wijaya, D. I. (2020). Industry 4.0 and society 5.0 through lens of condition based maintenance (CBM) and machine learning of artificial intelligence (MLAI). []. IOP Publishing.]. *IOP Conference Series. Materials Science and Engineering, 852*(1), 012022. doi:10.1088/1757-899X/852/1/012022

Rajashekara, K. (2013). Present status and future trends in electric vehicle propulsion technologies. *IEEE Journal of Emerging and Selected Topics in Power Electronics, 1*(1), 3–10. doi:10.1109/JESTPE.2013.2259614

Rajeshwari, B. S., Dakshayini, M., & Guruprasad, H. S. (2022). Workload Balancing in a Multi-Cloud Environment: Challenges and Research Directions. *Operationalizing Multi-Cloud Environments: Technologies, Tools and Use Cases.*

Ramachandran, P., Ranganath, S., Bhandaru, M., & Tibrewala, S. (2021). *A Survey of AI Enabled Edge Computing for Future Networks.* 2021 IEEE 4th 5G World Forum (5GWF), Montreal, QC, Canada. 10.1109/5GWF52925.2021.00087

Ramadhani, D., Kenedi, A. K., Helsa, Y., Handrianto, C., & Wardana, M. R. (2021). Mapping higher order thinking skills of prospective primary school teachers in facing society 5.0. *Al Ibtida: Jurnal Pendidikan Guru MI, 8*(2), 178–190. doi:10.24235/al.ibtida.snj.v8i2.8794

Ramesh Shahabadkar, S. (2017). *Secure Framework of Authentication Mechanism over Cloud Environment, CSOC.* Software Engineering Trends and Techniques in Intelligent Systems.

Ramezani, F., Lu, J., & Hussain, F. K. (2014). Task-based system load balancing in cloud computing using particle swarm optimization. *International Journal of Parallel Programming, 42*(5), 739–754. doi:10.1007/s10766-013-0275-4

Ramudu, K., Mohan, V. M., Jyothirmai, D., Prasad, D., Agrawal, R., & Boopathi, S. (2023). Machine Learning and Artificial Intelligence in Disease Prediction: Applications, Challenges, Limitations, Case Studies, and Future Directions. In Contemporary Applications of Data Fusion for Advanced Healthcare Informatics (pp. 297–318). IGI Global.

Rani, A. L. K. A., Chaudhary, A. M. R. E. S. H., Sinha, N., Mohanty, M., & Chaudhary, R. (2019). Drone: The green technology for future agriculture. *Harit Dhara, 2*(1), 3–6.

Rao, K. S., & Thilagam, P. S. (2015). Heuristics based server consolidation with residual resource defragmentation in cloud data centers. *Future Generation Computer Systems, 50*, 87–98. doi:10.1016/j.future.2014.09.009

Ravichandran, RSathyanarayana, NAli, A. A. (2022). AI-Based Smart Agriculture for Sustainable Growth-The Linkage between AI, IOT, Sustainable Growth and Development-An Indian Perspective. Adarsh Journal of Management Research, 1-9.

Raza, A., Friedel, J. K., & Bodner, G. (2012). Improving water use efficiency for sustainable agriculture. *Agroecology and Strategies for Climate Change*, 167–211.

Ren, K., Wang, C., & Wang, Q. (2012). Security challenges for the public cloud. *IEEE Internet Computing, 16*(1), 69–73. doi:10.1109/MIC.2012.14

Research Gate. (n.d.). *Artificial Intelligence techniques on renewable evergy systems*. Research Gate. https://www.researchgate.net/publication/361871065_Artificial_Intelligence_Techniques_Applied_on_Renewable_Energy_Systems_A_Review

Revathi, T., Muneeswaran, K., & Blessa Binolin Pepsi, M. (2019). *Hadoop History and Architecture*. IGI Global. doi:10.4018/978-1-5225-3790-8.ch003

Rizal, R., Misnasanti, M., Shaddiq, S., Ramdhani, R., & Wagiono, F. (2020). Learning Media in Indonesian Higher Education in Industry 4.0: Case Study. *International Journal on Advanced Science, Education, and Religion, 3*(3), 127–134. doi:10.33648/ijoaser.v3i3.62

Rodrigues, E. R., Navaux, P. O., Panetta, J., Fazenda, A., Mendes, C. L., & Kale, L. V. (2010, October). A comparative analysis of load balancing algorithms applied to a weather forecast model. In *2010 22nd International Symposium on Computer Architecture and High Performance Computing* (pp. 71-78). IEEE. 10.1109/SBAC-PAD.2010.18

Rong, C., Nguyen, S. T., & Jaatun, M. G. (2013). Beyond lightning: A survey on security challenges in cloud computing. *Computers & Electrical Engineering, 39*(1), 47–54. doi:10.1016/j.compeleceng.2012.04.015

Ryan, M. D. (2013). Cloud computing security: The scientific challenge, and a survey of solutions. *Journal of Systems and Software, 86*(9), 2263–2268. doi:10.1016/j.jss.2012.12.025

S., P. K., Sampath, B., R., S. K., Babu, B. H., & N., A. (2022). Hydroponics, Aeroponics, and Aquaponics Technologies in Modern Agricultural Cultivation. In *Trends, Paradigms, and Advances in Mechatronics Engineering* (pp. 223–241). IGI Global. doi:10.4018/978-1-6684-5887-7.ch012

Salah, K., Calero, J. M. A., Zeadally, S., Al-Mulla, S., & Alzaabi, M. (2012). Using cloud computing to implement a security overlay network. *IEEE Security and Privacy, 11*(1), 44–53. doi:10.1109/MSP.2012.88

Salimova, T., Vukovic, N., Guskova, N., & Krakovskaya, I. (2021). Industry 4.0 and Society 5.0: Challenges and Opportunities, The Case Study of Russia. *Smart Green City, 17*(4).

Salimova, T., Vukovic, N., & Guskova, N. (2020). Towards sustainability through Industry 4.0 and Society 5.0. *International Review (Steubenville, Ohio)*, (3-4), 48–54. doi:10.5937/intrev2003048S

Samikannu, R., Koshariya, A. K., Poornima, E., Ramesh, S., Kumar, A., & Boopathi, S. (2022). Sustainable Development in Modern Aquaponics Cultivation Systems Using IoT Technologies. In *Human Agro-Energy Optimization for Business and Industry* (pp. 105–127). IGI Global.

Sampath, B. (2021). *Sustainable Eco-Friendly Wire-Cut Electrical Discharge Machining: Gas Emission Analysis*.

Sampath, B., & Haribalaji, V. (2021). Influences of Welding Parameters on Friction Stir Welding of Aluminum and Magnesium: A Review. *Materials Research Proceedings*, *19*(1), 322–330.

Sampath, B., & Myilsamy, S. (2021). Experimental investigation of a cryogenically cooled oxygen-mist near-dry wire-cut electrical discharge machining process. *Stroj. Vestn. Jixie Gongcheng Xuebao*, *67*(6), 322–330.

Sampath, B., Naveenkumar, N., Sampathkumar, P., Silambarasan, P., Venkadesh, A., & Sakthivel, M. (2022). Experimental comparative study of banana fiber composite with glass fiber composite material using Taguchi method. *Materials Today: Proceedings*, *49*, 1475–1480. doi:10.1016/j.matpr.2021.07.232

Sanjay, G. H. G. S.-T. L. (n.d.). The Google File System, *Proceedings of the 19th ACM Symposium on Operating Systems Principles*. ACM.

Sankar, K. M., Booba, B., & Boopathi, S. (2023). Smart Agriculture Irrigation Monitoring System Using Internet of Things. In *Contemporary Developments in Agricultural Cyber-Physical Systems* (pp. 105–121). IGI Global. doi:10.4018/978-1-6684-7879-0.ch006

Sankar, K., Kannan, S., & Jennifer, P. (2014). On-demand security architecture for cloud computing. *Middle East Journal of Scientific Research*, *20*(2), 241–246.

Saptaningtyas, W. W. E., & Rahayu, D. K. (2020). A proposed model for food manufacturing in smes: Facing industry 5.0. In *Proceedings of the International Conference on Industrial Engineering and Operations Management*, Dubai, UAE.

Satav, S. D., & Lamani, D. G, H. K., Kumar, N. M. G., Manikandan, S., & Sampath, B. (2024). Energy and Battery Management in the Era of Cloud Computing. In Practice, Progress, and Proficiency in Sustainability (pp. 141–166). IGI Global. doi:10.4018/979-8-3693-1186-8.ch009

Satav, S. D., Hasan, D. S., Pitchai, R., Mohanaprakash, T. A., Sultanuddin, S. J., & Boopathi, S. (2024). Next Generation of Internet of Things (NGIoT) in Healthcare Systems. In Practice, Progress, and Proficiency in Sustainability (pp. 307–330). IGI Global. doi:10.4018/979-8-3693-1186-8.ch017

Saxena, D., Singh, A. K., Lee, C. N., & Buyya, R. (2023). A sustainable and secure load management model for green cloud data centres. *Scientific Reports*, *13*(1), 491. doi:10.1038/s41598-023-27703-3 PMID:36627353

Schaible, G., & Aillery, M. (2012). Water conservation in irrigated agriculture: Trends and challenges in the face of emerging demands. *USDA-ERS Economic Information Bulletin, 99*.

Schwarzkopf, R., Schmidt, M., Strack, C., Martin, S., & Freisleben, B. (2012). Increasing virtual machine security in cloud environments. *Journal of Cloud Computing: Advances. Systems and Applications*, *1*(1), 1–12.

Seng, K. P., Ang, L. M., Peter, E., & Mmonyi, A. (2023). Machine Learning and AI Technologies for Smart Wearables. *Electronics (Basel)*, *12*(7), 1509. doi:10.3390/electronics12071509

Şengönül, E., Samet, R., Abu Al-Haija, Q., Alqahtani, A., Alturki, B., & Alsulami, A. A. (2023). An Analysis of Artificial Intelligence Techniques in Surveillance Video Anomaly Detection: A Comprehensive Survey. *Applied Sciences (Basel, Switzerland)*, *13*(8), 4956. doi:10.3390/app13084956

Shafik, W., Matinkhah, S. M., & Ghasemzadeh, M. (2020). Internet of things-based energy management, challenges, and solutions in smart cities. Journal of Communications Technology. *Electronics and Computer Science*, *27*, 1–11.

Shaw, R., Howley, E., & Barrett, E. (2022). Applying reinforcement learning towards automating energy efficient virtual machine consolidation in cloud data centers. *Information Systems*, *107*, 101722. doi:10.1016/j.is.2021.101722

Shi, Q., He, T., & Lee, C. (2019). More than energy harvesting–Combining triboelectric nanogenerator and flexible electronics technology for enabling novel micro-/nano-systems. *Nano Energy, 57*, 851–871. doi:10.1016/j.nanoen.2019.01.002

Shock, C. C., Barnum, J. M., & Seddigh, M. (1998). Calibration of Watermark Soil Moisture Sensors for Irrigation Management. *Proceedings of the International Irrigation Show, September*, 139–146. https://www.researchgate.net/publication/228762944

Shortliffe, E. H. (1986). Medical expert systems—Knowledge tools for physicians. *The Western Journal of Medicine, 145*(6), 830. PMID:3811349

Siahaan, A. P. U. (2016). Comparison analysis of CPU scheduling: FCFS, SJF and Round Robin. *International Journal of Engineering Development and Research, 4*(3), 124–132.

Sileryte, R., Sabbe, A., Bouzas, V., Meister, K., Wandl, A., & van Timmeren, A. (2022). European waste statistics data for a circular economy monitor: Opportunities and limitations from the amsterdam metropolitan region. *Journal of Cleaner Production, 358*, 131767. doi:10.1016/j.jclepro.2022.131767

Singh, K. K. (2018, November). An artificial intelligence and cloud based collaborative platform for plant disease identification, tracking and forecasting for farmers. In 2018 IEEE international conference on cloud computing in emerging markets (CCEM) (pp. 49-56). IEEE. doi:10.1109/CCEM.2018.00016

Singh, M., Nandal, P., & Bura, D. (2017, October). Comparative analysis of different load balancing algorithm using cloud analyst. In *International Conference on Recent Developments in Science, Engineering and Technology* (pp. 321-329). Singapore: Springer Singapore.

Singh, S., Nikolovski, S., & Chakrabarti, P. (2022). GWLBC: Gray Wolf Optimization Based Load Balanced Clustering for Sustainable WSNs in Smart City Environment. *Sensors (Basel), 22*(19), 7113. doi:10.3390/s22197113 PMID:36236208

Singh, S., & Ru, J. (2023, January 21). Goals of sustainable infrastructure, industry, and innovation: A review and future agenda for research. *Environmental Science and Pollution Research International, 30*(11), 28446–28458. doi:10.1007/s11356-023-25281-5 PMID:36670221

Sirohi, A., & Shrivastava, V. (2015). Implementing data storage in cloud computing with HMAC encryption algorithm to improve data security. *International Journal of Advanced Research in Computer Science and Software Engineering, 5*(8), 678–684.

Situ, L. (2009). Electric vehicle development: the past, present & future. In *2009 3rd International Conference on Power Electronics Systems and Applications (PESA)* (pp. 1-3). IEEE.

Soares, L. F., Fernandes, D. A., Gomes, J. V., Freire, M. M., & Inácio, P. R. (2014). Cloud security: state of the art. *Security, Privacy and Trust in Cloud Systems*, 3-44.

Sołtysik-Piorunkiewicz, A., & Zdonek, I. (2021). How society 5.0 and industry 4.0 ideas shape the open data performance expectancy. *Sustainability (Basel), 13*(2), 917. doi:10.3390/su13020917

Someya, T., Bao, Z., & Malliaras, G. G. (2016). The rise of plastic bioelectronics. *Nature, 540*(7633), 379–385. doi:10.1038/nature21004 PMID:27974769

Song, M. H. (2014). Analysis of risks for virtualization technology. *Applied Mechanics and Materials, 539*, 374–377. doi:10.4028/www.scientific.net/AMM.539.374

Soni, V., & Barwar, D. N. (2018). Performance Analysis of Enhanced Max-Min and Min-Min Task Scheduling Algorithms in Cloud Computing Environment. In *International Conference on Emerging Trends in Science, Engineering and Management* (pp. 250-255). IEEE.

Srinivas, B., Maguluri, L. P., Naidu, K. V., Reddy, L. C. S., Deivakani, M., & Boopathi, S. (2023). Architecture and Framework for Interfacing Cloud-Enabled Robots. In *Handbook of Research on Data Science and Cybersecurity Innovations in Industry 4.0 Technologies* (pp. 542–560). IGI Global. doi:10.4018/978-1-6684-8145-5.ch027

Srinivas, J., Reddy, K. V. S., & Qyser, A. M. (2012). Cloud computing basics. *International Journal of Advanced Research in Computer and Communication Engineering*, *1*(5), 343–347.

Sriram, G. S. (2022). Green cloud computing: An approach towards sustainability. *International Research Journal of Modernization in Engineering Technology and Science*, *4*(1), 1263–1268.

Srivastava, A., Jain, S., Maity, R., & Desai, V. R. (2022). Demystifying artificial intelligence amidst sustainable agricultural water management. *Current Directions in Water Scarcity Research*, *7*, 17–35. doi:10.1016/B978-0-323-91910-4.00002-9

Strubell, E., Ganesh, A., & McCallum, A. (2020, April 3). Energy and Policy Considerations for Modern Deep Learning Research. *Proceedings of the AAAI Conference on Artificial Intelligence*, *34*(09), 13693–13696. doi:10.1609/aaai.v34i09.7123

Subashini, S., & Kavitha, V. (2011). A survey on security issues in service delivery models of cloud computing. *Journal of Network and Computer Applications*, *34*(1), 1–11. doi:10.1016/j.jnca.2010.07.006

Sugiono, S. (2020). Industri Konten Digital Dalam Perspektif Society 5.0 (Digital Content Industry in Society 5.0 Perspective). *JURNAL IPTEKKOM (Jurnal Ilmu Pengetahuan & Teknologi Informasi)*, *22*(2), 175-191.

Sumi, F. H., Dutta, L., & Sarker, F. (2018). Future with wireless power transfer technology. *J. Electr. Electron. Syst*, *7*(1000279), 2332–0796.

Sun, L., Jiang, X., Ren, H., & Guo, Y. (2020). Edge-Cloud Computing and Artificial Intelligence in Internet of Medical Things: Architecture, Technology and Application. *IEEE Access : Practical Innovations, Open Solutions*, *8*, 101079–101092. doi:10.1109/ACCESS.2020.2997831

Surianarayanan, C., Lawrence, J. J., Chelliah, P. R., Prakash, E., & Hewage, C. (2023). A Survey on Optimization Techniques for Edge Artificial Intelligence (AI). *Sensors (Basel)*, *23*(3), 1279. doi:10.3390/s23031279 PMID:36772319

Surianarayanan, C., Raj, P., & Niranjan, S. K. (2023). The Significance of Edge AI towards Real-time and Intelligent Enterprises. *2023 International Conference on Intelligent and Innovative Technologies in Computing, Electrical and Electronics (IITCEE)*, Bengaluru, India. 10.1109/IITCEE57236.2023.10090926

Surjeet, K., Sabyasachi, P., & Ranjan, A. (2021). *Turkish Journal of Computer and Mathematics Education*, *12*(11), 3885-3898.

Suryadi, S., Kushardiyanti, D., & Gusmanti, R. (2021). Challenges of community empowerment in the era of industry society 5. O. *Jurnal KOLOKIUM*, *9*(2), 160–176. doi:10.24036/kolokium-pls.v9i2.492

Sustainable Development. (n.d.). *The 17 Goals*. https://sdgs.un.org/goals

Syamala, M., Komala, C., Pramila, P., Dash, S., Meenakshi, S., & Boopathi, S. (2023). Machine Learning-Integrated IoT-Based Smart Home Energy Management System. In *Handbook of Research on Deep Learning Techniques for Cloud-Based Industrial IoT* (pp. 219–235). IGI Global. doi:10.4018/978-1-6684-8098-4.ch013

Szefer, J., Keller, E., Lee, R. B., & Rexford, J. (2011, October). Eliminating the hypervisor attack surface for a more secure cloud. In *Proceedings of the 18th ACM conference on Computer and communications security* (pp. 401-412). ACM. 10.1145/2046707.2046754

Taeihagh, A. (2021, April 3). Governance of artificial intelligence. *Policy and Society, 40*(2), 137–157. doi:10.1080/1 4494035.2021.1928377

Taherdust, H. (2023, April 4). Towards Artificial Intelligence in Sustainable Environmental Development. *Artificial Intelligence Evolution*, 49–54. doi:10.37256/aie.4120232503

Tai, X. Y., Zhang, H., Niu, Z., Christie, S. D., & Xuan, J. (2020). The future of sustainable chemistry and process: Convergence of artificial intelligence, data and hardware. *Energy and AI, 2*, 100036. doi:10.1016/j.egyai.2020.100036

Talib, A. M. (2015). Ensuring security, confidentiality and fine-grained data access control of cloud data storage implementation environment. *J. Inf. Security, 6*(2), 118–130. doi:10.4236/jis.2015.62013

Talwar, B., & Gupta, A. K. (2016). A Survey on Cloud Computing Model Configuration Security Issues with Proposed Solutions. *International Journal of Exploration in Science and Technology, 1*(2), 43-49.

Tapale, M. T., Goudar, R. H., Birje, M. N., & Patil, R. S. (2020). Utility based load balancing using firefly algorithm in cloud. Journal of Data. *Information & Management, 2*, 215–224.

Tari, Z. (2014). Security and privacy in cloud computing. *IEEE Cloud Computing, 1*(01), 54–57. doi:10.1109/MCC.2014.20

Thakare, V. R., & Singh, K. J. (2020). Cloud Security Architecture Based on Fully Homomorphic Encryption. In S. Goundar, S. Bhushan, & P. Rayani (Eds.), *Architecture and Security Issues in Fog Computing Applications* (pp. 83–89). IGI Global. doi:10.4018/978-1-7998-0194-8.ch005

Thakur, J., & Kumar, N. (2011). DES, AES and Blowfish: Symmetric Key Cryptography Algorithms Simulation Based Performance Analysis. *International Journal of Emerging Technology and Advanced Engineering.* www.ijetae.com

Thakur, S., & Chaurasia, A. (2016, January). Towards Green Cloud Computing: Impact of carbon footprint on environment. In 2016 6th international conference-cloud system and big data engineering (Confluence) (pp. 209-213). IEEE.

Thrampoulidis, E., Mavromatidis, G., Lucchi, A., & Orehounig, K. (2021). A machine learning-based surrogate model to approximate optimal building retrofit solutions. *Applied Energy, 281*, 116024. doi:10.1016/j.apenergy.2020.116024

Tomašev, N., Cornebise, J., Hutter, F., Mohamed, S., Picciariello, A., Connelly, B., Belgrave, D. C. M., Ezer, D., Haert, F. C. V. D., Mugisha, F., Abila, G., Arai, H., Almiraat, H., Proskurnia, J., Snyder, K., Otake-Matsuura, M., Othman, M., Glasmachers, T., Wever, W. D., & Clopath, C. (2020, May 18). AI for social good: Unlocking the opportunity for positive impact. *Nature Communications, 11*(1), 2468. doi:10.1038/s41467-020-15871-z PMID:32424119

Tran, M., Banister, D., Bishop, J. D., & McCulloch, M. D. (2012). Realizing the electric-vehicle revolution. *Nature Climate Change, 2*(5), 328–333. doi:10.1038/nclimate1429

Trehan, R., Machhan, R., Singh, P., & Sangwan, K. S. (2022). Industry 4.0 and society 5.0: Drivers and challenges. *IUP Journal of Information Technology, 18*(1), 40–58.

Trivedi, S., & Malik, R. (2022). Blockchain Technology as an Emerging Technology in the Insurance Market. In *Big Data: A Game Changer for Insurance Industry* (pp. 81–100). Emerald Publishing Limited. doi:10.1108/978-1-80262-605-620221006

Tuli, S., Casale, G., & Jennings, N. (2021). MCDS: AI Augmented Workflow Scheduling in Mobile Edge Cloud Computing Systems. *IEEE Transactions on Parallel and Distributed Systems. IEEE.* . doi:10.1109/TPDS.2021.3135907

Tumentsetseg, E., & Varga, E. (2022). Industry 4.0 and education 4.0: Expected competences and skills in society 5.0. *Acta Carolus Robertus, 12*(1), 107–115.

Ugandar, R. E., Rahamathunnisa, U., Sajithra, S., Christiana, M. B. V., Palai, B. K., & Boopathi, S. (2023). Hospital Waste Management Using Internet of Things and Deep Learning: Enhanced Efficiency and Sustainability. In M. Arshad (Ed.), (pp. 317–343). Advances in Bioinformatics and Biomedical Engineering. IGI Global. doi:10.4018/978-1-6684-6577-6.ch015

Ullah, A. (2019). Artificial bee colony algorithm used for load balancing in cloud computing. *IAES International Journal of Artificial Intelligence*, *8*(2), 156. doi:10.11591/ijai.v8.i2.pp156-167

Ullah, S., Khan, F. U., & Ahmad, N. (2022). Promoting sustainability through green innovation adoption: A case of manufacturing industry. *Environmental Science and Pollution Research International*, *29*(14), 1–21. doi:10.1007/s11356-021-17322-8 PMID:34746984

Vaidya, H., & Chatterji, T. (2020). SDG 11 Sustainable Cities and Communities. In B. Isabel, I. B. Franco, T. Chatterji, E. Derbyshire, & J. Tracey (Eds.), *Actioning the Global Goals for Local Impact* (pp. 173–185). Springer. doi:10.1007/978-981-32-9927-6_12

Van Erp, M., Reynolds, C., Maynard, D., Starke, A., Ibáñez Martín, R., Andres, F., Leite, M. C. A., Alvarez de Toledo, D., Schmidt Rivera, X., Trattner, C., Brewer, S., Adriano Martins, C., Kluczkovski, A., Frankowska, A., Bridle, S., Levy, R. B., Rauber, F., Tereza da Silva, J., & Bosma, U. (2021). Using natural language processing and artificial intelligence to explore the nutrition and sustainability of recipes and food. *Frontiers in Artificial Intelligence*, *3*, 621577. doi:10.3389/frai.2020.621577 PMID:33733227

Van Wynsberghe, A. (2021, February 26). Sustainable AI: AI for sustainability and the sustainability of AI. *AI and Ethics*, *1*(3), 213–218. doi:10.1007/s43681-021-00043-6

Vanitha, S., Radhika, K., & Boopathi, S. (2023). Artificial Intelligence Techniques in Water Purification and Utilization. In *Human Agro-Energy Optimization for Business and Industry* (pp. 202–218). IGI Global. doi:10.4018/978-1-6684-4118-3.ch010

Vaquero, L., Rodero-Merino, L., Caceres, J., & Lindner, M. (2008). *ACM Computer Communication Review*. ACM.

Varadharajan, V., & Tupakula, U. (2014). Counteracting security attacks in virtual machines in the cloud using property based attestation. *Journal of Network and Computer Applications*, *40*, 31–45. doi:10.1016/j.jnca.2013.08.002

Velmurugan, K., Venkumar, P., & Sudhakara, P. R. (2021). SME 4.0: Machine learning framework for real-time machine health monitoring system. *Journal of Physics: Conference Series*, *1911*(1), 012026. doi:10.1088/1742-6596/1911/1/012026

Venkateswaran, N., Vidhya, K., Ayyannan, M., Chavan, S. M., Sekar, K., & Boopathi, S. (2023). A Study on Smart Energy Management Framework Using Cloud Computing. In 5G, Artificial Intelligence, and Next Generation Internet of Things: Digital Innovation for Green and Sustainable Economies (pp. 189–212). IGI Global. doi:10.4018/978-1-6684-8634-4.ch009

Venkateswaran, N., Kumar, S. S., Diwakar, G., Gnanasangeetha, D., & Boopathi, S. (2023). Synthetic Biology for Waste Water to Energy Conversion: IoT and AI Approaches. In M. Arshad (Ed.), (pp. 360–384). Advances in Bioinformatics and Biomedical Engineering. IGI Global. doi:10.4018/978-1-6684-6577-6.ch017

Venkateswaran, N., Vidhya, R., Naik, D. A., Raj, T. M., Munjal, N., & Boopathi, S. (2023). Study on Sentence and Question Formation Using Deep Learning Techniques. In *Digital Natives as a Disruptive Force in Asian Businesses and Societies* (pp. 252–273). IGI Global. doi:10.4018/978-1-6684-6782-4.ch015

Vennila, T., Karuna, M. S., Srivastava, B. K., Venugopal, J., Surakasi, R., & B., S. (2023). New Strategies in Treatment and Enzymatic Processes. In *Human Agro-Energy Optimization for Business and Industry* (pp. 219–240). IGI Global. doi:10.4018/978-1-6684-4118-3.ch011

Vennila, T., Karuna, M., Srivastava, B. K., Venugopal, J., Surakasi, R., & Sampath, B. (2022). New Strategies in Treatment and Enzymatic Processes: Ethanol Production From Sugarcane Bagasse. In Human Agro-Energy Optimization for Business and Industry (pp. 219–240). IGI Global.

Verma, J., & Gagandeep. (2023). Embracing Fintech Applications in the Banking Sector Vis-á-Vis Service Quality. In *Contemporary Studies of Risks in Emerging Technology, Part B* (pp. 207-219). Emerald Publishing Limited.

Verma, J., Sharma, J., & Gupta, M. (2023). Digital Currency and Blockchain Technology in the Financial World. In *Perspectives on Blockchain Technology and Responsible Investing* (pp. 216–225). IGI Global. doi:10.4018/978-1-6684-8361-9.ch010

Vestin, A., Säfsten, K., & Löfving, M. (2018). On the way to a smart factory for single-family wooden house builders in Sweden. *Procedia Manufacturing*, 25, 459–470. doi:10.1016/j.promfg.2018.06.129

Vijay, Y., & Ghita, B. V. (2017, July). Evaluating cloud computing scheduling algorithms under different environment and scenarios. In *2017 8th International Conference on Computing, Communication and Networking Technologies (ICCCNT)* (pp. 1-5). IEEE. 10.1109/ICCCNT.2017.8204070

Vinuesa, R., Azizpour, H., Leite, I., Balaam, M., Dignum, V., Domisch, S., Felländer, A., Langhans, S. D., Tegmark, M., & Fuso Nerini, F. (2020, January 13). The role of artificial intelligence in achieving the Sustainable Development Goals. *Nature Communications*, 11(1), 233. doi:10.1038/s41467-019-14108-y PMID:31932590

Wadhwa, M., Goel, A., Choudhury, T., & Mishra, V. P. (2019, December). Green cloud computing-A greener approach to IT. In 2019 international conference on computational intelligence and knowledge economy (ICCIKE) (pp. 760-764). IEEE. doi:10.1109/ICCIKE47802.2019.9004283

Wang, Dong & Zhang, Daniel. (2023). *Real-Time AI in Social Edge*. Springer. . doi:10.1007/978-3-031-26936-3_5

Wang, Y., Xue, J., Wei, C., & Kuo, C.-C. (2023). *An Overview on Generative AI at Scale with Edge-Cloud Computing*. TechXriv. doi:10.36227/techrxiv.23272271.v1

Wang, J., Chen, T., & Xu, Y. (2020). Internet of Things-Based Demand-Side Management Techniques for Energy-Efficient Buildings: A Review. *IEEE Transactions on Industrial Informatics*, 16(6), 4016–4025.

Wang, P., Hu, M., Wang, H., Chen, Z., Feng, Y., Wang, J., Ling, W., & Huang, Y. (2020). The evolution of flexible electronics: From nature, beyond nature, and to nature. *Advancement of Science*, 7(20), 2001116. doi:10.1002/advs.202001116 PMID:33101851

Wang, T., Zhang, K., Thé, J., & Yu, H. (2022). Accurate prediction of band gap of materials using stacking machine learning model. *Computational Materials Science*, 201, 110899. doi:10.1016/j.commatsci.2021.110899

Wei, L., Zhu, H., Cao, Z., Dong, X., Jia, W., Chen, Y., & Vasilakos, A. V. (2014). Security and privacy for storage and computation in cloud computing. *Information Sciences*, 258, 371–386. doi:10.1016/j.ins.2013.04.028

Wen, T. Y., & Aris, S. A. M. (2022). Hybrid approach of eeg stress level classification using k-means clustering and support vector machine. *IEEE Access : Practical Innovations, Open Solutions*, 10, 18370–18379. doi:10.1109/ACCESS.2022.3148380

Wong, J. K. W., & Zhou, J. (2015). Enhancing environmental sustainability over building life cycles through green BIM: A review. *Automation in Construction*, 57, 156–165. doi:10.1016/j.autcon.2015.06.003

Wu, R. (2010). Information flow control in cloud computing. In *Collaborative Computing: Networking, Applications and Work sharing (Collaborate Com), 6th International Conference*. IEEE.

Wu, H., Ding, Y., Winer, C., & Yao, L. (2010, November). Network security for virtual machine in cloud computing. In *5th International conference on computer sciences and convergence information technology* (pp. 18-21). IEEE.

Wu, W., Huang, T., & Gong, K. (2020, March). Ethical Principles and Governance Technology Development of AI in China. *Engineering (Beijing)*, *6*(3), 302–309. doi:10.1016/j.eng.2019.12.015

Wu, Y., Sun, X., Zhang, Y., Zhong, X., & Cheng, L. (2021). A power transformer fault diagnosis method-based hybrid improved seagull optimization algorithm and support vector machine. *IEEE Access : Practical Innovations, Open Solutions*, *10*, 17268–17286. doi:10.1109/ACCESS.2021.3127164

Xiang, X., Li, Q., Khan, S., & Khalaf, O. I. (2021). Urban water resource management for sustainable environment planning using artificial intelligence techniques. *Environmental Impact Assessment Review*, *86*, 106515. doi:10.1016/j.eiar.2020.106515

Xiao, Z., & Xiao, Y. (2012). Security and privacy in cloud computing. *IEEE Communications Surveys and Tutorials*, *15*(2), 843–859. doi:10.1109/SURV.2012.060912.00182

Xin, Y., Kong, L., Liu, Z., Chen, Y., Li, Y., Zhu, H., Gao, M., Hou, H., & Wang, C. (2018). Machine learning and deep learning methods for cybersecurity. *IEEE Access : Practical Innovations, Open Solutions*, *6*, 35365–35381. doi:10.1109/ACCESS.2018.2836950

Xu, X., Lu, Y., Vogel-Heuser, B., & Wang, L. (2021). Industry 4.0 and industry 5.0 inception, conception and perception. *Journal of Manufacturing Systems*, *61*, 530–535. doi:10.1016/j.jmsy.2021.10.006

Yang, T., Zhao, L., Li, W., & Zomaya, A. Y. (2020). Reinforcement learning in sustainable energy and electric systems: A survey. *Annual Reviews in Control*, *49*, 145–163. doi:10.1016/j.arcontrol.2020.03.001

Yan, Z., Zhang, P., & Vasilakos, A. V. (2014). A survey on trust management for Internet of Things. *Journal of Network and Computer Applications*, *42*, 120–134. doi:10.1016/j.jnca.2014.01.014

Yao, X., Ma, N., Zhang, J., Wang, K., Yang, E., & Faccio, M. (2022). Enhancing wisdom manufacturing as industrial metaverse for industry and society 5.0. *Journal of Intelligent Manufacturing*, 1–21.

Yaqoob, I., Ahmed, E., Hashem, I. A. T., Ahmed, A. I. A., Al-Fuqaha, A., Gani, A., & Imran, M. (2017). Internet of things architecture: Recent advances, taxonomy, requirements, and open challenges. *IEEE Wireless Communications*, *24*(3), 10–16. doi:10.1109/MWC.2017.1600421

Yigitcanlar, T., & Cugurullo, F. (2020, October 15). The Sustainability of Artificial Intelligence: An Urbanistic Viewpoint from the Lens of Smart and Sustainable Cities. *Sustainability (Basel)*, *12*(20), 8548. doi:10.3390/su12208548

Yigitcanlar, T., Mehmood, R., & Corchado, J. M. (2021, August 10). Green Artificial Intelligence: Towards an Efficient, Sustainable and Equitable Technology for Smart Cities and Futures. *Sustainability (Basel)*, *13*(16), 8952. doi:10.3390/su13168952

Yli-Huumo, J., Ko, D., Choi, S., Park, S., & Smolander, K. (2016). Where is current research on blockchain technology?—A systematic review. *PLoS One*, *11*(10), e0163477. doi:10.1371/journal.pone.0163477 PMID:27695049

Younis, Y. A., & Kifayat, K. (2013). *Secure cloud computing for critical infrastructure: A survey. Liverpool John Moores University*. Tech. Rep.

Yu, S. (2010). Achieving secure, scalable, and fine-grained data access control in cloud computing. In IN- *FOCOM, 2010 Proceedings IEEE*, (pp. 1-9). IEEE.

Yu, D., Wenhui, X., Anser, M. K., Nassani, A. A., Imran, M., Zaman, K., & Haffar, M. (2023). Navigating the global mineral market: A study of resource wealth and the energy transition. *Resources Policy*, *82*, 103500. doi:10.1016/j.resourpol.2023.103500

Yu, H., Powell, N., Stembridge, D., & Yuan, X. (2012, March). Cloud computing and security challenges. In *Proceedings of the 50th Annual Southeast Regional Conference* (pp. 298-302). ACM. 10.1145/2184512.2184581

Yu, N. H., Hao, Z., Xu, J. J., Zhang, W. M., & Zhang, C. (2013). Review of cloud computing security. *Acta Electonica Sinica*, *41*(2), 371.

Zaz, Y., El Fadil, L., & El Kayyali, M. (2012). Securing EPR Data Using Cryptography and Image Watermarking. *International Journal of Mobile Computing and Multimedia Communications*, *4*(2), 76–87. doi:10.4018/jmcmc.2012040106

Zeb, S., Rathore, M., Hassan, S., Raza, S., Dev, K., & Fortino, G. (2023). Towards AI-enabled NextG Networks with Edge Intelligence-assisted Microservice Orchestration. *IEEE Wireless Communications*, *30*(3), 148–156. doi:10.1109/MWC.015.2200461

Zebulum, R. S., Pacheco, M. A., & Vellasco, M. M. B. (2018). *Evolutionary electronics: automatic design of electronic circuits and systems by genetic algorithms*. CRC press. doi:10.1201/9781420041590

Zengin, Y., Naktiyok, S., Kaygın, E., Kavak, O., & Topçuoglu, E. (2021). An investigation upon industry 4.0 and society 5.0 within the context of sustainable development goals. *Sustainability (Basel)*, *13*(5), 2682. doi:10.3390/su13052682

Zhang, B., Anderljung, M., Kahn, L., Dreksler, N., Horowitz, M. C., & Dafoe, A. (2021, August 2). Ethics and Governance of Artificial Intelligence: Evidence from a Survey of Machine Learning Researchers. *Journal of Artificial Intelligence Research*, *71*. Advance online publication. doi:10.1613/jair.1.12895

Zhang, F., & Chen, H. (2013). Security-preserving live migration of virtual machines in the cloud. *Journal of Network and Systems Management*, *21*(4), 562–587. doi:10.1007/s10922-012-9253-1

Zhang, F., Chen, J., Chen, H., & Zang, B. (2011, October). Cloudvisor: retrofitting protection of virtual machines in multi-tenant cloud with nested virtualization. In *Proceedings of the twenty-third acm symposium on operating systems principles* (pp. 203-216). ACM. 10.1145/2043556.2043576

Zhang, F., Wang, J., Sun, K., & Stavrou, A. (2013). Hypercheck: A hardware-assistedintegrity monitor. *IEEE Transactions on Dependable and Secure Computing*, *11*(4), 332–344. doi:10.1109/TDSC.2013.53

Zhang, L. (2022). Artificial Intelligence in renewable energy. *Energy Reports*, *8*, ●●●. https://www.sciencedirect.com/science/article/pii/S2352484722022818

Zhanna, M., & Nataliia, V. (2020). Development of engineering students competencies based on cognitive technologies in conditions of industry 4.0. *International Journal of Cognitive Research in Science, Engineering and Education*, *8*(S), 93-101.

Zhao, J., & Gómez Fariñas, B. (2022, November 28). Artificial Intelligence and Sustainable Decisions. *European Business Organization Law Review*, *24*(1), 1–39. doi:10.1007/s40804-022-00262-2

Zhao, Y., Yang, Z., Niu, J., Du, Z., Federica, C., Zhu, Z., Yang, K., Li, Y., Zhao, B., Pedersen, T. H., Liu, C., & Emmanuel, M. (2023). Systematical analysis of sludge treatment and disposal technologies for carbon footprint reduction. *Journal of Environmental Sciences (China)*, *128*, 224–249. doi:10.1016/j.jes.2022.07.038 PMID:36801037

Zheng, P., Wang, H., Sang, Z., Zhong, R. Y., Liu, Y., Liu, C., Mubarok, K., Yu, S., & Xu, X. (2018). Smart manufacturing systems for Industry 4.0: Conceptual framework, scenarios, and future perspectives. *Frontiers of Mechanical Engineering*, *13*(2), 137–150. doi:10.1007/s11465-018-0499-5

Zhu, F., Lv, Y., Chen, Y., Wang, X., Xiong, G., & Wang, F. Y. (2019). Parallel transportation systems: Toward IoT-enabled smart urban traffic control and management. *IEEE Transactions on Intelligent Transportation Systems, 21*(10), 4063–4071. doi:10.1109/TITS.2019.2934991

Zhu, H., Luo, W., Ciesielski, P. N., Fang, Z., Zhu, J. Y., Henriksson, G., Himmel, M. E., & Hu, L. (2016). Wood-derived materials for green electronics, biological devices, and energy applications. *Chemical Reviews, 116*(16), 9305–9374. doi:10.1021/acs.chemrev.6b00225 PMID:27459699

Žigienė, G., Rybakovas, E., & Alzbutas, R. (2019). Artificial intelligence based commercial risk management framework for SMEs. *Sustainability (Basel), 11*(16), 4501. doi:10.3390/su11164501

Zipfel, J., Verworner, F., Fischer, M., Wieland, U., Kraus, M., & Zschech, P. (2023). Anomaly detection for industrial quality assurance: A comparative evaluation of unsupervised deep learning models. *Computers & Industrial Engineering, 177*, 109045. doi:10.1016/j.cie.2023.109045

Zulueta, E. (2020). *Artificial Intelligence for renewable energy systems.* MDPI. https://www.mdpi.com/journal/sustainability/special_issues/artificial_intelligence_energy

About the Contributors

Vishal Jain is presently working as an Associate Professor at Department of Computer Science and Engineering, Sharda School of Engineering and Technology, Sharda University, Greater Noida, U. P. India. Before that, he has worked for several years as an Associate Professor at Bharati Vidyapeeth's Institute of Computer Applications and Management (BVICAM), New Delhi. He has more than 14 years of experience in the academics. He obtained Ph.D (CSE), M.Tech (CSE), MBA (HR), MCA, MCP and CCNA. He has authored more than 90 research papers in reputed conferences and journals, including Web of Science and Scopus. He has authored and edited more than 30 books with various reputed publishers, including Elsevier, Springer, Apple Academic Press, CRC, Taylor and Francis Group, Scrivener, Wiley, Emerald, NOVA Science and IGI-Global. His research areas include information retrieval, semantic web, ontology engineering, data mining, ad hoc networks, and sensor networks. He received a Young Active Member Award for the year 2012–13 from the Computer Society of India, Best Faculty Award for the year 2017 and Best Researcher Award for the year 2019 from BVICAM, New Delhi.

Meenu Vijarania received her B.Tech degree in Information Technology from MDU university, Haryana in 2005 and M.Tech(I.T) degree from GGSIPU, New Delhi in 2007. She has 8 years of experience in teaching. Since 2011 she is working at Amity University Haryana as faculty in Computer Science Department and Completed PhD in the field of Wireless Ad-hoc Network. Her research area include topics of Wireless Networks and Genetic Algorithm .

Sampath Boopathi is an accomplished individual with a strong academic background and extensive research experience. He completed his undergraduate studies in Mechanical Engineering and pursued his postgraduate studies in the field of Computer-Aided Design. Dr. Boopathi obtained his Ph.D. from Anna University, focusing his research on Manufacturing and optimization. Throughout his career, Dr. Boopathi has made significant contributions to the field of engineering. He has authored and published over 180 research articles in internationally peer-reviewed journals, highlighting his expertise and dedication to advancing knowledge in his area of specialization. His research output demonstrates his commitment to conducting rigorous and impactful research. In addition to his research publications, Dr. Boopathi has also been granted one patent and has three published patents to his name. This indicates his innovative thinking and ability to develop practical solutions to real-world engineering challenges. With 17 years of academic and research experience, Dr. Boopathi has enriched the engineering community through his teaching and mentorship roles. He has served in various engineering colleges in Tamilnadu, India, where he has imparted knowledge, guided students, and contributed to the overall academic development of the institutions. Dr. Sampath Boopathi's diverse background, ranging from mechanical engineering to computer-aided design, along with his specialization in manufacturing and optimization, positions him as a valuable asset in the field of engineering. His research contributions, patents, and extensive teaching experience exemplify his expertise and dedication to advancing engineering knowledge and fostering innovation.

Aarti Chugh is Associate Professor in CSE with SGT University, Haryana. She has 18+ years of teaching experience. She received her Ph.D. degree in Computer Science from Jagannath University, Jaipur and MCA degree from Maharishi Dyanand University, Rohtak. Her area of interest and research are Big Data, DBMS and Artificial Intelligence. She has published/accepted/presented more than 30+ papers in international journals /conferences (SCI+Scopus) and edited/authored three books. She has received reviewer recognition certificate from Elsevier and is part of editorial/advisory board of reputed journals.

Kunal Dhibar is an energetic and passionate college student working towards a B.Tech in CSE at the Bengal College of Engineering and Technology, Durgapur, West Bengal, India. Aiming to use my knowledge of Coding, Machine Learning, Software development, and Data Science strategies to satisfy the role fot the paper. Well-versed in numerous programming languages including C programming language, JAVA, C++, C#, Python MySQL. Strong background in Programming and Data Science.

Anuj Kumar Gupta is working as Professor & Head of CSE Dept. at CGC College of Engineering. He is PhD in Computer Science & Engineering. He has a vast academic & administrative experience of 20+ years. He has guided many PG & PhD research scholars. Hs has published more than 90 research papers in reputed international & national journals and conferences. He has filed more than 10 patents and published 4 books. He is a member of Computer Society of India & ISTE.

Anamika Lata (Member, IEEE) received the B.E. degree in electronics and instrumentation from Sathyabama University, Chennai, India, in 2013, and the M.Tech. and Ph.D. degrees in electronics and communication engineering from the Indian Institute of Technology (ISM), Dhanbad, India, in 2016 and 2022, respectively., She is currently working as an Assistant Professor with the School of Electronics Engineering, VIT AP University, Amaravati, India. She is the author of ten international journals and several conference proceedings. Her current research interests include sensors and transducer development.

Prasenjit Maji received a bachelor's degree in Computer Science & Engineering from the West Bengal University of Technology, West Bengal, in 2007, the master's degree in Computer Science & Engineering from the West Bengal University of Technology, West Bengal, in 2013 and currently pursuing Ph.D. from NIT, Durgapur. He is an Assistant Professor in the CSE Dept, Bengal College of Engineering & Technology, Durgapur since 2013. His research interests include Image Processing and Machine Learning. His Google Scholar h-index is 8, and his i-index is 8, with 217 citations.

Hemanta Kumar Mondal (M'13) received the bachelor's degree in electronics and communication engineering from the West Bengal University of Technology, West Bengal, in 2007, the master's degree in VLSI Design from the Guru Gobind Singh Indraprastha University, Delhi, in 2010, and the Ph.D. degree in Electronics and Communication Engineering from the Indraprastha Institute of Information

Technology, Delhi, in 2017. He was also associated with the National Centre for Scientific Research (CNRS) Lab- STICC, UBS University in France as a Postdoctoral Researcher in 2017. He is an assistant professor with the National Institute of Technology, Durgapur, West Bengal. His research interests include neuromorphic computing, parallel computing, energy-efficient interconnect architectures for manycore systems, heterogeneous system architecture (HSA) and IoT infrastructure for future healthcare and agriculture applications. He has authored 31 research articles. His Google Scholar h-index is 11, and index is 13 with 392 citations.

Pallavi Pandey is currently working as Assistant Professor, School of Engineering & Technology, K. R. Mangalam University, Gurugram, Haryana, India. She has done Ph.D in Computer Science & Engineering department, from Indira Gandhi Delhi Technical University for Women, Kashmere Gate, New Delhi, India and received M.Tech. degree in Computer Science and Engineering, from Jamia Hamdard, Delhi, India. Dr. Pallavi Pandey possesses nearly 9 years of teaching experience in B.Tech., BCA and MCA classes. Her research interest includes biomedical signal processing, AI and machine learning and data mining. She is working as reviewer of various reputed peer-reviewed international journals. She is IEEE memer.

Gayatree Parbat received her BTECH in Information Technology from West Bengal University of Technology in 2008, the MTECH in Software Engineering from National Institute of Technology, Durgapur in 2013. She is pursuing her PhD from National Institute of Technology, Durgapur in CSE Department. She is currently working as an Assistant Professor in CSE Department of Adamas University. Her research interest include Artificial Intelligence, Machine Learning and Sensor Network.

Yogita Yashveer Raghav is an Associate Professor in Dronacharya College of Engineering, Gurugram, Haryana. She has completed her PhD from Banasthali Vidyapith, Rajasthan and has already achieved impressive qualifications, including UGCNET and HTET. With research interests focused on cloud computing and data mining, she has published several articles in national and international journals and conferences, showcasing her expertise in these areas. As a faculty member, she is committed to teaching and mentoring students, sharing her knowledge and passion for computer science with the next generation of professionals. Their dedication to research and publication is a testament to their ongoing commitment to advancing the field and making meaningful contributions to the academic community. She is IEEE member.

Yogita Yashveer Raghav is an assistant professor in the computer science department at K R Mangalam University, Gurugram, Haryana is currently pursuing PhD from Banasthali Vidyapith , Rajasthan and has already achieved impressive qualifications, including UGCNET and HTET. With research interests focused on cloud computing and data mining, she has published several articles in national and international journals and conferences, showcasing her expertise in these areas. As a faculty member, she is committed to teaching and mentoring students, sharing her knowledge and passion for computer science with the next generation of professionals. Their dedication to research and publication is a testament to their ongoing commitment to advancing the field and making meaningful contributions to the academic community. She is IEEE member.

Yashna Sharma has been dedicated to sustainable practices, combined with her grasp of financial technologies, positions her as a promising young professional and an emerging expert in the field of finance and sustainability. These professional experiences have not only broadened her horizons but have also provided her with a deeper appreciation of the intricacies of the business environment. She has worked as an intern at A4 Solutions, where she gained invaluable insights into the dynamics of the corporate world, specifically in the context of HR. Additionally, she has served as a Super Interview Coordinator at the prestigious Indian School of Business (ISB). During her time as an intern at the University of Auckland, she also served as team leader and shared her knowledge as a specialist in Pacific Harvest's edible seaweed.

Arun Kumar Singh is an Assistant Professor in ECE at Amity University Haryana. He has 12+ years of teaching experience. He received his Ph.D. degree in Image Steganography. He has published/presented more than 20+ papers in international journals /conferences and authored three book chapters.

Juhi Singh is Assistant Professor in CSE at Manipal University Jaipur. She has 10+ years of teaching experience. She received her Ph.D. degree in Computer Science from Baba MastNath University Rohtak, Haryana and M.Tech in CSE from Maharishi Dyanand University, Rohtak and pursued B.Tech from UPTU in information technology. Her area of interest and research are Artificial Intelligence, Soft Computing, and Image Steganography. She has published/accepted/presented more than 30+ papers in international journals /conferences and authored three book chapters.

Manish Kumar Singh received his Bachelor of Technology (B.Tech.) degree from Dr. Ambedkar Institute of Technology for Handicapped(An Autonomous Institute – Established by Govt. of U.P. in 1997), Kanpur, Uttar Pradesh, India in 2011. Further he earned his Master of Technology (M.Tech.) degree from National Institute of Technology, Durgapur, West Bengal, India in year 2014. In year 2019, he has been awarded Ph.D. degree from Indian Institute of Technology (Banaras Hindu University) Varanasi. Dr. Singh has worked as Assistant Professor in department of Electronics Engineering, Harcourt Butler Technical University Kanpur, UP, INDIA during year 2018-2022 and currently he is working as Senior Assistant Professor in the School of Electronics Engg., Vellore Institute of Technology-AP University Amaravati from July 2022. His research area is microelectronics which mainly includes "engineered materials for fabrication and characterizations of Thin Film based Organic electronic/Optoelectronic devices".

Jyoti Verma is a faculty at Chitkara Business School, Chitkara University, Punjab, India. She graduated with a PhD from Punjabi University, Patiala and has qualified UGC NET in Management. With more than 20 research papers to her credit published in various journals and conferences at national & international levels, Dr. Verma has built her key competencies in entrepreneurship and financial technological services. She has published several book chapters in edited books at the world level and is the author of the book "Accelerating the Development of Quality of IT-Enabled Banking Services" by International Publishers. She has registered many patents and copyright. She is a Subject Matter Expert and Course Planner for MOOC courses of SWAYAM and UGC CEC. She is an Associate Editor (Finance & International Business) in Journal of Technology Management for Growing Economies, Chitkara University Publications and editor of many edited books published by Wiley, Nova Science and IGI Global Publishers. She is very optimistic and believes in continuous learning and hard work.

She has completed many online courses offered by IIM Bangalore, University of Illinois, Google Digital Unlocked, Coursera, Great Learning and many more. She has been invited as Guest Speaker for Financial Planning for New Business Plan at University of Technology, Bahrain.

Vaibhav Vyas is an Associate Professor, at the Department of Computer Science, Banasthali vidyapith, Rajasthan, India. With research interests focused on Block chain Technology, Cloud Computing, Requirement Engineering, Aspect Oriented Analysis and Design Distributed Systems, he has published several articles in national and international journals and conferences, showcasing her expertise in these areas.

Index

A

aeroponics 245-246, 255-257, 265
AI and solar energy management 62
AI-based drones 107, 241
analytics 3, 8, 18-19, 38, 40, 67, 70-71, 106, 126-127, 129, 131, 133-134, 136, 153, 182, 189-190, 198, 218-221, 224, 228-229, 231-234, 238, 240, 245-247, 249-250, 252, 256-257, 265, 276, 286
Applied Artificial Intelligence 152, 154, 162
aquaponics 108, 242, 245-246, 255-257, 265
ARIMA 229, 243
Artificial intelligence (AI) 1, 3-4, 7-9, 11-12, 18, 22, 25, 28-29, 37, 41, 45, 48, 62-64, 66, 69, 72-73, 79, 152-154, 159, 164, 218-221, 224-225, 239, 247, 264, 268-269, 271, 279, 281, 283
automated systems 245, 254

B

best practices 87-88, 92, 102, 104, 124-125, 132, 146, 203, 218, 237, 259-260, 262, 275

C

Case Studies 87, 89, 101-102, 106, 108, 127, 129, 132, 135, 153, 166, 174, 177, 218-221, 225-226, 228-229, 231-233, 235, 237, 240, 242, 245, 247, 258, 267-269, 279-280
Civilization 11, 17, 21, 25
Cloud Computing 18-19, 25, 38, 40, 45, 87, 89, 91, 99-101, 105, 107-109, 111-112, 115-117, 122-123, 134, 138-162, 164-165, 167-169, 174-176, 178-187, 189, 191, 193-204, 213-217, 238, 242-243, 265
Cloud Environment 151, 158, 165, 167, 169, 171-172, 179-180, 195-196, 199, 204, 216
CNN 158-159, 230, 243
CO2 65, 90, 110, 112, 117, 139
CPU 110, 175, 187, 196, 200, 208
Cryptography 55, 98, 194, 202, 205, 207, 214-217
cybersecurity risks 218

D

Data center 92-96, 99-102, 104, 115, 123, 138, 143-144, 146-147, 174, 183, 285
data privacy 12, 83, 103, 131, 157, 160, 196, 218, 220-221, 235-238, 261, 263
Database 25, 38, 166, 202, 205, 227
Design optimization 267, 271, 278-279
Digitalization 17-19, 22-23, 29-31, 33, 36, 39, 41, 44, 148

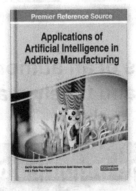

Ensure Quality Research is Introduced to the Academic Community

Become an Reviewer for IGI Global Authored Book Projects

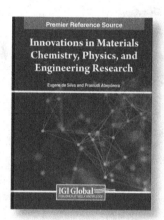

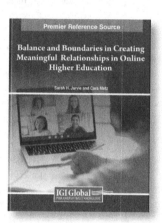

The overall success of an authored book project is dependent on quality and timely manuscript evaluations.

Applications and Inquiries may be sent to:
development@igi-global.com

Applicants must have a doctorate (or equivalent degree) as well as publishing, research, and reviewing experience. Authored Book Evaluators are appointed for one-year terms and are expected to complete at least three evaluations per term. Upon successful completion of this term, evaluators can be considered for an additional term.

If you have a colleague that may be interested in this opportunity, we encourage you to share this information with them.

Submit an Open Access Book Proposal

Have Your Work Fully & Freely Available Worldwide After Publication

Seeking the Following Book Classification Types:

Authored & Edited Monographs • Casebooks • Encyclopedias • Handbooks of Research

Gold, Platinum, & Retrospective OA Opportunities to Choose From

Easily Track Your Work in Our Advanced Manuscript Submission System With **Rapid Turnaround Times**

Double-Blind Peer Review by Notable Editorial Boards (*Committee on Publication Ethics* (COPE) Certified

Publications Adhere to All **Current OA Mandates & Compliances**

Affordable APCs *(Often 50% Lower Than the Industry Average)* Including Robust Editorial Service Provisions

Direct Connections with **Prominent Research Funders** & OA Regulatory Groups

Institution Level OA Agreements Available (Recommend or Contact Your Librarian for Details)

Join a **Diverse Community** of 150,000+ Researchers **Worldwide** Publishing With IGI Global

Content Spread Widely to Leading Repositories (AGOSR, ResearchGate, CORE, & More)

? Retrospective Open Access Publishing

You Can Unlock Your Recently Published Work, Including Full Book & Individual Chapter Content to Enjoy All the Benefits of Open Access Publishing

Learn More

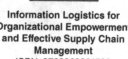

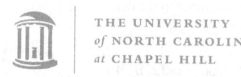

Printed in the United States
by Baker & Taylor Publisher Services

Printed in the United States
by Baker & Taylor Publisher Services